INSIDERS'
GUIDE®

COLUMBUS

THIRD EDITION

SHAWNIE KELLEY

Globe
Pequot

Essex, Connecticut

Globe Pequot

An imprint of the Globe Pequot Publishing Group, Inc.
64 South Main St.
Essex, CT 06426
www.GlobePequot.com

Distributed by NATIONAL BOOK NETWORK

British Library Cataloguing in Publication Information available

Library of Congress Cataloging-in-Publication Data available

ISSN 1556-4479
ISBN 978-1-4930-8484-5 (paper : alk. paper)
ISBN 978-1-4930-8485-2 (electronic)

∞™ The paper used in this publication meets the minimum requirements of American National Standard for Information Sciences—Permanence of Paper for Printed Library Materials, ANSI/NISO Z39.48-1992.

All the information in this guidebook is subject to change. We recommend that you call ahead to obtain current information before traveling.

CONTENTS

CONTENTS

Directory of Maps

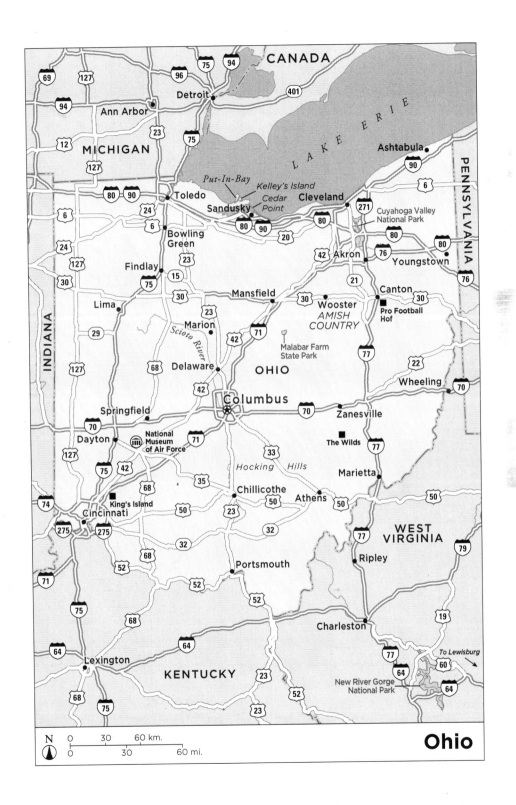

Ohio

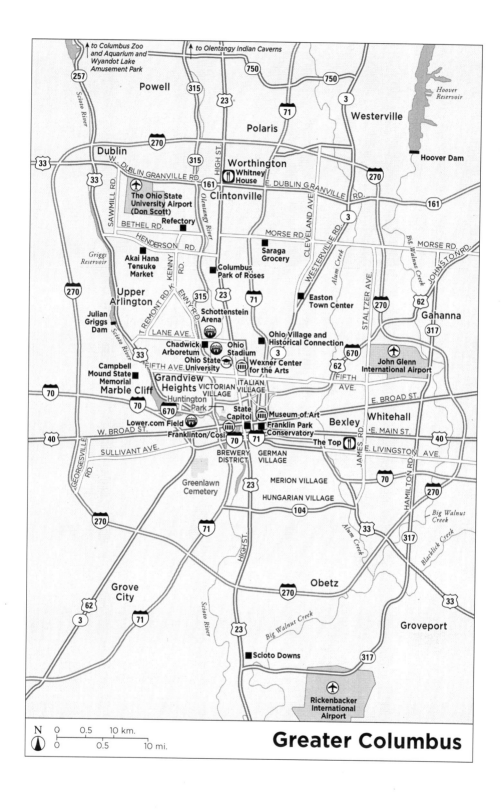

Greater Columbus

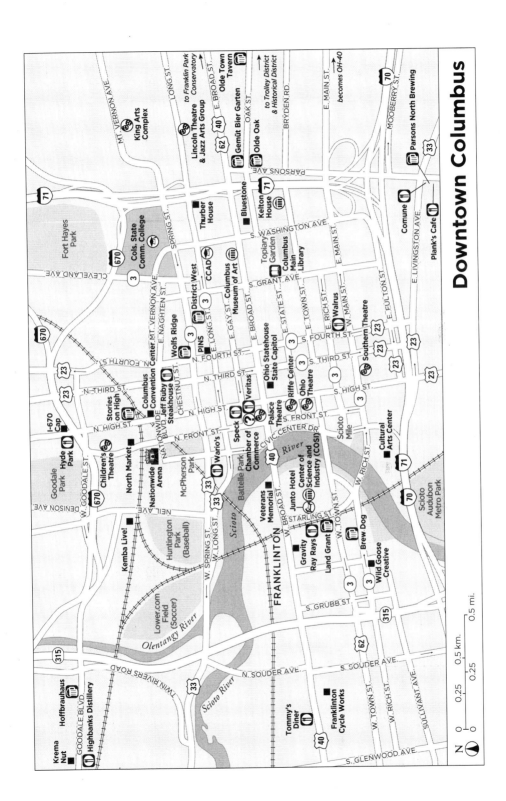

Downtown Columbus

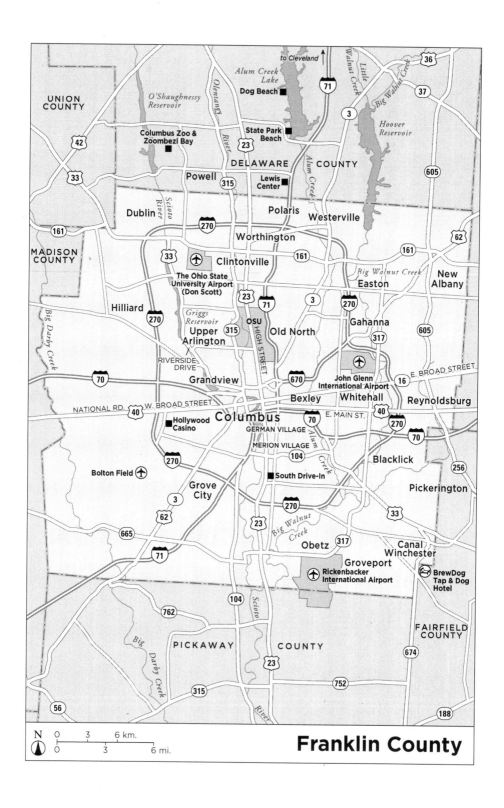

Franklin County

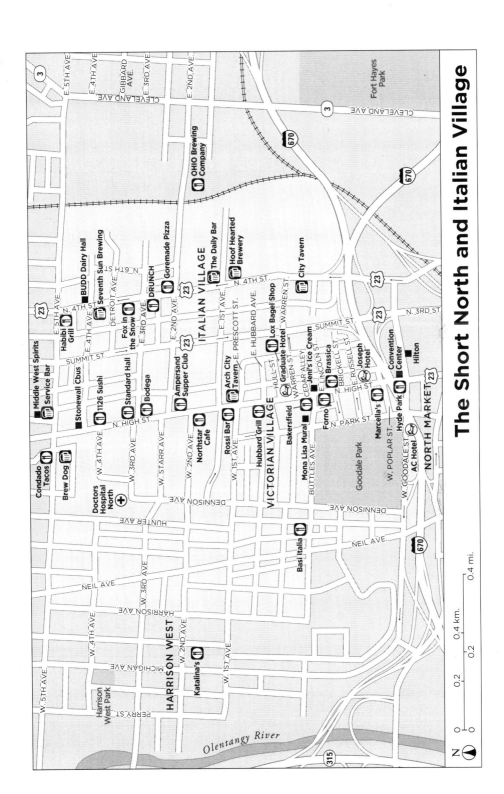

The Short North and Italian Village

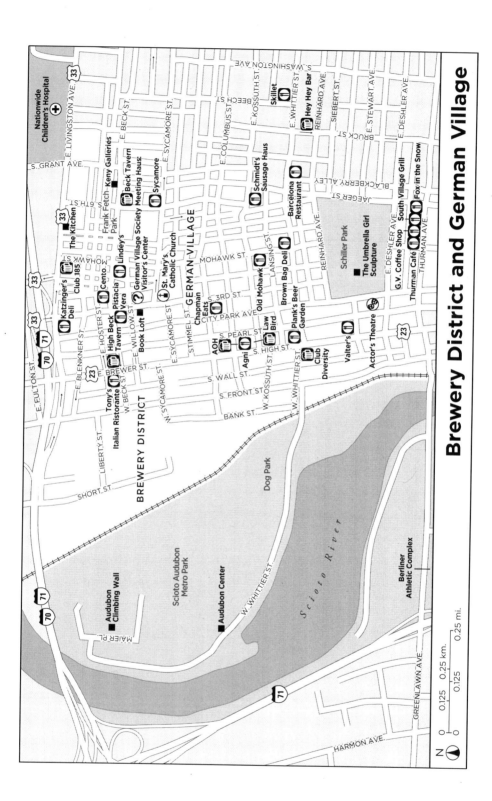

Brewery District and German Village

PREFACE

Columbus has changed dramatically in the 15 years since I wrote the city's first national travel guide. As the fastest-growing city in the Midwest, 90 percent of the state's population growth has happened in central Ohio. Approximately 1.8 million people now call the Columbus region home, with another million projected over the next 10 years. This population boom has moved us up the ranks to become the 14th-largest city in the country. Neighborhoods have been revitalized, and the culinary landscape is evolving in ways that I could have only hoped for a decade ago.

Columbus is often overshadowed by bigger cities like New York or Los Angeles, so it might be a pleasant surprise to learn that Columbus is the second-largest city in the Midwest after Chicago. When people visit for the first time, it is exciting to see the reactions when they recognize that Columbus is truly a large, energetic city with professional sports, world-class food, a thriving art scene, and urbane walkable neighborhoods that, just 10 years ago, were decrepit or totally abandoned but are now hip parts of town.

Neighborhoods, such as Italian Village and Franklinton, have been transformed through robust residential construction and repurposing of old industrial buildings in creative ways. These revitalization efforts are ongoing, and necessary to keep up with the city's projected population growth. Events like Columbus Fashion Week and the new fashion district, innovative chefs, rooftop bars, and thriving start-ups are helping shape our city into one that is truly cosmopolitan.

Over the years, I had a few lightbulb moments that changed the way I experience Columbus—such as not to overlook the small, nondescript strip malls, which are often home to wonderful immigrant food and international markets that emphasize Columbus's growing diversity. Staycations have been a great way to see the city through the eyes of a tourist. Staying in local hotels, behaving like crazy "woo-hoo girls" on the Pedal Wagon, and sniffing out new restaurants has allowed me to see Columbus from a perspective that I typically would not because I live here.

As one of America's most gay-friendly cities, the pride flag flies high around town. "Gayborhoods" have grown around the Short North, German Village, and Olde Town East. With one of the largest gay populations in the country, Columbus has a reputation for being accepting and welcoming of not only LGBTQ+ visitors but other minority communities too. Columbus now has the second-largest population of Somali Americans in the US and has a vibrant community of New Americans from a wide range of backgrounds. Even from the outside, Columbus is recognized as a city of inclusion.

The changes I have witnessed while living here for almost 25 years makes me proud of my hometown. I am inspired to showcase Columbus as the international capital city it has become. The *Insiders' Guide to Columbus* focuses on the independently owned, locally made, and unique offerings that make it a special place. My book encourages visitors and locals to explore Columbus in-depth, from its must-see world-class attractions to its off-beat experiences.

When it comes to finding something to do, every week brings some sort of festival, expo, or community event. Sports lovers can take in a Blue Jackets ice hockey game, Columbus Crew soccer, Clippers baseball, or a long list of Buckeye varsity and club sports. The city's quality visual and performing arts provide arts hounds year-round cultural events and international exhibitions. Families spend many a day at COSI, our science center, and at the world-class Columbus Zoo. Speaking of families, Columbus is a wonderful city in which to raise a family, but it's also a great place to be solo or a young professional, given downtown's evolving residential and social scene.

Get to know the city through neighborhood walks, culinary experiences, local libations, and all sorts of fun indoor and outdoor adventures. Themed itineraries help those visiting for a short time see the best of Columbus, while locals might enjoy finding hidden gems in other parts of town. Suggestions are made for getaways within a few hours driving distance that are totally worth the trip.

Once you start flipping through the *Insiders' Guide to Columbus,* you'll quickly realize there is a little bit of something for everyone in the "Capital City." The objectives of this guide are to help visitors make the most of a weekend, introduce Columbus to newcomers, and inspire lifelong residents to go exploring. As the city grows and evolves, there are always new experiences to be had. My hope is that you use this guide to enjoy all that Ohio's capital has to offer. I have had a great time discovering the "Discovery City" and hope you do too.

ACKNOWLEDGMENTS

Many years ago, I learned a friend was coming to work in Columbus and attempted to purchase a travel guide for her, but there was none to be found. After corresponding with Globe Pequot Press, it was determined I would write *Insiders' Guide to Columbus*. This project remains special to me for many reasons, but mostly because it was the first comprehensive travel guide written about the very deserving capital of Ohio. I would like to thank the publisher for investing in this much-needed third edition, and my editor, Greta Schmitz, for her engaged and patient feedback.

I want to extend my thanks to many people for their support, but especially to my partner, Dan Ralley, whom I have been able to count on for so many things peripheral to writing this book, including lending an editorial eye and insights to Columbus business and government, taking photos, providing shoulder massages, making meals, and entertaining the kids while I write. You are my Renaissance Man and hero! And to Madalyn and Gabe Ralley, who bring their kid expertise, incredible sense of adventure, and curiosity to all the family-fun stuff.

Thanks to Mandy Jones, my sister and traveler extraordinaire, for taking time to go exploring, and who, along with my mother, Kitty, is always ready and willing to read through chapters. I am grateful for your ongoing input. Brian Jones, Sam, and Mira always embrace the family fun when we sniff out new things to do.

Special thanks to my besties, the "ladies who lunch" (and happy hour), and all the wonderful women who open my eyes to different experiences in and around Columbus: Sherri Noll, Missy Garland, Annie Vian, Tamra Fuscaldo, JoAnne Schorsten, Sarah Bacha, Meredith Scott, Julie Kriss, Shawn Ireland, and Doreen Rogers. We never need an excuse to celebrate, but always find one!

Again, to my dear friend JoAnne Schorsten for the thoughtful conversations about the state of Columbus real estate and development, dining and cocktails—and for your retail connoisseurship. Thank you, Jean Ralley, for keeping us on the Afternoon Tea circuit and in constant search for local rye bread. And Dr. Lisa Hinkelman and Lauren Hancock for their tireless efforts through ROX to help Columbus girls grow up healthy and confident.

My guys: Gary L., Michael, L. Nick K., Stephen H., Kent K., Tom M., Nate E., Justin M., Aaron G., and Lee L.: I adore your willingness to do the "heavy foodie" research. I always look forward to eating in and out with all of you. Thanks for keeping Columbus fun and entertaining! And to my Columbus-emeritus guys: Chet Domitz and Rob Pilarski, Paul Feeney and Dr. Chad, and Steven Weber and Malcolm Riggle. Columbus misses you.

Thanks, Rod Chu, for letting me ride your coattails into exclusive dining experiences and always being at the ready to school me in Chinese food; Tommy Tucker for running a top-notch recreational cooking program at The Mix and making sure I know of every karaoke bar in town; and Phil Wells, our favorite *homme de chanson-et-danse*.

Many thanks go out to the family and friends who each have added to our adventures in Columbus in different ways: Dan Noll, Dan Fuscaldo, Marty Vian, Jim Bacha, Meredith and Kip Wahler; and to David Ralley and Jonathan Ralinovsky's ongoing search for immigrant food and for suggesting all the thrift stores, knowing this is not quite my wheelhouse.

I value so many of the foodie folks that help bring visibility to the Columbus culinary scene, like Bethia Woolf of Columbus Food Adventures and Nick Dekker, Dr. Breakfast himself. I appreciate Dr. Mark Arceño's input about the Ohio wine industry and all of you who run the great local farmers' markets.

One of the most exciting aspects of writing this guide is having legitimate reasons to explore new parts of town, experience new places, and meet new people. If it weren't for so many of you taking the time to return calls, meet with me, and offer personal or professional opinions about Columbus, I would not have accumulated such a broad base of information over the years.

Special thanks to BJ Leiberman of Chapman Eats Market, Ashley Dominici of Luftig Loft, and Cameron Mitchell Restaurants, along with Bethia at Columbus Food Adventures, Karen Chrestay at Worthington Farmers' Market, Experience Worthington, The Ohio State University, Mandy Jones, Norm Hall, and Amy Paulin for contributing photos. Much appreciation to the Omni Hotels for their hospitality in helping me showcase Columbus's close proximity to such unique and beautiful regions and being the custodian for so many beautiful properties.

It has been very special indeed to revise this third edition, and I welcome the opportunity to learn even more about my hometown on an ongoing basis.

Insiders' Guide to Columbus is dedicated to my fun little family—Dan, Madalyn, and Gabe—who are always up for an adventure and exploring new places, and are very good eaters!

HOW TO USE THIS BOOK

When you first get a new travel guide, what do you usually do? Head straight to the history chapter to try to figure out what the place is all about? Delve into the dining and nightlife sections to figure out how much food and entertainment you can consume in one night? Or, like me, do you just thumb through, anticipating that "something special" will catch your eye? Whatever your technique, *Insiders' Guide*'s user-friendly format doesn't require reading from front to back—unless you want to, of course. *Insiders' Guide* veterans and beginners alike will find that any approach to using this guide is the right approach.

When I first relocated to Columbus 25 years ago, I could have used a comprehensive, in-depth resource like this—with the pivotal word being *used*. The second edition of *Insiders' Guide to Columbus* builds on the original base of information gathered through research, observations, conversations, and debates. This revision is the result of a year of research, tweaking, and fine-tuning—not to mention an equal amount of eating, drinking, and merriment. I took a very interactive approach to compiling this information, so one suggestion for using this guide is to take the same approach and really use it. Consider this book a manual to be annotated, highlighted, discussed, and shared. It's very special to have written this guide, and I invite you to begin your exploration of Columbus here.

Insiders' Guide to Columbus is written for you, the tourist. The chapters on Accommodations, Restaurants, and Nightlife are organized according to cuisine and neighborhood, so you can easily determine what you want to eat and where you want to stay. When passing through Columbus, this guide should help you easily find quality accommodations, good eats, and something fun to do.

First-time visitors to Columbus have been pleasantly surprised at the variety and caliber of shopping, dining, and other activities often associated with much bigger cities. Of course, we have our high-end shopping, such as Saks Fifth Avenue, Nordstrom, and Williams-Sonoma. We have our fair share of chain restaurants, like The Cheesecake Factory and P.F. Changs, and can boast the original Wendy's and White Castle headquarters. As many a fine meal that can be had at national chains, this guide's objective is to highlight the local, independent restaurants, bars, and shops offering a distinct Columbus experience.

Insiders' Guide to Columbus is written for you, the transplant. If you are relocated, working long-term, or attending college in Columbus, this guide will familiarize you with our communities, traditions, and events. The Relocation chapter describes Columbus neighborhoods, detailing libraries, post offices, local utilities, and other practical information. Those with a family may be particularly interested in the Family Fun and Education chapters. Animal lovers will be happy to learn that *Purina Magazine* ranked Columbus the eighth Pet Healthiest City in the US in their most recent study. The Pet-Friendly Columbus chapter includes details about kennels, vets, and other animal services.

Newcomers may also want to spend a little extra time looking over the chapters unique to Columbus. Golf lovers can read up on the Golden Bear, Jack Nicklaus, and his annual Memorial Tournament. The chapter dedicated to The Ohio State University will provide students and parents with pertinent information about campus living, Buckeye sports, university facilities, and various organizations. Here you will be introduced to the "Best Damn Band in the Land" and learn to navigate one of the largest universities in the country. No chapter about OSU is complete without a list of campus pizza shops and watering holes. Hopefully, this fundamental information will make your transition to Columbus a little smoother and, most of all, fun.

Finally, *Insiders' Guide to Columbus* is written for you, the native. It is amazing how Columbus is growing and evolving. In fact, Columbus's population has increased in every census since 1830 and is estimated to grow by another million over 10 years. No matter how long you have lived here, there are always new experiences to be had and different parts of town to explore. You may discover your new favorite restaurant, find a romantic getaway, or attend a festival for the first time. Permanent "Insiders" may even learn a new tidbit of trivia about the "Capital City."

The Attractions and Worth the Trip chapters reinforce Columbus's centralized location, though represent only a handful of interesting places you can easily visit. History buffs revel in bygone days at Historic Zoar or Roscoe Villages or make the short drive to Serpent Mound, a spectacular Native American effigy recently made a UNESCO World heritage Site. Sports fans pilgrimage to the Football Hall of Fame, and outdoorsy types get back to nature in a short drive south to the Hocking Hills. Step into another world by visiting Ohio's heartland, home to the world's largest Amish and Mennonite population. Here you can buy fine handcrafted furniture, crafts, and remarkable cheese. Read on to learn why Sugarcreek is called "Little Switzerland." Many locals don't realize there is a taste of Europe on our doorstep.

HOW THIS BOOK IS ORGANIZED

Insiders' Guide to Columbus is not meant to be an exhaustive directory of restaurants and hotels but rather an organized guide explaining what makes Columbus "what it is." It highlights the special attractions and features that make our city unique and fun. For example, where can you have a sophisticated business lunch at noon, a rowdy happy hour after work, and listen to live music at night? Lots of places! Where can you go for a fun family Friday, rock climbing on Saturday, and run off the dog's energy on Sunday? Lots of places! The format of the *Insiders' Guide* is designed to make sense of an overwhelming amount of information.

After finding out how you can get to and around the city in the chapter not surprisingly titled Getting Here, Getting Around, take a little time to bring yourself up to speed on Columbus's history and our famous (and infamous) sons and daughters. The History chapter will explain how a little town along the banks of the Scioto River grew into the cosmopolitan city it is today.

If you're new to Columbus, you may want to linger a bit in Area Overview, an introduction to Columbus today. It discusses the current state of the city, its ambience, cost of living, and people. It offers vital statistics and information about its political atmosphere as the capital of Ohio and its diverse people and economy.

If you already know the basics about Columbus, it's time to dig in. Are you looking for restaurants, live music, theaters, or lodging for a staycation? Or perhaps you're seeking more practical information. General discussions of schools, worship, retirement, and wellness are included in their respective chapters. Restaurants, bars, and retail therapy are self-explanatory. Restaurants are listed by neighborhood, but short lists call out the top 10 of various categories of dining, such as Breakfast, Burgers, and Mexican classics.

Entries organized geographically begin downtown and work their way through the Franklinton, Arena District, Short North, and slightly farther north to OSU's campus. The entries then move east, south, and west through the city neighborhoods, finishing up north of the city in Dublin. Standardized listings include the name, address, telephone number, website (if available), and price code (if applicable) for each entry, as well as a description. If no town name is listed, assume the location is within the city limits of Columbus.

Each entry strives to maintain the most up-to-date information; however, if you find inaccuracies, feel an important tip has been left out, or discover a place that deserves mention, we'll be glad to explore these suggestions for subsequent editions. Please send a note to editorial@GlobePequot.com.

Relocating can be stressful, and having to feel your way around a new city only compounds that stress. Entertaining visitors can be equally nerve-racking. No matter what your status—tourist, transplant, or lifer—*Insiders' Guide to Columbus* is written for you. Whatever the reasons and how you decide to use this guide is up to you. It is a resource to help you discover Columbus in a fun, easy—and personal—way.

AREA OVERVIEW

Christopher Columbus. Our namesake—but why? When researching this book, I assumed there was some profound reason the founders chose to name the capital of Ohio after the great explorer, but there wasn't. The best (and very anticlimactic) explanation I found is that the name was arbitrarily selected. Columbus could just as easily have been named Ohio City or High Bank, but they passed on both. The History chapter will go into greater detail about the original city of Franklinton being moved from the west bank of the Scioto River to higher ground on the east due to perpetual flooding. It was at this point, in 1812, that Franklinton was renamed Columbus and this same year designated the "Capital City" of Ohio.

Many people are surprised to learn Columbus is the 14th-largest city in the country, with a population of more than 1.8 million. Along with this booming development comes big-city sprawl. Yet somehow Columbus has been able to retain a small-town, middle-America charm. Navigating the city is still manageable, even given its continuous growth. Columbus was planned from conception and has two ring roads that are cut by a north–south and an east–west highway, making it easy to get around.

Columbus is privileged enough to boast four proper seasons. Summers are beautiful, with billowing clouds floating lazily in the big blue sky, but they are often accompanied by sweltering temperatures and high humidity. Autumns tend to linger, warming up residential streets with flaming trees, reviving harvest festivals, farmers' markets, and Ohio State football. Indian summer sometimes hangs around well into the holiday season. When winter finally sets in, it is crisp, cold, and often very snowy. Central Ohio is frequently subjected to subfreezing temperatures, so spring is a welcome reprieve despite the rain.

Speaking of which, not much is more American than Benjamin Franklin—another namesake—for whom the original city, Franklinton, was named in 1797, as well as Franklin County, established in 1803. Columbus lies in Franklin County, along with 12 other cities, 12 villages, and 18 townships. As of the 2023 estimated census, a population of almost 1.3 million resides within Franklin County, making it the country's 32rd-largest metro area. Another half million people live in seven surrounding counties that, along with Franklin, comprise the Columbus Metropolitan Statistical Area (MSA). These seven counties are Delaware, Fairfield, Licking, Madison, Pickaway, Morrow, and Union.

Now that you know how we got our name, read on to learn how we got our reputation. The remaining chapters will introduce you to our city, people, and economics—the heart, soul, and lifeblood of Columbus. Get a quick snapshot of the city by checking out the vital statistics. You may be surprised to learn what people and ideas were born in our city.

DOWNTOWN: A 21ST-CENTURY RENAISSANCE

Columbus has one of those skylines that may not be immediately recognizable, but several distinct buildings do make it memorable. One can't help but be awe-inspired by the oldest skyscraper in the skyline, the LeVeque Tower, with its verticality and sculptures that scream 1920s art deco. One Nationwide Plaza is reminiscent of the former twin towers of New York's World Trade Center in the way they stand a solid and seemingly unmovable mass of 1970s concrete and steel. And then there is Miranova, the crescent-shaped condominiums that marked Columbus's move into the new millennium.

Downtown Columbus encompasses 2.2 square miles bound by I-670, I- 71, Highway 315, and CSX Railroad, making it one of the nation's largest downtowns. Geographically speaking, Columbus's size is comparable to San Antonio or Charlotte. This area is home to nearly 20 hotels, 4 theaters, and nearly

Downtown Columbus skyline at night Norm Hall

200 eating and drinking establishments. Good thing, because nearly 50 million visitors pass through the Capital City annually.

Several new builds since the last edition include Huntington Park, the baseball stadium for the Columbus Clippers; Lower.com Field, home to MLS champions Columbus Crew; the Grange Insurance Audubon Center, the nation's first urban ecological center; and a bunch of new hotels with rooftop bars. The historic Lazarus Building was the Midwest's largest "green" project and the city's first environment-conscious building. The Scioto Mile, a series of interconnected, riverfront park systems featuring river-walks, promenades, bridges, and continuous bike paths between parks all make downtown Columbus a more pleasant place to work, visit, and live.

The development of urban green spaces is essential to making any downtown living attractive, but even more vital is housing. Downtown residential development is booming; with 114 high-rises and more condos and other units being built, there is no shortage of options for those who prefer city living. And fear not, city dwellers; there is no need to venture to the suburbs for "proper" grocery shopping, as the Brewery District is home to a full-scale Kroger grocery, while Hills Market also has a smaller store on Grant Street.

Keep in mind that with all these new plans and changes happening in downtown Columbus, many of the surrounding communities are undertaking their own revitalization efforts, like Franklinton and Italian Village. As Columbus grows and changes, so too will subsequent editions of this guide.

THE NECKLACE OF NEIGHBORHOODS

If you have an opportunity to explore the sprawling Columbus area outside downtown, you will find a varied landscape ranging from highways and scenic roads to rural farmland and developing suburbs.

Barns are found around the corner from major shopping malls and homes worth seven figures a short distance from low-income housing.

With such a variety of neighborhoods, it is impossible to pinpoint an architectural style typical to Columbus. There are many neighborhoods with cavernous Victorian homes, but even they vary in terms of their location and style. Take a drive (or a stroll) through Olde Towne East or Victorian Village and you'll find a number of homes built between the 1850s and 1890s, spanning the spectrum from traditional to garish. Both the Italianate and Queen Anne styles are heavily represented, but the Victorians' obsession with period revivals is evident as well. You'll find Tudor Revivals, Neoclassical Revivals, Georgian Revivals, and Colonial Revivals, not to mention the eclectic homes that go unclassified.

The wealth and eccentricity of the Victorian period continue to set these parts of town apart from others, but eclectic building styles exist all over Columbus. Historic homes in Old Worthington, giant Georgians of New Albany, monstrous mansions in Bexley, tight-quartered brownstones in German Village, and new developments in just about every part of town offer unique living experiences in each neighborhood.

HIGH STREET

As it leaves the cobbled streets of German Village, High Street passes through the center of downtown Columbus, flanked by austere government buildings, modern hotels, and parking lots. Just outside the city center, the Short North, with its storefront boutiques, restaurants, and town houses, has a SoHo feel to it, while a mile farther up High Street are the unmistakable signs of campus life: cheap eats, tattoo and music shops, beautiful university architecture, and not-so-beautiful off-campus housing—not to mention the occasional protest or street performer seen along High Street at The Ohio State University.

At Hudson Avenue, the neighborhood begins to transition from a university to a residential setting. Clintonville and Beechwold are quintessential tree-lined streets, with character-ridden older houses that are still affordable when compared with Worthington, the next community north. Old Worthington, with its many pubs, restaurants, and shops, is a good place to finish a tour of High Street.

From German Village to Worthington, this 10-mile stretch of road passes through six altogether different neighborhoods, six completely different cityscapes with six different local flavors. Keep in mind that this is just the north–south axis. If you drive east–west through town, you'll experience the same thing. No matter which side of Columbus you venture to, you'll come across distinctive neighborhoods, each with its own identity and sense of community.

Encircling the city is a "necklace of neighborhoods." These suburbs likewise each have a distinct character. Columbus maintains a reputation for being safe and clean and offering an affordable cost of living when compared with other cities of its size. This is part of what makes Columbus family-friendly. People are born and raised here, and often they stay here. People move here, and they stay too.

THE EVERYMAN

When you come to Columbus, what sort of people do you expect to encounter? Columbus is diverse. It has a unique population for a Midwestern city, so much so that major news outlets have referred to Columbus residents as "the 'Everyman' of America," because the city's population mirrors the rest of the US. Politicians woo Ohio to no end; we are a test market for new products, a breeding ground for new wining and dining concepts. But why?

Columbus is culturally, religiously, and ethnically diverse. In fact, there are more multiracial people in Franklin County than any other county in Ohio. Minorities comprise 25 percent of the population, while Franklin County has the largest number of Asians, Pacific Islanders, and Native Americans in the whole of Ohio. The city's population has burgeoned over the past 20 years, with the greatest increase seen in Hispanic and Asian populations, and is projected to grow by another million in the next 10 years

The state of Ohio might be a more representative cross section of America than Columbus, which on average is younger and more educated, with a higher disposable income than that of typical metros the same size. This makes our locals very attractive for new test markets.

Columbus offers up the youthful demographics considered to be "risk takers" or "early adopters," meaning if a Columbusite latches onto a new product or trend (or politician), there's the likelihood the vast middle of the American population will latch onto it as well. As a side note, advertising is more affordable here than in other cities, which may add a little to Columbus's test market appeal.

Columbus also is educated. Thirty-five percent of Franklin County's population holds a bachelor's degree, while almost 10 percent have graduate or professional degrees.

There is, however, a lot more to the Columbus population than trendsetting, smarty-pants, or making and breaking political campaigns. On the whole, we are a fun lot. We are families, and we are singles. We are gay, and we are straight. We love a good football game, and we love a good festival. We are good neighbors and responsible members of the community.

One thing that stands out about the general population is that, along with the strong sense of community comes a tremendous love of giving. Columbus residents are social minded and community service oriented, giving back when and how we can. This can be seen in fund-raisers of the most creative types for charities of all sorts. From small, nonprofit organizations like A Kid Again to massive, corporate campaigns for the United Way, Columbus residents are very passionate about making our city a better place to live and visit.

COLUMBUS SPEAK

People of Columbus speak with a rather nondescript Midwestern accent, but a few words will raise an eyebrow when it comes time to actually verbalize them. Here is a pronunciation guide for the few that might cause a little grief.

Bellefontaine—For you French-speaking purists, forget about it! In the ongoing effort to butcher the beautiful French language, this town is pronounced Bell Fountain.

Morse Road—When a local says "Morse Road," it often comes out sounding like "Morris Road." Morse Road, which runs east–west, dead-ends into High Street in Clintonville, so be sure not to drive around in confusion looking for "Morris Road."

Newark—One might be inclined to pronounce this like the city in New Jersey, but this Columbus suburb's name has been condensed into one slurred syllable. Call us lazy, but we call it "Nerk."

Olentangy (River and Boulevard)—It is *not* pronounced O-len-tangy (as in a tangy sauce), but O-len-tan-gee (as in "gee"-whiz; that's how it's pronounced).

Riffe Building (and Theaters)—I have heard this mistakenly called the Riff Building. It is named for a longtime Columbus senator Vernal Riffe, and rhymes with wife.

Scioto—This river's name has a silent c: Sigh-OH-tuh, not Sky-OH-tuh.

STRICTLY BUSINESS

Columbus never had the geographical advantage of being on a major water port like Cincinnati or Cleveland, so the opportunity to develop into a big industrial base was never part of its history. While Columbus has some manufacturing, it was during the late 20th century that the city came into its own with a booming service and distribution economy, holding true to its market town roots.

Without the weighty legacy of its sister Ohio port cities, Columbus has a nimbleness and willingness to innovate that has allowed it to develop a reputation as a leader in modern economies of banking, insurance, health care, finance, government, and biomedical research. In additional to being the state capital and the home of one of the largest universities in the country, the city is well known for its progressive, high-tech businesses, but retail and distribution have long been the driving forces behind the economy. Columbus is headquarters for 5 Fortune 500 companies and another 20 Fortune 1000 companies. It was also the launching pad for top corporations such as L Brands, Wendy's International, Abercrombie & Fitch, and Nationwide Insurance. The presence of these major companies has now inspired a whole series of related businesses that call central Ohio home. A diversified economy, as well as its outstanding workforce, is the key to the city's and region's strength. Consequently, Columbus has

Vital Statistics

- **Founded** by Lucas Sullivant in 1797 as Franklinton
- **Mayor of Columbus (2016):** Andrew Ginther (D)
- **Governor of Ohio (2018):** Mike DeWine (R)
- **Nicknames:** "Discovery City," "Capital City"
- **Population (2022):** Columbus, 907,000 (est.); Franklin County, 1,321,820 (est.); Columbus metro area, approximately 1.8 million
- **Land area:** 223 square miles (5.9 square miles is water)
- **Counties:** Columbus Metropolitan Statistical Area consists of eight counties: Franklin, Delaware, Fairfield, Licking, Madison, Pickaway, Morrow, and Union
- **Airports:** John Glenn International Airport (CMH), Rickenbacker International Airport (LCK), Bolton Field (TZR), Ohio State's Don Scott Field (OSU)
- **Interstates:** I-70, I-71, I-270, I-670
- **Temperatures:** Average temperature in January 28°F, July 75°F
  Average temperatures (°F):

	High	Low
Winter	35	19
Spring	62	41
Summer	84	63
Autumn	65	43

- **Precipitation:** Average 38 inches of rainfall, 22 inches of snowfall annually
- **Local time:** Eastern Standard Time (EST)
- **Public transportation:** COTA bus system
- **Bureau of Motor Vehicles:** 1970 W. Broad St.; (844) 644-6268. There are about 15 centers in Franklin County. Driver's licenses, vehicle registration, titles, and new resident information can be found online at www.bmv.ohio.gov.
- **Driving age:** 16
- **Driving facts:**
  - If you hit a deer, you are entitled to take the carcass, but the collision must be reported to a game protector or law enforcement within 24 hours.
  - The blood-alcohol level for Columbus is 0.08. Your license will be revoked if you are found guilty of driving under the influence of alcohol or if you refuse to take a chemical or physical test.
- **Alcohol laws:** Age 21 to purchase and consume alcohol. Beer and wine can be purchased in grocery and convenience stores, while hard liquor is sold in licensed stores, sometimes located within grocery stores.

- **Marriage:** In order to get married in Columbus, both parties must be 18 years of age. Both parties must apply in person at the Franklin County Probate Court, 373 S. High St.; the license fee is $65 cash or credit.
- **Sales tax:** 7.5 percent
- **Columbus Chamber of Commerce:** 150 S. Front St.; (614) 221-1321; www.columbus.org
- **Daily newspaper:** *Columbus Dispatch*
- **Visitor center:** Experience Columbus, 277 W. Nationwide Blvd., Arena District, and at Easton Town Center
- **Major colleges/universities:** Capital University, Columbus State University, Denison University, Franklin University, Ohio Dominican University, The Ohio State University, Ohio Wesleyan University, Otterbein College, Wittenberg University, Muskingum College
- **Key business sectors in Columbus:** Professional and business services, government, health, education, retail, logistics, e-commerce, R&D, manufacturing
- **Top Columbus employers:** State of Ohio, The Ohio State University, JPMorgan Chase, federal government, Nationwide Insurance, OhioHealth, City of Columbus, Columbus public schools, L Brands, Honda, Amazon

an unemployment rate below the national average and has been able to endure national economic downturns.

Columbus is a "smart city" and is now one of the top 10 cities for cloud computing, including Amazon, Facebook, and Google data centers, and Intel is now taking up residence. Research and development is Columbus's best-kept secret. Battelle, headquartered in Columbus, coupled with the hospitals at OSU, Children's Hospital, and Cardinal Health, to name a few, provides the world with cutting-edge R&D in biotechnology. Honda and the Transportation Research Center, near Marysville, is where hundreds of new automobiles are tested each year. This has led to the creation of the US-33 Smart Mobility Corridor where autonomous vehicles are being tested in a real-world environment.

This growth in research and development was built on an already strong foundation of advanced logistics. Rickenbacker Airport is a designated Foreign Trade Zone that helps distribute many of the global online goods that consumers now purchase from major online clothing retailers. Columbus's location within a day's drive of over 50 percent of the US and Canadian markets makes Columbus one of the most cost-effective locations in the country to do business.

The information in the following chapters provides more than a glimpse of what makes the quality of life in Columbus so attractive for those who choose to live here and what keeps people coming back.

Famous and Infamous

George Bellows—born in Columbus; The Ohio State University; Ashcan School artist

Milt Caniff—The Ohio State University; creator of comic strips "Terry and the Pirates" and "Steve Canyon"

Ellen Walker Craig-Jones—born in Urbancrest; first African American woman elected mayor of a US municipality (1972)

Mildred Gilars, aka "Axis Sally"—studied theater arts at Ohio Wesleyan University; broadcasted for Nazi propaganda radio during World War II, jailed as the first woman convicted of treason against the US, then returned to live out life in central Ohio

John Glenn—Muskingum College; first American astronaut to orbit the earth and oldest human to go to space; Ohio senator

Archie Griffin—born in Columbus; The Ohio State University; professional football player, only player to win the Heisman Trophy twice

Benjamin R. Hanby—Otterbein College; early Ohio songwriter; composed popular Christmas tune "Up on a Housetop"; museum home in Westerville

Jack Hanna—Otterbein College and Capital University; director emeritus of the Columbus Zoo, "Jungle Jack" Hannah TV personality

Rutherford B. Hayes—born in Columbus; 19th president of the US

"Woody" Hayes—Denison University and The Ohio State University; very outspoken (and very successful) OSU football coach

Curtis E. LeMay—born in Columbus; The Ohio State University; controversial general headed World War II bomber forces, youngest and longest-serving four-star general

Anne O'Hare McCormick—grew up in Columbus; Ohio Dominican University; first woman to win a Pulitzer Prize (1937) for her foreign journalism with the *New York Times*

Geraldine "Jerrie" Mock—born in Newark, Ohio; first woman to fly solo around the world (1964) in a Cessna 180 named *Spirit of Columbus*

Jack Nicklaus—born in Upper Arlington; The Ohio State University; golfer, course designer, and founder of the Memorial Tournament

Jesse Owens—The Ohio State University; track-and-field star, first American to win four gold medals in a single Olympics at the 1936 Olympics in Berlin

Bobby Rahal—Dennison University; race car driver and team owner, ranked first in career starts, second in career earnings when he retired in 1998

Eddie Rickenbacker—born in Columbus; premier World War I combat pilot; race car driver

Branch Rickey—Ohio Wesleyan University; coach of Brooklyn Dodgers, integrated Major League Baseball by recruiting Jackie Robinson; pioneered the use of baseball statistics and batting helmets

Alice Schille—born in Columbus; Columbus College of Art and Design; America's foremost female watercolorist, renowned for impressionist and postimpressionist paintings

James Thurber—born in Columbus; The Ohio State University; writer, journalist, humorist, playwright, and cartoonist

GETTING HERE, GETTING AROUND

I f you look at a detailed map of the city, you'll see downtown Columbus is oriented north-south along the Scioto River at a point near its confluence with the Olentangy River. The preface to this book notes that Columbus is within a day's drive of over 50 percent of the US population, and the mileage chart shows how this is the case. Many large Midwest and East Coast cities are within a reasonable driving distance, which is why I have included some fun weekend getaways in the Worth the Trip chapter.

GETTING HERE

Roadways

Columbus sits at the junction of two major highway intersections: I-70 is the major east–west thoroughfare, and I-71 is the major north–south highway through the city. Both of these roads connect to beltways around the city. I-270 (Outer Belt) is the bypass loop that runs the entire way around Columbus. It connects to I-70 and I-71 from all directions. I-670 (Inner Belt) rings only the downtown and provides a hassle-free route between the airport and the city center.

There are several roads in Columbus where the route numbers and street names are used interchangeably. Columbus, having been settled by Europeans, has a few High Streets. There is one in Dublin and another in Gahanna, but US 23 is *the* High Street. It runs all the way north halfway to Toledo and dead-ends on the southern border of Ohio in Portsmouth. It is referred to as High Street in the 12-mile vicinity of Columbus, but farther north and south of the city the road is referred to as US 23.

Broad Street, which runs east–west through the city, is slightly more confusing. Broad Street is the same as the historical US 40 to the east of the city, but the road splits a mile to the west of Bexley where Broad Street becomes US 16, and is referred to as such farther east of the city. The picturesque Riverside Drive, also known as US 33, runs north–south along the Olentangy River. It is a nice diversion from the main drag if you have some spare time to enjoy the scenic route.

Highway 315 is another important highway that runs north–south through the city and intersects all the other highways. The major exits to The Ohio State University and the Schottenstein Center are off Highway 315. The Lane Avenue, Fifth Avenue/King Avenue exit ramps back up quickly on game days and during concerts, so be sure to allow yourself time to get through the congestion or find an alternate route during major events. When the Buckeyes are playing a home football game, you can see (and hear!) the stadium from Highway 315—it is quite a sight.

The Ohio Department of Transportation has embarked on a 10-year plan to rebuild stressed roads and to address issues of congestion and high-crash areas on freeways. Needless to say, we must all get used to navigating an obstacle course of orange barrels or driving at a snail's pace through construction zones, but given the layout of Columbus, it's never difficult to find alternate routes.

Mileage Chart from Columbus

Baltimore	420
Chicago	311
Cincinnati	101
Cleveland	143
Detroit	204
Indianapolis	175
Lexington	197
Louisville	210
Nashville	384
New York City	589
Pittsburgh	195

 **Close-up**

America's Golden Highway, US 40

US 40 once stretched 3,200 miles between Atlantic City, New Jersey, and San Francisco, passing directly through Columbus. It was believed by some that it was designated "40" because the route closely follows the 40th parallel, but this is not the case. The highway naming system, developed in the 1920s, just happened to come up with that numerical coincidence.

US 40 became a certified highway in 1926, but its predecessor, the "National Road," was created by an act of Congress in 1806 under President Thomas Jefferson. The goal was to connect the Atlantic Ocean and the Ohio River over land, making the National Road the first federally funded highway. Prior to this approval from Congress, Colonel Ebenezer Zane and his brothers were anxious to start cutting their way into the Northwest Territory (now central Ohio), so in 1796, they forged ahead with their own road, following even earlier Native American footpaths.

This important road was, at one point, rerouted to run through Columbus's business district at the request of influential politicians and businessmen. This explains the little jog that US 40 takes through downtown Columbus near Bexley. The road was meant to link various capital cities, but nearby Dayton, feeling slighted by the road bypassing it altogether, created a misleading "alternate" route through the community. By the time railroads were being built in the 1830s, the National Road crossed Ohio into Indiana.

When the interstate highways were built, 800 miles of this transcontinental road were decommissioned. Ohio is fortunate to have escaped with most of the historic road still in use, even after I-70 was built parallel to it.

If you have the opportunity to drive US 40 east of Columbus, certain parts of the road become very narrow and rural. One gains a sense of what it was like to travel along the "Main Street of America" before the road-building boom of the 1920s and '30s. A stop-off at the Zane Grey/National Road Museum along the way or viewing www.route40.net provide further insight into America's Golden Highway history, its milestones, and other tidbits of trivia.

Air Travel

Columbus has two international airports: John Glenn International Airport and Rickenbacker International Airport. Their accessibility and competitive airfares are just two reasons Columbus is a valuable choice for a business location and an affordable travel location. Check out the quick fly times—even to the West Coast.

i In 1984 the city of Columbus received the commissioned sculpture titled *Brushstrokes in Flight* from Roy Lichtenstein. It is located inside the main terminal of John Glenn International Airport, and you can't miss it. The 26 feet of brightly painted aluminum make it a great meeting spot.

Flight Times from Columbus

Most of the flights here are direct, but the timing for a few includes one stop.

Atlanta   1 hour, 30 minutes
Austin   3 hours
Baltimore/Washington, DC   1 hour, 20 minutes
Boston   2 hours
Charleston   3 hours, 30 minutes
Chicago   1 hour
Denver   2 hours, 30 minutes
Houston/Dallas   2 hours, 30 minutes
Kansas City   2 hours, 30 minutes
Los Angeles   4 hours, 15 minutes
Miami/Fort Lauderdale   2 hours, 45 minutes
New Orleans   4 hours
New York   2 hours
Seattle   5 hours
St. Louis   1 hour, 30 minutes

JOHN GLENN INTERNATIONAL AIRPORT (CMH)

(formerly Port Columbus International
  Airport)
4600 International Gateway
(614) 239-4000
https://flycolumbus.com

John Glenn International Airport (CMH) is situated 15 minutes east of downtown Columbus and is easily accessible from all parts of town. In fact, this location makes it one of the most easily accessible airports in the country. It is also one of the fastest-growing airports in the Northeast, which is reflected in the recent renovation of all concourses, the expansion of food and retail operations, and the opening of the new air traffic control tower.

Served by 12 airlines with nearly 400 daily flights, including more than 50 nonstop destinations, John Glenn is an international airport that is relatively hassle-free. Despite its 35 gates and 730,000-square-foot main terminal, a user-friendly layout makes the airport manageable. With 6.7 million annual passengers and tight security measures in place, allow ample time for check-in. Watch for a possible $2 billion airport rebuild in the next six years, which will boost capacity and ease of commutes.

If you have time to kill, "cool your jets" at a few chain restaurants such as Bob Evans and Donoto's Pizza or at a local original such as Columbus Land-Grant Brewing Co. Stop in at Starbucks for a morning coffee "on the fly," or a salad from the Farmer's Fridge or treat from the Jeni's Ice Cream or illy Coffee kiosks. Grab last-minute souvenirs from Columbus Marketplace or Scioto Mercantile. It is nearly impossible to leave Columbus without acquiring some sort of Buckeye paraphernalia.

If you have a little time to check in for your flight, you can save some money by parking in the remote lot and catching the shuttle to the airport. The Parking Spot is just outside the airport at 1399 Stelzer Rd. The app makes it convenient to prepay and scan in to the secured lot where you can choose covered or uncovered parking. The circulating shuttle picks up and delivers you to the terminal and vice versa. Get more information at www.theparkingspot.com.

Besides food and drink, John Glenn International provides other services for the weary traveler. An interfaith meditation room is located on the baggage claim level across from carousel 6. Also on the baggage claim level is an information center where you can pick up maps of Columbus, get visitor information, or have your party paged.

With luggage in hand, it is an easy jaunt to access ground transportation via the terminal walkway or the ground level near baggage claim. Here, you can hail a cab or grab a shuttle to your hotel or the parking lots. Taxi service is offered by a number of companies, and the fare into downtown from the airport is on average around $22. It takes anywhere from 20 to 30 minutes to get into the city center, depending on the time of day.

Be advised that when picking up passengers, you are not permitted to stop your car outside the passenger pick-up area. Security will wave you on, so just keep moving. You can either park in the garage and go into the airport or just keep looping around through the arrival area until your party exits the building. It is here you find jet-lagged souls waiting with their deer-in-the-headlights gaze, examining each car as it slowly passes by—similar to travelers catatonically watching baggage glide past on the belt, until that glimmer of recognition lights up their faces when they see the familiar bag (or in this case, the car) roll up alongside them.

MAJOR AIRLINES

Many major airlines are represented in Columbus, including a few low-cost airlines.

Air Canada—Concourse B
(888) 247-2262
www.aircanada.ca

Alaska Airlines—Concourse C
(800) 252-7522
www.alaskaair.com

American Airlines—Concourse B
(800) 433-7300
www.aa.com

Breeze Airways—Concourse C
www.flybreeze.com

Delta—Concourse C
(800) 221-1212
www.delta.com

Frontier Airlines—Concourse C
(801) 401-9000
www.flyfrontier.com

Spirit Airlines—Concourse B
(855) 728-3555
www.spirit.com

Southwest—Concourse A
(800) 435-9792
www.southwest.com

Sun Country Airlines—Concourse C
(651) 905-2737
www.suncountry.com

United Airlines—Concourse B
(800) 241-6522
www.ual.com

Vacation Express—Concourse C
(800) 309-4717
www.vacationexpress.com

PARKING

Parking is convenient in the attached six-level parking garage that offers short- and long-term parking. Short-term parking costs $3 per hour up to a maximum of $30, while long-term parking runs $5 for the first hour up to $22 per day.

Two outdoor, uncovered lots offer a more economical solution to long-term parking needs, especially if you have time to park and ride to the airport. The lots are safe and well lit, and free 24-hour shuttle service to and from the terminal is provided from covered stations located throughout the lot.

The Blue Lot, which is closest to the terminal, may shave a few minutes off your shuttle ride and offers both uncovered and covered parking at $10 per day. Another perk of the Blue Lot is a shuttle drop-off service from a shuttle stop. The slightly farther Red Lot offers long-term uncovered parking for $8 per day, while the farthest Green Lot is $6 per day. All daily rates are based on a 24-hour parking period but are otherwise prorated for each additional hour up to the maximum daily rate. Most important, take note of the row in which you park (for example, B14), so you can easily be dropped off on your return.

Electric vehicle charging stations are also available in all CMH lots and garages and at the complimentary Cell Phone Waiting Lot, about a minute's drive from the terminal.

i For the frequent traveler, the EZ-Park Program is ideal. Prepay for an automated vehicle identification device for your car window. This acts as an electronic key, giving access to any airport-owned lot without having to stop. Applications are on the John Glenn International Airport website.

CAR RENTALS

Listed below are the eight on-site car rental agencies at John Glenn International Airport. They can be found on levels 1 and 2 of the parking garage, which is helpful in the winter, as you will not have to brave the elements to get to your car.

Alamo
(800) GO-ALAMO (462-5266)
www.alamo.com

Avis
(800) 331-1212
www.avis.com

Budget
(800) 527-0700
www.budget.com

Dollar
(800) 800-4000
www.dollar.com

Enterprise
(800) 325-8007
www.enterprise.com

Hertz
(800) 654-3131
www.hertz.com

National
(800) CAR-RENT (227-7368)
www.nationalcar.com

Thrifty
(800) 367-2277
www.thrifty.com

Airport Shuttle Service

If you prefer not to use Uber or Lyft, shuttle service can be arranged by calling ahead. View the shuttle, limo, and charter options at https://flycolumbus.com/getting-to-from. Shuttles leave from the ground transportation level of the airport, and cost varies according to distance and number of passengers. It usually takes about 20 minutes to get downtown. Bigger hotels sometimes have their own transportation service at extra charge.

Taxis and Rideshares

On-demand transportation is found at the ground transportation level of the airport 24 hours a day. The airport is one of the few places in town you can spontaneously grab a cab, as they do not cruise in Columbus. With the popularity of ridesharing, traditional taxi services should be contacted ahead of time for transport back to the airport—or anywhere, for that matter. Cost into downtown, Easton, or the Short North averages $25.

AAA Express Airport Taxi Service
(614) 262-3333 or (800) 434-5149

Yellow Cab
(614) 444-4444 or (800) 551-4222

Limousines and Private Cars

The rates will be more costly than a shuttle or taxi, but if you want to accommodate a large group in luxury or just prefer privacy, contact any one of the following companies to get where you are going in style. Rates will vary depending on the type of vehicle, but you can get VIP luxury cars, more traditional stretch limos, and even the trendy super-stretch Hummers and Excursions.

Arch Express Limo Service
(614) 252-2277
www.ohiolimoexpress.com

R Man Limo and Luxury Car Service
(614) 477-0737
www.rmanvan.com

Xtreme Limo
(614) 483-3300
www.xtremelimocolumbus.com

Rickenbacker International Airport (LCK)
Rickenbacker International Airport
2241 John Circle Dr.
(614) 491-1401
https://flycolumbus.com/cargo/
Rickenbacker, predominantly an international cargo airport, is one of the few Foreign Trade Zones (FTZ) in the US. Rickenbacker started out as the Lockbourne Army Airbase the day after Pearl Harbor was attacked in 1941, and opened in 1942. The base grew and expanded during the Korean and Vietnam Wars. In 1974 it was renamed Rickenbacker Air Force Base in honor of World War I combat pilot and Congressional Medal of Honor winner Eddie Rickenbacker, a Columbus native. Holding true to its military roots, branches of the US Army, Navy, and Marine Reserve and the National Guard remain active here.

Rickenbacker has since grown into a large distribution hub, with the first development happening at Rickenbacker in 1985, with the establishment of an air cargo hub and bulk-sorting facility for Flying Tigers (now owned by Federal Express). To encourage development, Rickenbacker was established as FTZ No. 138 in 1987, and now, with 10.5 million square feet of warehouse space and trucking access, more than 30 worldwide cargo carriers are represented, including Federal Express, UPS, Polar, Evergreen, and Nippom Express.

Year-round passenger flights are offered through Allegient Air to sunny southern locations out of Rickenbacker International Airport, situated 15 miles south of downtown Columbus.

Parking and Shuttle Service

Parking rates are $2 for the first hour and $1 for each additional hour up to $5 per day. Enterprise Rent-a-Car (614-239-3200) is located at the Charter Terminal. The same shuttle and taxi services available at John Glenn are available here (phone numbers are listed with the John Glenn International Airport information). Cab fare into downtown Columbus will run around $40.

Other Airports

There are two other private fields in Columbus, so if you have the good fortune to own your own plane, or at least be able to fly one, you have options to land in Columbus.

Bolton Field (TZR)
2000 Norton Rd.
(614) 851-9900
www.columbusairports.com/bolton
Bolton is a private airport 9 miles southwest of Columbus dedicated to corporate and recreational aviation. It has air traffic control service daily from 7:30 a.m. until 7:30 p.m. Piston, turbo-prop, jet aircraft, and helicopters can use this facility. Events such as fly-ins, aerobatic competitions, banner towing, and ballooning also take place on airport grounds. Hungry pilots and crew can fill up on local barbecue at JP's Barbecue Ribs, at the north end of the terminal. Contact the airport general manager for more information at (614) 851-9900.

The Ohio State University Don Scott Field
2160 W. Case Rd.
(614) 292-5460
www.osuairport.org
The Ohio State–owned Don Scott Field, named after a former OSU All-American who died in World War II, is among Ohio's five busiest airports. It is an educational facility for OSU's School of Aviation and provides aircraft and flight services to the Columbus community. Don Scott can accommodate piston, turboprop, and single- and twin-engine aircraft. An array of services is available to pilots, ranging from computerized weather and flight-planning spaces to event rooms or car rentals and an on-site restaurant. The interpretive

i Foreign Trade Zones are sites within the US legally considered outside customs territory, so duty-free goods are brought into the site without formal customs entry. An FTZ provides users with the opportunity to lower costs and boost profits by delaying, reducing, or eliminating duties, while the entry procedures save time.

exhibit throughout the lobby tells the story of Don Scott's history since its inception in 1943. The website offers comprehensive information about the airport, ranging from arrival and departure procedures to the history of the airfield.

GETTING AROUND

If you need to get around Columbus, public transportation is available but can be tedious and time-consuming. Unless you're staying in an area on a bus line *or* can easily walk to restaurants or attractions, renting a car is recommended.

General rules of thumb in Columbus: Front-seat passengers must wear seat belts, and children under the age of 4 or weighing less than 40 pounds must be in a child safety seat. It is also legal to make right turns at red lights, unless signs state no turn on red.

If you happen to need directions while exploring Columbus, people are usually friendly and willing to offer their assistance, but be prepared for them to say, "Go south on this street and east on that street." It is just the nature of the locals, who may have driven Columbus's gridlike streets all their lives. For those of you who are not used to using compass directions to find your way around, you can easily orient yourself if you just remember that no matter where you are, the sun always sets in the west.

i Be sure to watch for reduced speed limits through certain parts of town, such as Arlington, Dublin, Gahanna, and Worthington. Speed limits can decrease from 45 or 35 to 25 mph in a block or two. Police are diligent about enforcing speed limits.

Getting around Downtown

Getting around downtown Columbus is easy by car, bus, or on foot. Walking from one end of downtown to the other doesn't take more than 30 minutes, but when in a hurry, a COTA bus will carry you up the street for a nominal fee. Downtown's roads are in pretty good shape, well marked, and uncomplicated. Like anywhere, rush hour can become a waiting game, but most other times the traffic flow is good, and getting around downtown takes a matter of minutes. Traffic also tends to get backed-up around the Arena District, Schottenstein Center, and Ohio Stadium during games and concerts, but this is easy to avoid if you are aware of the events.

Downtown streets aren't too idiosyncratic, but one road to watch out for is Main Street. Main runs all the way east out of the city, but coming west it dead-ends at Grant Street and forces you to turn right (north). Like other big cities, a few streets, such as High and Broad, have two-way lanes, while most of the others are only one-way. Curb lanes along High Street are bus lanes between the hours of 7 and 9 a.m. and 4 and 6 p.m., which means right turns are not permitted at a few major intersections during rush hour. Overall, navigating downtown Columbus is pretty straightforward.

Downtown Parking

Parking is free in most outlying neighborhoods around Columbus except downtown and first-ring neighborhoods where zoned paid parking is enforced. Paid multilevel garages, surface lots, and street meters are in abundance. When lucky enough to find a meter during business hours, be sure to read the details, since there's a wide range of time limits from 15 minutes to 12 hours. Parking meters are often free on Sundays and holidays, but there are some exceptions to this. Certain meters or zones have 24/7 enforcement, many of which are in the Short North and Victorian Village, so pay attention.

i Forget about parking at downtown street meters between the hours of 7 and 9 a.m. and 4 and 6 p.m. Violators will be towed and ticketed.

If you work downtown and prefer to park in garages near the LeVeque Tower, State House, or Nationwide, be prepared to pay premium parking rates as high as $250 per month. On average, monthly parking rates are around $150, but if you're willing to walk 5 or 6 blocks to work, monthly parking exists for as little as $80. Daily rates at lots and garages range from $5 to $25.

For a quick jaunt into town, the Columbus Commons Garage is reasonably priced if your visit is contained to a few hours and it is central enough to be walkable to a lot of places. Other centrally located parking garages are in the Huntington Building (41 S. High St.) and the Vern Riffe Garage (78 S. Front St.).

Most parking facilities charge flat rates for special events or weekend parking, and a few garages, particularly near the theaters, have "twilight" rates for when you enter after 5 p.m. Here are a couple of parking options:

Columbus Commons
Main entrance on Rich Street (between Third and High Streets), alternate entrance on Main Street
$3 for the first hour, $1 for each additional hour up to $27 for 24 hours
Early-bird rates: $5.50 if in by 9 a.m.; when parking after 7 p.m., the flat fee is $3.00

State House Underground Parking
Entrances on Broad and Third Streets
$5 for the first 2 hours, $1 for each additional hour up to $12 for 24 hours

i Download the ParkCbus app for convenient street parking downtown and in the Short North, Victorian Village, and Arena District. Each enforced street has signage with a zone number to input along with a set duration of time. Your license plate(s) and vehicle description(s) are added to the app profile at setup. Time can be added remotely, and pricing is reasonable. Another app, Parking.com, is used in some private surface lots, so make sure you are using the correct app.

Buses

Central Ohio Transit Authority (COTA)
33 N. High St.
(614) 228-1776
www.cota.com
The city bus system has 41 fixed-routes lines and four on-demand service zones served by nearly 500 vehicles, 212 of which are hybrid. Twenty-four Park & Ride facilities are located around the city, so park for free and let someone else drive you into the city. Bikes ride for free on all COTA buses, which are equipped with racks. COTA also provides free Wi-Fi across its fleet.

View detailed maps of bus routes and time-tables on COTA's website or by calling customer service. Weekly and monthly passes are available, but individual fares are $2 one-way for local buses and $4.50 for a day pass of unlimited rides. COTA LINK costs 50 cents, and transfers are free. Seniors can get a reduced fare ID card, Discount Children (ages 5 to 12 years old) pay $1, and children under 4 ride for free.

Ohio State, Capital University, and Columbus College of Art and Design students can use their school ID to ride the bus unlimited for free, as it is included in the tuition. See www.cota.com for extensive bus routes from each campus. All Columbus City High School students in grades 9 through 12 can use a Student Success Card for unlimited rides on fixed routes for free to after-school activities, jobs, or tutoring.

Greyhound Bus Lines
845 N. Wilson Rd.
(614) 221-2389
www.greyhound.com
Buses may not be the most comfortable form of transportation, but they're certainly one of the more affordable ways to travel long distances.

Columbus's Greyhound station moved from downtown to the west side of the city in 2022. The Greyhound website lists routes and fares, including student rates and internet super-saver fares. Keep in mind that Greyhound buses do not serve meals, provide blankets, or show movies, but you are allowed to carry on food and nonalcoholic beverages. Electronic equipment is permitted as long as it does not disturb your fellow travelers.

Although there is no train service in Columbus, Amtrak offers Amtrak Thruway bus connections from Columbus to Cleveland, where there are Amtrak services to Buffalo, Boston, New York, Washington, DC, and Chicago. Amtrak service is available out of Pittsburgh as well. Purchase rail and bus tickets together through Amtrak or separately from Greyhound and Amtrak.

Bike Paths

A number of multiuse trails run throughout the city and parks. Please see the "Happy Trails to You!" Close-up in the Parks and Recreation chapter for details of the different paths.

i Columbus Cogo Bike sharing is a great way to explore the city without a car. The city boasts 80 stations with more than 600 bikes in the system. Use the app to locate and check out a bike from any automated bike station, then ride it around from there to explore all Columbus has to offer. When you've reached your destination, dock your bike at the nearest station to complete your session. Learn more and download the app at www.cogobikeshare.com.

HISTORY

Summing up a city's history in just a few pages is daunting. Ohio, our nation's 17th state, celebrated its bicentennial in 2003 and looks ahead to its 225th anniversary in 2028. Though settled in its current form for only a few hundred years, much of American history and its large, colorful cast of characters have passed through the city.

As the "Mother of Presidents" and the "Birthplace of Aviation," Ohio has sent seven sons to the White House and a few into space—all of whom spent some time in Columbus. These giants of science and politics were not alone in putting the state and the city on the map. Writers, musicians, athletes, and inventors also have contributed to the city's fascinating story.

An honorable mention should go to the unnamed heroes and heroines, farmers and laborers, Native Americans and immigrants, lest we forget the folk who never made it into the history books. This faceless majority had a huge hand in shaping Columbus.

Founding father Lucas Sullivant was a forward-thinking man who had great plans for the land at what was referred to as the Forks of Scioto. By the time the Capital City was established in 1812, visionary businessmen, politicians, and doctors had begun a new chapter in a story already rich with Indian and frontier history. Columbus, once at the edge of the Wild West, deep in Indian Territory, quickly became the breadbasket of America and a center of trade. The need to supply the nation with agricultural goods lured stagecoaches, the National Road, and canals to the city, making Columbus a strategic hub of transportation and distribution, which it remains to this day.

Wars, canals, and railroads came and went. Much of Ohio ended up part of the Rustbelt, but Columbus rose from the industrial ashes to become a financial and retail powerhouse. As a hub of research, development, aviation, and trade and as home to one of the nation's great universities, Columbus continues to attract visionaries. The founders' spirit of exploration and discovery has been kept alive into the 21st century.

This is our story.

THE MOUND BUILDERS

We can thank the last ice age for Ohio's agricultural windfall. Eleven thousand years ago our state was buried under a glacier that stopped moving just short of Columbus, leaving in its wake the hills and rivers near Cincinnati. This massive chunk of ice pushed the topsoil into the central Ohio region, giving Columbus its fertile farmland and buckeye trees. As the land warmed and the ice melted away, a wide variety of prairie grasses, wetlands, and deciduous trees took hold.

Several thousand years later, the vast forest that covered the region was finally able to sustain a variety of animal life. A group of people eventually emerged to become the area's first inhabitants. These ancient nomadic hunters and gatherers mastered crops and began establishing permanent villages. As society became more complex, so did their views of death and ritualistic approach to burial.

The earliest Mound Builders, known as the Adena, Hopewell, and Fort Ancient cultures, date from 100 BC to AD 1000. During the course of the millennium, they developed sophisticated burial and ceremonial rituals, which included the construction of a vast network of earthen mounds all over Ohio. The mounds progressively became more elaborate and sometimes reached upward of 50 feet tall and 30 feet wide.

i The Buckeye State's nickname is derived from a type of chestnut tree that has been nearly eradicated from the landscape. The nut of the buckeye tree looks like a buck's eye.

By the time European settlers arrived in central Ohio, there were thousands of mounds in the Ohio Valley but no sign of the builders. There is still no definitive reason why these ancient cultures faded away, but theories contend it may have been due to disease, wars, or overpopulation. It is, however, quite clear why fewer than 1 percent of these mounds exist today.

The early settlers attributed these extraordinary burials to everyone but the Indigenous people they were displacing. Local savages couldn't possibly build something so sophisticated, and the mounds were explained away with theories of Peruvians, Vikings, and even extraterrestrial aliens. Hundreds of mounds were documented in the Columbus area alone, but by the mid-19th century most were gone—plowed over, leveled, and, in the case of the one for which Mound Street is named, used to make bricks for the first statehouse.

The Great Serpent Mound is a 1,300-foot-long, 3-foot-high prehistoric effigy mound located about 2 hours south of the city in Adams County. The mound is the largest serpent effigy known in the world, and after decades of petitioning, Serpent Mound was finally made a UNESCO World Heritage Site in 2023.

EARLY SETTLERS

The Native Americans who replaced the Mound Builders had established villages by the time English and French explorers arrived in the 1650s. The first documentation of Native Americans in Ohio was by French missionaries from Canada. The Iroquois, Delaware, Shawnee, and Huron people were a long way from their original homes, pressed into central Ohio by the French and British from every direction. Some tribes were acquiescent, but most wouldn't give up their lands without a fight.

By 1749, the governor of Canada had claimed Ohio for France. During the French and Indian War, both French and British frontiersmen worked their way into the Midwest to set up trading posts. It was at this time that the first written description of Franklin County was given by Christopher Gist of the Virginia Land Company.

While little of the French and Indian War touched Ohio, isolated incidents occurred between the Indians (French loyalists) and the British. Such was the case when Matthew McCrea was killed during an Ottawa attack on a trading post at the Forks at Scioto, making him the first person to die on the site of what was to become Columbus. England ultimately won the struggle for control of North America and banned settlement north and west of the Ohio River as a means to monopolize the fur trade. British troops were sent to suppress Indian revolts, and so began the wresting of the Northwest Territory from the Native Americans.

As a new nation emerged, little of the Revolutionary War was fought in central Ohio. By 1785, plans were made to bring the Northwest Territory into the Union, and campaigns were undertaken to negotiate (or force) treaties with the Indians. By the 1790s, Native villages were systematically destroyed, and the Native Americans were pushed to the northern third of the state. Shortly thereafter, the Forks at Scioto was permanently settled by Europeans.

i Many local place names are Indian words, including Ohio, which is Iroquois for "Great River." Other names are Wyandot, or "River at Rest," and Scioto, or "Hairy River," named for the hundreds of deer that would shed their fur on the banks of the river.

FRANKLINTON'S FOUNDING FATHER

It didn't take long for the government to begin surveying the Northwest Territory. It was surveyed once in 1785, when township measurements were created and governing rules put in place for when the Northwest Territory became a state. Surveyors were again sent from Kentucky in 1795, at which time many of the familiar streams and natural landmarks like Darby Creek were named.

Among these surveyors was Lucas Sullivant, founder of Franklinton and later Columbus.

Our young country had no money to pay many of the Revolutionary War veterans or the government employees such as these surveyors, who subsequently took their pay in real estate. Lucas Sullivant took an immediate liking to the Forks at Scioto. Realizing the area near the river was on low ground and regularly flooded, he claimed thousands of acres on higher ground slightly to the west of the river, which soon became known as Sullivant's Hill.

Sullivant, an ardent admirer of Benjamin Franklin, named the new town Franklinton in his honor. In just two years, the city was planned and attempts were made to draw people into the heart of Indian Country. The names of the earliest settlers are woven into the very fabric of the city: Dr. Lincoln Goodale, Dr. James Hoge, Pelatiah Webster Huntington, and David Deardurff, to name a few. Floods whisked the city away several times over, but Lucas Sullivant was not deterred from making his city prosper.

Today, the city is undergoing a renaissance, with new development and hotels being built and with more phases to come.

THE CAPITAL CITY IS BORN

By 1801, the frontier village of Franklinton was a fully functioning town, with brick homes, a church, and a jail. For forward-thinking Sullivant, his city was about the future. When Ohio became a state in 1803, Franklinton's centralized location gave Sullivant hope it would become the state capital.

The capital was originally moved between Zanesville and Chillicothe a few times, but politicians weren't thrilled with either decision. Several suggestions were made to move the capital to Delaware, Worthington (established the same year Ohio became a state), Franklinton, or the area that would soon become Dublin. The Ohio General Assembly rejected Sullivant's city simply because it was just too wet.

At this point in the state's history, the biggest industry was not agriculture or trapping, as one might think, but land. Sullivant, as a former surveyor and one of the biggest landowners, rallied four others to purchase a strip of land across the

i Senator John Glenn, the first American to orbit the earth, is honored at the John and Annie Glenn Historic Site. His boyhood home is in New Concord, east of Columbus. Neil Armstrong, the first astronaut to walk on the moon, is memorialized in his hometown of Wapakoneta with a lunar-shaped Air and Space Museum.

river from Franklinton. This tract was allotted to Canadian refugees from Nova Scotia who had supported the American cause during the Revolution. Most of the refugees were destitute and more than willing to sell their land deeds to this group.

After acquiring the Refugee Tract of land, they went about proposing this new area, which was called High Banks, to the Ohio General Assembly. The proposition was accepted on February 12, 1812, and the "Capital City" was born. The next dilemma: what to name the new legislative center of the state. On February 20, for whatever reasons, the General Assembly chose the name Columbus over Ohio City, in honor of Christopher Columbus.

The founders quickly planned a grid of streets that aligned with the established roads across the river in Franklinton. All that existed on the east bank of the Scioto River was the High Trail through a dense forest and a 40-foot-tall Indian mound at the corner of what is now High and Mound Streets. Ten acres each were set aside for the statehouse and a penitentiary. The capital was under way.

i *Blue Jacket* is a dramatization of the story of a white settler adopted by the Shawnee Indians who later becomes their war chief. The action takes place on a 3-acre outdoor stage. The season runs from mid-June to early September. For information, call (937) 376-4318 or (937) 427-0879 or view www.bluejacketdrama.com.

With the increasing stability of the economy and a growing number of people identifying themselves as Americans, the presence of British troops on American soil was challenged. Ohio, particularly Franklinton, feared invasion by the British in Detroit, consequently putting the new capital in a vulnerable position.

THE WAR OF 1812

Coincidentally, on June 18, 1812, the day Columbus was officially established as the seat of Ohio's government and the first day of land sales, was the same day the US declared war on Great Britain. Because of this, the capital was not physically moved from Chillicothe to Columbus until 1816.

Once again, Ohio escaped much of the war, but Columbus and Franklinton served as a mobilization and supply center for troops. A ditch was dug around the statehouse, a stockade was created, and a makeshift prison (named British Island) was built on a sandbar, which no longer exists, in the middle of the Scioto River. Future president William Henry Harrison undertook the construction of forts just north of Columbus and led a successful invasion of Detroit and Canada. He expelled the British troops at the Battle of the Thames and brought about the collapse of Tecumseh's Confederacy, marking the downfall of the Native Americans in Ohio.

BOOM OR BUST

Columbus saw an enormous boom between the War of 1812 and the Civil War, but not without the usual postwar bust. After a period of economic hardship, flooding, and disease, many people chose to move on to other cities. In 1832, 2,000 people lived in Columbus. In just two years the city's population more than doubled to 5,000, making it the fastest-growing city in Ohio. Lucas Sullivant died in 1823, but his legacy was carried on by a few friends and fellow visionaries.

As the country pushed westward and grew, so did the need for reliable modes of transportation and road systems. Enter the ruthless businessman William Neil. He recognized central Ohio's lack of water transportation and knew land was the best way to get to the capital. By the 1840s, he had acquired most of the stagecoach lines in Ohio, earning him the nickname "The Stagecoach King." Neil opened a tavern and hotel at Broad and High Streets, convenient to the statehouse. The Neil House Hotel quickly became the place to stay in downtown Columbus. He also played a part in having the National Road (US 40) rerouted through Columbus's business district.

William Neil's name lived on, not in his short-lived stagecoach business or even his hotels but in what he chose to invest his money: land. He purchased a farm just north of downtown Columbus, which, upon his death in 1870, became the Ohio Agricultural and Mechanical College and later The Ohio State University. Neil Avenue was once the private lane onto his estate.

Like William Neil, Alfred Kelley had a passion for transportation, only he was into canals. In 1816 Kelley came to the capital from Cleveland in a political capacity and remained here permanently. Seeing how the Erie Canal changed the face of American trade and commerce elsewhere, he was adamant about linking Columbus to the canal system, which he did via Canal Winchester and Lockbourne.

By 1837 the canal projects were over budget, and the state was behind in repayment. Realizing that the success of central Ohio depended on the quick distribution of Ohio's farm goods, Alfred Kelley put his house up as collateral on the unpaid interest on the canal bonds. Thankfully, the legislature did not pull funding, and he kept his house. Kelley's deep integrity and unwavering belief in these modern modes of transportation began the transformation of Columbus into the hub of distribution that it is today.

In less than three decades, stagecoaches, the National Road, and canals saw their heyday and were displaced by locomotives. Both Neil and Kelley had the good sense to get involved in sponsoring the first railroad into Columbus. In 1851, a crude terminal was built on High Street, where the Hyatt Regency is now located. By 1853, locals could take the 3C train direct from Cleveland to Columbus to Cincinnati, thus ushering in a period of rail travel that lasted for 120 years.

Columbus's train traffic peaked around 1916, but it slowly declined with the increasing popularity of the automobile. Union Station, which was located along High Street where the present-day Greater Columbus Convention Center is situated, fell into disrepair by the 1970s and was altogether demolished in the 1980s. The only existing part of the original station is a classical-style arch that now stands at the head of McFerson Park in the Arena District.

i Lucas Sullivant, the man who transformed central Ohio, died in 1824 as one of the largest landowners in Ohio. He was originally buried in the Franklinton Cemetery but was moved to Greenlawn Cemetery in 1849. A 17-foot-tall bronze statue of Sullivant, by local artist Michael Foley, stands looking out over the west bank of the Scioto River. Its plinth contains a sculptural story of the founding of Franklinton.

THE CIVIL WAR

The Civil War left its mark on Columbus in subtle and unusual ways. A plaque commemorates a speech Abraham Lincoln gave from the south side of the statehouse on September 16, 1859, just prior to the Civil War. Within two years, Union soldiers occupied Columbus and remained here until the very end of the war.

Ohio provided more troops per capita to the Union than any other Northern state, although it fell third behind New York and Pennsylvania in the total number of men who served. Ohio was represented by artillery, cavalry, and infantry units in all the major battles and campaigns, while the 5th and 27th US Colored Troops were primarily made up of Ohioans.

Columbus was one of the major centers of mobilization and training of the Union army. A historical marker near the convention center commemorates the site of Tod Barracks, one of the five military outposts located in Columbus during the war.

Named for Governor David Tod, the barracks were built in 1863 and served as headquarters for central Ohio's military administration. They ran along High Street, where the new Union Station shops are located, and could accommodate up to 5,000 soldiers. Conveniently adjacent to the train station, they also served as a recruiting depot and transfer point for soldiers on their way to new assignments.

Columbus was also home to Camp Chase, one of the Union's largest prisoner of war camps. More than 2,000 Confederate political and military prisoners from Kentucky and western Virginia died of disease and malnutrition between 1861 and the end of the Civil War. This 160-acre site was located near present-day Westgate on the West Side. Now all that exists is Camp Chase Cemetery on Sullivant Avenue. It comes as no surprise that many consider this burial ground for Confederate soldiers haunted.

One of the primary disputes of the American Civil War was slavery. When the Northwest Territory was first surveyed in 1785, a law was established making slavery illegal north of the Ohio River, thus leaving Ohio as a crucial station on the Underground Railroad. It was, however, a dangerous state for escapees.

Ohio's Black Laws, enacted in 1804, regulated and monitored the lives of African Americans, while stringent additions to the law made it nearly impossible for African Americans to settle or work in Ohio. In 1850 the National Fugitive Slave Law was enacted, thus spurring an active manhunt of runaways. This prompted the development of the Underground Railroad, a network of safe houses and "conductors" who helped guide the escaped slaves north to freedom.

The Underground Railroad route through Ohio began at the Ohio River and passed through Chillicothe, Circleville, Columbus, Worthington, and Westerville, then north to Lake Erie and into Canada. No one was permitted to harbor slaves and by law the public required to turn them in. The Kelton family house in East Columbus is confirmed as one of these safe houses. Several others have unofficial but strong Underground Railroad connections, including the Benjamin Hanby House in Westerville, the Livingston House in Reynoldsburg, and the Southwick-Good Funeral Chapel in Clintonville. Most remain as clandestine now as they were 150 years ago.

The Ohio Historical Society has extensive information about Civil War–era Columbus, and the National Freedom Center in Cincinnati is the premier place to explore the Underground Railroad. Some 500 men from Franklin County lost their lives in the Civil War, many of whom are buried in Greenlawn Cemetery.

COMING OF AGE

In the years following the Civil War, technological developments occurred and industry began to emerge in Columbus. German immigrants established breweries. Shoe, cigar, machinery, furniture, and carriage manufacturers took advantage of the established transportation systems, an infrastructure put in place only 30 years earlier by William Neil and Alfred Kelley.

As the capital of the state, Columbus was becoming a center of education and social activity. By the late 19th century, two universities, two medical colleges, an art school, libraries, and musical societies had been established. Hospitals were also associated with these reputable medical schools, and Columbus reputedly had the largest insane asylum in the world. City records indicate that by the late 1880s, Columbus had more than 50 churches and 600 saloons.

In the 1860s, a single horse-drawn streetcar was pulled up and down High Street on one track, leading to the development of residential suburbs. People no longer had to live near their place of employment. By the turn of the century, horse-powered trolleys were a thing of the past. From 1905 to 1914, a system of electrified metal arches powered the streetcars, earning Columbus the nickname "Arch City." The 17 arches, running the length of the Short North, have recently been reinstalled and illuminated, a sentimental throwback to yesteryear.

By the close of the 19th century, Columbus saw many notable births, including World War I ace Eddie Rickenbacker (b. 1889) and the humorist James Thurber (b. 1894). The urban face of the city was changed with the addition of several towering skyscrapers, posh hotels, and theaters. Automobiles were also beginning to appear on city streets, prompting the nation's first gas station to open in Columbus on June 1, 1912.

20TH-CENTURY COLUMBUS

By the turn of the 20th century, a third of Columbus's population was of German descent, so World War I brought about a zealous move to "Americanize" the German Village part of town. A push to rename the streets and foods showed the growing sentiment against the city's German community: Sauerkraut, for instance, became "victory cabbage."

The Great War was also used as a propaganda tool to bring about Prohibition. Developments in mechanical refrigeration contributed to the increasing number of saloons, and in response to this "liquor problem," the Anti-Saloon League was formed in 1893. The organization had its first offices outside Columbus and was eventually relocated to Westerville, where their primary focus was the single issue of Prohibition.

World War I gave the League an opportunity to develop a frenzied patriotism by associating booze with the enemy, as most brewers were German. It also purported that the resources used for alcohol production were diverted from the war effort. On January 17, 1920, the 18th Amendment was passed, banning the production and consumption of alcoholic beverages.

During the Roaring '20s Columbus saw the opening of the first White Castle and the construction of some of Columbus's landmarks: the LeVeque Tower, City Hall, and Central High School (now COSI). Prohibition brought about home brews, bathtub gin, and speakeasies, of which the Ringside Cafe and Larry's (on campus) still exist. This was also when Charles Lindbergh recommended Columbus as an important link for coast-to-coast air travel. The Port Columbus (now John Glenn) Airport was opened a few months before the Great Depression struck and took 15 years before turning a profit.

When the stock market crashed in 1929, over half of all Ohioans lost their jobs, but this did not affect Columbus as much as other cities because of the diversity of the local economy and its primary function as a center of government rather than industry. The lifting of Prohibition and the start of World War II breathed new life into Columbus's economy.

It was during the 1936 Olympics in Berlin that the impending threat of Adolf Hitler was felt in central Ohio. Jesse Owens, of The Ohio State University, is perhaps one of the most famous Olympians of all time. He was the first American in the history of Olympic track-and-field events to win four gold medals in a single Olympics and set records in three of the four events. Hitler

i **Columbus-born Elsie Janis was the country's first female actress and singer sent to entertain troops in France during World War I.**

refused to acknowledge Owens's accomplishment, despite his being given a standing ovation by German fans. Owens is now memorialized at Ohio State's Jesse Owens Memorial Stadium.

During World War II Columbus became the modern city that it is today. It prospered through the manufacture of warplanes, particularly the Curtiss-Wright "Helldivers," and once again, Columbus became a major supply center. Rickenbacker Air Force Base was built the day after Pearl Harbor. Local boy Curtis LeMay became a major war hero and retired as the armed forces' longest-serving general.

In 1953, Mayor Jack Sesenbrenner coined the slogan "Come to Columbus and Discover America." Columbus was officially dubbed "Discovery City," and during the second half of the 20th century, it became a leader in retail, insurance, technology, and software development and became home to the world's largest private research facility, Battelle Memorial Institute. Columbus entered the 21st century with a sound economic climate and a dynamic business community—a city, I imagine, Lucas Sullivant would be proud of.

HISTORICAL SOCIETIES

Included here are just a few of Columbus's active and better-known historical societies. Some of them maintain their own collections or work out of interesting landmark buildings. Most put on annual holiday events, offer walking tours, and are dedicated to preserving the neighborhoods' cultural and architectural heritage.

Columbus Historical Society
717 W. Town St.
(614) 224-0822
www.columbushistory.org
This society, established in 1990, is dedicated to the preservation of city heritage and artifacts, as well as annual awareness programming. It is working toward the creation of a local history exhibition space, virtual museum, and heritage bus tours.

Gahanna Historical Society
101 S. High St., Gahanna
(614) 475-3342
www.gahannahistory.com
This society sponsors the annual May Herb Festival and offers a 1-mile walking tour of Olde Gahanna's 16 historic landmarks, which include the Log House and two historic churches.

German Village Society
588 S. Third St.
(614) 221-8888
www.germanvillage.com
The society is housed in the historic German Village Meeting Haus and is the tireless caretaker of the charming neighborhood established in 1814. German Village Tours (www.germanvillagetours.com) offers resident-led walking tours of the village, where historical plaques and cobbled brick streets speak to its history. The visitor center in the Meeting Haus has a short video, maps, and books about the area. Other souvenir items and information about the village are also available. It also organizes the annual Haus und Garten Tour the last Sunday in June.

Ohio History Connection
800 E. 17th Ave.
(614) 297-2510
www.ohiohistory.org
Formerly the Ohio Historical Society, the Ohio History Connection is dedicated to preserving tangible history throughout the state. The main organization works closely with other local groups, forming the nation's largest historic site and museum network. The Ohio History Center is located near the Ohio Fairgrounds at the intersection of I-71 and 17th Avenue. You cannot miss the "brutalist" 1970 building's massive concrete cap hovering over the square building. The permanent collections tell the story of Ohio's Indigenous people, geography and nature, and the general history of statehood. It is also home to Ohio Village, a re-created 19th-century town that hosts an annual Dicken's Christmas around the holidays.

Upper Arlington Historical Society
1670 Fishinger Rd., Ste. 220, Upper Arlington
(614) 470-2610
www.uahistory.org
A volunteer board takes an active role in maintaining the architectural integrity, material culture, and oral histories of the Arlington neighborhood. It also organizes walking tours, formal home and garden tours, and educational programs for both adults and children. A book titled *History of Upper Arlington* can be purchased from the UA Historical Society. Digitized material can be found online at www.uaarchives.org.

Short North Civic Association
120 W. Goodale Blvd.
(614) 228-2912
www.shortnorthcivic.org
The Short North Civic Association promotes restoration, preservation, and maintenance of this historic district. It is a nonprofit civic association that sponsors social events in the Short North and Victorian Village neighborhoods. It has hosted an annual Short North Tour of Homes each September for the past 50 years.

Worthington Historical Society
50 W. New England Ave., Worthington
(614) 885-1247
www.worthingtonhistory.org
Working out of the Old Rectory, this society preserves the history and heritage of the community and operates historic properties such as the Orange Johnson House. It organizes annual home and garden tours, reenactments, and special holiday events.

ACCOMMODATIONS

Whether you're in town for an extended business trip or are a weary traveler looking for a place to rest your head, Columbus offers a wide range of lodging at rates suitable to most travelers' budgets. In fact, there are over 32,000 rooms citywide from which to choose, 5,000 of which are downtown. The goal of this chapter is to let you know where you can sleep in style, where to find basic comfort at a low price, and which parts of town offer the best values.

In a city this size, almost every national chain is represented. Some of the nicest hotels are affiliated with big names like Hilton and Marriott, while most of the moderately priced hotels have equally familiar names.

Where to stay really depends on what you plan to do in Columbus. Hotels have been built near the conference center, entertainment districts, shopping areas, and the airport. The breakdown of this chapter reflects these different pockets of lodging. Downtown is home to Columbus's financial and government districts. The Short North and the Arena District are big convention and entertainment areas, while the airport has plenty of hotels near the terminal for that quick in-and-out. The suburbs, particularly Dublin and Worthington, have business parks offering the usual suspects of extended-stay hotels.

It's fair to say that the most expensive places are located downtown and Columbus's room rates are relatively stable throughout the year. Prices seem to spike more during conventions and annual events rather than follow a traditional "low" or "high" season.

For a purely Columbus experience, stay downtown at the historic Great Southern Hotel or at one of the hotels with a rooftop patio. You'll be within walking distance to many restaurants, galleries, and theaters. The downtown locations allow you to easily shop at the North Market, see a show, and top off the evening with a meal in the trendy Short North. If you prefer to surround yourself with antiques and are looking for a low-key getaway, read more about the inns of Amish Country in the Close-up in this chapter.

The Ohio State University has plenty of newer lodging options near the campus. The campus's upscale hotel, the Blackwell Inn, is located in the heart of OSU and is worth the splurge if you want total convenience and a little luxury. There are, however, less expensive options a few blocks away on Olentangy River Road. Hotels in various price ranges are included, but check out Ohio State's website (www.osu.edu) for suggestions around the university.

People from the tristate area come to shop themselves silly at Easton Town Center, where plenty of hotels are walkable in Easton proper and several more are just a mile or two away. Many choose stay at the Hilton Columbus, but there are two other less expensive options also conveniently located on-site. The three Easton hotels included in this chapter boast an 80 percent occupancy rate, so be sure to make your reservations well in advance.

If you are just passing through Columbus, you will not have any problem finding a quick place to lay over for the night. Clusters of fair-priced hotels are situated around the beltway (I-270) and along the major highways (I-70/I-71). Unless unforeseen nasty weather conditions strike or major festivals are going on in central Ohio, you'll have little trouble getting a room spontaneously.

Two distinct parts of town have sprawling office developments with a good number of mid-priced rooms and extended-stay suites;

Worthington Crosswoods and MetroPlace in Dublin are slightly older facilities with standard amenities and free parking, but nothing really distinguishes them from other run-of-the-mill mainstream lodging. The upshots to staying in these areas are the competitive rates.

Newer hotels, such as Hyatt House, Aloft, and Springhill Suites are convenient to the Ohio State Wexner Center, and the Polaris area has plenty of hotels if you need to stay north of the city.

Hotel descriptions are kept to a minimum and only note the extra amenities such as complimentary Wi-Fi, breakfast, fitness center, or swimming pool.

Low-budget accommodations are not included, but it is worth mentioning that East Dublin–Granville Road (OH 161) is teeming with budget and express hotels such as Super 8, Comfort Inn, Days Inn, and Knights Inn. Many of these places charge under $60 for a room and are easily accessed from all the major highways.

The number of bed-and-breakfasts and guesthouses has grown over the years, some booked through Airbnb. The few included here are quite charming and offer a refreshing change of pace from the hotel experience. What B&Bs lack in traditional hotel amenities they make up for with their homey atmosphere and charm. Whether staying at a unique inn, a humble chain hotel, or a plush executive suite, expect to be greeted with a smile and met with the warm hospitality the Midwest is famous for.

The price code is the average "rack" rate for a double room during the week. Keep in mind that most hotels have cheaper weekend rates and more expensive single rooms and suites. Many also offer romance, theater, or dinner packages and internet discounts directly through the website. All the hotels listed here accept major credit cards and require plastic to guarantee the room.

Price Code

$	$150
$$	$151–200
$$$	$201–$250
$$$$	More than $250

View Columbus's most comprehensive visitor's information at www.experiencecolumbus.com or call them at (614) 221-6623. Another great source of travel information is the Ohio Department of Tourism at www.ohio.org or 1-800-BUCKEYE (282-5393).

DOWNTOWN/FRANKLINTON/ARENA DISTRICT

The downtown hotels are a 15-minute drive ($25 ride) to John Glenn International Airport. One of the better values downtown is in a primo location right at the edge of German Village.

AC Hotel $$
517 Park St.
(614) 227-6100
www.marriott.com
The stylish, European-style hotel is fairly central in downtown and walkable to the Greater Columbus Convention Center, Nationwide Arena, and KEMBA Live! venue. Its nicest feature is the rooftop restaurant and bar, Lumin Sky Bar and Kitchen.

Doubletree Guest Suites $$$
50 S. Front St. at State St.
(614) 228-4600, (800) 222-8733
www.doubletree.com
The newly remodeled Doubletree is the only all-suites hotel in downtown Columbus and the only one with rooms overlooking the Scioto River. It is adjacent to the Huntington Bank Building and is a short walk to the capitol building, Vern Riffe State Office Tower, and American Electric Power. The spacious suites feature a living room and bedroom separated by French doors. The rooms come equipped with a sofa bed, mini fridge, microwave, two TVs, and phones. Internet access is available for a fee, and pets up to 100 pounds are permitted but require a deposit. The Presidents Dining Room, a full-service restaurant and bar, is open for breakfast, lunch, and dinner. Other amenities include free Wi-Fi and complimentary EV charging. The self-parking fee in the attached garage is $25 per day. This is an easy choice for extended stays downtown.

ACCOMMODATIONS

Drury Plaza Hotel $$
88 E. Nationwide Blvd.
(614) 221-7008
www.druryhotels.com

This small, affordable hotel adjoins the Greater Columbus Convention Center via covered walkway and is situated within a short walk of the State Capitol and a short drive to The Ohio State University. This hotel features an indoor and outdoor pool, whirlpool, exercise facility, and laundry room. Complimentary coffee and breakfast are served each morning in the lobby. Pets are allowed at the Drury.

Hilton Columbus Downtown $$$$
402 N. High St.
(614) 384-8600
www.hilton.com

Boasting 1,000 rooms and 28 floors, the Hilton Downtown is the largest and tallest hotel in Columbus. The second, newer tower is linked to the Greater Columbus Convention Center via a skywalk. Stories on High, on the 28th floor, is the highest rooftop bar in the city—for now—serving up sushi and cocktails with a view. FYR is the signature restaurant at the Hilton Columbus Downtown. It is a live-fire restaurant led by executive chef Sebastian La Rocca and offers breakfast, dinner, and craft cocktails.

Hotel LeVeque $$$$
50 W. Broad St.
(614) 224-9500
www.hotelleveque.com

The Leveque Tower has been a beacon of the Columbus skyline since 1927. This iconic art deco building was built by the American Insurance Company as an office building with 600 hotel rooms. The attached Palace Theatre remains one of the city's landmark show venues. Standing 555 feet, 5 inches tall, the tower was purposefully constructed 5 inches taller than the Washington Monument in Washington, DC, making this the fifth-tallest building in the world at the time. The Leveque's 47 stories were topped with floodlights that could be seen up to 20 miles away, serving as a navigational aid to planes. Since then, the Tower has gone through decades of incarnations and states of disrepair. New life was breathed into the building in 2017 when Marriott's Autograph Collection developed several floors into a luxury boutique hotel with 143 rooms and suites. Keeping in line with the building's art deco roots, the guest rooms hearken back to an era known for its glitz and glamour. Accents of gold, bold geometric shapes, opulent marble, intricate metal work, and touches of animal prints evoke the sumptuousness of the Roaring '20s and '30s. The standard bedrooms are quite spacious, while the suites are nearly 800 square feet with attached living and dining room, along with an efficiency-style kitchenette. The Keep is the hotel restaurant, located on the mezzanine Level.

Hyatt Regency $$
350 N. High St.
(614) 463-1234
www.hyatt.com

The Hyatt is one of the premier convention hotels and is attached to the convention center via walkway. It is situated between the Arena District and Short North Arts District. The rooms have views of the city and some over the Ohio State campus. The rooms include large work stations, Wi-Fi access, and cable, and the property is pet-friendly, providing dog beds, bowls, and treats for furry friends up to 50 pounds with a $100 service fee.

Junto Hotel $$$
77 Belle St., Franklinton
(614) 976-2106
www.thejuntohotel.com

The Junto is a 198-room, independent lifestyle hotel located across the river in Franklinton, so it is not in downtown proper, which means its rooftop bar, The Brass Eye, has panoramic views of the city skyline and all along the river. The Junto is a sleek, new independent hotel with various styles of rooms, lofts, studios, and suites. The Little West Tavern serves hearty wood-fired dishes with a bit of Wild West flare in a high-end saloon setting. Guests have two bar options, a market and cafe, and different types of areas to socialize in, whether around the fireplace or the outdoor patio. Bikes, scooters, skateboards, kayaks, and other games are available to rent. Keep in mind if staying here, you will have to walk or catch a ride across the bridge into downtown.

LC GuestHouse $$
245 S. High St.
(614) 918-2183
www.lc-guesthouse.com

LC GuestHouse is a luxury short-term rental-suite property in downtown, walkable to restaurants and shops. Room rates are reasonable when compared to a hotel, and the patio suite is popular with guests.

Renaissance Columbus $$$
50 N. Third St. at Gay St.
(614) 228-5050, (800) 417-1057
www.marriott.com

The Renaissance is well situated a few blocks between the Statehouse and the convention center and only 2 blocks from the Arena District. Its upscale, contemporary decor and modern amenities make it a fine choice for both ambience and value. Some rooms on the higher floors have Club Lounge access. The hotel features a large fitness center, seasonal rooftop pool, and Latitude 41 Restaurant and Bar. Valet parking costs $45 per day.

Sheraton at Capital Square $$$$
75 E. State St.
(614) 228-1234, (800) 400-5400
www.sheraton.com

Located near theaters and conveniently across the street from the Ohio Statehouse, this premier downtown hotel has a lot going for it—location for starters. Government figures and business bigwigs are often found milling about the hotel, as it is in the heart of Columbus's government and financial district. A wander through the lobby will take you to the adjacent Ohio Theatre's box office.

It boasts 400 spacious guest rooms, 13 suites, club lounge floors with all-day snacks, and fantastic service. The concierge services are outstanding. Pamper yourself with turndown service, get tickets to a show, or schedule a massage. This property has no pool, but the views from a top-floor health club will help you forget about it. The fitness center is equipped with top-of-the-line exercise equipment, free weights, and a sauna. The express breakfasts cater to the hotel's large number of business travelers.

Sonesta Hotel $$$
33 E. Nationwide Blvd.
Arena District
(614) 461-4100
www.sonesta.com

This four-star, dog-friendly hotel is located on the doorstep of the Arena District and within walking distance of the restaurants, bars, and shops of the Short North.

An enclosed walkway connects this 12-story facility to the Greater Columbus Convention Center, making it a very popular hotel during conventions. Guests on business trips will appreciate the complimentary wireless internet and business center and personal work pods in The Hub. The Sonesta was renovated in 2019 and includes a fitness center, concierge, and outdoor courtyard with a fire pit. The Vine and Forge restaurant on-site serves breakfast, lunch, and dinner, but you'd be remiss not to venture out to the fine-dining establishments nearby. Valet parking costs $42 per night.

Westin Great Southern Hotel $$$
310 S. High St.
(614) 228-3800
www.marriott.com

It was with great pride, on August 23, 1897, that the city was presented with the Great Southern Fireproof Hotel and Opera House. The hotel was built in response to tragic fires claiming several fine downtown hotels. This masterpiece, which is attached to the Southern Theatre, was built entirely of fire-resistant material and has survived to become the grande dame of Columbus. The historic hotel was restored to its original splendor by the Columbus Association of the Performing Arts (CAPA) in 1995 and remains a bastion of classic elegance and gracious service.

Ideally situated on the corner of Main and High Streets, the 196-room Westin has been tastefully updated to suit 21st-century travelers' needs while retaining its 19th-century sophistication. The Great Southern is deservingly one of two downtown hotels awarded Four Diamonds by AAA.

The French Renaissance provided inspiration for the exquisite detailing found throughout the hotel. The lobby makes quite a first impression, glowing pink and gold with marble, gilding, and cherry furniture. Original stained glass and sparkling chandeliers are a reminder that, at one time, no expense was spared on this hotel. The Great Southern has bedded many famous and fashionable people, including Eleanor Roosevelt and Presidents William McKinley, Theodore Roosevelt, and Woodrow Wilson.

The rooms are luxurious, with Queen Anne–style furniture, marble baths, and rich colors. All the rooms (and public spaces) provide free wireless internet access. Solo travelers might like to stay in the Victorian Cozy, a small double room equipped with all the amenities of a standard room. Twenty-three spacious suites range from a standard one-room Executive to the immaculate Thurber Suite, touted as the Crown Jewel of the Westin.

Other hotel services include a fully equipped fitness room, business center, and valet parking. The hotel's restaurant, Bar Cicchetti, features modern Italian dishes by owner and *Top Chef* alum, Fabio Viviani. It is open for breakfast, lunch, and dinner. The cool bar is great place to grab a drink before a show at the Southern Theatre.

GERMAN VILLAGE

German Village Lofts $$
145 E. Livingston Ave.
(614) 295-9455
www.germanvillagelofts.com
Location, location, location. The GV Lofts are centrally located within walking distance of most restaurants and shops in the charming historic German Village. Accommodations come in the form of five unique spaces ranging from a studio to two-bedroom lofts, some with city views. Off-street parking is generally easy to find, so you can just stay parked and walk.

The Luftig Loft $$
171 E. Livingston Ave.
(231) 342-8181
Instagram: @luftigloft
The spacious urban loft on Livingston right on the edge of the German Village can be booked through Airbnb. The surprisingly large one-bedroom apartment has a fully equipped kitchen and coffee bar, king-size bedroom with a working fireplace, a large rainshower in the master bath and a powder room off the open living and dining space. A spiral staircase leads to a small upstairs level that can be used as a workspace. The Luftig Loft is perfectly situated for an extended stay while working downtown or a staycation to carouse about the village. The building is within walking distance of most German Village eateries and shops, and two parking spaces are provided outside the door. Another upside is the congenial owners live in the same building and are accessible for any questions and suggestions. Club 185 is around the corner, while the Sycamore and Lindey's restaurants are a few minutes stroll. Do yourself a favor. Take a staycation.

SHORT NORTH/ITALIAN VILLAGE

50 Lincoln Short North Bed
** and Breakfast $$**
50 E. Lincoln St.
(614) 299-5050
www.columbus-bed-breakfast.com
A beautiful 1917 Italianate brick home is perfectly situated to explore the Short North while staying in modern comfort. 50 Lincoln has been around since 1986, making this one of the oldest B&Bs in Columbus. Each of the seven cozy rooms is uniquely appointed, with queen beds, comfortable sitting areas, and private bathrooms with bathtub/shower combos. A house-made breakfast, which includes a daily entree, is served in the dining room or to-go for those on the go. The inn provides complimentary off-street parking.

Canopy by Hilton $$$
77 E. Nationwide Blvd.
(614) 223-1400
www.hilton.com
One of Columbus's newer hotels is located in the Short North Arts and Arena Districts, conveniently across from the Greater Columbus Convention Center and a few blocks from Nationwide Arena and the Crew's MLS Soccer stadium at Lower.com Field. It is walkable to downtown, or you can explore farther on a Canopy bike. The rooftop bar and restaurant, Goodale Station, serves up local fare and handcrafted cocktails, while the rooftop fitness center offers views of downtown Columbus.

The Graduate Hotel Columbus $$$
750 N. High St.
(614) 484-1900
www.graduatehotels.com/columbus
Buckeye traditions permeate this stylish boutique hotel in the heart of the Short North Arts District. Graduate Columbus is just a few miles south of The Ohio State University and within walking distance to all the Short North nightlife and downtown Columbus. The rooms are warm, tailored spaces sporting collegiate scarlet and gray details that sort of mimic dorm rooms. Complimentary bikes are available to go exploring. Kings, doubles, studios, and suites scream with school spirit. Homage Bar is open daily for food and drinks, including breakfast and coffee in the morning. Bonus: The Shake Shack is right next door.

Le Méridien Columbus, The Joseph $$$$
620 N. High St.
(614) 227-0100
www.marriott.com
Get a little bit of art and soul at the Short North's premier boutique hotel, which is part of the Marriott brand. The Joseph is a sophisticated 135-room, art-themed hotel featuring artworks donated from the Pizzuti family's private collection, which hang throughout the public spaces and some guest rooms.

The third-floor fitness center overlooks the Short North, and the spa suites are a great place to relax during a special occasion. The hotel's Soul Bar hosts live local music every Thursday evening. Both the Soul Bar and the hotel restaurant, the Guild Room, serve innovative farm-to-table dishes in an elegant setting.

Moxy Columbus Short North $$$
808 N. High St.
(614) 412-7664
www.marriott.com
This is no ordinary hotel check-in experience. At Moxy Short North, you can check in 24/7—at The Bar, where you get your room key along with a free drink token. The open lobby layout with contemporary furniture is designed to allow you commune with other guests by playing pool or games with the staff. Moxy has 24/7 food and beverage offerings with a wide selection of snacks and drinks at the Grab and Go market. The Bar has three daily happy hours. The hotel has a gym and rooftop terrace as well. All guest rooms are equipped with 55-inch smart TVs, built-in USB ports, and free enhanced Wi-Fi.

THE OHIO STATE UNIVERSITY CAMPUS

Only one hotel is located directly on campus, but newer, less expensive chain options, such as Fairfield Inn, Hampton Inn and Suites, Springhill Suites, and Hilton Garden Inn, can be found a short distance away on Olentangy River Road. John Glenn International Airport is a 15-minute drive ($25 taxi) away. Don Scott Airport is 5 minutes ($15 taxi) away. Most of these hotels have their own restaurant or are within a few minutes of a variety of restaurants.

The Roger D. Blackwell Inn $$$
2110 Tuttle Park Place
Fisher College Campus
(614) 247-4000, (866) 247-4003
www.theblackwell.com
Columbus's newest deluxe hotel is found on OSU's Fisher College of Business campus. The Blackwell serves as the executive residence for the college's Executive Education Program. With a management team pulled together by the university's Hospitality and Conference Services Department,

you are guaranteed the very best guest service and state-of-the-art technology at your disposal. The Blackwell's location is hard to top, as the hotel is directly across the street from Ohio Stadium and a short walk from the Schottenstein Center and Wexner Center for the Arts. Amenities include complimentary internet access in each room, a fitness center, concierge services, and shuttle service to the airports. Each floor has fully equipped meeting rooms and conference suites. You won't have to go far for good food and drink either. The Blackwell has a full-service lounge with its own grill menu and a separate restaurant with a respectable selection of Continental and Asian cuisine. Guests dining at Bistro 2110 can use the hotel's complimentary valet parking.

WORTHINGTON

Located at a major intersection of I-270 and US 23, most of the hotels in this area are ordinary, but newer, chains and extended-stay suites, like Hyatt Place, WoodSpring Suites, Courtyard, and Double-Tree. These hotels are close to major businesses including Worthington Industries and the Polaris area. Worthington Crosswoods is 25 minutes ($40 taxi) from John Glenn International Airport and close to restaurants, grocery stores, and charming downtown Old Worthington. If you have a car, there is no shortage of complimentary parking in the huge lots. You can also enjoy a broad selection of dining and entertainment options without leaving the Crosswoods complex.

Holiday Inn Express and Suites $$
55 Hutchinson Ave.
(614) 977-0520
www.holiday-inn.com
The hotel might be your run-of-the-mill chain, but it is a newer build with guest rooms featuring one king or two queen beds with a separate workspace, mini fridge, and microwave. In addition to a complimentary breakfast, this hotel has a heated indoor pool and fitness center. It is located in Worthington Crosswoods, where a wide variety of dining is available.

Worthington Suites $$$
7300 Huntington Park Dr., Crosswoods
(614) 885-0799
www.worthingtonsuites.com
The 104 apartment-style suites come with fully equipped kitchens and are a very good value for an extended stay. The living and sleeping areas are spacious and separate from one another, and free high-speed internet service is provided. There is an outdoor pool and fitness center. A daily hot/cold breakfast is included, along with Wi-Fi, free parking, and concierge services. Worthington Suites is a pet-friendly facility.

EASTON TOWN CENTER

This "city within a city" is one of the largest mixed-use developments in the country and has several lodging options in the heart of Easton, all walkable to dozens of restaurants, shops, and bars. Quite a few chains have been built over the past few years just outside Easton proper, such as TownPlace Suites by Marriott, Hampton Inn and Suites, Homewood Suites, and Hilton Garden Inn. The airport is only a few miles from Easton and takes about 10 minutes to reach by car ($20 taxi).

Aloft Columbus Easton $$
4176 Brighton Rose Way
(614) 762-9162
www.aloftcolumbus.hotelmaestros.com
The Aloft Columbus is a three-star hotel at Easton. The hotel has 136 rooms, including family rooms with trendy decor, an open-plan layout, a lounging area, and a small fridge. The rooms are quiet and well appointed. The hotel has a fitness center, bar, and complimentary parking. It is within walking distance of all the shops and restaurants in Easton Town Center.

Courtyard by Marriott $$
3900 Morse Crossing
(614) 416-8000
www.courtyard.com
The 126-room Courtyard is an affordable substitute for the posh Hilton without compromising location. With rooms ranging from $119 to $139 per night, the hotel attracts business people

during the week and families on the weekends. Plus, it is only a few steps to the heart of Easton Town Center. The guest rooms have a few extras, such as "on-command" movie rental and complimentary internet access. High-speed wireless internet is available in the Business Library, along with private workstations, copiers, and fax machines. The hotel has its own cafe, where a daily breakfast buffet is served at an additional charge, and a convenience market is open 24 hours a day. Parking is free.

Hilton Columbus $$$$
3900 Chagrin Dr.
(614) 414-5000, (800) HILTONS (445-8667)
www.hiltoncolumbus.com

Enter the Hilton and you could be in any top-notch hotel in the world. This sprawling, seven-story hotel is located in one of Columbus's hottest shopping, dining, and entertainment districts, but you won't have to step foot inside to understand why it has been awarded a Four Diamond rating from AAA. The approach to this monumental, Georgian-style hotel is truly striking.

The Hilton is as equally magnificent on the inside as it is from the outside. High ceilings and marble floors give the vast lobby a timeless elegance. Contemporary chairs, sofas, and a sleek bar in the Lobby Lounge entice you to drop everything and indulge in a cocktail (or Starbucks coffee) while piano music wafts through the air.

The marble doesn't end at the lobby. The Hilton's 313 standard rooms are luxurious and generously sized at 400 square feet. Italian marble bathrooms boast heated mirrors and plush bathrobes, while the rooms feature oversize beds, a large work desk, an ergonomic chair, and two phone lines. Sixty-eight Club-level rooms have upgraded amenities, personal concierge services, and complimentary breakfast. Internet access is available in rooms for a daily fee, but Wi-Fi is free in all public spaces.

The Hilton is one of Columbus's premier conference locations, so rooms are often booked several months in advance. The hotel has a variety of meeting rooms equipped with high-speed internet and a full-service business center with copiers, printers, and fax services. Recreational facilities include a complete fitness center, massage therapy room, and game room. The indoor pool is a knockout, with its soaring atrium, whirlpool, and soft lighting. The concierge can arrange tennis and golf outings at nearby facilities.

Despite the fact that there is a bevy of dining and drinking options just a few steps from the hotel, the Hilton adds two more to the mix. The stylish dining room serves breakfast, lunch, and dinner from an a la carte menu and buffets at breakfast and lunch. In the evening, the Easton Sports Club is an easy place to grab a beer and appetizers. The casual tavern-like atmosphere features seven plasma TVs, two pool tables, and video games.

Marriott Residence Inn $$
3999 Easton Loop W.
(614) 414-1000, (800) 331-3131
www.residenceinn.com

Easton's extended-stay hotel is an excellent option when you want a home away from home. The inn's complimentary airport shuttle service will drop you off at the hotel, conveniently located on the west side of Easton. Each newly renovated one- or two-bedroom suite provides a full range of services that echo your home: a fully equipped kitchen, furnished living and dining rooms, and complimentary internet access. Nice touches include a complimentary breakfast buffet, free newspaper, daily housekeeping, and a grocery service for those who want the basics picked up during a busy day. A pool and fitness center are also on-site. Pets are allowed with a $75 nonrefundable fee, but must be restrained or caged while housekeeping is in the room. Complimentary parking is available on-site.

AIRPORT AND EAST

Looking to stay near the airport while you're in town? A bunch of hotels are located on the grounds of John Glenn International Airport, all providing 24-hour shuttle service to and from the terminal. Other chain hotels are just a few miles away on Taylor Road and Stelzer Road.

Fairfield Inn $$
4300 International Gateway
John Glenn International Airport
(614) 237-2100
www.marriott.com

Staying 2 minutes from the airport terminal can certainly take the edge off a hectic travel day, but this 147-room hotel boasts more than a prime location. The rooms are inviting and offer guests extras, such as a microwave, refrigerator, complimentary internet access, and free local calls. The bathrooms have extra amenities of their own: plush bathrobes, a TV, and a phone. Work off your stress at the indoor pool or fitness center and relax on the outdoor patio. If drinking is your means to relaxation, then the hotel bar should do the trick. The Fairfield provides 24-hour shuttle service to the terminal.

Hilton Garden Inn $$
4265 Sawyer Rd.
John Glenn International Airport
(614) 231-2869, (800) 445-8667
www.hilton.com

The 156 well-appointed guest rooms with spacious work desks, multiple phone lines, and data ports make the Hilton Garden Inn ideal for busy travelers. The hotel also features a complimentary 24-hour business center. You can relax in the whirlpool, swim a few laps, or knock out a few miles on the treadmill in the fitness center. The on-site restaurant serves breakfast every morning, and the in-house Pavilion Pantry is open around the clock.

Holiday Inn Hotel & Suites $$
John Glenn International Airport
750 Stelzer Rd.
(614) 237-6360
www.holidayinn.com

The newly renovated Holiday Inn Hotel & Suites Columbus Airport is located near the city's major expressways and has 210 guest rooms and suites. All rooms feature complimentary wireless high-speed internet access, and business-class rooms have microwaves and refrigerators.

The hotel has a first-class fitness room, game room, and toddler room for the kids. The Holidome houses an atrium-style indoor pool and

hot tub sure to get you itching for that tropical vacation. The hotel is a five-minute drive ($8 taxi) from the airport, but it also offers complimentary shuttle service to the terminal.

DUBLIN

A number of hotels and extended-stays can be found around Metro Center Business Park and along Tuller Road in Dublin. These hotels are close to such businesses as Ashland Chemical, Cardinal Health, Honda, Nationwide, and Wendy's International. It is also close to the Columbus Zoo, Dublin Bridge Park, and the Muirfield Village Golf Club. Newer budget hotels such as the Red Roof Inn and Courtyard by Marriott can be found nearby on Post Road. This area is 25 minutes northwest of downtown Columbus. A taxi from the airport will run about $30. If you're staying in the area, try a fabulous local restaurant, Hyde Park Prime Steakhouse, just around the corner at 6360 Frantz Rd.

Doubletree by Hilton $$
600 Metro Place N.
(614) 956-3400
www.hilton.com

The three-story hotel is conveniently located in Dublin's Metro Center Business Park and has 215 spacious guest rooms, which include a king- or two queen-size beds and a workspace. The four-star hotel has a 24-hour fitness center and late-night room service. Other features include a good-size indoor pool and an outdoor fire pit. The hotel also has a full-service restaurant with a separate lounge, but if you are looking to get out, try venturing along Frantz Road, where a number of restaurants and bars are located.

Embassy Suites Hotel $$$
5100 Upper Metro Place
(614) 790-9000
www.embassysuites.com

The Embassy Suites can be a bit pricey but are known for consistently good service and well-appointed extended-stay suites. You get what you pay for here. This recently renovated eight-story hotel has 284 suites built around a garden-style atrium lit from above by a diamond-shaped glass ceiling. If the lobby's glass-encased elevators, lush greenery, and waterfall aren't dramatic enough, then the four-story wooden pagoda should get your attention.

Each suite has one private bedroom, living room with sleeper sofa, work/dining table, wet bar, refrigerator, microwave, two TVs, and high-speed internet access. The hotel amenities go beyond the complimentary breakfast and daily paper to include an evening manager's reception, business center, and babysitting services. Plenty of family fun can be had in the indoor pool, whirl-pool, and fitness center. The on-site restaurant, Urban Craft, is open seven days a week, but for a change of scenery, Stoney River Legendary Steaks is right next door.

Hilton Garden Inn $$
500 Metro Place North
(614) 766-9900
www.hilton.com

The Hilton Garden Inn is located in Dublin's Metro Center Business Park, close to the Columbus Zoo and highways. Each spacious guest room has a refrigerator, microwave, and 27-inch TV with Nintendo and movie options. The business fea-tures of each room include a large work desk, an ergonomic chair, refrigerator and microwave, and complimentary high-speed internet access. The hotel has a 24-hour fitness center, indoor pool, whirlpool, and valet parking. Breakfast is served in the Garden Grill and Bar, while the Pantry sells a variety of sundries, beverages, microwave foods, and snacks. This hotel is pet-friendly.

BED-AND-BREAKFAST INNS

Guesthouses and inns offer a homelike alterna-tive to the standard hotel. A handful of privately owned B&Bs are scattered about town, and unlike hotels, reservations are almost always required. As their names imply, breakfast is included, and some even provide airport transportation.

Bexley Bed & Breakfast $$
519 S. Drexel Ave., Bexley
(614) 935-1863
www.bexleybedandbreakfast.com

The modern five-bedroom inn is just a block from Capital University, making this a convenient place to stay during a college visit and an easy walk into downtown Bexley's restaurants and shops. Each guest room, named for a major city, has an en suite bathroom with heated floors, a flat-screen TV, and plenty of outlets for charging devices. A con-tinental breakfast is served each morning around the table in the bright, cheery gathering room or alfresco on the covered front porch. On-site park-ing is available, and individual door codes to the house and bedroom doors are issued at check-in.

Lily Stone Bed and Breakfast $
106 S. High St., Gahanna
(614) 440-2715
www.gahannahistory.com/lilystone

Gahanna's most unique lodging is a two-story 1920s bed-and-breakfast owned and operated by the Gahanna Historical Society. It is the only one in Ohio owned by a historical society and run by a volunteer staff. Three guest rooms are decorated in the Victorian style, and the facilities from a hotel vary in that all rooms have a sink and share two half and two full baths. Only one room has a TV, and a kitchen phone is available for free local calls. Lily Stone is usually rented out in its entirety for local events and family functions. All rooms are $65 per night and include a continental breakfast. It is well placed within walking distance of several restaurants and bars, and is a short drive from the airport and both beltways (I-670 and I-270).

Luftig Loft $$
171 E. Livingston Ave., German Village

A spacious urban loft within walking distance of German Village restaurants. Read more about this beautiful accommodation in the German Village section of this chapter.

Ohio Log House Bed & Breakfast $
9640 Slough Rd., Canal Winchester
(614) 206-0432
www.loghouseandbb.com

A short drive southeast of the city lands you a world away. History and architecture buffs will appreciate the Ohio Log House for its rustic charm and handmade furniture and cabinetry. The 19th-century log structure was reassembled on the property near a large fishing lake that provides catch-and-release fishing or paddle-boating and a waterfront swing set for kids. The cabin has central air, but the amenities are otherwise primitive, such as a wood-fire baking oven in the kitchen. Guests can rent a single bedroom with a private bathroom or take over the entire three-room cabin. Each bedroom has either a shower or claw-foot tub. The large communal living room is a great place to cozy up next to the fireplace. A homemade country breakfast is included.

Short North Bed & Breakfast $$
50 E. Lincoln St., Short North
(614) 299-5050, (800) 516-9664
www.columbus-bed-breakfast.com
This restored 1917 brick town house is in the Italian Village section of the Short North, just a few blocks from the Greater Columbus Convention Center and a short drive from The Ohio State University. Each of the seven rooms offers a comfortable blend of antique and modern furnishings, wireless internet, and full private baths. Local art fills the house with an ever-changing display of works. A gourmet continental breakfast is included, and parking is available in the private lot.

Timbrook Guesthouse $$$$
5811 Olentangy River Rd., northwest
  Columbus
(614) 634-2166
www.timbrookguesthouse.com
The Timbrook Guesthouse is a wonderful alternative to a traditional hotel stay or a romantic staycation. The beautiful property is located 10 minutes northeast of the city between Worthington and Linworth. The *Old Jack Antrim Farmhouse* was built in 1875 and, after only three owners, was turned into a stately bed and breakfast inn. Each of the six multi-room suites features a smart TV, walk-in shower, plush linens, toiletries, and luxurious touches like robes and slippers. A few of the themed rooms have gas fireplaces and claw foot tubs, but all are luxuriously appointed with handcrafted Amish, Stickley, or Arts and Crafts furniture.

The common areas are cozy enough to belly up to the living room fireplace in the winter, enjoy quiet time in the sunny reading room, or sip a summer cocktail on the gazebo. Guests can

spread out around the pool on plush loungers or soak your stress away in the jetted spa tub surrounded by greenery. For those preferring to hunker down for a night or two, the dining area offers access to a refrigerator, microwave, coffee maker, dishware, and grazing snacks. After a gourmet breakfast (often using eggs from their own happy hen house), take a walk to the aviary to see their collection of pet parrots. If you are looking for a sophisticated retreat with luxurious touches and a convenient location, pay a visit to the Timbrook Guesthouse.

LODGES AND RESORTS

Cherry Valley Hotel $$$
2299 Cherry Valley Rd., Newark
(740) 788-1200
www.cherryvalleyhotel.com
Cherry Valley is the nation's only hotel to carry the distinction of being a hotel-arboretum and botanical garden. The recently renovated lodge is nestled on 17 acres about 30 miles east of Columbus near Granville. This 200-room resort-style lodge is geared toward group meetings and romantic getaways. It is a popular place for family reunions, wedding parties, and family weekends. The lobby has a rustic atmosphere with soaring stone fireplaces, hardwood floors, and wood beam ceilings. Beautifully landscaped courtyards and unique common areas allow for group gatherings or private moments. The spacious guest rooms have coffeemakers and mini fridges, while some have ceiling-to-floor windows overlooking the grounds.

Wander the tranquil gardens through a collection of rare heirloom and native plants that encompass some 2,000 plantings and 400 species. Birdhouses and feeders are strategically placed throughout the property to attract butterflies and birds. Fresh herbs from the chef's herb garden are used in the Craftsman Kitchen, where you can also have a private igloo dining experience during winter. The gazebo and Cascade Gardens provide great photo ops.

The hotel's facilities boast a fitness center, heated indoor pool and hot tub, and full-service Cherry Valley Spa.

ℹ View www.ohiocamper.com to find campsites in the Columbus area. Tree Haven Campground, located at 4855 Miller Paul Rd., Westerville, is closest to the city. It has 130 sites with water and electric, showers, and a pool. Call (740) 965-3469 for information. Read more about camping in the Parks and Recreation chapter.

Deer Creek Resort and Conference
   Center $$
22300 State Park Rd., Mount Sterling
(740) 869-2020
www.deercreekparklodge.com
This beautiful resort is located 30 minutes south of Columbus in 3,100-acre Deer Creek State Park. All of the lodge's 110 guest rooms have a balcony or patio, many overlooking the lake or pool. The rooms come in a variety of configurations including bunk bed lofts for bigger families. Resort amenities include large indoor and outdoor pools, sauna, whirlpool, fitness room, and cafe. The lodge is less than 2 miles from the Deer Creek State Park Golf Course and has dining facilities on-site. Breakfast or pizza dinners can be bundled with some packages.

   Slightly more expensive options include newly renovated one- and two-bedroom cottages with full living and dining areas and bathrooms, as well as a screened porch, outdoor grill, and fire pit. The historic Harding Cabin is a spacious three-bedroom cottage that was once a presidential retreat of President Warren G. Harding. Its lakefront location allows for a private boat dock and full-length screened porch with a fabulous view. Cabin rates vary, and year-round packages can be viewed online.

Hocking Hills State Park Lodge $$
20020 OH 664, Logan
(740) 270-6100, (800) At-A-Park (282-7275)
The new-ish full-service lodge in the Hocking Hills is a fun and affordable place to base yourself for adventures in Hocking Hill State Park. The modern space has a rustic elegance in the lobby and minimalist but new guest rooms and cabins. Property activities are plentiful, from swimming in indoor and outdoor pools, soaking in the all-season hot

tub, or working out at the fitness center, to relaxing by the first-come, first-served individual fire pits. Get in a quick game of Ping Pong or billiards before heading out for a hike to one of the many caves and waterfalls just steps from the lodge. Fuel your adventures with breakfast at the café and lunch or dinner at the restaurant, then kick back by the cozy fireplace with a drink at the Rock House Pub.

AMISH ACCOMMODATIONS

Amish Country Inns
Berlin Village Inn
5135 Hwy. 39, Berlin
(330) 893-2861, (800) 869-7571
www.berlinvillageinn.com

Carlisle Village Inn (Dutchman Hospitality
   Group)
1357 Old Rte. 39 NE, Sugarcreek
4949 Walnut St. (Hwy. 515), Walnut Creek
(330) 893-3636, (855) 411-2275
www.dhgroup.com/inns

Guggisberg Swiss Inn
5025 Hwy. 557, Charm
(330) 893-3600, (877) 467-9477
www.guggisbergswissinn.com

Swiss Village Inn
206 S. Factory St., Sugarcreek
(800) 792-6822
www.swissvillageinn.com

BED-AND-BREAKFASTS

Carlisle Country Inn
5676 Township Rd. 362, Berlin
(330) 674-3975
www.visitamishcountry.com
The Carlisle Inn is located just off Berlin's busy shopping district, but you will feel a world away once you tuck into the warm inn with its spectacular views, warm hospitality, and country elegance. The inn's seven queen and king rooms have private baths, Jacuzzis, and fireplaces. The wraparound porch is a great place to relax with a

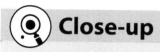 **Close-up**

Amish Country Escape

Columbus may abound with chain hotels, but a one-hour drive northeast of the city will land you in the rolling hills of Amish Country, where character-ridden inns, rustic cabins, and privately owned B&Bs are the norm. Ohio's heartland has a handful of hotels near the cities of Wooster and New Philadelphia, but a much more personalized experience can be found at one of the small, scenic inns or bed-and-breakfasts.

Amish country inns are independently owned facilities, usually located in or near the more popular towns, such as Berlin, Charm, and Walnut Creek. The rooms are set up hotel style, with private bathrooms and cable TV, and some have indoor swimming pools. Most also have restaurants on-site and include breakfast. These are a nice, affordable choice for family fun in the country.

Listed here are a small number of unique accommodations, but it's best to call for reservations since some Amish-owned facilities do not have websites. Most places are open year-round and accept major credit cards.

book and take in the scenery. A farmstead breakfast is included in the rates.

Garden Gate Get-A-Way Bed & Breakfast
6041 Township Rd. 310, off Hwy. 39 in
   Millersburg
(330) 674-7608
www.garden-gate.com
Garden Gate's four rooms are a reflection of its country charm, and its beautiful perennial gardens are brought indoors with guest rooms named the Briar Patch Room and Rose Garden Room. All have private baths but share a common area with kitchen facilities and lounge. Escape to the solitude of a porch swing or socialize with other guests around the popular evening campfire.

Hotel Millersburg
35 W. Jackson St., Millersburg
(330) 674-1457
www.hotelmillersburg.com
Located near the well-preserved town square, this interesting Victorian hotel has been welcoming visitors since 1847. The 24 rooms have private baths and offer old-world charm alongside modern-day amenities. A restaurant and tavern are on-site.

Miller Haus Bed and Breakfast
3135 Cty. Rd. 135, 1.5 miles southwest of
   Walnut Creek
(330) 893-3602
www.millerhaus.com
Kick back in a rocking chair and take in the stunning views of the surrounding farms from one of the highest points in Holmes County. This Amish-style home has nine rooms with private baths and air-conditioning. Quilts and antiques add cozy touches to the rooms, and the homemade breakfasts and desserts served daily are heavenly. Though seeming like a secluded sanctuary, this authentic Amish homestead is very close to major attractions and shopping.

CABINS AND LODGES

Coblentz Country Cabins
Berlin Area
(877) 99-SLEEP (997-5337)
www.amishcountrylodging.com
These high-end log cabins can accommodate anywhere from four to eight people per unit, making this a great group getaway. Linens, towels, and TVs make it feel like home, but the cathedral ceilings, hardwood floors, lofts, and fire pits gives the cabins a lodge-like feel. They are spacious enough for a large family to spread out, while the

Jacuzzi, fireplace, and peaceful surroundings provide romance for couples as well. This group also owns Pine Cove in Millersburg and cottages and treehouses in Berlin.

Donna's Premier Lodging
Berlin Area
(330) 893-3068
www.donnasofberlin.com

Indulge in pure luxury at any one of the cozy cabins, Jacuzzi villas, bridal suites, chalets, and honeymoon cottages. All accommodations come with a fully equipped kitchen, Jacuzzi, fireplace, TV, and outdoor grill. Looking for a Poconos-style retreat but don't want to drive 8 hours for it? Look no further than the "Romancing the Stone" cabin, with its indoor waterfall, mood lighting, and remote-control gas logs in a massive stone fireplace. If you prefer "city dwelling," the villas are Cape Cod–style units that are within walking distance of downtown Berlin.

Landoll's Mohican Castle
561 Township Rd. 3352, Loudonville
(419) 994-3427, (800) 291-5001
www.landollsmohicancastle.com

This 1,100-acre estate is fit for a king with its luxury cottages, log cabins, and, yes, castle. King-size beds, hardwood floors, Gothic carved doors, fully equipped kitchens, Italian baths with heated tile floors, Jacuzzis, and stone fireplaces will leave you feeling majestic. If that isn't enough, rent a golf cart and explore the 30 miles of trails that run through your royal forest. Pamper yourself in elegant solitude or indulge in winter skiing only 90 minutes from Columbus.

37

RESTAURANTS

This is likely the longest chapter in the book, but frankly, it could easily be twice as long, given the number of wonderful restaurants in our city. Those new to Columbus sometimes struggle to see the "ethnicity" here, but the diversity of the people who live here is seen in the diversity of our restaurants. This chapter is organized according to neighborhood and provides a representative cross section of the city's eateries. Writing this chapter was a lot of fun, but the most difficult part was choosing selectively which places to include.

Admittedly, I have not eaten everywhere in Columbus, but not for lack of trying! Through years of research, conversations, and basic word-of-mouth recommendations, hundreds of independently owned dining establishments have been whittled down to a selection of greasy spoons, breweries, campus haunts, upscale dining, and comfortable coffeehouses. There are plenty of romantic places to take your sweetheart for an intimate setting. There are the ever-changing trendy spots where the "hipper than thou" crowd goes to see and be seen. There are the cheap-ish (but good!) eats for the shoestring budget. Hopefully, after reading this chapter you will find at least a few places to tempt your taste buds.

When I first moved to Columbus, the one thing that immediately stood out—and is still the case—was how many restaurants are located in (sometimes unattractive) strip malls, many of which have been included here. Don't let a shopping center locale scare you away. Some of the best food is hidden behind unassuming glass doors or advertised with a generic storefront sign. You'll discover fine dining tucked in the lower levels of buildings and along out-of-the-way dead-end streets.

Columbus does, however, have several trendy pockets of restaurants that should not be missed, especially if you are only visiting for a brief time. Park your car and do a little progressive eating and drinking in German Village, the Short North, and Bridge Park in Dublin, but if you don't have access to a vehicle, several buses travel along High Street, allowing you to experience the different flavors of Columbus with little effort. The "Cap" at Union Station, linking downtown and the Short North, is home to several local restaurants, including Hyde Park Prime Steakhouse and the more casual Local Cantina.

This chapter's goal is to help you find a feast unique to Columbus—but what exactly is this? Cincinnati is known for its chili, Kansas City for its barbecue, but what is Columbus known for? Even after long interviews with local foodies and restaurateurs, it is still impossible to say. Even they had a tough time nailing down a cuisine specific to our city, so for now, let's just say that dining in Columbus will satisfy any craving. Whether it's unpretentious comfort food, global immigrant cuisine, or menus of sheer genius, we have a lot of diversity in our dining.

In the past 10 years, we have seen several pockets of immigrant restaurants grow along Morse Road, Cleveland Avenue, Dublin-Granville Road, and, more recently, Bethel Road. These stretches of road are home to wonderful Thai, Vietnamese, African, Indian, Korean, and Mexican food, usually very authentic and served in simple no-frills dining rooms. Columbus pop-ups and special-event menus are ever evolving too, with collaborations between established and up-and-coming chefs, food trucks, breweries, and, in some cases, at the homes of local celebrity chefs.

When it comes to fast food, we have that too—and, unfortunately, a lot of it. Columbus has one of the nation's highest ratios of national fast-food chains per capita. Besides being corporate headquarters to Bob Evans, two other chains are headquartered in Columbus. White Castle, the first ever fast-food burger chain, began selling its five-cent burgers in 1921 in Kansas City. The company moved corporate headquarters to Columbus in 1934, but we consider Whiteys ours because the white-and-blue castle motif was conceived here. White Castle remains privately held, and the restaurants are company-owned, not franchised, so I have made it a point to mention "our" Whiteys for sentimental value, if for no other reason.

The late Dave Thomas, founder of Wendy's International, made his contribution to the weight problem of America starting right here in Columbus with square hamburgers and addicting Frosties. The original Wendy's, which opened in 1969, was located downtown but closed its doors in 2007 and moved the museum of Wendy's memorabilia to its corporate campus in Dublin, Ohio.

Another local restaurateur, who has been redefining the Columbus dining scene for 30 years, is Cameron Mitchell. His flagship restaurant, Cameron's American Bistro in Worthington, along with his 49 other countrywide restaurants, has brought consistently good dining concepts to Columbus. Rather than include them among the regular entries, Mitchell's restaurants are featured in a Close-up later in this chapter.

Chains and fast-food restaurants are clustered at Easton Town Center and around the Polaris area, which generally requires a car to get to. This chapter is meant to promote dining at the independently owned restaurants responsible for feeding a hungry Columbus, which they do with creativity and imagination. Entries for most of these restaurants are listed in their respective neighborhoods.

And for those evenings when you are not looking for innovative food and just want a simple slice of pie, some of the favorite neighborhood pizza places are included here, yet necessitates a disclaimer. Everyone has their own opinion about what makes a pizza special, but not all beloved pizza shops are included. I have kept the descriptions of what they offer to a minimum and focused more on what the locals prefer about it.

Pizza shops located on campus are listed separately in The Ohio State University chapter.

When it comes to general protocol, assume the restaurants accept major credit cards unless otherwise noted. Cash-only places are few and far between, but they do still exist, so this is pointed out specifically when applicable. Most Columbus restaurants do not require a dress code of more than business casual. Even the priciest restaurants permit business casual dress most nights of the week, providing for an elegant but relaxed dining experience.

As for wheelchair accessibility, only exceptions are pointed out. Columbus is modern enough that this doesn't seem to be much of a problem as in other cities where restaurants may be located in older buildings not up to compliance.

Smoking is banned in public places, including restaurants, bars, and patios. Outdoor smoking areas must be situated away from an enclosed area, and violators can face civil charges and a $150 fine.

Drinkers don't have it so bad. Just don't go looking for a Bloody Mary before 11 a.m. on Sunday, as restaurants are not permitted to serve alcohol before then. Any other day of the week, alcohol can be served beginning in the wee hours of the morning. Many of the restaurants included here are known more for their full-service bars, but there is often the case of that blurry line between restaurant and pub. If you don't see your favorite restaurant-bar here, have a look in the Wine, Bars, and Breweries and The Ohio State University chapters.

One last but strongly recommended piece of advice on dining in Columbus is to try to make reservations, as many of the popular places open online reservations at the beginning of each month for the following month. Weekends and holidays fill up fast. I also recommend calling smaller mom-and-pop restaurants before going. Columbus has long been known as a test market for new forays into food, so it comes as no surprise that restaurants come and go at a high rate in our city, but this also means some fantastic dining is to be had when new concepts stick.

If to eat well is to live well, then we are living quite large in Columbus.

Price Code

The following price codes are based on the average price of two entrees, excluding tax, tip, appetizers, desserts, and drinks.

$	Cheaper Eats	Less than $30
$$	Moderate	$31–$50
$$$	Indulgent	$51–$75
$$$$	Worth the Splurge	$75 and more

DOWNTOWN

Bar Cicchetti $$
310 S. High St.
(614) 228-5300
www.bar-cicchetticolumbus.com

The historic Westin Great Southern Hotel is home to TV personality and *Top Chef* Fabio Viviani's modern Bar Chiccetti. The name means "to share," which is exactly what guests are encouraged to do with the number of fantastic small plates, salads, pizzas, and pastas. Menu items range from crowd-friendly focaccia and (darn good!) meatballs to more refined shareables of octopus and black rice arancini. All the bread, pasta, and pizza doughs are made in-house and served in a variety of main entrees along with other "big bites." The cioppino is definitely something to write home about! Keep in mind, this is technically a hotel restaurant so it is open for breakfast, lunch, and dinner and offers menus for each. The bar and restaurant are separate but equally atmospheric. Belly up to the bar for lunch or a cocktail and it will be a different experience than in the dining room.

Degrees Restaurant $$
250 Cleveland Ave., Mitchell Hall
(614) 287 5578
www.degrees.cscc.edu

The full-service, student-run restaurant located on the ground level of Mitchell Hall is a testimony to the top-notch hospitality department at Columbus State Community College. The small-but-mighty menu changes with the season and includes scratch-made soups, flatbreads, sandwiches, and salads with optional proteins. The main entrees run the gamut of proteins and vegetables, offering a little something for everyone. Do not miss out on dessert, as the school's budding pastry chefs bring their A-game with cakes, tortes, and seasonal sweets. Degrees might be one of the more underrated spots to grab a bite, especially given the price point for the fantastic quality of food and service. Enjoy your meal on the seasonal outdoor patio. Degrees is open for lunch (11 a.m. to 2 p.m.) and dinner (4 to 8 p.m.) Mon through Thurs, with a brief closing between meals. Check the website to confirm hours as they may change through the academic year. Keep an eye out for special foodie events that are regularly held here and open to the public.

Dirty Franks Hot Dog Palace $
248 S. Fourth St.
(614) 824-4673
www.dirtyfranks.com

One always thinks of Vienna when you mention the word *palace*; in this case, it is Vienna beef hot dogs at Dirty Franks Palace, a popular and casual restaurant specializing in all things wiener, including vegetarian and vegan dogs. Some of the top dogs on the menu include the Chicago-style, sauerkraut dog, Hot Tot-cho Dog, and Puff the Magic Popper. If none of the signature flavors tickle your fancy, build your own dogs, choosing from almost fifty toppings. If frankfurters aren't your thing, salads, fries, and all sorts of other delicious carbs are among the side dishes. The Palace can become quite busy on the weekends, but it is still a family-friendly place. Appease your late-night munchies, as Dirty Franks is open until 10 p.m. weeknights and 1 a.m. on Fri and Sat. One can also get a Dirty fix at locations in Ohio Stadium, Crew's Lower.com stadium, Huntington Park, and Hollywood Casino.

Due Amici $$$
67 E. Gay St.
(614) 224-9373
www.due-amici.com

Due Amici has been a Gay Street mainstay for 20 years. The restaurant, located within a beautiful historic building, has a sophisticated atmosphere, but with a relaxed vibe. It serves up classic Italian entrees such as chicken parmesan, gnocchi, lamb, and veal. Salads, pizzas, desserts, and an Italian-forward wine list round out the menu. Due Amici serves Sunday brunch with brunchy cocktails and offers a changing seasonal menu. Seating options include booths, tables, or an outdoor patio overlooking Gay Street. Reservations are recommended.

Flatiron Tavern $$
129 E. Nationwide Blvd.
(614) 461-0033
www.flatirontavern.com

If you pass through downtown and notice a triangular, tapered building and think, "Gee, that looks like the Flatiron Building in New York," well, this is Columbus's version, built in 1910 as a saloon and grocery store. The Tavern serves up traditional pub grub and drinks at fair prices, drawing a faithful after-work crowd. You will find various sandwiches, burgers, salads, wings, and a la carte sides on the menu, but their signature is build-your-own Phillys. The interior has recently undergone a much-needed update, while maintaining the historic marble and wood bar. This popular watering hole offers decent happy hour specials, is open until midnight on weeknights and late on the weekends, and has seasonal outdoor patio seating.

Hank's Low Country Seafood and
Raw Bar $$
6 W. Gay St.
(614) 992-5447
www.hanksseafoodrestaurant.com/columbus

Hank's Columbus is the second location of the beloved Charleston-based fish house known for its low-country flavors and sophisticated white-jacket service. Seafood lovers will rejoice in this menu full of Southern specialties like she-crab soup, shrimp and grits, grilled grouper, and bouillabaisse. There is no shortage of oyster options— on the half shell, stewed, grilled, and casino style. The Raw Bar has an extensive selection of shareables and an over-the-top seafood tower. Meat lovers will appreciate the few thoughtful chicken and beef options. Save room for dessert, as you are sure to find something among the dozen or so sweet offerings. The restaurant has a classic coastal fish-house vibe with warm wood and brass details. The saloon-style bar serves up South

Carolina craft beers, global wines, and signature cocktails, both classic and modern. This is the place to get your vesper or sazerac. Reservations are a must.

Indian Oven Restaurant $$
427 E. Main St.
(614) 220-9390
www.indianoven.com

This popular North Indian restaurant offers a contemporary dining experience with its airy, industrial dining room. The usual curries and tandoori dishes are available in whatever degree of spice you can handle, and more sophisticated house specialties have been added to the menu. The Indian Oven offers plenty of vegetarian and vegan entrees and a wonderful selection of breads from the open kitchen. The sleek stainless-steel bar carries a full complement of liquor, wine, and beer, while the patio accommodates outdoor dining during the summer months. Open for lunch and dinner.

Jeff Ruby Steakhouse $$$$
89 E. Nationwide Blvd.
(614) 686-7800
www.jeffruby.com/columbus

The glitzy steakhouse sports a glamourous gilded-age ambience to go with its heady dining experience. Reds, golds, and purples combined with Venetian mirrors and stained glass create a luxurious art deco–inspired dining room and bar. The upscale menu features world-class handcrafted steaks and seafood dishes, including wagyu beef, sushi, and the signature steak Diane. Be sure to get the mac and cheese, which the Food Network ranked among its "Most Magnificent Sides." Jeff Ruby is one of the premier dining experiences in Columbus, so be prepared to pay for it.

The Keep Kitchen and Liquor Bar $$$
50 W. Broad St.
(614) 224-9500
www.thekeepcolumbus.com

The Keep is tucked away on the mezzanine level within the historic LeVeque Tower, making it a great spot for dinner or drinks when attending a show at the neighboring Palace Theatre. The menu is modern American, and the ambience is warm and contemporary even though it's located within the city's iconic 1927 art deco building. The bar, restaurant, and lounge spaces are beautiful, but be cognizant that The Keep also serves as the restaurant for Hotel LeVeque, so it is open for breakfast, lunch, and dinner and has regular happy hour specials—and hotel prices might make for a pricey meal.

Market 65 Local Eatery and Bar $$
65 E. State St.
(614) 564-6565
www.market65.com

Looking for a healthy lunch option? Head to the ground-level Market 65 in the Sheraton at Capitol Square for farm-to-table fare between 11 a.m. and 3 p.m. on weekdays. In 2011, Anthony Micheli and Patrick Katzenmeyer were ahead of the curve when it came to the build-your-own-meal concept. Choose from signature salads, wraps, paninis, and daily scratch-made soups or build your own loaded salad from a laundry list of fresh, organic ingredients. Market 65 grows much of its own produce and herbs to reinforce the philosophy of serving good, clean food. A once-a-week happy hour is offered on Thurs from 4 to 6 p.m., when you can get a stone-fired flatbread washed down with a local craft beer or lovely glass of wine. Market 65 is closed on weekends.

Milestone 229 $$
229 Civic Center Dr.
(614) 427-0276
www.milestone229.com

Solid, modern American food at a good price point makes Milestone 229 a popular and convenient downtown spot to meet for lunch or dinner when attending a theater show. The open, airy dining room with ceiling-to-floor windows offers views of the Scioto River and downtown Columbus. A large outdoor patio overlooks the Scioto Mile fountains, which, during the warmer months, makes for fun people-watching while dining alfresco. Milestone is open for lunch and dinner and has happy hour specials and a great Sunday brunch.

Rishi Sushi Kitchen and Bar $$
114 N. Third St.
(614) 914-5124
www.rishicolumbus.com

Rishi has been keeping downtown bellies full of fish and ramen since 2014. Its location near the corner of Third and Long makes this is an easy place to grab a bento box during the lunch hours between 11 a.m. and 2 p.m. or pop in for a few of the specialty rolls and a drink or sake at the long bar during the dinner hours. The spacious interior is modern industrial, and a colorful outdoor patio is open seasonally.

Sidebar Columbus $$
122 E. Main St.
(614) 228-9041
www.sidebarcolumbus.com

Literally tucked on a side street, the dimly lit Sidebar is a cozy, popular downtown restaurant serving South American and Spanish-style tapas, meat, and seafood-heavy entrees. Salads and pizzas also nod toward Spanish flavors. The wine list focuses on European varieties, and the bartenders are known for specializing in Prohibition-era cocktails. The weeknight happy hour menu is one of the best around, offering a generous selection of reasonably priced small plates, pizzas, and drinks.

Speck Italian Eatery $$$
89 N. High St.
(614)754-8544
www.speckrestaurant.com

Simply put, this vibrant Italian eatery in the heart of downtown serves really good food. If mortadella is making a comeback, chef Josh Dalton is making sure Columbus gets in on the meaty action. Lunch is a great value, especially given the quality of ingredients and price point. It is common knowledge that in Italy, certain shaved-meat sandwiches have risen to cult status, and Speck's signature sammies on house-made focaccia could become Columbus's elevated equivalent. Dinner is another delicious story! Handmade pasta is front and center, while starters and other main dishes showcase exquisite interpretations of Italian classics. The open kitchen and bar helps create a lively atmosphere. The wine and cocktail list is very well curated, and dessert is not to be missed. Dinner reservations are practically compulsory.

Veritas $$$$
11 W. Gay St.
(614) 745-3864
www.veritasrestaurant.com

If food with bravado is your thing, look no further than Veritas. For the past decade, chef Joshua Dalton has helped shape the culinary landscape of Columbus into one that is modern and inventive, becoming one of the best chefs in the region. Veritas was the first restaurant to offer a tasting menu only for dinner and continues to create fixed menus offering innovative global fine dining. The five-plus courses guide eaters from bread to starters to salad, entree, and dessert. Premium side dishes can be added on, and wine pairings for each course are included at an additional charge. The bar is first-come, first-served and has its own abridged bar menu. Coveted reservations are opened the first of each month, one month at a time—and they fill up fast.

GERMAN VILLAGE/BREWERY DISTRICT

Agni $$$$
716 S. High St.
(614) 674-6600
www.dineatagni.com

Columbus's very own *Top Chef* alum, Avishar Barua, opened his second restaurant in the Brewery District to much acclaim. The six-course tasting menu melds his Bangladeshi heritage with Midwestern ingredients, regional classics, and love for fire. Agni, appropriately named for the Hindu god of fire, says it all about the techniques used for many of the dishes. Chefs maintain the fire by hand, stoking wood on the Grillworks hearth in the partially open kitchen. It's an intensive labor of love that shows in every bite. Most of the dishes change every few months, and of course wine pairings can be added on, or drinks can be ordered individually. With advance notice, the menu can be made vegetarian or pescatarian, and the bar is first-come, first-served with an abridged bar menu available. Agni's unique menu

is worth every cent for eaters and those who truly appreciate high-end dishes that you can't find anywhere else. Reservations open a month in advance, require a per-person deposit, and fill up fast.

Barcelona $$$
263 E. Whittier St.
(614) 443-3699
www.barcelonacolumbus.com

Barcelona is a longtime German Village favorite. The consistently good food and service maintains its popularity. Barcelona's menu features regional Spanish dishes, including several paellas with various protein combinations, and a classic assortment of tapas. The tapas tower is large enough to serve several people as a starter, and different size charcuterie boards are great if you are just feeling grazey. The wine list is heavy into Spanish bottles and flights, but a few French and Italian wines also make the cut. Sangria by the glass or pitcher is a popular choice on a hot summer day.

The dining room is elegant, and the caliber of food could justify a stuffier atmosphere, yet it remains casual and comfortable. It's the outdoor patio, however, that brings something truly special to this restaurant. Enclosed with lush greenery, hanging baskets, old-fashioned street lamps, and twinkly lights, Barcelon's remains one of the most desirable patios in the city. I have bestowed it the honor of most romantic patio in Columbus. Barcelona has midweek live music and happy hour specials. Reservations are recommended on the weekends, and valet parking is available.

Bistrolino Old World Kitchen and Bar $$
495 S. Fourth St.
(614) 928-3898
www.bistrolino614.com

A laid-back bistro is tucked in an intimate brick house with a slight Middle Eastern vibe to the decor. The menu features great ingredients in rustic old-world Lebanese and Italian cuisine. Guanciale and speck turn up on pizzas, while lamb and labne top rustic mankoushe flatbreads. Oven-baked entrees include parmigiana dishes, pastas, and chops. Bistrolino offers a wonderful blend of familiar and unfamiliar flavors. The wine list is Italian heavy with some Lebanese wines in the mix. The adjacent sister bar, Ferdinand Lounge, is an eclectic bar with interesting drinks.

Cento $$$
595 S. Third St.
(614) 696-6565
www.centogermanvillage.com
Read details in the Close-up about Cameron Mitchell Restaurants.

Chapman Eats $$$
739 S. Third St.
(614) 444-0917
www.eatchapmans.com
When Chapman Eats first opened in the iconic (original) Max and Erma's space, it made the *New York Times*' list of the 50 Most Exciting Restaurants in the Country. It has been nonstop popular ever since. Husband and wife team BJ Lieberman and Bronwyn Haines conceived a clever seasonal menu offering an Ohio twist on global comfort food. Think General Tso's cauliflower, confit duck leg "shake 'n bake," or Ohio maple budino. Asian flavors are laced throughout the menu, as are a lot of local ingredients. Ice cream is the hot-ticket dessert, and seasonal pints are available to carry out. Being voted a James Beard semifinalist for the Best Chef: Great Lakes category (which includes Chicago and Detroit) brings another level of recognition to Columbus's increasingly innovative food scene. Reservations open a month in advance and fill up fast, but occasionally the lucky soul can walk in and get seated and eat at the bar.

Comune $$$
677 Parsons Ave.
(614) 947-1012
www.comune-restaurant.com
Vegetarians and vegans rejoice as Comune is elevating plant-based cuisine to a point where meat eaters won't miss the meat, which is impressive in carnivorous Columbus. Roasted root sandwiches, bean stews, watermelon carpaccio, and meaty mushrooms have been in rotation on the menu, but the "bread + spread" is the original fan favorite, with house-made pita and seasonal

i Street parking in German Village, the Short North, and the campus area can be nearly impossible on weekends. Allow ample time to find a space, or take advantage of valet parking offered by many of the restaurants. It isn't always cheap, but it may be the least frustrating way to go. Also, be aware of signage in certain zones that charge for parking using the ParkCBUS. com app.

trios of dips. The food is inspired yet unfussy, just like the hip minimalist atmosphere. Comune is all about creating satisfying vegetarian dishes using great produce and simple techniques that allow the ingredients to shine.

Emmetts Café $
744 S. High St.
(614) 826-0679
www.emmettscafe.com
Your friendly neighborhood cafe serves breakfast and lunch from 8 a.m. to 3 p.m. Pick up a drip, pour-over, or specialty coffee to go with the popular breakfast burrito or The Lox. Parfaits, breakfast sandwiches, and muffins are also among the offerings. This hole-in-the-wall breakfast spot does a great carryout, but it only has a small dining room with a few tables and an outdoor patio. A second location is at 2571 Neil Ave.

Katzinger's Delicatessen $
475 S. Third St.
(614) 228-3354
www.katzingers.com
This German Village institution is open for breakfast, lunch, and dinner seven days a week. People come from all over to what is possibly the best deli in town. Presidents, rocks stars, and astronaut-senators (John Glenn) have visited Katzingers for its famously big sandwiches and outstanding selection of deli meats, cheeses, and breads.

Create your own sandwich, go for one of the monstrous Reubens, or order off the vegetarian and vegan menus. Throw in some garlic pickles, potato salad, and rugelach for dessert, and your takeout is officially gourmet. Enjoy your sandwich alfresco if you are quick enough to get a sidewalk table or eat in where the bustling atmosphere is unpretentious and the service is friendly. Katzinger's is also a specialty store that carries Jewish, kosher, and other artisanal groceries. A second location is at 7160 Muirfield Dr. in Dublin.

Lindey's $$$
169 E. Beck St.
(614) 228-4343
www.lindeys.com

Lindey's has been voted one of Columbus's top 10 restaurants every year since opening in 1981, and for good reasons: the charming location, sophisticated clubby atmosphere, and consistently exceptional food. It's one of the longest-serving fine-dining restaurants in Columbus.

The restored brownstone is a natural home for this New York–style bistro that harkens back to the turn of the 20th century. The tin ceilings are intricately decorated. A copper-topped bar, polished brass railings, chandeliers, and hardwood floors give the bar area a warm, cozy feeling. Of the three separate dining areas, the front room is the liveliest and is often a stage for the movers and shakers of Columbus.

The kitchen turns out decades-long favorites, such as lobster bisque, tournedos of beef, and steak frites, as well as more modern-day specials. Be sure to leave room for the dessert appropriately called Lindey's Post Mortem: coffee ice cream topped with Kahlúa hot fudge sauce. Some of the special offerings are happy hour and brunch on both Saturday and Sunday.

Lindey's has two of the most coveted alfresco dining options in Columbus: a tranquil ground-level terrace with a full bar and a patio perched on the rooftop with decent views of the city skyline. Reservations are a must on any weekend, even during lunch.

Plank's Cafe & Pizzeria $
743 Parsons Ave.
(614) 443-6251
www.plankscafe.com

Columbus residents love their Buckeyes, and it's obvious at Plank's. The walls of this sports-themed, family-friendly restaurant are a shrine to OSU, but there is a strong showing of Blue Jacket, Clippers,

and Crew memorabilia, too. It will be a stretch, but if you can't find your college pennant tacked up somewhere on the overloaded walls, bring one in to hang up.

As for the food, they've been in the same digs since 1939, if that says anything. Plank's serves a full breakfast, lunch, and the usual pizzeria fare, such as burgers, bratwursts, subs, sandwiches, and the gamut of fried appetizers The pizza crust is sweeter than usual, which makes it a neighborhood favorite. Expect to be welcomed with open arms by a very friendly and accommodating staff. If you must stay at home to watch the football game, this is one of the only places in Columbus that delivers everything on the menu. Plank's Cafe is not to be confused with Plank's Biergarten, which is listed in the Wine, Bars, and Breweries chapter.

Schmidt's Restaurant und Banquet Haus $$
240 E. Kossuth St.
(614) 444-6808
www.schmidthaus.com

This German Village landmark is located in a historic brick livery stable and serves traditional German American fare in a classic (touristy) beer hall setting. The Schmidts began sharing their recipes with Columbus from a concession stand at the Ohio State Fair in the 1920s (currently the second-oldest food booth at the fair). The restaurant is actually part of a family-owned business started in 1888, so it's not surprising to learn some of the restaurant's recipes have been in the Schmidt family for over 100 years.

Their hospitality does the homeland proud as you are bid "Guten Essen!" and pointed toward the buffet by Bavarian-costume-clad servers. If table service is your preference, order the popular Bahama Mama sausage from the menu. And what would a German restaurant be without a fine selection of beers? Probably not German! Schmidt's is open seven days a week and has live music Wed through Sat.

The Sycamore $$$
262 E. Sycamore St.
(614) 407-3071
www.sycamoregv.com

The popular neighborhood restaurant is open for breakfast, lunch, and dinner. Like many German Village restaurants, it is situated in house and therefore has a narrow bar and a few rooms of booths and tables, which can be quite busy most evenings. Grab a pastry and coffee at breakfast time and enjoy nice weather on the patio, or swing by for a burger or sandwich for lunch until 3 p.m. The dinner menu is upscale Ohio comfort food—hangar steak, short rib ragu, and trout—while the large entree salads are unique with house-made vinaigrettes and optional protein add-ons. Be sure to make reservations, as the Sycamore is one of the favorite go-tos for locals.

Tony's Italian Ristorante $$$
16 W. Beck St.
(614) 224-8669
www.tonysitalian.net
Straightforward, upscale Italian food served in a straightforward, upscale setting. There is no escaping the historic brick buildings of the Brewery District, and Tony's is located in yet another one. The timeless decor is kept simple and elegant, with white tablecloths, pastel colors, and a baby grand piano. Arches break up the space, giving the dining area intimacy and privacy, which makes Tony's a draw for local politicians. Even the TV over the bar is as subtle as one could be. There is no arguing the number of excellent house specialties on the menu—classics such as homemade pastas, cioppino, and various parmigianas—but loyal patrons say Tony's serves the best veal in central Ohio. You be the judge. The covered veranda is a pleasant outdoor dining option in good weather.

Valter's at the Maennerchor $$
976 S. High St.
(614) 444-3531
www.valtersatthemaennerchor.com
What would German Village be without a German restaurant? The 1907 brick house is home to America's largest and longest continually active German singing society, founded in 1848. It also houses Valter's restaurant with two dining rooms, a bar, and a small outdoor patio. The walls are decked with historical photos and the menu chock-full of German classics. Fun starters like sauerkraut balls, bier cheese soup, and Jagermeister wings warm up the stomach for traditional bratwurst, käsespätzle, and schnitzel entrees. The elusive weisswurst is also on the menu. Saturday and Sunday adds additional skillet breakfasts and sandwiches on the menu. Open 11 a.m. to 11 p.m., except for Sun when it closes at 10 p.m.

FRANKLINTON

Ray Rays Hog Pit Franklinton $
424 W. Town St.
(614) 404-9742
www.rayrayshogpit.com
Ray Rays is Columbus's go-to barbeque spot. The stationary food trucks have six locations around town. Old-school smoke is combined with new-school magic as the meats are hardwood smoked daily on-site. Among the meaty offerings are smoked ribs, pulled pork, and brisket with sides of waffle fries, mac and cheese, and more. All you have to do is follow your nose for legendary barbecue. Other locations are in Clintonville, Powell, Westerville, and farther out in Granville and Flint.

Tommy's Diner $$
914 W. Broad St.
(614) 224-2422
www.tommysdiner.com
This west-side institution has been slinging breakfast and lunch since 1989. The food is a little more upscale greasy-spoon fare. Loaded omelets and hefty french toast or waffles are served alongside the typical eggs, hash browns, and Benedicts. Grab a bright red booth or sit at the counter to take in the fun diner vibe. It is easy to find Tommy's—just watch for the big art deco sign with an arrow pointing toward breakfast all day.

Yellow Brick Pizza $$
415 W. Rich St.
(614) 372-5983
www.yellowbrickpizza.com
Get your deep dish here! The casual pizza shop makes fantastic hand-tossed 'za with signature toppings, or you can build your own custom pie. Many of the ingredients are sourced locally and the meat is very high quality. Yellow Brick is most popular, however, for the Chicago-style stuffed

pizza that takes about 45 minutes to prepare. So, either order in advance or plan to wait while enjoying a glass of vino or a cocktail from the full bar. The menu also offers vegetarian and vegan options. A second location is in the East End Market.

ARENA DISTRICT

Kooma $$
37 Vine St.
(614) 224-3239
www.koomacolumbus.com
Kooma opened in 2001, and the cozy restaurant is located across from the North Market and Greater Columbus Convention Center. The menu is a fusion of Korean and Japanese. Sushi fans can belly up to the bar for an artful chirashi or any number of traditional rolls and tempura dinners. In the mood for Korean? The stone-pot bibimbap or bulgogi are solid choices. Kooma is open for lunch with an abridged version of the dinner menu. You might even bump into a Columbus Bluejacket here during hockey season.

Nada $$
220 W. Nationwide Blvd.
(614) 715-8260
www.eatdrinknada.com
Tacos and margaritas—need I say more? The decor is colorful and modern, while the classic taco and fajita dishes are a hit with fun flavors and friendly twists to keep each bite interesting. Nada serves lunch and dinner as well as a weekend brunch.

Wario's Beef and Pork $
111 W. Nationwide Blvd.
(614) 914-8338
www.wariosbeefandpork614.com
Wario's sandwich window is tucked inside a small courtyard of Nationwide Boulevard in the Arena District. The popular carryout sandwich shop can get quite busy on weekends, before games, and even if it is just a sunny day. People flock to the Wario window for hearty East Coast–inspired sandwiches. Great seeded rolls are stuffed with shaved steak, rib eye, rosemary pork, or Italian cold cuts topped with the secret Wario sauce. Add

i The Arena District and Short North afford you the luxury of parking in one place and walking to a large selection of restaurants. The area around Nationwide Arena has several chain restaurants like Ted's Montana Grill and Rodizio Brazilian. A few blocks away, you will find locally owned spots. Parking garages are located throughout the Arena and Arts Districts, and parking zones and meters are strictly enforced in the Short North, Victorian Village, and into downtown.

on a heap of Wario spuds and call it a very satisfying meal. There are several umbrella tables on the courtyard patio, but you can also call ahead to grab and go.

SHORT NORTH

1126 Sushi $$$
1126 N. High St.
(614) 725-3435
www.the1126restaurant.com
The modern Japanese restaurant on the Cap serves primarily sushi a la carte, signature rolls, and hand rolls. The menu has a small selection of hibachi and udon noodle bowls, craft cocktails, and sake. 1126 is open midday through dinner seven days a week.

Bodega $$
1044 N. High St.
(614) 299-9399
www.columbusbodega.com
As one of the Short North's original restaurants and bars, Bodega (which is Spanish for small market) has been offering inventive American pub fare in a lively atmosphere since 2005. It takes its beer seriously with 47 taps, 150 beers, and carefully crafted cocktails! The curated draft menu is always changing, and the chefs keep the food menu fresh with new items like the Big Mic burger and the Famous Grilled Cheese, which is still served for $2 on Mondays. The servers and patrons are full of character, which has kept Bodega a neighborhood favorite for nearly 20 years.

Domo Sushi $$$
976 N. High St.
(614) 465-7005
www.domoskb.com

Domo takes pride in sourcing the highest-quality ingredients that they can get their hands on—and it shows in the sophisticated starters and entrees as well as the artful plating of the sushi nigiri and rolls. Expect your meal to be photogenic and Instagram worthy. The restaurant is a cute little place, serving big trays of sushi for dinner only. Domo opens at 4 p.m. daily and is closed on Mon.

The Eagle $$
790 N. High St.
(614) 745-3397
www.eaglerestaurant.com

The Short North beer hall wins local awards for its fried chicken brined in a secret spicy honey and its cast-iron spoon bread. Southern sides of collards, coleslaw, mac and cheese, and sweet potatoes ensure you will not go hungry. It's a popular place to grab a beer and snack of hush puppies or pimento cheese and hang out with a group of friends. The Eagle is a lively place during the summer with its garage door windows rolled up and bustling patio lined with overflowing flower boxes.

Forno Kitchen and Bar $$
721 N. High St.
(614) 469-0053
www.fornoshortnorth.com

American-Italian cuisine and pizzas finished in a stone oven form the bulk of the pizza- and pasta-laden menus available in different incarnations for lunch and dinner. Forno's hosts a popular happy hour, and weekends can become quite lively, especially during patio season when the modern space is often full of fashionable twenty- and thirty-somethings. The same group owns popular sister restaurants, the Pint House at 780 N. High St. and Standard Hall at 1100 N. High St., both in the Short North.

Happy Greek Restaurant and Pub $
660 N. High St.
(614) 463-1111
www.happygreek.com

If the architectural details around the bar and the wall murals don't give away the Mediterranean theme of this restaurant, the menu with 25 specialties from all over Greece will. The pita sandwiches are very popular, as are the Greek salads. The restaurant serves traditional kebabs, moussaka, and several interesting vegetarian dishes in a casual and relaxed setting. It's no surprise the wine list features Greek wines. Sit at a table in the front window and gawk at passersby on High Street, or spend time gawking at the beautiful dessert case. You can't go wrong with either. Some say this is Columbus's Greek food at its best.

Hyde Park Prime Steakhouse $$$$
569 N. High St., The Cap
Four Columbus locations
(614) 224-2204
www.hydeparkrestaurants.com

Hyde Park Prime Steakhouse is a steak lover's paradise in a spectacular space, on the Cap near the Greater Columbus Convention Center. When it comes to red meat, Hyde Park tops the list of steak houses in Columbus, with daily specials as well as the usual Hyde Park selection of premium beef dishes named for Ohio sports figures. One of the longtime favorites is Steak Kosar (filet mignon topped with lobster, béarnaise sauce, and vegetables), while the Ryan Day Steak (a beefy, 36-day dry-aged bone-in rib eye), which has come onto the menu more recently, is also popular. The a la carte side dishes are portioned large enough to serve two, and the sides are more interesting than the usual baked potato or rice. The wine list is extensive, with dozens of wines offered by the glass, along with a menu of rare spirits and weekday happy hour specials.

Anyone familiar with the other Hyde Park locations will notice this steak house is a lot larger and glitzier, especially with its sleek indoor/outdoor bar next door. Don't wait for a special occasion to try any one of the Hyde Park restaurants, whether it's just for a drink or a romantic dinner on the patio. It is open for dinner seven days a week and offers valet parking. The original Hyde Park Steakhouse is on Olde Henderson Road in Upper Arlington.

Lemongrass Fusion Bistro $$
641 N. High St.
(614) 224-1414
www.lemongrassfusion.com

East meets West meets NYC at this industro-bistro. A modern ambience serves as the setting for the American-Thai fusion cuisine. Popular options include pad thai, sake with peanut sauce, and an extensive selection of sushi and sashimi. Vegetarians love Lemongrass for their meatless entrees, while the lemongrass salad comes highly recommended by everyone. In keeping with the artsy spirit of the Short North, exhibitions are rotated through the restaurant on a monthly basis, and live music is regularly offered in the piano court. The stylish bar is a little claustrophobic but a good locale for people-watching when you can get a seat.

Mikey's Late Night Slice $
1030 N. High St. (original food truck)
Multiple Columbus locations
(614) 333-5386
www.latenightslice.com

Someone was craving a late-night slice when this concept was born. Mikey's Late Night Slice started life as a food truck serving New York–style pizza after hours. You can get Plain-Ass or Spicy-Ass pizza by the slice as well as a half dozen other flavors. Also popular is the Pizza Dawg, a butterflied pepperoni-stuffed hot dog in a slice of pizza as the bun. Mikey's still maintains the pizza-only truck in the Short North, but also has "pizza and booze" brick-and-mortar restaurants that can be family-friendly by day and crowded with hungry bar hoppers by night. All locations serve lunch beginning at 11 a.m. and stay open well into the wee hours of the morning. The sit-down restaurants are located at 268 S. Fourth St. in Italian Village, 457 N. High St. and 892 Oak St. in Olde Towne East, and a spot in Hollywood Casino on the west side.

Northstar Cafe $$
941 N. High St.
(614) 298-9999
www.thenorthstarcafe.com

Focusing on locally grown, organic products and healthy preparation, Northstar serves a menu full of healthy-ish breakfast, lunch, and dinner options like veggie-forward salads, brick-oven pizzas, and handhelds. The veggie burger has been voted the best in town since its opening. The Cloud-9 pancakes with ricotta and Ohio maple syrup likewise have been on the menu from the beginning. Brunch and lunch may require a bit of a wait, but this only speaks to Northstar's booming popularity. There is a lot of loyalty to this brand. Northstar is also open for dinner and offers a selection of wine, local beers, cocktails, and non-alcoholic drinks. With floor-to-ceiling windows and a generous outdoor patio, this cafe is no greasy spoon— so don't anticipate greasy spoon prices. As one of Columbus's consistently best-rated restaurants, you can expect a farm-to-table menu that supports local farmers and tastes great, too. A second location is at 4241 N. High St. in Clintonville and another at Easton Town Center.

'plas $$$
21 E. Fifth Ave.
(614) 725-5700
www.plasfoodanddrink.com

'Plas is named after the ethos of its food. The Italian- and French-inspired menu features local ingredients, house-made charcuterie, scratch pastas, and breads rooted in classic culinary traditions. The modern rustic menu is true to its philosophy with bright seasonal salads and house-made pastas with lamb, duck, and vegetables that transports diners to the French or Italian countryside. The restaurant also offers gluten-free, vegetarian, and vegan options. It offers rustic fine dining in a warm space with a lot of character. Indoor and outdoor seating is available.

Rooh $$$
685 N. High St.
(614) 972-8678
www.roohcolumbus.com

Do not expect a typical Indian buffet here. Rooh's progressive pan-Indian menu is extremely modern as many of the dishes meld classic Indian recipes with Midwestern concepts (like shepherd's pie and pinwheels). Butter chicken, paneer pinwheels, beef short rib kofta, lamb shanks, and garlic and plain naan are among the offerings. The atmosphere is as cosmopolitan as it gets, and the cocktails are inventive. Plan to drop some coin for a two-person dinner—it is totally worth it.

ZenCha Café and Tea $$
982 High St.
(614) 421-2140
www.zen-cha.com

ZenCha was the first tea salon in central Ohio. This full-service restaurant and tea shop carries teas ranging from international teas from China, Britain, Germany, India, and the Middle East to refreshing bubble teas and fruit teas. ZenCha may offer the most extensive tea list in Columbus with nearly 50 types. Asian-inspired entrees and afternoon-tea-inspired sandwiches and sweet treats are available from lunch through the dinner hour. The shop is open from 11 a.m. until 6 or 8 p.m. (closed on Tues). This location is under different ownership than the ZenCha in Bexley.

ITALIAN VILLAGE

Budd Dairy Food Hall
1086 N. Fourth St.
(614) 505-2630
www.budddairyfoodhall.com

The chef-driven restaurant incubator allows diners to sample a variety of local restaurateurs' food. Ten chef-partners offer their menus from food stalls located throughout the former milk processing plant. The historic brick building, built in 1917, has multiple floors with a few patios for dining and a rooftop bar with lots of seating and games. Be sure to take a lap around the entire first floor to check out the offerings, which include Filipino street food, poke bowls, tacos, loaded fries, and pizza. Cousins Maine Lobster transports you to the East Coast with its generous lobster rolls and clam chowder, while the Modern Southern Kitchen turns out fantastic gumbo, fried chicken, and

catfish with awesome classic sides like Geechee red rice and collards. Owner Daisy Lewis became a local celebrity, having won Food Network's *Food Court Wars*, and is always smiling from behind the counter.

GoreMade Pizza $
936 N. Fourth St.
(614) 725-2115
www.goremadepizza.com

What started as a pizza Sunday with friends grew into a brick-and-mortar restaurant in Italian Village. Pizzas come in 12-inch sizes or as a half-size pizza boat. Load it up with fresh mozzarella and your choice of local toppings, or choose from one of the set signature flavors like the Clintonvillian or Porkistopheles. You can add a simple salad or cheesy bread and beer or wine; non-alcoholic beverages are also on the menu. Get your wood-fired 'za on at GoreMade.

Habibi Grill $$
1131 N. Fourth St.
(614) 999-9909
www.habibigrill614.com

Quite a few Columbus restaurateurs got their start wanting to fill a need for late-night noshing. After more than a decade running Mr. Hummus and Falafel food trucks, owner Tarek Albast is channeling his heritage into a new restaurant serving authentic Lebanese cuisine. Start with flavorful falafel and fried kibbeh, traditional dips, or one of the many vegetarian options or platters. Gyros, beef and lamb kebabs, Lebanese salads, and Mediterranean-inspired pizzas and burgers are among the many main entrees on the menu. Habibi does not serve alcohol, but you can get a variety of hot and cold teas or coffees and smoothies.

Hiraeth $$$
36 E. Lincoln St.
(614) 824-4516
www.hiraeth614.com

From the folks at Chapman Eats and Ginger Rabbit (BJ Lieberman and Bronwyn Haines) comes a wood-fire concept just a few blocks off High Street. The restaurant is an exquisite space. The airy, minimalist bar with a small dining area is upstairs, where full-size windows open to the sidewalk, while the restaurant and open kitchen is downstairs. Sit at the chef's counter to watch the team working their magic on the grills and their meticulous plating. As expected, the menu is creative and delicious, offering global comfort food and huge hunks of meat. The flavorful nods to Spain, Thailand, and North Africa incorporate lots of spices with a bit of heat. The texture from grilling over the hand-stoked grill makes for beautiful bites. *Note:* Closed and now a private event space.

The Lox Bagel Shop $
772 N. High St.
(614) 824-4005
www.theloxbagelshop.com

The Lox Bagel Shop makes bagels that are a cross between New York and Montreal style, hand-rolled, boiled, and fired in a live oven. Order individual or dozens of bagels at a time, choosing from plain, everything, sesame, and sea salt herb. The spreads are all house-made and any fancy jam is sourced locally. Breakfast sandwiches run the gamut from egg and cheese to lox with cream cheese, and lunch sandwiches are loaded with egg salad, pastrami, or tuna. The Lox Bagel Shop is a study in doing a few things very well. There is a fairly spacious dining room to eat indoors and a nice outdoor patio. The shop is open daily from 7:30 or 8 a.m. until 2 p.m. A small parking lot has a few spaces right in front.

VICTORIAN VILLAGE/ HARRISON WEST

Basi Italia $$$
811 Highland St.
(614) 294-7383
www.basi-italia.com

This little gem of Victorian Village is in a nondescript house off an alley-like street where a relaxed yet upscale dining experience can be had in a few cozy rooms or the garden patio. The intimate little trattoria has only a few dozen seats and serves knockout Italian food. The attention is to upscale food without the stuffiness often associated with

fine dining. The menu moves through the traditional Italian courses of insalata and primo to Basi's classics and main meat and seafood dishes. Basi Italia is worth seeking out, but seating is by reservation only and it is closed Sun, Mon, and Tues.

Katalina's $
1105 Pennsylvania Ave.
(614) 294-2233
www.katalinas.com

Katalina's serves up a great breakfast with character, both its food and setting in a former 100-year-old gas station. The Latin- and Southern-inspired menu has earned Katalina's best breakfast awards since opening in 2009. Come hungry because the scratch-made, organic menu choices are generous and filling. Quite a few of the breakfast entrees come with Katalina's Purple Craze Hash, local Shagbark corn chips, or house-made salata. Get the pancake balls! There is a reason more than a million have sold. The quirky little cafe has limited indoor dining and patio seating. Katalina, Too! is the second location at 3481 N. High St. in Clintonville.

Pelino's Pasta $$
247 King Ave.
(614) 298-9986
www.pelinospasta.com

Pelino's serves scratch-made pasta using local, organic ingredients and specialty Italian imports. The atmosphere is warm and energetic while the menu is well thought out and nicely executed. The owners and servers are really friendly, which makes this neighborhood eatery quite popular and inviting. Each month the changing three- and four-course prix fixe menus feature choices of starters, pasta, and desserts, while the seven-course Chef's Tasting is a tour de menu. The in-house sommelier helps pair the perfect wines, as the wine list is extensive. Wine flights are also an option. Pelino's newer concept, Piazza Pelino, is an Italian sandwich and gelato shop at 772 N. High St. in the Short North.

OHIO STATE CAMPUS/OLD NORTH

Walk along High Street and you'll find no shortage of affordable eateries, cafes, and dive bars. This section includes only the most popular and unique dining spots; pizza shops and South Campus Gateway restaurants are listed in The Ohio State University chapter. Popular chains like Panera, Chipotle, Bruegger's Bagels, and Noodles and Co. are mixed in with locally owned casual spots like Piada, Barrio Tacos, and HangOverEasy.

Alqueria $$
247 King Ave.
(614) 824-5579
www.alqueriacolumbus.com

The cozy, romantic farmhouse kitchen is a hidden gem bringing refined rustic dining to the university district with a regularly changing seasonal menu. The homey, hearty offerings begin with cheeses and cured meats, and vegetable-forward starters, soups, and dips. The farmhouse-style entrees might include burgers, fried chicken, gnocchi, and pork chops, with whispers of Spanish flavors running through some of the dishes. The cocktail menu is well conceived, while a separate menu features bourbon, whiskey, and rye pours. Drinks and charcuterie are among the weeknight happy hour specials.

El Vaquero $
3230 Olentangy River Rd.
Eleven Columbus locations
(614) 261-0900
www.vaquerorestaurant.com

The mostly Mexican/Spanish-speaking staff has fooled many a local into thinking this restaurant is a "mom-and-pop" shop, but the fact that it is corporate owned does not diminish the quality of the authentically Americanized Mexican food. You can find every combination of tortillas, tacos, burritos, meat, beans, and rice you can dream of somewhere in the 160 menu options. Be careful not to fill up on the complimentary chips and salsa, as the servers will diligently replenish the baskets as they pass by. The menu has reasonable prices, but definitely divert some savings into one of the tasty house margaritas. Other El Vaquero locations are in Dublin, Gahanna, Grove City, Hilliard, Powell, Upper Arlington, and Worthington.

MODA Restaurant and Bar $$$
3100 Olentangy River Blvd.
(614) 447-9777
www.modacolumbus.com

Fashion and sports come together at this upscale modern gastropub in the Marriott Ohio State Hotel. The New American comfort food menu is crowd-friendly with primarily pizzas, shareables, and a few stick-to-the-ribs main dishes. The service is good and the drinks are plentiful. It's a solid choice if staying near campus.

Moy's Chinese Restaurant $
1994 N. High St.
(614) 297-7722

This small mom-and-pop restaurant has been a campus staple for more than 40 years. Moy's is an easy option for good, convenient Chinese food on campus. It was started by a couple from Hong Kong and is always packed with students, faculty, and locals who know about the authentic eat-in or carryout options at reasonable prices. The service is good and the place is clean, especially given its prime location on the main drag of one of America's largest university campuses. Get the Peking duck or Mongolian beef.

NE Chinese Restaurant $
2620 N. High St.
(614) 725-0880
www.nechinese.com

For a quick, inexpensive meal, pop into the tiny cafe at the north end of OSU's campus. This unassuming storefront restaurant has a few tables for dine-in and serves manageable portions of northeastern Chinese dishes like fried rice, noodle dishes, and plenty of vegetarian entrees. The menu is split—one with Americanized favorites and another main menu that has much more adventurous, authentic options. Crowd favorites are the mala green beans and any of the specialties and spicy chicken entrees. People go here for the food and not necessarily the ambience.

Service Bar $$$
1230 Courtland Ave.
(614) 947-1231
www.middlewestspirits.com/servicebar

When the purveyor of one of Columbus's most beloved local spirits opens a restaurant at their distillery, chances are the food will be quite good too. The Service Bar's beautiful space and lively atmosphere set the tone for a great dining experience. The food (and drink) speaks for itself. Innovative Midwestern modern describes the hearty but sophisticated small and large plates. Who doesn't love triple-cooked duck fat french fries or a Szechuan chicken sandwich? Middle West Spirits' bourbon, vodka, and gin are used to make fantastic cocktails, while a selection of wine and local beers is also available.

Yaus Chinese Bistro $
1493 N. High St.
(614) 299-1272
www.yauschinesebistro.com

This family-owned campus favorite serves up big portions of Cantonese cuisine. The extensive menu has almost 20 soups to choose from and a dozen hot pot options. You will find all the usual appetizers and starter-size soups like egg rolls, dumplings, and wonton soup. It also offers a build-your-own stir-fry for a very reasonable price. Yaus is a fine option for a carryout dinner since it is open until 10 p.m.

CLINTONVILLE/BEECHWOLD

Aladdin's Eatery $
2931 N. High St.
Five Columbus locations
(614) 262-2414
www.aladdinseatery.com

This quiet, casual eatery, just north of campus, draws a student crowd as well as neighborhood regulars. Aladdin's serves healthy, inexpensive Middle Eastern food, so healthy you won't feel guilty racing for the amazing dessert case as soon as you finish your meal. Hummus, tabouli, and falafel are among the standard fare, while pita pockets filled with just about anything are the house specialties. Aladdin's serves freshly squeezed fruit juice and has one of the most

extensive tea lists in town. "Eat healthy. Eat good" is its motto, and you can do both in this environmentally friendly restaurant. Other locations are in Bexley, Dublin, Gahanna, and Grandview.

Dante's Pizzeria and Restaurant $
3586 Indianola Ave.
(614) 268-5090
www.dantespizza614.com

This well-known local pizza shop is found in an unassuming, outdated strip mall, but the homemade pasta and thin, crispy pizza make it the unofficial-official favorite among Clintonville residents. You can taste wine in the sauce and garlic in the sausage. 'Te's, as it is affectionately nicknamed, also serves the usual fried pub grub. Don't expect much in the way of atmosphere. You can eat in and have drinks at one of the few tables, but the paneled dining area is small and practically indistinguishable from the kitchen. There's nothing fancy about Dante's, which is probably why the locals like it so much.

Gatto's Pizza $
3420 Indianola Ave.
(614) 262-2233

www.gattosclintonville.com

Clintonvillians love their 'za, and Gatto's has put Columbus-style thin crust pizza on the local map. A neighborhood favorite since 1952, Gatto's makes a meal easy with one-stop shopping. Pick up your pizza, sub, wings, or salad along with a six-pack of rotating craft or domestic beer or a house bottle of wine and prego—It's dinner!

Harvest Bar and Kitchen $$
2885 N. High St.
(614) 947-7133
www.harvestpizzeria.com

Harvest Pizzeria is a family-owned restaurant in Clintonville that serves gourmet farm-to-table pizza, small plates, and great cocktails. The menu includes individual-size pizzas, sandwiches, pastas, salads, desserts, and fun starters. The pizzas are just large enough that one hungry person can finish it off, or two people can easily share along with a few small plates or a salad. Harvest Pizzeria also offers a kids' menu and non-alcoholic beverages.

Parking in the lot behind the building is plentiful, and the indoor atmosphere is really pleasant, as is the patio. Harvest has three other Columbus locations, in Bexley, Dublin, and the Brewery District.

Hot Chicken Takeover $
4203 N. High St.
(614) 754-1151
www.hotchickentakeover.com

You don't have to go to Tennessee to get an authentic-tasting Nashville hot chicken sandwich. High Street's Hot Chicken Takeover is all about using the best quality meat slathered in your choice of six levels of Nashville hot sauce. Choose from tenders, thighs, drums, wings, and even meatless meat, then pick your heat from plain ol' Southern ("just fried chicken") to the Unholy hot sauce. Meals come with bread and pickles, but you can add on classic sides of mac, beans, or slaw. Don't miss Miss B's banana pudding! Hot Chicken Takeover has garnered national attention through the years since opening in 2014 as a pop-up window, and now has seven brick-and-mortar restaurants throughout Columbus, including in Gahanna, Grandview, Westerville, and the North Market. Lunch combinations, family meals, and daily specials are also on the menu. Parking is available in a lot behind the restaurant in Clintonville.

Lavash $
2985 N. High St.
(614) 263-7777
www.lavashcafe.com

Craveable Middle Eastern and Mediterranean food in a no-frills, super-clean dining room with a super-friendly owner has been the hallmarks of this Clintonville staple since 2008. The menu has plenty of vegetarian, vegan, and gluten-free options that span the flavors of the Levant, as well as being halal. The great-tasting food comes from recipes that owner Nasir Latif learned in his mother's kitchen, which is why every dish tastes homemade. Sandwiches are served on a choice of pita or delicious lavash bread, and every day brings a different special. The restaurant has a prayer room and does not serve alcohol. Lavash is closed on Mon.

Pat and Gracie's Kitchen and Tavern $
138 Graceland Blvd.
(614) 987-5147
www.patandgracies.com

The name says it all. The casual family-friendly restaurant in Graceland Shopping Center has earned a reputation for serving great burgers and a variety of delicious tavern-style sandwiches. The rest of the menu consists of above-average bar food and entree salads. The second location downtown has a slightly different menu and a little more refined ambience.

Preston's: A Burger Joint $
2973 N. High St.
(614) 400-1675
www.prestonsburgers.com

Preston's is a very popular, locally owned burger joint in Graceland Shopping Center. The menu is small, but the burgers are mighty. And when I say small menu, I mean there are literally only a dozen things to choose from, four of them being burgers. The Spicy Boi is by far the fan favorite, but you can keep it classic with a regular or mushroom Swiss burger; serious meat lovers enjoy the pastrami bacon burger. Order a single or make it a double, add on fries, mac and cheese, or pimento cheese dumplings, and save room for banana or chocolate pudding. Preston's has an eat-in dining room and outdoor patio.

Smith's Deli $
3737 N. High St.
(614) 263-1855
www.smithsdeli.com

For more than six decades, family-owned Smith's Deli has been serving up homemade deli sandwiches, toasted subs, pizzas, and traditional pastas. The unassuming Clintonville classic started life as a frozen meat center and morphed into a deli, so it's no wonder they make a mean sub. Also worth mentioning is that they crank out handmade potato and macaroni salad and coleslaw from a longtime family recipe.

Villa Nova Ristorante $$
5545 N. High St.
(614) 846-5777
www.villanovacolumbus.com

Villa Nova has been a Clintonville fixture since the 1970s, and the proof is in the food, which remains an assortment of old-time Italian entrees and bar food. The restaurant is family-friendly, as are the prices. The food may consist of breadsticks, heaps of pasta and red sauce, Italian subs, and pizzas, but this place is more about ambience—and, boy, do you get it. The walls are packed with enough memorabilia to cause sensory overload. License plates, posters, and copper pots are among the eclectic and continuously growing collection. The bar area, which is a separate space from the restaurant, offers happy hour food and drink specials. Villa Nova is a low-key neighborhood place where the line between restaurant and bar is blurry—especially after happy hour.

WORTHINGTON/LINWORTH

Dewey's Pizza $$
640 High St.
(614) 985-3333
www.deweyspizza.com

Dewey's pizza is ranked among the best in the city for its perfect bubbly, wood-fired crust, not-too-sweet red sauce or optional garlic white sauce, and high-quality toppings. The pre-set pizzas use interesting flavor combinations such as the Porky Fi, with jam and lots of melty cheese, or the Bronx Bomber, loaded with meat and veggies. You can create your own pizza or choose one of the well-thought-out seasonal pies. The house salad with dried cranberries, pine nuts, and goat cheese is always on the menu and always a good choice. Kids (and adults) enjoy watching the pizza makers toss and twirl the dough through the kitchen windows. Parking is available in a lot, as well as at the second location at 1327 W. Fifth Ave. in Grandview.

Everest Cuisine $$
652 High St.
(614) 601-6004
www.everestcuisinecolumbus.com

i Meat rationing during World War II forced White Castle to sell hot dogs and eggs rather than burgers. An impressive list of firsts includes being the very first fast-food chain, the first to use industrial-strength spatulas, the first mass-produced paper hat, the first to sell a million and a billion hamburgers, and the first frozen fast food to be carried in stores.

This authentic Nepali, Tibetan, and Indian restaurant right in Old Worthington allows you to get a taste of the Himalayas without having to climb a mountain. The cavernous space has a bar in the back and can accommodate large parties with advance reservations. The menu is divided into Everest appetizers ranging from Indian *pakoras* to Nepali *sadheko* (meaning "sharply seasoned") starters. You might need a minute to study the expansive menu as it covers quite a bit of regional culinary turf: soups, salads, Tibetan specialties, biryani and tandoori, seafood, lamb, goat, vegetarian, and the list goes on. Everest serves beer, wine, and cocktails from a full bar, and traditional yogurt drinks and desserts. This is solid food in a casual setting. Everest is open daily, with a weekday lunch buffet and dinner hours, as well and lunch and dinner on weekends.

George's Linworth Diner $
2245 W. Dublin-Granville Rd.
(614) 396-6401
www.linworthdiner.com

This modern take on a classic diner provides the greasy spoon experience with early breakfast hours, swivel seats at the counter, family-filled booths, and line cooks slinging hash browns and hotcakes in the open kitchen. Giant three-egg omelets are loaded with different meats, veggies, and cheese. The diner is open until 3 p.m. so specialty sandwiches, gyros, and burgers make an appearance. Early birds can grab a full dinner of diner standards: meat loaf, chopped sirloin, and fried fish. Owner George Cela was brought up under the tutelage of Tommy's Diner and has a second location offering the same menu at 4408 Indianola Ave. in Beechwold.

Joya's $
657 High St.
(614) 468-1232
www.eatatjoyas.com

Columbus's very own *Top Chef* alum, Avashar Barua (of Agni in the Brewery District), opened his Bengali-American cafe in the heart of Old Worthington to much acclaim. It is open for breakfast and lunch, serving super innovative breakfast sandwiches, fried rice, kati rolls, and noodle dishes. A variety of drip, cold brew, and specialty coffees round out the menu. When Avashar is involved, expect unexpected flavors and brilliant textures. The storefront shop is small, so there is no indoor seating, which is no problem since downtown Worthington is a charming place to carry out your sandwich and coffee and take a stroll. In warmer months there may be a few chairs outside. Parking is available in the public lot behind the building off New England Avenue.

La Chatelaine French Bakery and Bistro $
627 High St., Old Worthington
Three Columbus locations
(614) 848-6711
www.lachatelainebakery.com

Some might consider the casual bistro food "French Dining 101," but the pastries and breads are masterful. If you have ever been to Paris, you have probably stood with your nose pressed against a bakery window, gazing in awe at the rows of edible art. You'll do that here. Newcomers "oooh" and "ahhh" at the fruit-topped tortes and bulging eclairs, while regulars drive out of their way to have La Chatelaine's baked goods.

It isn't at all unusual to find people munching only a baguette along with a cup of coffee or sharing intimate conversation over a bottle of wine. Full breakfasts and lunches are served cafeteria style, while a refined dinner menu and table service add a formal touch to the otherwise light and airy French countryside–inspired bistro. There's an outdoor patio, which is open seasonally. The other two locations are on Lane Avenue in Arlington and West Bridge Street in Old Dublin, both with patios.

Stone Bar and Kitchen $$
1045 Bethel Rd.
(614) 914-5142
https://stonebarandkitchen.com

Stone is always busy, which speaks to the great food and service. The contemporary bistro-like setting is a fun place to gather with friends for dinner in one of the big horseshoe-shaped booths or enjoy a drink and small plates at the beautiful bar while watching a game on one of the big screens scattered around the restaurant. The well-conceived menu is full of global seafood, entree salads, sandwiches, and pastas. The main dishes range from lamb and steaks to salmon and fish-and-chips.

Subourbon Southern Kitchen and Spirits $$$
2234 W. Dublin-Granville Rd.
(614) 505-0773
www.subourboncolumbus.com

From the same owners as Alqueria Farmhouse Kitchen, Southern hospitality is front and center in this relaxed restaurant and bar serving upscale low-country fare. Gumbo, fried green tomatoes, and cast-iron corn bread for starters transport diners to the Deep South. Country-fried chicken, shrimp and grits, and short ribs are menu favorites. Subourbon's low-country boil is something special, loaded with shellfish, sausage, and potatoes. Only a few places in Columbus serve authentic Southern cuisine, but Subourbon does it with contemporary flair. It's open for dinner Mon through Sat, and there is plentiful parking in the side lot.

Whitney House $$$
666 High St.
(614) 396-7846
www.thewhitneyhouserestaurant.com

Nicely conceived American comfort food in a bistro-like setting makes the Whitney House a destination dining spot in Old Worthington. The restaurant consists of two spaces—a modern, cozy bar in the back of the building and a bright, open dining room in the front facing High Street. It's open for lunch, then closes between lunch and dinner. Certain items change seasonally, but the Ohio Burger, Adult Grilled Cheese, and roasted tomato soup have been menu fixtures from the start. Sun brunch is usually very busy, so try to make reservations. It's worth it for the brioche french toast. The restaurant is closed on Mon.

WESTERVILLE/NORTHLAND AREA

Asterisk Supper Club $
14 N. State St.
(614) 776-4633
www.asterisksupperclub.com

Asterisk Supper Club has an English country manor vibe with floor-to-ceiling bookshelves and glittery chandeliers. The menu is rustic yet elegant with comfort food like potpie, meat loaf, and duck sliders. It serves cocktails, beer, wine, and classic desserts and is one of the few places in town that does an afternoon tea. Choose from cream tea, petite tea, or a full tea with sandwiches, scones, and desserts and enjoy it in the charming dining room or on the patio during warmer months.

Carfagna's Kitchen $$
1440 Gemini Place
(614) 846-6340
www.carfagnas.com

Since 1937, this third-generation Italian specialty market-meets-restaurant just off Polaris Parkway has kept Columbus in Italian specialties, gourmet imports, cheese, meats, and wine. The family-owned store has an attached sit-down ristorante and bar reminiscent of a Tuscan *ritrovo* ("gathering place"). Grab a glass of wine at the bar, do a little shopping, and stay for lunch or dinner. The menu covers all the bases from arancini to zuppa and all the pastas, parmigianas, and pizzas in between. More than two dozen pasta entrees are on the menu, along with seasonal specialties and a long list of cocktails, beer, and wine. Carfagna's also hosts great cooking classes a few times a week in a villa-inspired teaching kitchen. The restaurant is open seven days a week until 9 or 10 p.m.

Carsonie's Restaurant $
6000 Westerville Rd.
(614) 899-6700
www.carsonies.com

Bocce, anyone? Carsonie's is about as well-known for its regulation-size bocce court as it is for its strombolis. Once you satisfy your hunger with huge portions of pasta, calzone, or the unusual Italian fries, satiate your competitiveness with a game of bocce on the fenced-in patio. This family-friendly restaurant has a second location at 1725 W. Lane Ave. in Upper Arlington. Outdoor seating is available at each.

City BBQ $
600 S. State St.
Six Columbus locations
(614) 755-8890
www.citybarbeque.com

Thought you had to go to Kansas City to get good barbecue? Well, think again. City BBQ has developed quite a cult following in Columbus, and word is spreading throughout Ohio and the Midwest. The goal is simple: to make the best barbecue anywhere! According to the most discriminating barbecue lovers, City BBQ is putting Columbus on the map with its extraordinary (secret) sauce and pure smoked meats. The menu features ribs, beef brisket, pork, and chicken. The sides are scratch-made Southern dishes like baked beans, corn pudding, and hush puppies. A sandwich and side dish can be filling, but don't leave without trying the peach cobbler. The service is nothing fancy; it's more or less an indoor picnic. You order at a counter and eat at wooden tables. Five other locations are in Upper Arlington (the original), Gahanna, Polaris, Powell, and Reynoldsburg.

Koble Greek Italian Grill $$
7 N. State St.
(614) 882-6366
www.koblegrill.com

Belly up to the large center bar or grab a table in the dining room for a Greek version of tapas. The *meze* small plates are shareable, and appetizers range from grilled octopus to smelts and meatballs to falafel. Spreads and dips can be ordered individually or in combination. A soup and salad with optional proteins or a gyro make for a lighter meal. Or stuff yourself silly with pastitcio, moussaka, or any number of meat and seafood entrees. A bit of Italiano is brought into the menu by way of flatbreads, paninis, and a few classic pastas.

There's a little something for everyone at Koble's, including a Greek/Italian-inspired kids' menu. The restaurant is open from lunch until 10 p.m. Koble Grill has a second location at 176 W. Olentangy Rd. in Powell.

Ming Chinese Restaurant $
475 Lazelle Rd.
(614) 885-8836
www.mingfloweroh.com
Ming's extensive menu is full of reasonably priced pan-Asian food, ranging from traditional starters of spring rolls and soups to noodles, stir-fries, and pad thai. The atmosphere is warm and slightly upscale, with lazy Susans in the center of the tables for sharing multiple courses. The lunch specials are a deal, as an additional soup and egg or spring roll is bundled in.

Pasquale's Pizza & Pasta House $
14 N. State St.
(614) 882-6200
www.pasqualespastahouse.com
Westerville's answer to pizza pie lies just around the corner and through the somewhat evasive side door of this building. Just follow the arrow painted on the window. The popularity of this pizzeria lies in the details and family recipes. The sweet sauce–covered crust is loaded with toppings. The meatballs are handmade. The staff is service oriented and well-known for their ability to get special orders right the first time. The restaurant is casual and homey feeling, well suited for a family dinner and well priced for families too. It offers both delivery and takeout.

Polaris Grill $$
1835 Polaris Pkwy.
(614) 431-5598
www.polarisgrill.com
The longtime defunct 55 Restaurant was reincarnated 25 years ago as Polaris Grill but still serves some of 55's beloved menu items alongside newer American dishes. Pasta, seafood, grilled chops, and ribs are among the entrees, while Aztec chowder and mushroom bisque are among the favorite appetizers.

In keeping with 55 tradition, the belly-busting Sunday brunch offers a nice selection of Benedicts, omelets, mimosas, and Marys along with a variety of brunchy entrees. This Columbus original is a casual restaurant with spacious booths and tables, often filled with businesspeople during the week, giving it a dressier atmosphere than on the weekends. Polaris Grill is open for lunch and dinner and Sunday brunch.

Thai Grille $$
15 E. College Ave.
(614) 865-4515
Thai Grille is such a mom-and-pop operation they do not have a website. Just sniff out the little brick building a few doors off Main Street. It is like stepping into someone's dining room, with about a dozen of tables and booths and incredible aromas wafting from the kitchen just a few feet away. The food is authentic while the service is friendly. You really can't go wrong with any dish from the menu. Thai Grill is open 11 a.m. to 9 p.m. daily except on Mon.

Westerville Grill $
59 S. State St.
(614) 794-7200
www.westervillegrill.com
A classic American diner in Uptown Westerville serves hearty breakfasts all day, lunch classics like Reuben and turkey club sandwiches, and pot roast for dinner. The interior is decorated with nostalgic 1950s artworks, and the covered patio allows you to enjoy your meal outdoors anytime. And hold my beer! You can wash down a burger or chicken sandwich with a cold one. The parking lot is small, but there is usually ample street parking nearby.

EASTON

Upscale chain restaurants such as Cooper's Hawk, J. Alexander's, and the Cheesecake Factory abound at Easton Town Center, but a few locally owned restaurants are able to hold their own next to these giants. More casual, mainstream chains like Melt, Chuy's, Shake Shack, and Pies and Pint are also located around Easton. Cameron

Mitchell's Ocean Club is located above the mall and is discussed in the Close-up in this chapter.

Afra Grill $
3922 Townsfair Way
(614) 591-3399
www.afragrill.com
Afra Grill has introduced Columbus to traditional Somali flavors, but the menu features several regional dishes in a build-your-own-bowl concept within a contemporary restaurant setting. Take a culinary tour d'Africa as you choose your base, a protein, which could include goat, habo steak, or jerk chicken. Add your hot topping like beans or veggies, then select salsa, pickled veggies, and various mild or spicy sauces. Non-alcoholic drinks, savory sides, and dessert are also on the menu. Afra Grill is a great way to introduce your palate to African flavors or if you enjoy experimenting with different combinations. The original location is nearby at 1635 Morse Rd.

Brio Tuscan Grille $$$
3993 Easton Station
(614) 416-4745
www.brioitalian.com
Escape to the Tuscan countryside for a few hours and find *la dolce vita* ("the good life") at Brio. The innovative menu includes not only the heavy, red-sauced cuisine so often associated with Italian restaurants but also lighter grilled and seafood dishes inspired from all regions of Italy. Brio is as much a purveyor of steak and seafood as pasta.

The wood-fired ovens are used to roast steaks, fish, and chops as well as turn out gourmet pizzas and flatbreads. The ovens were actually imported from the homeland, and the decor simulates a sprawling Tuscan villa. Arches, columns, and palm trees break up the dining area, which is quite large, while mosaics, plaster walls, and earthy colors lend it intimacy. This upscale version of Bravo! Italian Kitchen opened in 1999, and like Bravo! it rarely disappoints. Brio continues to leave an impression on Columbus visitors and locals.

Café Istanbul $$
3983 Worth Ave., Easton
(614) 473-9144
www.cafeinstanbul.com
Outstanding Turkish cuisine can be found in the part of Easton with the least amount of foot traffic. You'll forget you are anywhere near the Easton sprawl. The red-and-white-striped arches and iron chandeliers are most striking. Carpets, brass, and ceramic decorations scream of the Arabesque.

The bar is modern, while the waiting area has traditional low tables at which to enjoy a glass of wine or Turkish coffee. Aside from the chic decor, the authentic food is what sets Café Istanbul apart from the dozens of other Mediterranean-inspired restaurants in Columbus. The gastronomically curious will not be disappointed with anything on the menu, but there's also an extensive range of the familiar: hummus, falafel, and kebabs, just to name a few. The restaurant features Turkish wines, coffees, and teas and an outdoor patio. A second location is at 6125 Riverside Dr. near OH 161.

Condado Tacos $
4077 Fenlon St.
(614) 532-5956
www.condadotacos.com
A build-your-own taco concept in an edgy rock 'n' roll atmosphere, this Columbus-born taqueria serves up 50 whiskeys, 50 tequilas, and a laundry list of local craft beers. Oh, and tacos. Grab a high-top table and one of the checklist notepads to begin marking off the type of tortilla or shell for the base, then figure out which tacos, queso, and sides you might enjoy and the server will return with your custom order. And probably some tequila.

Cumin and Curry Indian Kitchen $$
4155 Morse Crossing
(614) 470-8975
www.cuminandcurryoh.com
The freestanding building is open and spacious, which is a good thing because the lunch buffets packs in the eaters. There might be about twenty items on the buffet, but the turnover and replenishing is very timely, as the food disappears rather quickly. The a la carte menu has the standard

Indian offerings, which are ordered at a counter at the entrance then delivered to your table with any specialty or alcoholic drinks. Self-service machines are in the back of the restaurant for non-alcoholic beverages. Parking is plentiful, as the restaurant is at the edge of Easton where parking lots reign supreme.

Dos Hermanos $
3946 Morse Crossing
(614) 383-7930
www.doshermanoscolumbus.com

A former taco truck now offers tableside service at this popular Oaxacan-style Mexican restaurant located in a stand-alone building just outside Easton proper. Mexican street tacos and chicken mole speak to the owner's heritage. Order at the counter, grab a seat in the cool dining room, and your food will be delivered. A full bar including frozen margaritas are available. Other locations are at the North Market in downtown and Bridge Park in Dublin.

Piada Italian Street Food $
4025 Easton Station
(614) 532-6551
www.mypiada.com

Piada is a type of Italian flatbread wrap popular as a carryout lunch in Italy. The name is fitting for the local fast-casual eatery where you can customize your own piada with protein and other fillings. Piada also serves a variety of pre-set pastas and fresh salads. There are many locations all around the city. Check the website to find one near you.

NEW ALBANY/GAHANNA AREA

Asian Gourmet and Sushi Bar $$
1325 Stone Ridge Dr.
(614) 471-8871
www.asiangourmetgahanna.com

This large pan-Asian restaurant is focused on Thai, Korean, and Japanese cuisine, as well as having a sushi bar. The chef's specials range from General Tso's, teriyaki, and sesame chicken to Thai curries. In terms of sushi, there's a wonderful selection of nigiri, sashimi, and more than a dozen types of rolls. The atmosphere is modern but comfortable

for both individuals and families, who can be accommodated at large tables. A traditional tatami room can be reserved for private dining. It is open for dinner seven days a week and for lunch Sun through Fri.

Eagle Pizza $
2 N. High St.
(614) 855-7600
www.eagle-pizza.com

This family-style pastaria is considered the best deal in New Albany. The casual atmosphere is seen in the fact that there are no regular menus, just a posting by the entrance. The fare is simple: pizzas, subs, and the very popular twice-baked spaghetti. It's a neighborhood eatery where patrons likely know one another and their children work here. The table service is good, but keep in mind they do not accept credit cards.

Elliot's Wood Fired Kitchen & Tap $$
266 E. Main St.
(614) 924-0223
www.elliotswoodfiredkitchenoh.com

If you are hankering for a freshly fired pizza or a tasty trio of tacos, Elliot's Wood Fired Kitchen & Tap offers gourmet tavern fare in a relaxed atmosphere. The menu features Neapolitan-style pizza, street tacos, fish-and-chips, and interesting starters. Wash it all down with one of the 16 beers or four wines on tap, or a specialty cocktail. Enjoy lunch or dinner in the wide-open dining room with lots of TVs or on the beautiful patio, where there is the occasional live musician. Elliot's is open seven days a week from 11 a.m. to 10 p.m.

Gahanna Grill $
82 Granville St.
(614) 476-9017
www.gahannagrill.com

So what if you have to fix a wobbly table with a few matchbooks under the leg, or the decorations consist of laminated advertisements for local businesses and pictures of people who have put away a Triple Beanie burger? Locals don't come here for the ambience. They come for the company of others who just like to hang out in a nice neighborhood restaurant—and they come for the burgers. Which side of town you live in determines which way your burger loyalty swings. Those who live in this neck of the woods swear the Gahanna Grill makes the best burgers on earth. It certainly makes one of the biggest! The Beanie burgers, loaded with toppings and slaw, are nothing compared to the Triple Beanie, while the faint of heart can wimp out with the smaller Academy version. If you finish off a Triple Beanie, you get a free T-shirt and a picture of your mug on the wall. It also serves regular fried pub grub, soup, and salads, as well as a whole gamut of meat and seafood entrees.

Gahanna Pizza Plus $
106 Granville St.
(614) 428-9878
www.gahannapizzaplus.com
If you want some pizzazz in your pie, look no further. Taking first in the 2003 Mid-America Pizza Pizzazz and first in the 2002 Columbus Pizza Challenge, the Gahanna Pizza Plus crew must be doing something right. The competitive prices

and baker's dozen of specialty pies keep the place popular among Gahanna and New Albany residents, so popular it has won first place three years in a row at the Taste of Gahanna. The crust is bready and the sauce is tart. The most popular specialty pies are the mega meat and three-mushroom pizzas, but there are more than 35 high-quality toppings to choose from if you prefer to create your own. If blue-ribbon pizza isn't your craving, subs and salads are also available.

Lola & Giuseppe's Trattoria $$
100 Granville St.
(614) 473-9931
www.lolaandgiuseppes.com
A quaint mom-and-pop trattoria in downtown Gahanna has been serving traditional Italian favorites, from pasta to seafood, for almost 20 years. The food here is legit! The menu moves through the traditional antipasti, zuppa, insalata, pasta, and entree courses like any down-home Italian restaurant. Quite often Lola will make an appearance to greet diners and make you feel like one of the

 # Close-up

Cameron Mitchell: 30 Years of Hospitality

No one can pass through Columbus without encountering the name Cameron Mitchell. This ambitious restaurateur has propelled dining in Columbus to new levels beginning in 1993 with Cameron's American Bistro. The Mitchell empire has grown to include 100 restaurants in 15 states and recently has focused on new steak house, Italian, and food hall concepts. This book typically does not include chains, but with most of his restaurants located here in Columbus, a great disservice would be done not to include the Upper Arlington native in this chapter. Even more importantly, you will not be disappointed with the thoughtful ambience of each place and the consistently high quality of food and service. Visit www.cameronmitchell.com for more details.

Cameron's American Bistro $$$
2185 W. Dublin-Granville Rd., Linworth
(614) 885-3663
www.cameronsamericanbistro.com
Cameron Mitchell's flagship restaurant remains innovative even after 12 years. The atmosphere around the art deco bar is intimate and cozy, while the candlelit restaurant is romantic and comfortable. If you've visited one of Mitchell's glitzy steak houses or seafood restaurants, the Bistro may seem a bit passé, but one look at the menu and you'll know there is nothing outdated about the place where Columbus's restaurant mogul made his start. American cuisine is showcased in all its eclecticness on both the regular menu and the changing specials. Dieters beware! The portions are large, the sauces rich, and the desserts plentiful. Like the food, the wine list is all-American, with a heavy nod toward California. Cameron's has been packed elbow-to-elbow with regulars from day one. That says it all.

family. You can't go wrong with anything on the menu! Besides the restaurant, there's also a bakery selling traditional Italian sweets. Lola's is open for dinner Tues through Sat, and closed Sun and Mon.

Cap City Fine Diner & Bar $$
1301 Stone Ridge Dr., Gahanna
(614) 478-9999
1299 Olentangy River Rd., Grandview Heights
(614) 291-3663
www.capcityfinediner.com
Despite the shiny chrome, neon, and mirrors, these diners are no greasy spoons. Bright colors and pop art murals give the Fine Diners a cool retro ambience. As for the food, who knew meat loaf would ever be considered fine dining? Leave it to Cameron Mitchell to make the most sophisticated of comfort food, but come hungry because portions are super-sized. In 2006 and 2007, Cap City was voted Columbus's number one diner for its extensive menu, massive desserts, and family-friendly atmosphere. Both locations have a killer Sunday brunch and weeknight happy hour.

Cento $$$
595 S. Third St., German Village
(614) 696-6565
www.centogermanvillage.com
Cameron Mitchell recently opened his 100th restaurant, Cento, in the bustling heart of historic German Village. An intimate entrance through canopies of green dancing with sparkly lights evoke fine-dining experiences throughout Tuscany. The atmosphere, hospitality, and upscale Italian menu transport you to Italy by way of modern interpretations of regional classics. Start with a few antipasti and decide if you are going the route of eggplant pasta alla Norma or the unusual Lombardian "shoe-shaped" scarpinocc pasta. Or choose an entree of beautiful branzino, chicken saltimbocca, or Piedmontese-style filet mignon. Fresh vegetables channel the Italian countryside, while the wine list is a tour d'Italia. A private room is available, and alfresco dining on the patio is open seasonally. Cento is open for dinner only, beginning at 4 p.m., seven days a week. Reservations open up a month in advance and are highly recommended.

Marcella's Ristorante $$
615 N. High St., Short North
1319 Polaris Pkwy., Westerville
(614) 223-2100, (614) 844-6500
www.marcellasristorante.com
Marcella's is more than just a pizzeria; it's an upscale Tuscan-style cafe replete with tile, brick, and padded bistro chairs. The Short North location has a lively, urban wine bar vibe. The tight seating and large bistro windows opening directly to the sidewalk give Marcella's a distinctly European flair. The menu traverses Italy, as does the wine list. You'll find all the usual suspects like pizza, pasta, and Chianti. The *cicchetti*, or small plates, along with meat, cheese, and olive selections, are designed for sharing among the table. Wine can be purchased by the bottle, half bottle, or *quartino* (quarter liter). While Cameron Mitchell's Short North Marcella's seems trés Euro, expect a different experience at the Polaris location, which caters to suburbanites who appreciate large parking lots. It is also more family-friendly than the Short North location.

Martini Modern Italian $$$
445 N. High St., Arena District
(614) 22-ITALY (224-8259)
www.martinimodernitalian.com
Martini's is a glossy place that lures in the fashionable types after a hard day's work. It's a lively bar full of carousing professionals often putting back a lot of drinks. The wine list is extensive and, as the name suggests, Martini's serves nearly 20 kinds of martinis. The food isn't bad either. The menu includes contemporary Italian dishes, and the weekday 4 to 6 p.m. happy hour has cocktails and antipasti on special. The individually portioned tiramisu is still rated among the best in the city.

Mitchell's Ocean Club $$$
Easton Town Center
(614) 416-2582
www.ocean-prime.com
Mitchell's upscale seafood restaurant has a sophisticated supper club vibe, complete with cocktail lounge and a seasonal wraparound terrace with an indoor/outdoor fireplace. The menu features inventive seafood with a strong showing of meat entrees and steak-house-style side dishes.

The Ocean Club offers a dining experience that shouldn't be rushed, and with this attitude, the somewhat slow (but impeccable) service can be overlooked. A classy touch is the optional black lint-free napkins for anyone wearing dark clothes.

Molly Woo's Asian Bistro $$
1500 Polaris Pkwy., Polaris Fashion Place
(614) 985-9667
www.mollywoos.com
Mitchell's Asian-themed Molly Woo's is very Oriental, to say the least. Giant red lanterns hang from the soaring industrial ceilings, and Chinese sculpture and ceramics fill all the nooks and crannies. This spacious, bamboo-accented restaurant is filled with businesspeople at lunch and shoppers at dinner—and with good reason. The pan-Asian food is artistic and flavorful. Sushi and firecracker chicken are among the popular menu items, but the spring roll remains a favorite with patrons. Patio and bar seating are also available.

Valentina's $$$
4595 Bridge Park Ave., Dublin
(614) 957-0074
www.valentinasitalian.com
Mitchell's beautiful Italian bistro, Valentina's in Bridge Park, is open for lunch and dinner, catering to business professionals, dinnergoers, and us ladies who lunch. The menu is a self-proclaimed "Barolo-inspired culinary journey," which is evident in the northern Italian offerings. The menu spans the Italian spectrum of meats and chesses, wonderful carpaccio, truffled this 'n' that, veal dishes, and classic entrees. In typical Mitchell form, crowd-friendly pastas and pizzas are also on the lunch and dinner menus. The interior space is sleek and opens up to the outdoor patio surrounded by flower planters. Valentina's cocktails are inventive and well worth their priciness.

BEXLEY/OLDE TOWNE EAST

Bexley Pizza Plus $
2540 E. Main St.
(614) 237-3305
www.bexleypizzaplus.com
This family-owned carryout has been a Bexley staple since 1980. Bexley locals say it's the thick and chewy handmade crust, topped with tangy sauce, that makes this pizza so good. But it may also be the head-spinning number of toppings and gourmet combos such as Greek pizza. Subs, garlic bread, and salads are also available. Beer and wine is served in the dining room. Las Vegas judges also think the pizza is pretty good, as it won the International Pizza Challenge in 2014, beating out 60 pizzerias worldwide.

Brassica $
2122 E. Main St.
Other locations in Upper Arlington, Short
  North, and Easton
www.brassicas.com
Brassica serves Lebanese and Mediterranean food including incredible falafel sandwiches, pita sandwiches, and addicting hand-cut brassica fries topped with a signature sauce. Build-your-own bowls and wraps allow diners to customize the proteins, crunchy toppings, pickled veggies, and sauces any which way they like. Most locations have indoor and outdoor seating. The commitment to organic and sustainable practices shines through in the fresh, healthy ingredients that form the base of solid, tasty food. Brassica serves beer, wine, and a house-made minty lemonade.

Gemút Biergarten $
734 Oak St.
(614) 725-1725
www.gemutbiergarten.com
The German-style biergarten and brewery in Olde Towne East is located in former Engine House 12. Friendly bartenders serve up bratwurst, schnitzel, giant pretzels, and other Bavarian fare along with a whole bunch of *gemütlichkeit* (friendliness) in a classic beer garden setting. Communal picnic tables, open spaces, and lots of prost-ing with steins of beer take place inside the former fire station and on the large outdoor patio.

Giuseppe's Ritrovo $$
2268 E. Main St.
(614) 235-4300
www.giuseppesritrovo.com
The incredibly rich southern Italian cuisine is a telltale sign of the owner's roots in Calabria.

Ritrovo, which means "gathering place," is a store-front eatery that has long been drawing regulars and attracting new patrons with its solid classic dishes. The interior captures the essence of Italy with its black-and-white photography on the walls, and the homemade dishes, some that have been on the menu for a very long time, transport you to the motherland. Egg pasta is handmade daily using traditional Italian techniques, and the sauces vary. The spinach rollati (rolled lasagna noodles stuffed with spinach and four cheeses) is the house favorite. The ambience is cozy and the bar is lively, but be prepared to wait for a table as seating is first-come, first-served. Seasonal outdoor seating is available on a small patio along the sidewalk. Giuseppe's is a longtime Columbus staple where you can get quality Italian food for a fair price.

HangOverEasy $
51 Parsons Ave.
(614) 928-3778
www.hangovereasy.com

If you are looking for comfort breakfast food, HangOverEasy will take care of business with breakfast tacos, chicken and waffles, pork belly Benedicts, and cinnamon roll french toast. Throw in a Bloody Mary for the hair of the dog and your day just got much better—and fuller.

Khaab Indian Kitchen and Bar $$
2400 E. Main St.
(614) 237-5500
www.khaabofcolumbus.com

Upscale Indian in a classy, contemporary atmosphere makes for a wonderful dining experience, whether inside the sleek restaurant or on the pretty covered patio. The menu features traditional Punjabi tandoori dishes and lots of appetizers, and is a bit meat heavy with many options for chicken, lamb, and seafood. There are some vegetarian dishes but be cognizant of the limited options. The Indian-themed cocktails creatively use ingredients like chili mango to customize drinks. A full bar is available.

The Lifestyle Café $$
891 Oak St.
(614) 344-6686
www.thelifestyle.cafe

Feeling a little health-conscious? Get your lifestyle in check and head for this laid-back vegan eatery that serves nutritious, delicious meatless meals that substitute all sorts of plant-based ingredients, including for eggs. The menu clearly describes the ingredients, grains, and other foodie facts on the menu for full transparency. When you see the vegan food that comes out of this kitchen, it might make you a believer.

The Olde Oak $
62 Parsons Ave.
(614) 223-1010

This bar is so trendy it doesn't have a website. Head to the Olde Oak for classic tavern food and drinks like burgers and wings, craft cocktails, and growlers, along with a game of pool. It has happy hour specials and serves lunch and weekend brunch.

The Top Steakhouse $$$$
2891 E. Main St.
(614) 231-8238
www.thetopsteakhouse.com

The black-and-white-striped awning with the Top logo is a landmark on East Main Street. Although Bexleyites lay claim to this old-school steak house, you will find a diverse clientele from all around town, from old-timers who have frequented the Top since it opened in the 1950s to the 20-somethings dressed to impress.

After you allow your eyes to adjust to the dimly lit, cavernous interior, you will find the ultimate timeless steak house—fireplace, copper-topped bar, black Naugahyde booths, and all. The decor remains unchanged. The menu is timeless and extensive. The clientele is unwavering. The serpentine bar is perfectly campy. All this makes for a true supper club experience where you can envisage Rat Pack crooners slinging martinis with Hitchcockian blondes.

The menu features all sorts of fine cuts of beef, pork, and lamb with classic steak-house sides. The seafood options are equally impressive, but the hefty surf and turf goes unmatched. The Top is open seven days a week and has a daily lineup of live piano music.

ZenCha Café and Tea $$
239 E. Main St.
(614) 237-9690
www.bexleyzencha.com
ZenCha is a full-service restaurant and tea salon serving an extensive menu of teas ranging from international teas from China, Britain, India, and the Middle East to refreshing bubble teas and fruit teas. ZenCha may offer the most extensive tea list in Columbus with nearly 50 types. It also scratch-makes fresh salads, sandwiches, and Asian-inspired entrees from lunch through the dinner hour. ZenCha is open from 11 a.m. until 9 p.m. This location is under different ownership than the ZenCha in the Short North.

WHITEHALL

Lalibela Restaurant $$
1111 S. Hamilton Rd.
(614) 235-5355
www.lalibelarestaurant.net
Named for an Ethoipan town famous for extraordinary rock-cut churches, the down-to-earth namesake restaurant features fantastic Ethiopian food with a full bar and warm service, making this one of the most popular Ethiopian eateries in Columbus. The unassuming storefront has a decent-size dining room and can accommodate bigger groups, which is perfect for sampling a wide variety of vegetarian dishes simmered in spicy sauces and flavorful marinated meat stews with rice. The selection of menu items arrives on a communal tray with rolls of *injera*, a spongy, tangy bread meant to sop up the meat and sauce by hand. The large bar serves beer and cocktails, which help tame the notoriously spicy dishes. Lalibela is a great option for vegetarians who aren't afraid of a little heat.

TAT Ristorante di Famiglia $$
1210 S. James Rd.
(380) 235-6135
www.tatitalianrestaurantcolumbus.com

This east-side restaurant has been serving homemade Italian dinners to Columbus since the late 1920s, officially making it the oldest Italian and family-owned restaurant in the city. Over the years, it has moved a few times but retained that old-school Italian restaurant ambience. Pastel colors and twinkly lighting, along with cushy booths and packed tables, give off the image of one big family in one giant dining room. Unlike the decor, the menu has been updated a few times to reflect the city's changing tastes. One can have American, Chinese, and vegetarian dishes, as well as the trademark Italian. Favorites include the wedding soup, chicken cacciatore, and baked lasagna. If you come before 6 p.m., you can take advantage of early-bird dinner specials, but this restaurant can be quite busy most days of the week. It's closed on Mon.

HILLIARD

Alladeen Grill and BBQ $
5394 Roberts Rd.
(614) 363-5011
www.alladeengrill.com
The Mediterranean restaurant features flavors from Morocco to Pakistan in its house-made dishes and build-your-own bowls. Super-fresh ingredients, herbs, and fine olive oil form the base of traditional dips with made-to-order naan bread. High-quality rotisserie-grilled meats are shaved for shawarma sandwiches and entree combos. Pakistani flavors are showcased in the slow-cooked stew and chili-laden goat Karahi as well as the rich Nehari beef. Tandoori barbecue, gyros, and kebabs are among the more familiar dishes. The dessert menu is sweet with delicious baklava, tiramisu, Hareseh "semolina cake," and Rasmalai "juicy cream" cake. Alladeen opens at 10 a.m., serving a light Mediterranean-style breakfast, and is open until 10 p.m. daily.

Center Street Market $
5354 Center St.
(614) 219-1500
www.crookedcanohio.com
Downtown Hilliard Station's locally owned food hall is a centralized spot to enjoy a variety of food

options from different vendors serving burgers, meatballs, sandwiches, and desserts. The market is anchored by the Crooked Can Brewing Company, so grab an award-winning handcrafted beer or cocktail from the bar. Plenty of seating is available inside. In nicer weather, have a seat on the patio, which during summer months is a popular spot to enjoy live music at the weekly Celebration at the Station.

Crazzy Greek II $$
3640 Main St.
(614) 876-5303
www.crazzygreek2.com

Yes, the name is spelled correctly. Two decades of tasty home-style Greek cooking makes Crazzy a popular family-friendly restaurant. The chef shares family recipes from the homeland, including well-received appetizers of falafel, kibbeh, and baba ghanoush. Soups and entrees come with home-made pita, while the lamb and beef is rotisserie grilled for gyros, salads, and bowls. It has a full bar and is open 10:30 a.m. to 9 p.m. Mon through Sat.

Habanero's Fresh Mexican Grill $
3650 Main St.
(614)850-7255
www.habanerosfmg.com

Habanero's is just a little different from your typical Americanized Mexican fare. The popular go-to menu item is the tortas sandwich made on fresh-baked bread and stuffed with your choice of protein, including less common beef tongue or tripe. A dozen types of quesadillas, street tacos, burritos, and bowls provide lots of options for lunch and dinner. Platters with chimichangas, fish tacos, and tortilla soup make the short list of entrees. The locally owned eatery has a second Hilliard location in at 3680 Fishinger Blvd. in Mill Run.

HillGarten Beer and Wine $$
4131 Main St.
(614) 319-3427
www.hillgarten.com

HillGarten is a charming outdoor craft wine and beer hall in Old Hilliard inspired by German beer gardens. Just look for the pretty landscaped garden with HillGarten signage lining the spacious patio. The menu leans toward Bavarian with high-quality bratwursts, sausages, pork and beef hot dogs, and the biggest, priciest pretzel around. The beer cheese is house-made, and the warm German potato salad and käsespätzle are popular sides. This is a very well-done concept with 16 Ohio microbrews on tap, as well as domestic and N/A (non-alcoholic) cans. Wines are reasonably priced and served by the glass and bottle. During winter, eight-person, heated domed igloos are available for two-hour rental and a minimum food and beverage order.

Legacy Smokehouse and Rickhouse 41 $
3987 Main St.
(614) 541-9022
www.legacysmokehouse.com

From Wed through Sun, central Ohioans can get their hands on central-Texas-style barbeque in downtown Hilliard. The restaurant is located on the first floor of a charming old house, recently renovated to include the Rickhouse 41 bourbon bar on the second floor with a seasonal rooftop space. The menu features craft-smoked brisket, turkey, pork, and sausages that can be ordered by the pound or in sandwich form. The usual side suspects, like corn, mac, or baked beans can be added on, while kids can get slider-size meals. If you have any room after all the meat, grab one of the classic Southern desserts and head upstairs for a cocktail or beer.

Mala Hotpot $$
3777 Park Mill Run Dr.
(614) 971-3045
www.mala-hotpot.com

The interactive dining experience at Mala allows diners to customize their own hot pot and cook ingredients in a simmering broth right at the table. Choose from a wide selection of raw meats, vegetables, tofu, and noodles. A pot of broth is placed on the burner inset into the table. Once it gets rolling, use tongs to dunk your bite-size bits of food into the broth to cook, then enjoy with rice and sauces. Hot pot is a fun way to get the whole family involved in "making" dinner.

Sexton's Pizza $$
5460 Franklin St.
(614) 353-6876
www.sextonspizza.com

Brothers Sexton moved from a wood-fired pizza trailer to the brick-and-mortar shop that quickly became a neighborhood favorite. The pizza crust is not too thick and not too thin and perfectly wood-fire-charred for New York–style 'za. The dough ferments for two days making a fantastic "chew," and local meats from Ezzo Sausage Co. bring premium flavor. The restaurant is family-friendly, with a few free video games in the back room to keep the kiddos busy. Cauliflower crusts are available for a tasty gluten-free option. The full bar features lots of local canned craft and domestic beer, wine, and cocktails. Happy hour runs from 3 to 6 p.m. Mon through Fri.

Starliner Diner $$
4121 Main St.
(614) 529-1198
www.starlinerdiner.com

This Cuban-fusion restaurant is a kitschy, colorful place to experience cuisine that's just a little different in a setting that's just a little different. The furniture doesn't match. The murals and wall decorations are whimsical. Your senses are overloaded with fragrant aromas and festive music. Fun and affordable is the best way to describe a dining experience here.

Many locals don't realize this eatery has been around for nearly 30 years, but Starliner Diner has developed quite a loyal following that swears by the Cajun jambalaya and Creole macaroni. The food ranges from Southwestern to Cajun to Caribbean, but the menu offers plenty of crowd-friendly options, like pizzas, chili, big burritos, or fresh salads for those preferring something diet-esque. Pasta lovers go for the fettuccini caliente, while vegetarians opt for the pan-roasted vegetables with black beans and rice. Often overlooked are the desserts (which come in epic portions), so save plenty of room for the famous flan. Over the decades, Starliner has won awards for best breakfast, particularly the huevos rancheros. Come hungry and prepare for a hefty meal.

Taj Palace $$
3794 Fishinger Blvd.
(614) 771-3870
www.tajpalacehilliard.com

Don't let the ancient shopping mall setting put you off. This staple of Indian dining has been in the same location for nearly 30 years and has bragging rights as the first Indian restaurant in Columbus. The family-owned business is still serving up authentic regional Indian dishes, with a heavy nod toward tandoori and Punjabi flavors. The a la carte menu is extensive, offering more than a dozen types of bread, lots of vegetarian options, and a popular lunch buffet. Indian beers, wine, and a full bar is available.

Zaytoon Mediterranean Grill $
5450 Westpointe Plaza Dr.
(614) 363-4131
www.zaytoonrestaurant.com

The easy, fast-casual eatery is a build-your-own-bowl-style restaurant in yet another strip mall off Rome-Hilliard Road. This is one of the few locally owned places in a sea of chains. Start with your base of salad or pita wrap and add chicken, beef, lamb, chicken, or falafel; choose your vegetable toppings; then sauce it up. The usual dips, grape leaves, and salads are among the offerings. Zaytoon has modern indoor seating and easy parking.

GRANDVIEW

Aab $$
1470 Grandview Ave.
(614) 486-2800
www.aabindiarestaurants.com

Grandview's go-to Indian restaurant has been bringing traditional wood-fired cooking from the Punjab region to Columbus since 2013. Customers are incredibly loyal to the rustic northern Indian cooking turned out of this kitchen. Some of the favorite award-winning dishes include some of the almost 20 breads, roti and poori, tandoori specialties, curries, and chef specialties. Dinner specials rotate through family-favorite combinations that include entrees, rice, breads, and dessert. Aab has plenty of vegetarian-friendly dishes and a full bar.

Agave & Rye $$
479 N. High St.
(380) 229-3742
www.agaveandrye.com

Prepare for epic tacos that come doubly rein-forced with both hard corn shells tucked into flour tortillas to hold the massive amount of fillings. The tacos are piled high with creative combinations that can be made vegetarian, vegan, or gluten free with only corn shells. The pre-set tacos have names like the Filthy Fajita, giving away its sizzling filling of steak and grilled onion and peppers. Or the Rico Suave with herbed chicken and cowboy caviar (aka corn salsa). For an even more loaded taco, add on the "love cushion" of refried beans and queso between the duo of shells. The tacos are pricey but gigantic. If you have room for start-ers, a variety of queso and salsas can be ordered in combination. The margaritas are pretty epic, too. A second location is at 479 N. High St. in the Short North. Both places have outdoor patio seating.

Barrio Tacos $
1416 W. Fifth Ave.
(614) 665-9960
www.barrio-tacos.com

You had me at tacos. And tequilia. And whiskey. Here you can craft your own custom tacos to be as traditional or unusual as your palate desires. Grab a table and ordering pad, then check the boxes for each type of shell, one of more than a dozen meat and vegetarian proteins, toppings, salsa, and sauces. If you are overwhelmed with choices, check out El Jefe's suggestion for popu-lar combinations. The bar serves margaritas and other cocktailian libations in mason jars. Barrios is super casual and has outdoor seating. It also has a traveling food truck. The restaurant is open seven days a week from 3 p.m. and a little earlier on Sun for brunch.

Bonifacio $$
1577 King Ave.
(614) 914-8115
www.bonifacio614.com

Columbus's best authentic Filipino food is located in a nondescript building on the corner of King and North Star. The exterior looks deceivingly "fast food" as the bright, airy interior is full of light wood, lots of windows, and a shiny bar. While the menu features some truly traditional dishes like chicken adobo and curry mussels, the more modern signature dishes surprise and delight! The appetizer list is varied enough that you could make a meal of three or four. The full-service bar offers set cocktails, beer, and wine. Bonifacio is open for lunch with an abridged version of the dinner menu, and there's a completely different Sunday brunch that features the likes of Spam, brisket, and a Filipino version of fried chicken and waffles.

Cambridge Tea House $
1885 W. Fifth Ave.
(614) 486-6464
www.cambridgeteahouse.com

Pinkies up! The charming little teahouse is very popular among the ladies who lunch and those wanting an afternoon tea experience. The space is cozy, but during warmer months, the out-door patio has several umbrella tables for dining alfresco. The most appealing part of Cambridge Tea House is the quality of food for the price. The thoughtful signature dishes, like curried egg salad, daily quiches, and the best scones in town have created loyal customers since the shop's opening in 2011. The tea selection is nicely curated, as is the three types of tea service: full afternoon tea with tiers of finger sandwiches, scones, and sweets; teas and sweets including a scone, mini desserts, and a pot of tea; or cream tea with just a scone and tea. Kids can choose from a prince or princess tea as well. The Tea House is open Wed through Sun 9 or 10 a.m. until 3 p.m. and serves breakfast all day.

Dewey's Pizza $$
1327 W. Fifth Ave,
(614) 487-8282
www.deweyspizza.com

See the entry for Dewey's Pizza in the Worthing-ton section.

Eastern Bay $$
2055 Riverside Dr.
(614) 487-1198
www.easternbayrestaurant.com

This pan-Asian restaurant has been around for almost 25 years. The cozy booths afford couples a quiet, intimate dinner, while larger groups can share their meals across big, round tables. Now, about the food: It looks good, it tastes good, and it always comes out piping hot. If you come here a handful of times, you will be recognized and acknowledged. The service is prompt and courteous, even on the busiest of days. The extensive menu of entrees is divided into the usual categories of rice and noodle stir-fry, meat, seafood, and vegetarian. While the main menu serves up good-quality Americanized Asian cuisine, the separate Korean menu is legitimately authentic. Familiar bibimbap, Korn wings, and bulgogi are listed along with Spam-laden hot pots, salty lemon mackerel, and goat stew—all written in Korean, but described in English. Eastern Bay is open for lunch and dinner all week.

Figlio Wood-Fired Pizza $$
1369 Grandview Ave.
(614) 481-8850
www.figliopizza.com
For 30 years, Figlio (pronounced "feel-ee-oh") has been a buzzy neighborhood eatery offering quality wood-fired gourmet pizzas and homemade pastas at prices that do not gouge. This is the sort of place where you bump into people you know. The kitchen turns out high-end yet approachable dishes. The spicy chicken diablo, drunken shrimp, and pear and brie pizzas have been on the menu forever. Designer, wood-fired pizzas have been carefully crafted with toppings that range from hot honey and proscuitto to truffled mushrooms. Pasta selections are just as varied, as is the wine list. The restaurant is fancy family-friendly, and the small outdoor patio is first-come, first-served. Street parking and a nearby free lot makes parking easy, but pay attention to a few paid zones within a few blocks. Figlio is closed Sun.

FUSIAN $
855 W. Fifth Ave.
www.fusian.com/grandview
Other locations in Clintonville, Dublin,
  Westerville, and Easton

The flagship location in Grandview is an easy, casual sushi joint that has indoor seating but does a lot of carryout. The menu hanging above the counter lists a number of mainstream 10-piece rolls, like crispy shrimp, spicy tuna, and California rolls. The other non-roll options are build-your-own bowls or salads, with proteins like poke or crunchy tofu and customizable toppings, potstickers, and soup. No booze here, but rather serve-yourself organic teas and flavored lemonades. FUSIAN is a great option for fresh, fast food.

High Bank Distillery Co. $$
1051 Goodale Blvd.
(614) 826-5347
www.highbankco.com
The modern distillery pub is a cavernous restaurant serving award-winning, locally distilled spirits, craft cocktails, and modern American cuisine with a nod toward Korean flavors. The High Bank Vodka, Statehouse Gin, and Whiskey War labels used in many of the restaurant's cocktails are made on-site, where Saturday tours of the facility are given. Choose from shareables like blistered shishitos and bison potstickers, or fill up on pizza, Gochujang salmon, a Korean Philly, or classic fish sandwich. Parking can be tight. The restaurant is open seven days a week for lunch and dinner, and brunch on the weekends. A second location is at 1379 E. Johnstown Rd. in the Gahana–New Albany area.

Hot Chicken Takeover $
1417 W. Fifth Ave.
(614) 914-5068
www.hotchickentakeover.com
Read the full description under the Clintonville section.

La Tavola $$
1664 W. First Ave.
(614) 914-5455
www.latavolagrandview.com
Looking for great scratch-made Italian food? Check out La Tavola, where chef Rick Lopez turns out exceptional old-world specialties that are just a little different from a lot of other Italian restaurants. The nightly menu changes up starters and

seasonal entrees with creativity. There are usually a few house-made gnocchi dishes on the menu, along with more unusual Tuscan specialties like tortellini en brodo and steak tagliata. The purist wine list is strictly Italiano, while most of the beers are Italian, too. Chef Rick is also the mind behind Upper Arlington's Spanish tapas restaurant, Lupo.

Panzera's Pizza $
1354 Grandview Ave.
(614) 486-5951
www.panzeras.com

Often rated at the front of the pizza pack, Panzera's has been creating pizza addicts since 1964, with no changes to the recipes since then. Some say it's the thin, crispy crust, while others claim it's the super tomato-y sauce, and still others love the sharp, greasy cheese. Whatever it is, the dough and sauce are scratch-made daily, and the pepperoni is thick and salty, quite bacon-like. The menu also includes subs and pasta, but don't forget to grab a bundle of homemade pizelles for dessert. This Grandview institution has a seasonal outdoor patio; otherwise, you have to get the pie to go.

Paul's Fifth Avenue $
1565 W. Fifth Ave.
(614) 481-8848
www.paulsonline.com

Paul's has two different personalities under one unassuming roof. Down-home cooking is served for breakfast and lunch, while full-on lunch fare is turned out until 3 p.m. daily except Mon. For 50 years this Grandview institution has filled local bellies with pancakes and eggs for breakfast and burgers and pasta for lunch. The morning hours attract the greasy spoon crowd looking for corned beef hash and omelets, while the afternoon draws locals wanting soup, salad, or one of many classic diner sandwiches, like Reubens, chicken salad, burgers, and all sorts of different melts. Don't miss out on the house-baked pie. The Panzera family also started Panzera's Pizza, the other Grandview fixture just around the corner.

Rotolo's Pizza $
1749 W. Fifth Ave.
Multiple locations
(614) 488-7934
www.rotolospizza.com

This is not just another Grandview pizzeria. Folks from Grandview Heights have been calling Rotolo's meaty, cheesy pizzas a tradition since 1976. The rest of Columbus seems to like it too, as it has claimed numerous awards over the years. Lovers of thick-crust pizza will enjoy the pliable crust, lightly covered with a sweet sauce and loaded with lots of mozzarella. The pepperoni is small, thick, and crispy, but there's a bevy of high-quality ingredients to pile on—and that they do! The menu also features subs, salads, and a handful of pasta entrees. Keep in mind this is takeout only; Rotolo's does not deliver and does not have a dining room.

Si Señor Peruvian Sandwiches $
146 W. Fifth Ave.
(614) 369-1500
www.sisenor-columbus.com

Si Señor is one of Columbus's beloved sandwich shops. Authentic Peruvian sandwiches are made in-house on grinder-style bread baked at a local bake house. The vibe is totally Latin, meaning colorful, with friendly service and a lively energy. Despite long lunch lines at the counter, the wait is pretty reasonable. The menu is meat heavy, but there are a few vegetarian sandwich offerings and a half-dozen protein-optional salads. They have a decent amount of indoor seating and some on the patio. Si Señor is a great place to be exposed to South American flavors in a crowd-friendly way and to get a fabulous sandwich.

Trattoria Roma $$
1447 Grandview Ave.
(614) 488-2104
www.trattoria-roma.com

Trattoria Roma is the upscale Italian restaurant of Grandview, and it doesn't get more intimate than cozy tables with white linens nestled in a deep red dining room with the likes of Dean Martin crooning in the background. The fare is classic Italian cuisine from central and northern Italy. The menu falls somewhere between traditional and adventuresome. You can have fresh, handmade pasta in a rich cream sauce or a simple marinara, but the kitchen is known for its slow-roasted osso buco and amazing rotolo di pasta. Regulars concur that the service is impeccable, and the sidewalk patio is truly romantic. There's a small bar, and the restaurant is open for dinner seven days a week.

Z Cucina
1368 Grandview Ave.
(614) 486-9200
www.zcucina.com

This neighborhood favorite puts a modern spin on its Mediterranean menu. Updated classics and creative modern entrees can be washed down with a bottle of Italian wine from a solid wine list, or quench your thirst with Z's signature drinks: a Z Royale or a variety of martinis. The menu features a nice selection of seafood, meats, and vegetables and is open for dinner at 5 p.m. (closed on Sun). Reservations are recommended. The second location in Bridge Park, Dublin, is a beautiful space with a patio facing the river.

UPPER ARLINGTON

Akai Hana $$
1173 Old Henderson Rd., Kenny Center
(614) 451-5411
www.akaihana.japanmarketplace.com

This casual strip-mall restaurant has a traditional, understated atmosphere. The dining room is large and unpretentious; the sushi bar is small and often busy. There isn't anything trendy about this place, but the sushi menu is extensive, and the fish is very fresh and well prepared. If you are struggling to decide what to get, order the Columbus Box, which comes with a selection of just about everything. There are Korean selections alongside the cooked Japanese fare. Tempura, deep-fried tofu, and udon noodles are house favorites. Sushi lovers claim this is the best Japanese restaurant because of the portions, price, and atmosphere. Or alternatively, pop in to its fast-casual Tensuke Express a few doors over for sushi and noodle bowls.

Chef O'Nette $
2090 Tremont Center, between Tremont and Redding Rd.
(614) 488-8444
www.chefonette.com

Diner seats have been swiveling at the counter since 1955, making the Chef-O an Upper Arlington tradition for many generations. It has recently come under new ownership, and while it is undergoing a refresh, it will preserve much of the original decor and continue to serve up the same menu full of nostalgic favorites. Old-time comfort foods like tuna melt, fried bologna, and fish sandwiches are on offer, but the mainstays of the menu are the Hangover Sandwich and the Chef-O-Burger. Some people go just for the soda fountain malts and shakes. Chef-O is open for breakfast, lunch, and dinner. Pick up your carryout from the vintage drive-through window; Chef-O claims to be one of the earliest drive-throughs in the region.

Cuco's Taqueria and Grill $$
2162 W. Henderson Rd.
(614) 538-8701
www.cucostaqueria.com

An unassuming storefront eatery serves up some of the most authentic Mexican food in Columbus—and at great prices. Tucked in the corner of a little strip mall, this bright and cheerful restaurant could be considered one of the city's hidden gems! Try the chef specialty, Guadalajara lamb stew, or any number of home-style dishes from south of the border. Cuco's also is a Mexican market. It has great hours of operation, from 10 a.m. to 10 p.m.

Dosa Corner $
1077 Old Henderson Rd.
(614) 459-5515
www.dosacornerrestaurant.com

The family-run hole-in-the-wall Indian restaurant has been around since 2000. It is well-known for its bold-flavored South Indian vegetarian food. When dining in, don't expect anything fancy, but you can expect enormous dosas served on a silver platter. Dosas are the Indian version of crepes made from fermented lentil and rice flour then filled with a variety of curried potatoes, chutneys, and other vegetables. There are more than a dozen dosas to choose from, as well as combinations that include appetizers, bread, and dosas. You can also order a variety of vegetarian curries and rice dishes. Dosa Corner does not sell alcohol, but the mango lassi should put out the fire from the Indian spices.

El Vaquero Mexican Restaurant $
2195 Riverside Dr. (US 33)
Eight Columbus locations
(614) 486-4547
www.vaquerorestaurant.com
Most people living west of the Olentangy will say to go to El Vaquero for good authentic Mexican food, thinking this corporate-owned restaurant is a mom-and-pop shop. The decor is nothing fancy, and though there are some piñatas and blow-up Corona bottles hanging from the ceiling, it's not as garish or contrived as some Mexican chains. The Spanish-speaking waitstaff is very attentive, and your refillable basket of chips and spicy salsa will seem bottomless. The food never fails to come out very fast, as if Speedy Gonzales himself made it. It will probably take you longer to figure out what you want from the 160-plus menu options than to actually get your food. Be careful, because the plates and the food arrive steaming hot, and the refried beans are like liquid lava at times.

Gallo's Kitchen and Bar $$$
2820 Nottingham Rd.
(614) 754-8176
www.galloskitchen.com
This could just as easily be listed in the pubs chapter because the bar is almost always lively and full of locals. The menu is not big, but the food is quality Creole and Italian. It might seem like an odd mix of offerings, but the dishes from both cuisines are deeply flavored. The pastas are cooked to order, and it's hard to choose between the equally fabulous gumbo and jambalaya. The space is modern and bustling, and parking is available in a lot.

Hyde Park Grille $$$
1615 Old Henderson Rd.
(614) 442-3310
Four Columbus locations
www.hydeparkgrille.com
I hesitate to call anything the "best," but I will go out on a limb here and say you should come to this dark, clubby steak house with high expectations. Valet parking is complimentary, and one could say the caliber of cars parked outside reflects the caliber of dining you will find inside. A friendly host will guide you past the bar, where cigar smokers and the over-30 set look equally at home, into one of the cozy, wood-paneled dining rooms.

The menu is loaded with top-quality cuts of meat, which can be enhanced with any of the gourmet sauces named for Ohio sports celebrities. Steak Rahal (as in Bobby) is a bacon-wrapped filet mignon with caramelized Dijon hollandaise sauce. The house favorite is Steak Kosar (named for the Browns' Bernie Kosar). This huge filet is topped with lobster and served in bordelaise sauce. Seafood lovers won't be disappointed with classics such as oysters Rockefeller, lobster tails, and king crab. Like the other Hyde Park restaurants, the side dishes are varied and come portioned for two. The quality of service matches the food—world-class. Hyde Park Prime Steakhouses are located at 6360 Frantz Rd. in Dublin and on the Cap in the Short North.

Local Cantina $
1670 W. Lane Ave.
(614) 674-6269
www.localcantina.com
The locally owned cantina serves up fresh-made tacos with unusual names and fillings that are equally playful. The menu is not like the typical Mexican list of burritos and beans, but rather good-quality meats, sauces, and veggies tucked into soft flour or hard corn shells—or both, known as "weezy" style. The casual, modern restaurant is family-friendly, but the bar can become crowded on evenings and weekends. On nice days the front garage-door wall is raised, opening to a large outdoor patio, perfect for hanging out with a margarita and Local Cantina's delicious queso.

Lupo on Arlington $$$
2124 Arlington Ave.
(614) 914-6134
www.lupoonarlington.com

If Spanish tapas are what you are craving, head to the Mallway in Arlington where Lupo's serves up a wide range of Spanish-inspired small plates. While the menu changes seasonally, a few popular pintxos and tapas remain the same. Can't have a mutiny on our hands by taking away the meatballs or mussels! The atmosphere as a neighborhood restaurant is somewhat casual, but that doesn't take away from the upscale nature of the food and service. The wine list is well curated, with more than just Spanish wines. A pretty outdoor patio overlooks Arlington Avenue. It also has a nice happy hour.

Moretti's of Arlington $$
2124 Tremont Center, between Tremont and
**   Redding Rd.**
(614) 486-2333
www.morettisofarlington.com

First-rate, zesty southern Italian food is served in a modern setting in this storefront restaurant located in a part of town where strip malls are called "plazas." Behind the smoke-colored glass door is a small but lively bar leading into a small but festive dining area where the walls are deep red and the paintings are cheerful. Once you settle in to the (lived-in) chairs, you may not be able to get up after stuffing yourself with hand-rolled pasta piled with meats and cheese and canoli for dessert. Though you will find hearty classics and pizzas on the menu, the kitchen turns out some sophisticated dishes and nightly specials. Moretti's is open for dinner only and closed on Sun.

Nicola Bar and Restaurant $$
4740 Reed Rd.
(614) 459-7000
www.nicolacolumbus.com

This fine neighborhood Italian eatery is tucked on the end of a strip mall, making it easy to drive right by. I highly recommend checking out Nicola's for the fabulous handmade pasta dishes and several quality starters, like the carpaccio and calamari. The wine list is equally thoughtful. The atmosphere is lively at the bar and can be rather warm and romantic in the dining area, making for a great date night or happy hour meetup with friends. In good Italian form they also celebrate the holidays with a Feast of the Seven Fishes and a Christmas menu and host various special events through the year.

Original Pancake House $$
1633 W. Lane Ave.
(614) 695-6810
www.ophcentralohio.com

Head to the Shops on Lane Avenue for a breakfast that will leave you ready to go home and take a nap. The omelets are the size of footballs and come with a side of pancakes. Crepes likewise are either huge or come in a three-pack. The quality of ingredients and flavors is great, but be prepared for large portions. The OPH can be quite busy on weekends, but the table turnover is pretty quick. Parking is available. A second location is at 715 Worthington Rd. in Westerville.

South of Lane $
1987 Guilford Rd.
(614) 586-2233
www.southoflanecafe.com

This cute little vintage cafe sits off a side street around the corner from the Mallway. The small restaurant is a popular neighborhood breakfast spot that serves breakfast, brunch, and lunch in a cozy cafe-like space, as well as on the small sidewalk patio. The menu features upscale classics, like Greek and caprese omelets, but gets creative with house specialties like sweet potato hash and bourbon pecan french toast. Waffles are encouraged! Lunch comes in the form of salads, sandwiches, and chili. This is a great spot to grab a coffee and enjoy brunch with a friend. SOL is open from 7 a.m. through lunch until 2 p.m.

SŌW Plated $$
The Shops on Lane Avenue
1625 W. Lane Ave.
(614) 826-0028
www.sowplated.com

SŌW (pronounced so, with a long o) is a cheery restaurant with a menu that puts wellness and healthy eating front and center. SŌW, which stands for "sustainable, organic, wellness," lives up to its name, as ingredients are locally sourced and pesticide free. The executive chef designs menus with the seasons, using the highest-quality ingredients to ensure every dish is good for you. SŌW's philosophy in a nutshell is that food is directly linked to physical and mental well-being. The spacious dining room is modern but warm and welcoming, while the large double-sided bar opens to a pretty covered patio. The menu has thoughtful meat and seafood dishes, but vegetarians and vegans rejoice in the many plant-based options, salads, and creative bowls. The desserts are creative, the juices cold-pressed, and the cocktails handcrafted using local spirits.

Tai's Asian Bistro $
1285 W. Lane Ave.
(614) 485-0016
www.taisasianbistrocbus.com
Tai's is situated between Upper Arlington and Ohio State's campus, so it sees plenty of action seven days a week as college kids strap on their feed bags and busy parents pick up carryout fried rice for dinner. The pan-Asian menu has just about anything you might want, from dumpling or won ton soup to Mongolian beef and stir-fries of every kid. Pad thai, banh mi, and pho are also on the expansive menu. If you can't find anything among the 100 menu items, there is also a full-service sushi bar, as well as alcohol and bubble tea. The best part of Tai's is that the price is right and quantities are huge. Parking is available in a lot.

Tommy's Pizza $
1350 W. Lane Ave.
(614) 486-2969
www.tommyspizza.com
Some locals will go to their graves swearing that Tommy's makes the best pies in the universe. The pizzeria has had plenty of practice, having been around for almost 75 years. The pizzas are cheesy, the pepperoni curls up at the edges, and the crust is crispy and not too thick, not too thin. The menu includes subs, salads, and full dinners. This restaurant is totally family-friendly, which adds to the appeal for those who live in the neighborhood.

Tommy's has a second location up the street on Ohio State's campus.

XiXia $$
1140 Kenny Rd.
(614) 670-7736
www.xixiacuisine.com
XiXia specializes in western Chinese cuisine and is known for its daily house-made noodles and rich, flavorful bone broth. The restaurant serves a bit more atypical Chinese food than what our American palates are used to, which makes the noodle soups, rice bowls, and appetizers just a little different and interesting for adventurous eaters. In keeping with the idea of the affordability of *gaifan* (rice or noodles topped with meat or vegetables), the price points are quite reasonable for the quality and creativity of the dishes. The warm and inviting storefront restaurant is located in Kenny Center Mall and is open for lunch and dinner.

Windward Passage $$
4739 Reed Rd.
(614) 451-2497
www.windwardpassageua.com
This is another Upper Arlington institution where time has stood still. Looking for a classic Waldorf salad and lobster? This is your place! Upper Arlington's tried-and-true seafood restaurant hangs in there amid the opening of high-profile seafood places thanks to an unwavering clientele, old-school service, and only the freshest seafood. The dining room is dark and cozy, and the bar is comfortable with low seats around a sunken bar. Regulars swear by Windward Passage's walleye and perch, but as the fish is flown in daily, you can't go wrong with any seafood. The oysters on the half-shell are among the best in the city, and the steaks are generously sized. Best thing about Windward Passage? You won't break the bank having a fabulous meal.

DUBLIN

101 Beer Kitchen $
7509 Sawmill Rd.
(614) 210-1010
www.101beerkitchen.com

Even though beer is in the name of this chef-owned restaurant, the rustic, local-ingredient-driven kitchen turns out wonderful food. The appetizers are elevated bar food, and modern spins are put on classic salads. Creative starters include butternut squash pierogies or black garlic Caesar salad. The entrees are approachable, but not your run-of-the-mill bar food, with options like roasted pork and green chili, Creole walleye, and a turkey pesto panini. The 101 Burger pairs perfectly with the dozens of regional craft beer offerings, but cocktails and wine are also on the menu. Even the kids' menu has fancy twists on the standards. The restaurant is quite large and great for big groups, but is also family-friendly. The bar is large, too, and has a warm, welcoming vibe. 101 Beer Kitchen has two other Columbus locations, in Gahanna and Westerville.

J. Liu of Dublin $$
50 W. Bridge St.
(614) 718-1818
www.jliudublin.com

When looking for a menu that caters to a variety of palates, Jason's fits the bill. The extensive pan-Asian menu traverses the globe, offering Asian, Italian, American, and a variety of steak and seafood entrees. You can kick off the meal with Asian pot stickers, have an entree of Italian chicken parmesan, and top it off with a slice of New York–style cheesecake. Sushi, stir-fries, soups, and salads are also in the mix. The decor is as modern and eclectic as the menu. The bar features a weeknight happy hour and special holiday events.

Kitchen Social $$
6791 Longshore St., Dublin Bridge Park
(614) 763-1770
www.ourkitchensocial.com

If warm and industrial can be used in the same breath, then the atmosphere at Kitchen Social is just that. The spacious, bright restaurant serves upscale American and global comfort food. It is a lively, family-friendly space with consistently good service and even better cocktails. The menu features things like fantastic fish-and-chips, Korean BBQ cauliflower, pizzas, tacos, and Nashville hot chicken sandwiches, but the cheddar scallion

biscuits are most popular. A second Columbus location is on Gemini Place at Polaris.

Matt the Miller's Tavern $$
6725 Avery-Muirfield Rd.
(614) 799-9100
www.mtmtavern.com

The casual pub serves upscale tavern food like fish-and-chips, great flatbreads, soups, salads, and a wide range of steaks and ribs. MTM is a popular place to get together and watch games on the televisions in the bar area, but it is also a family-friendly dining room. It is open seven days a week for lunch and dinner.

Mezzo $$$
12 W. Bridge St.
(614) 889-6100
www.mezzodublin.com

Mezzo is modern destination Italian dining nestled in the heart of historic Dublin. The menu serves upscale takes on regional Italian classics. The restaurant, located in a charming brick building, is warm and contemporary and has three outdoor patios to enjoy the bustle of old Dublin during warmer months. A happy hour menu with half-off pizzas and appetizer and drink specials is offered every day except Sat. It also hosts live music.

Song Lan Restaurant $$$
6628 Riverside Dr.
(614) 389-2736
www.songlanrestaurant.com

Song Lan in Bridge Park makes some of the best sushi in town. Here, you definitely eat with your eyes first, beginning with the dining room and bar areas, which are modern and sophisticated. Frankly, it's just a beautiful space with a seasonal covered patio. The menu is full of traditional Japanese dishes including soups, salads, and a large selection of hot and cold appetizers. There are a few noodle dishes and hibachi combinations to choose from, but most people come for the fish. The dozens of specialty rolls are exquisitely executed and plated. Song Lan serves the full range of nigiri, maki rolls, and hand rolls. The chef's special rolls are quite large, but sharing several rolls is manageable. The most popular rolls are the Triple Three, Dancing Yellowtail, and Kiss of Fire. This can become a fairly expensive outing, depending on how much sushi you can put away, but it is absolutely worth the experience in terms of ambience and quality of food and service.

Sunflower Chinese Restaurant $$
7370 Sawmill Rd.
(614) 764-7888

Sunflower is one of the longtime go-to Chinese restaurants tucked in the corner of a shopping center off Sawmill. The restaurant has a menu full of the usual stir-fries, noodles, and appetizers, but many locals have been coming for years for the dim sum. This is one of a just a few places that serves house-made dim sum, so be patient with the wait. The traditional cart will eventually roll out with whatever options you chose from the long list of items, like lotus buns, barbecued meats, chicken feet, and bean curd rolls. Sunflower is also one of the few restaurants in town that serves congee. The hot pot takes around 45 minutes to make to order, too, so be sure to have some appetizers in the pipeline.

Tucci's Wood-Fired Bistro $$
35 N. High St., Old Dublin
(614) 792-3466
www.tuccisdublin.com

This lively, modern Italian-style bistro has been getting rave reviews for its wood-fired pizzas and other chef-driven dishes since it opened in 1998, but it receives particularly big kudos for its attentive customer service. The dining room is intimate and sophisticated, but the seating is somewhat tight, so be warned it can become noisy and crowded on the weekends. But that's a good thing for a restaurant! Tucci's opens at 3 p.m. for dinner daily and offers a brunch Sat and Sun. Happy hour appetizers and drink specials are available Mon through Fri until 6 p.m.

Ty Ginger Asian Bistro $$
5689 Woerner Temple Rd.
(614) 889-8885
www.tyginger.com

Ty's serves up classic, authentic Thai and Chinese cuisine in a bright, spacious restaurant in Emerald Town Center, near Tuttle Crossing. What sets Ty's apart from most other Chinese eateries is the extensive dim sum menu offered seven days a week. The ingredients are really good quality, and you can rely on solid, attentive service. You can order the usual Chinese soups, salads, classic stir-fries, noodles, and curry dishes for lunch and dinner daily. The more than 50 dim sum offerings are made in-house and served tableside via the traditional cart delivery. Steamer baskets arrive with all sorts of two-bite delicacies ranging from dozens of different dumplings to steamed buns, turnip cakes, and fish balls. Ty's is one of only a few restaurants in Columbus that serves dim sum and, lucky for us, it is very good.

BETHEL AND SAWMILL CORRIDOR

Awadh India Restaurant $$
2584 Bethel Rd.
(614) 914-8884
www.awadhrestaurant.com

Indian and Indo-Chinese cuisine is the specialty at Awadh. This is the sort of restaurant where you share a bunch of starters to explore dishes like Manchurian chicken and lamb samosas. Choose from a dozen breads to sop up any number of saucy entrees. There are plenty of options for meat eaters and vegetarians alike.

Bamboo Thai Kitchen $$
774 Bethel Rd.
(614) 326-1950
www.bamboothaikitchen.com

Be advised this restaurant is not open for dine-in service, but it is totally worth ordering carryout when craving Thai food. It is among the best in town. The soups and noodle dishes are top notch, and the kimchi dumplings are highly recommended for those who enjoy a bit of heat. The business is run by a very nice family, and the chef takes great care with the quality and consistency of the food.

Buckeye Pho $
761 Bethel Rd.
(614) 451-2828
www.buckeyepho.net
This longtime popular Vietnamese storefront eatery is located in a shopping center, so parking is easy, and the pho is fine! Buckeye Pho is among the top two or three places recommended when asked where to go for great banh mi or vermicelli bowls. The bar serves beer, wine, and a decent amount of liquor options. The restaurant does a thriving lunch business, and carryout is constant through the day as it is open from 11 a.m. until 8 p.m. Closed on Wed.

Donpocha Korean BBQ $$
4710 Reed Rd.
(614) 459-9292
www.donpocha.com
Korean barbeque and sushi make for a traditional dining experience at Donpocha. Authentic dishes such as bibimbap, hot pot, and bulgogi are prepared and delivered tableside, while two or more people can get a table with a built-in barbecue to cook a variety of combinations of meat and vegetables. The sushi bar has been around for about 25 years and serves a nice selection of nigiri and rolls.

Gogi Korean $$
1138 Bethel Rd.
(614) 670-4790
www.gogikbbq.com
The large restaurant serves fantastic Korean barbeque and soups, and has many grill tables for you to cook your own meat and vegetables in broths. The portions are generous, and the ambience is lively with K-Pop videos playing on a bunch of TVs in the background.

Los Guachos Taqueria $
5221 Godown Rd.
(614) 538-0211
www.losguachostaqueria.com
The fun, festive atmosphere at this colorful Mexican restaurant, combined with its great food, has drawn in folks from all around Columbus. This is one of the most popular taco spots in the city. It began life as a food truck and opened its first brick-and-mortar place in 2011. The al pastor gringas is hands down the crowd favorite. Also extremely popular are the meat-filled tortas, a Mexican-style panini. Traditional Mexican-style tacos and food truck tacos are among the offerings, and giant burritos, sopes, and volcanes round out the menu. Let's not forget the handcrafted margaritas, Mezcal cocktails, and a full complement of beer and wine.

Meshikou Ramen $
1506 Bethel Rd.
(614) 457-1689
www.meshikou.com
Consistently ranked among the best ramen shops in Columbus, Meshikou serves authentic Japanese noodle dishes and Asian street-fried chicken. The casual contemporary eatery offers both traditional appetizers like gyoz and wings alongside more interesting options like spicy crab tacos and octopus hush puppies. Choose from a few rice bowls or a dozen types of ramen with a wide range of add-on toppings. Meshikou is closed on Mon.

Min-Ga Korean $$
800 Bethel Rd.
(614) 457-7331
www.min-ga.com
This is one instance where terrific Korean food can be found in a nondescript strip mall off Bethel Road. The no-frills dining room is divided into two sides, so it is bigger than you might think. Hot stone-pot meals, bibimbap, fried fish, and traditional meat dishes are on the extensive menu for both lunch and dinner. The service here is consistently good and the restaurant has been around for more than 20 years, making it one of the oldest Korean establishments in the city. It serves wine, beer, and sake and is open seven day a week from 11 a.m. until 9 p.m.

Moretti's Restaurant $$$
5849 Sawmill Rd.
(614) 717-0400
www.morettisofdublin.com
Moretti is a family name synonymous with fine Italian dining, and this location has been a longtime fixture in yet another nondescript strip mall

full of ethnic grocery stores. The interior decor is old-world Italian (with a few Greek statues thrown in), and the cuisine is authentic and homey. The menu consists of old reliables, like four types of lasagna, casseroles, pizzas, pastas, and entrees like chicken cacciatore and veal parmigiana. Don't expect frozen breaded cutlets. Everything including the pasta noodles is made from scratch, and you'll know it.

New India Restaurant $$
5226 Bethel Rd.
(614) 442-7705
www.newindiarestaurant.com
Authentic pan-Indian cuisine is on the menu at New India, continually voted one of the best Indian restaurants in Columbus since opening. It comes as no surprise given the owners introduced Columbus to various Indian cuisines at several of their restaurants in 1970. The offerings span Punjabi tandooris, rich curries, aromatic Awadhi specialties, and more than a dozen types of breads drawing on the Mughal influence on Indian cuisine. Popular dishes include biryanis, masalas, and kormas. Many of the dishes are halal, and vegetarian selections are extensive. The unassuming restaurant in Bethel Center Mall is open for lunch until midday, then closes a few hours until dinner. There is a small outdoor patio.

Panini Opa $$
4799 Sawmill Rd.
(614) 336-8830
www.paniniopa.com
Panini Opa serves some of the best Greek food in the city. The fairly extensive menu has all the usual Mediterranean favorites like falafel with dips and spreads, gyros, soups, and salads with optional proteins. The house specialties, like enormous moussaka, pasticcio, and Aegean-style dishes, are what set Panini Opa apart from other places. Wine and beer are available for dining in, or eat alfresco on the patio that is bedazzled with bits of sculpture and architecture to resemble a Greek temple.

The Refectory Restaurant $$$$
1092 Bethel Rd.
(614) 451-9774
www.therefectoryrestaurant.com
This entry could end right here with a laundry list of awards—Wine Spectator's Grand Award and Best of Award of Excellence, DiRona Award for Distinguished Restaurants of North America, AAA Four-Diamond Award for three decades straight, and five stars locally—but there is so much more to say about this landmark of great dining.

The website has a detailed history of this unique and distinguished building, which began as a church in the 1850s and took its place as Columbus's premier French restaurant in 1982. The spirit of the past can be felt in the handhewn wooden beams of the high ceilings and the exposed brick walls, while the stained-glass windows are a reminder of the spiritual place this once was.

Whether you love classic or contemporary French fare, "spiritual" is a good way to describe a dining experience here. It begins with a candlelit dining room and ends with a symphony of desserts. In between, an exquisite meal prepared with flair by chef Richard Blondin—a native of Lyon, France—is served from a seasonally changing menu. The attention to detail is staggering, and the service is superb. In the tradition of true French dining, nothing is hurried. You are not supposed to eat your dinner; you are supposed to experience it. Order from the a la carte menu or enjoy a few different fixed-price Chef's Tasting menus with optional paired wine. Owner Kamal Boulos is often in-house rubbing elbows with guests.

The original schoolhouse is now the lounge and sit-down bistro. The long, mirrored bar is a cozy place to order from an appetizer menu and enjoy a glass of wine or one of the many whiskeys. Wine lovers will be pleased to know The Refectory has a Cruvinet wine preservation system, allowing staff to pour many special wines by the glass from its world-class wine cellar.

Reservations are strongly recommended and especially well in advance of the holidays. Aside from the main dining room, The Refectory offers alfresco dining in the courtyard during the summer months and a private room in the wine cellar, which is loaded with character and allows you to dine among the bottles. The Refectory is closed Sun.

Sun Tong Luck Asian Cuisine $
2500 Bethel Rd.
(614) 442-3375
www.suntongluck.com

Sun Tong Luck has been garnering great local reviews since it first opened in 1982 in east Columbus. The current incarnation has been in the Carriage Place Plaza location since 2002. The menu is full of pan-Asian offerings like Singapore noodles and pad thai, and the restaurant also serves more than a dozen tofu and vegan options. Sun Tong Luck is nothing fancy but makes good-quality Asian food for a reasonable price.

MORSE AND CLEVELAND CORRIDORS

Addis Ethiopian Restaurant $
3750 Cleveland Ave.
(614) 269-8680
www.addis-restaurant.com

The family-owned Ethiopian restaurant serves traditional dishes as well as a good selection of vegetarian, vegan, and gluten-free options. Everything is made to order, so you can decide how spicy you want your meal, which can get quite hot if you go with a meat dish simmered in berber sauce. Ethiopian cuisine is typically vegetable heavy, often served with spicy meat stews. The spongy house-made injera bread is used in lieu of utensils, as it is traditional to eat with your hands and use the injera to scoop up the delicious meat and veggies. Order platters to share or go with one of the few individual entrees or salads. The dining room is covered with pictures of the motherland, and a small patio is open seasonally.

Brazilian Grill and Bakery $
5818 Columbus Sq.
(614) 392-9254
www.instagram.com/braziliangrillandbakery.com

If you like grilled meat, then this is the place for you, especially during the rare all-you-can-eat weekend buffet (and the pay-by-the-pound

during the week), when multiple types of meat are served on a carving station, and the hot and cold buffets are loaded with sides like rice and chimichurri sauce. The food is as authentic as it gets, and the dining room full of Brazilian patrons proves that. The spacious restaurant is attached to a Brazilian market where you can find Portuguese, Latin, and Brazilian specialties ranging from linguiça sausage to Brazilian cookies and candy.

Drelyse Ghanaian African Restaurant $
1911 Tamarack Circle N., Northland Area
(614) 430-3350
www.drelyseafricanrestaurant.com

Drelyse specializes in traditional African food from around the continent, but particularly from the chef-owner's home country of Ghana. She takes pride in serving great-tasting and beautiful-looking food using high-quality African ingredients. Her offerings range from traditional jollof rice and lamb and goat dishes to bean or okra dishes, and the popular beef and spinach stew. Unlike many other African restaurants, Drelyse serves a limited selection of beer and wine.

Ginevre Somali Café $
2285 Morse Rd.
(614) 475-4880

Somalian meets Mediterranean cuisine at this fusion restaurant known for its generous portions of homey comfort food. If you like spicy hot food, have the dishes cooked traditionally; otherwise, you can choose your spice level. The most popular items are the chicken suqaar, lamb shank, and lentil soup. Ginevre shakes up the Somali menu a bit with a few non-African options like osso buco, falafel, and salmon and pasta. The cafe has a clean minimalist interior, where you can dine in at tables or booths or carryout. Ginevre is known for friendly, fast service and reasonable prices.

Golden Phoenix $
4542 Cleveland Ave.
(614) 471-3105
www.goldenphoenixcbus.com

The Golden Phoenix has been around for quite a while and could use a bit of a refresh, but it is generally busy, especially on weekends. The casual sit-down restaurant is the classic old-school Chinese dining room with booths, tables, and traditional decorations. The menu offers the gamut of Asian fusion food, soups, and stir-fries, with the house suggestions being the most popular items. This is an affordable place to go with a group to sample a variety of dishes.

Huong Vietnamese Restaurant $
1270 Morse Rd.
(614) 825-0303
www.huongvr.blogspot.com
Columbus is lucky to have a few solid Vietnamese restaurants, and one of the longest-established is located in a small shopping center near the I-71 exit. The owners take pride in serving only Vietnamese food and not adding the usual pan-Asian suspects to the menu. And you'll never miss them, as the multiple-page menu ranges from the familiar to lesser-known regional specialties, illustrated with pictures. Be sure to check through the whole menu, as daily specials change through the week. The dining is room is sizable and cheery with a colorful landscape mural and, quite often, American music cranking from a speaker.

Intercontinental Nigerian Restaurant $
5777 Cleveland Ave.
(614) 259-3951
www.intercontinentalnc.com
West African fare has been served at Intercontinental (formerly known as Lagos Peppersoup Corner) since 2011. The menu is small but represents regional dishes from quite a few different western countries. Choose from the classic spicy jollof rice topped with various proteins, yam dumplings, or okra stew. More adventurous eaters might appreciate the authentic amala soup with cow feet or tripe. A pleasant dining room awaits just inside a storefront in a shopping center.

Layla's Kitchen $
6152 Cleveland Ave.
(614) 882-5522
www.laylaskitchenonline.com
Laya's is one those gems you feel lucky to stumble on. It is known for well-seasoned, great-tasting Southeast Asian food and service with a smile. Come here for the fantastic home cooking

featuring mostly Indian cuisine, but also Tibetan momos. The menu is expansive, and you can choose your own heat level for most dishes. Layla's also has one of the hard-to-find Indian lunch buffets that is also a good value. Some of the go-to favorites are the chicken makhana (butter chicken), paneer specialties, and tandoori kebabs.

Mi Li Café $
5858 Emporium Sq.
(614) 899-9202
www.milicafe.com
Some say Mi Li serves the best banh mi in town, but you be the judge. Speaking from experience, I must admit it is a very good version. You will find all the traditional Vietnamese offerings done well. The pho, summer rolls, and vermicelli bowls are also popular with patrons. Having opened in 2005, Mi Li is a long-established and beloved anchor in Emporium Square. Parking is plentiful.

Riziki Swahili Grill $$
1872 Tamarack Circle S., Northland Area
(614) 547-7440
www.rizikiswahiligrill.com
The menu features authentic Swahili dishes from Zanzibar, an East African island known for its exotic spices and Arab and Portuguese influences on flavors. The female chef–owned restaurant showcases dishes inspired by street food and infused with heady spices like cardamom and cumin. The sit-down dining room pops with colors and decor that nods to island life. Chef Riziki Yussuf works tirelessly to turn out fantastic, flaky chapati flatbread to dip in anything you order. No alcohol is served, but grab a drink from the self-serve cooler or order a hand-pressed juice drink to take the edge off some of the fiery curries.

Wycliff's Kenyan Food $
2492 Home Acre Dr.
(614) 772-3461
www.wycliffskitchen.com
Humble Kenyan food is presented in the form of grilled meats in rich sauces, tender bone-in goat stew, and lots of vegetable side dishes, along with chapati flatbreads and samosa-like fried starters. Try out the traditional mukimo made of mashed potatoes, corn, and beans or the ugali, which is a

grits-like corn porridge topped with grilled meats. The storefront eatery is no-frills, but the food is truly authentic.

Yemeni Restaurant $$
5426 Cleveland Ave.
(614) 426-4000
www.yemenirestaurant.us

As the name suggests, truly authentic Yemeni food is on the menu, and this is one of only one or two other restaurants in the city serving it. East African, Indian, and Arab influences on the country's cuisine are seen in the variety of lamb, meat, and fish plates on the menu. Beautiful biryani, tandoori breads, and chicken cooked over hot stones are among the offerings. A favorite bite is the lamb consommé with spicy sauce served in a blazing hot stone bowl, sopped up with delicious flatbread. Aromatic spices waft throughout the dining room, and the service is attentive. If you have never tried Yemeni food, it is a rich and flavorful cuisine, and this no-frills restaurant is worth seeking out.

IMMIGRANT FOOD CORRIDORS

Rather than write an entry for every immigrant restaurant, it is easier to suggest a few parts of town where clusters of Indian, Mexican, African, and Asian restaurants have opened in the past decade. Although I did include many of these restaurants among the entries, Columbus has a few hubs of global dining that stretch several blocks along major roads. Look to Bethel Road for Indian, Thai, Vietnamese, and Korean. Morse Road and OH 161 are home to several African, Mexican, and Southeast Asian restaurants. The Japanese Marketplace on Kenny Road is home to one of Columbus's best Japanese restaurants, a casual noodle place, and a Japanese bakery. Nearby are more Thai, Indian, and Mexican. Check the top 10 lists throughout the chapter for suggestions on specific global cuisines.

OUTSKIRTS

Restaurants located outside the city, but within a reasonable drive.

BrewDog Tap Columbus $$
96 Gender Rd., Canal Winchester
(614) 908-3051
www.brewdog.com

The craft beer brewery, restaurant, and dog-friendly hotel is about 15 miles southeast of the city. The spacious, industrial taproom is one of the most popular breweries in the area for its almost 40 types of beer, an epic menu available for lunch and dinner, and the unique DogHouse Hotel with 32 beer-themed rooms. The menu features a lot of meat, ranging from huge rib eyes, juicy burgers, and crispy wings to brisket mac, tacos, and loaded fries. But vegetarians will appreciate that half the menu is plant-based, vegetarian, or vegan. Grab a beer and pick up a game of table-top shuffleboard, giant Jenga, corn hole, or any number of arcade games. The outdoor patio is huge and overlooks a lake and fenced-in dog park. The hotel is a beer lover's dream with in-room taps, shower beer fridges, and sleeping accommodations for your furry friend.

Ghostwriter Public House $$$
49½ S. Main St., Johnstown
(740) 809-1104
www.ghostwriterph.com

Go for dinner and stay the night. Ghostwriter is a modern riff on a tavern with food and accommodations. The seasonal menu of very well-curated American comfort food features locally sourced cheese and responsibly raised beef, chicken, and eggs. The guest rooms can be reserved through Airbnb.

Granville Inn $$$
314 E. Broadway, Granville
(740) 587-3333
www.granvilleinn.com

Charming downtown Granville, just 30 minutes east of Columbus, is as Americana as it gets. The historic inn was designed by local architect Frank Packard in 1924 as a golf club for railroad magnate

John Sutphin Jones. It remained in the family until Denison University purchased it in 2013 to serve as destination for lodging and fine food. The restaurant prides itself in serving classic appetizers and entrees but with a modern twist. The Old Oak Room is open for breakfast, lunch, dinner, and brunch on Sat and Sun. The cozy tavern has a beautiful central bar and fireplace, and is a lovely place to get a cocktail and small plates. In warmer months, the large flagstone patio is an ideal spot for dining alfresco.

Local Roots, Powell $$
15 E. Olentangy St., Powell
(614) 602-8060
www.localrootspowell.com
A menu full of all-Ohio chicken, pork, bison, and beef shows that the owners take their name seriously. All the meats are hormone-free, bread is sourced from local bakers, and even the produce comes from a nearby family farm. The offerings change often and seasonally, making for fresh dishes of even fresher food. The menu is a bit meat-heavy, but there are plenty of options for vegetarians to enjoy. Especially the desserts, many of which are also gluten free!

The Syndicate $$
213 S. Main St, Bellefontaine
(937) 210-5165
www.syndicatedowntown.com
In a small town about an hour from Columbus is a surprisingly nice restaurant housed in the former Jackson News Stand—hence the name. The dining room is airy and open and decorated with historical features from its past life, like newspapers and salvaged glass. The food makes headlines too, with chef-driven dishes using organic, locally sourced ingredients. The shareables are just a little different from what you generally see on a modern American menu, and the cheesy French onion soup alone makes it worth the drive. The mains are meaty but interesting, like pork schnitzel, Cajun shrimp, and cola-braised short ribs. The outdoor patio is large and festive.

COOKING CLASSES

The Mix Recreational Cooking Classes
Columbus State Community College
250 Cleveland Ave., downtown
(614) 287-5126
www.mix.cscc.edu
Columbus State's recreational program is open to the public, offering year-round hands-on cooking classes for adults and children, mixology workshops, and specialized baking courses. Learn to make sushi, paella, and beef Wellington or any number of global cuisines like Thai, Vietnamese, Indian, and Korean. Sign up for a multi-week French Sauce series or bring your best person for a date night where you together make a full menu and enjoy your sit-down meal with wine. Check out the website for ongoing class listings. Classes average around $90 per person and include wine with the meal. Parking in the lot and on the street must be paid through ParkCBUS or parking.com parking apps.

Quinci Emporium
11 Buttles Ave., Short North
(614) 370-2038
www.quinciemporium.com
The Short North's gourmet Italian market is both a retail shop carrying imported pastas, sauces, kitchenware, and table decor and a private kitchen for recreational cooking classes. A majority of the small classes are hands-on and focused on Italian dishes. Learn to make handmade pasta, various pestos, doughs, and sweet treats. Check the website frequently as classes fill up fast, though more are added every few months.

The Seasoned Farmhouse
3674 N. High St., Clintonville
(614) 230-6281
www.theseasonedfarmhouse.com
The boutique cooking school is an intimate place to take hands-on and demonstration-style cooking classes in a charming English country farmhouse-style kitchen. Small classes learn to make appetizers, entrees, and desserts in specialized seasonal classes, date nights, technical series, and

TOP 10 RESTAURANTS BY CATEGORY

AFRICAN
Addis Ethiopian Restaurant, Cleveland Avenue
Dabakh Senegalese Restaurant, Cleveland Avenue
Drelyse Ghanaian African Restaurant, Northland Area
Ginevre Somali Café, Morse Road Corridor
Hoyo's Somali Kitchen, North Market and Bridge Park, Dublin
Intercontinental Nigerian Restaurant, Cleveland Avenue
Lalibela Ethiopian Restaurant and Bar, Whitehall
Riziki Swahili Grill, Northland Area
Wycliff's Kenyan Food, Cleveland Avenue

BREAKFAST
Brekkie Shack, Grandview
DK Diner, Grandview
Emmett's Café, German Village
Fox in the Snow, Italian Village and German Village
HangOverEasy, Olde Towne East
Jack and Benny's Old North Diner, OSU
Katalina's, Victorian Village and Clintonville
La Chatelaine, Worthington and Upper Arlington
Starliner Diner, Hilliard
Tommy's Diner, Franklinton
Westerville Grill, Westerville

BRUNCH
Alchemy, Grandview and Parsons Ave.
The Guild House, Short North
Kitchen Social, Dublin and Polaris
Lindey's, German Village
Milestone 229, Downtown
Northstar Café, Short North and Clintonville
South of Lane, Upper Arlington
Tupelo Honey, Upper Arlington
Whitney House, Worthington
The Woodbury, Downtown

BURGERS
101 Beer Kitchen, Dublin and Westerville
Johnnie's Tavern, Trabue Road
O'Reilly's, Clintonville
Pat and Gracie's, Clintonville
Press Grill, Short North
Preston's: A Burger Joint, Clintonville
The Rail, Grandview and Dublin
The Ringside Café, Downtown
Rossi Bar and Kitchen, Short North
Thurman Café, German Village

CHINESE
Golden Phoenix, Cleveland Avenue
Mala Hotpot, Hilliard
Ming Flower, Westerville
Moy's, Ohio State's campus
NE Chinese Restaurant, Upper Arlington
Sun Tong Luck, Bethel Road
Sunflower Chinese Restaurant, Sawmill Road

Ty Ginger Dim Sum and Asian, Dublin
XiXia, Upper Arlington
Yaus Chinese Bistro, University District

COLUMBUS CLASSICS
Akai Hana, Upper Arlington
Barcelona, German Village
Basi Italia, Victorian Village
Giuseppe's Ritrovo, Bexley
Lindey's, German Village
Old Mohawk, German Village
The Refectory, Bethel Road
Schmidt's Sausage Haus, German Village
TAT Ristorante di Famiglia, East Columbus
Thurman Café, German Village
The Top, Bexley
Windward Passage, Upper Arlington

DONUTS
Buckeye Donuts, OSU Campus
Destination Donuts, Clintonville & North Market
DK Diner, Grandview
Donna's Delicious Donuts, Gahanna/New Albany
HoneyDip Donuts & Diner, Arlington
Lil Donut Factory, Hilliard
The Original Goodie Shop, Upper Arlington
Peace, Love, and Little Donuts, Worthington
Resch's Bakery, Whitehall
Schneider's Bakery, Westerville

ESSENTIAL EATERIES
Agni, Brewery District
Chapman Eats, German Village
La Tavola, Grandview
Lola & Giuseppe's Trattoria, Gahanna
Lupo on Arlington, Upper Arlington
Speck, Downtown
The Sycamore, German Village
Veritas, Downtown
Whitney House, Worthington

FOOD TRUCKS
www.centralohiofoodtrucks.org
Ajumama Korean, 1655 Old Leonard Ave.
Bella Lao Food, traveling locations
Cilantro Latin Bistro, 993 King Ave.
Cousins Maine Lobster, traveling locations
Dos Hermanos, traveling locations
Fetty's South African, traveling locations
Los Agavez Taqueria, 3166 N. High St.
Moon Pizza, 3861 Park Mill Run, Hilliard
Pitabilities, traveling locations
Ray Ray's Hog Pit, Franklington/6 locations
Schmidt's Sausage Truck, traveling locations
Street Thyme, traveling locations
Taqueria Los Primos, 233 W. Fifth Ave.
Texas Steel BBQ, 1060 King Ave.

GREEK/MEDITERRANEAN
Agape Mediterranean, Gahanna
Brassica, Bexley, Upper Arlington, Short North
Café Istanbul, Bexley, Dublin, Easton
Habibi Grill, Italian Village
Happy Greek, Short North
Lavash, Clintonville
Mazah, Grandview
Panini Opa, Sawmill Road
Yanni's, Cleveland Avenue
Yemeni Restaurant, Cleveland Avenue
Zaytoon Mediterranean Grill, Hilliard

INDIAN/HIMALAYAN
Aab, Grandview
Amul India, Sawmill Road
Awadh India, Bethel Road
Dosa Corner, Arlington
Everest, Worthington
Haveli Indian Bistro, Downtown
Layla's Kitchen, Cleveland Avenue
Momo Ghar, North Market
New India, Bethel Road
Taj Palace, Hilliard

JAPANESE/SUSHI
The 1126 Restaurant, Short North
Akai Hana, Upper Arlington
Domo Sushi Kitchen and Bar, Short North
Mr. Sushi, Historic Dublin
Rishi Sushi, Downtown
Song Lan, Dublin Bridge Park
Sushiko, Worthington Crosswoods
Tensuke Express/Sushi Ten, Upper Arlington
Wild Ginger, Hilliard
Yoshi's Japanese Restaurant, Dublin and Down-
town

MEXICAN
Agave and Rye, Short North and Grandview
Casa Mezcal Mexican Grill, Northland area
Cuco's Taqueria, Arlington
El Vaquero, several locations
Habanero's Fresh Mexican Grill, Hilliard
La Favorita, Sawmill Road
La Plaza Tapatia, Georgesville Road
Local Cantina, Grandview, multiple locations
Los Gauchos, Bethel Road
Nada Modern Mexican, Arena District

Latin/Spanish
Barcelona, German Village
Brazilian Grill and Bakery, Cleveland Avenue
Choripan Argentine Grill, Dublin

Cilantro Latin Restaurant, Sawmill Road
El Arepazo Latin Grill, German Village
Los Galopagos, South Grener Avenue, West Side
Lupo on Arlington, Upper Arlington
Si Señor Peruvian Sandwiches, Grandview
Starliner Diner, Hilliard

PAN-ASIAN/FUSION
Ampersand Asian Supper Club, Short North
Bonifacio Modern Filipino, Grandview
Eastern Bay, Upper Arlington
Helen's Asian Kitchen,
J. Liu, Dublin and Worthington
Jiu Thai Asian Café, Bethel Road
Lemongrass Fusion Bistro, Short North
Tai's Asian Bistro, Upper Arlington
Tiger + Lily, Downtown
Wild Ginger Asian Fusion, Hilliard and Worthington

RAMEN/NOODLES
Fukuryu Ramen, Upper Arlington, Dublin, Polaris
Hiro Raman and Tea, Sawmill Road
Kirin Noodle Bar, Clintonville
Kyushu Ramen Noodle Bar, Grandview
Lan Zhou Noodles, OSU Campus
Meshikou Ramen, Bethel Rd.
Red Rabbit Ramen, Grandview
Satori Ramen Bar, North Market
Tensuke Express, Arlington

SANDWICHES
Broad Street Bagels and Deli, Downtown
Brown Bag Deli, German Village
Goood Friends, inside Jackie O's, Downtown
Hot Chicken Takeover, Clintonville and Grandview
Katalina's Cafe, Harrison West and Clintonville
Katzinger's Delicatessen, German Village
The Lox Bagel Shop, Short North
Si Señor, Grandview
Smith's Deli, Clintonville
Warios Beef and Pork, Arena District and Clinton-
ville

THAI/VIETNAMESE
6-1-Pho, Clintonville
Buckeye Pho, Bethel Road
Erawan Thai, Refugee Road
GC Pho, Georgesville Road
Huong Vietnamese, Morse Road
Mi Li Vietnamese Café, Cleveland Avenue
Pho Asian Noodle House, Upper Arlington
Siam Orchid Thai Restaurant, Dublin
Thai Bamboo Kitchen, Bethel Road (carryout only)
Thai Grille, Westerville

other special events. Parking is found behind the building in a small lot or along High Street.

Young Chef's Academy
425 Beecher Rd., Gahanna
(614) 933-9700
www.ganannaoh.youngchefsacademy.com
The recreational cooking program is a great place for your budding chefs to take weekly one-off classes, or sharpen their skills in age- and skill-appropriate programs. KinderCooks teach ages 4 to 7 basic kitchen safety and culinary skills, while JuniorChefs and SeniorChefs build on the culinary skills. The academy also hosts culinary camps, workshops, and summer programming.

CATERING

You can easily order heaps of bagels from Panera or towers of Chipotle burritos, but the following are the best-rated locally owned catering companies that have been around for at least a decade. Among the services offered are menus with full buffets, heavy hors d'oeuvres, brunch, afternoon tea parties, barbecues, and backyard tented parties.

Bleu and Fig
(614) 348-3328
www.bleuandfig.com

Caterers Three
(614) 486-1330
www.caterersthree.com

Catering by Scott
(614) 237-1949
www.cateringbyscott.com

Milo's Catering
(614) 224-0272
www.cateringbymilos.com

Pastaria Catering Classics
(614) 228-2850
www.pastarianorthmarket.com

Simply Plated Catering
(614) 736-3771
www.simplyplatedco.com

Steven's Catering
(614) 486-1221
www.stevenscatering.com

Taste of the Best
(514) 358-4559
www.tasteofthebestcatering.com

BAKERIES AND SWEET SHOPS

**Anthony-Thomas Chocolates Factory
and Retail Store**
1777 Arlingate Ln.
(614) 272-9221, (877) CANDY-21 (226-3921)
www.anthony-thomas.com
This family-owned and -operated business produces an average of 50,000 pounds of chocolate, including the popular Buckeye candies, every year. Free tours of the factory are offered every Tues through Thurs from 10 a.m. to 2 p.m. More than a dozen retail stores are located throughout the Columbus area; see the website for locations and contact information for each retail store.

Bake Me Happy
500 E. Whittier, German Village
(614) 477-3642
www.bakemehappygf.com
Every item on the Bake Me Happy menu is gluten-free, and the bakers take their wheat-free work environment very seriously. They bring fun flavors to their sweets while using local ingredients like Krema peanut butter and Snowville cream. Some of the baked goods include brownies, scones, muffins, cookies, delicious mini bundts, and oatmeal cream sandwiches. Gluten-free cakes can be ordered in advance.

Belle's Bread Japanese Bakery and Café
1168 Kenny Centre Mall
(614)451-7110
www.bellesbread.com
A fun French-Japanese bakery is located within the Japan Marketplace in Kenny Centre. Everything is

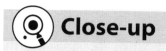

Close-up

Redefining Columbus Dining

Over the past decade, the Columbus food scene has evolved into a vibrant, global culinary land-scape thanks to brilliant chefs turning out innovative, modern dishes. Many of them cut their chops at fine-dining establishments in Columbus, while a few brought their global flavors from other states and countries. One of our nationally recognized chefs, Avishar Barua, made it far on *Top Chef* and hosts special events with other TC alum. After training in NYC, Avishar returned here to his hometown to share a unique fusion of his roots in Midwestern and Bangladeshi cuisine. Joya's is his casual breakfast place serving creative handhelds and other dishes with Southeast Asian flavors, while Agni is Chef Barua's live-fire fine-dining restaurant named for the Hindu god of fire. The six-course chef's menu is a culinary journey showcasing incredibly clever and playful combinations of techniques, flavors, and plating.

Meanwhile, it was chef Josh Dalton who led the charge in a tasting-menu-only dining experience when Veritas opened more than 10 years ago. The menus change seasonally, keeping it fresh for everyone. Chef Dalton's Italian concept, Speck, brings a little slice of Tuscany to downtown Colum-bus with new twists on old classics. Chef Andrew Smith and partner-wife, Devoney Mills, have been hosting the "by invite only" Roys Avenue Supper Club, where every menu is different and each small plate is thoroughly modern. We anticipate delicious things at their new restaurant, Isla in Merion Village. The small restaurant will seat only a handful of diners over two seatings and, like Roys, will be a coveted dining experience.

French/Italian-inspired 'Plas in the Short North is the brain-child of Jamie George, who chan-nels the Mediterranean countryside with house-made charcuterie and a rustic fine-dining menu with upscale, but unpretentious food. Argentinian-born chef Sebastian La Rocca has had a bit of a nomadic culinary career that took him to NYC, Miami, South America, and into kitchens and television in Costa Rica. La Rocca now leads Columbus's first live-fire restaurant, Fyr in the Hilton Hotel. As Food and Wine Ambassador of Argentina, he is bringing a sophisticated taste of Latin America to our city.

Rick Lopez is known for his small eateries, La Tavola in Grandview and Lupo in Upper Arlington, that prove how understated neighborhood restaurants can become destination dining. Yes, La Tavola is Italian, but upon closer inspection of the menu, you'll find some things that just aren't served on other local menus. Lupo on Arlington, with its Spanish-inspired small plates, gives Chef Lopez freedom to keep the tapas fresh and ever-evolving, which is a win for all of us.

A final place to point out would be Freedom a la Carte. Paula Haines is behind the wonderful scratch-made food and pastries with an extraordinary mission to create a safe place for victims of sex-trafficking. Here survivors work, heal, and learn self-sufficiency. Talk about food changing the landscape for someone!

Whether you want high-end tasting menus or whimsical handheld sandwiches, Columbus has no shortage of fantastic dining experiences that you can only find here. These visionary restaurateurs and chefs are redefining Columbus dining. There are many other chefs also doing great things, and we look forward to seeing how our food scene grows and evolves in the coming years.

made from scratch in-house daily. Not only does Belle's turn out traditional loaves of white and raising bread, but they also make a dozen flavored kashi-pan (sweet breads). The list of pastries and confections is impressive, ranging from Danishes and macarons to cookies and madeleines. The coolers carry pre-packaged cake pieces, and with advance notice, you can order great-quality round, sheet, tiered, or rolled cakes. If the bread and desserts weren't enough, Belle's also serves ice cream, sweet crepes, and savory sandwiches. There is small outdoor patio and a few benches.

The Cheesecake Girl
5354 Center St., Hilliard
Other locations in Dublin and Italian Village
(614) 787-1753
www.thecheesecakegirl.com
Who doesn't want to be friends with someone called the Cheesecake Girl? Local pastry chef Samantha Strange's mantra—"There are so many ways to cheesecake"—shines through on a menu full of classic full-size and mini cakes and not-so-traditional forms of the cheesy dessert. Creative and delicious cheesecake cookies and sandwiches, along with the more unusual cheesecake dip and push pop is why The Cheesecake Girl is consistently voted among the best desserts in town.

Crème de la Crème Bakery & Café
5311 Westpointe Plaza Dr., Hilliard
(614) 319-3005
Eastern Europe meets Italian and French bakery at this busy cafe off Hilliard Rome Road. The cases are packed full of colorful, unique pastries, tarts, macarons, eclairs, and slices of cakes and cheesecake. Coffees range from basic drip to fancy macchiatos. One of the special finds here is the affogato coffee—a shot of espresso over vanilla gelato. The savory menu is small but offers interesting items like khachapuri cheese–filled bread boats, salmon tartines, and Tuscan soup and sandwich combos. The quality of food is very good, but be patient with the service, as the place can become very busy, especially on the weekend. The indoor dining space is large and will be expanding, while the outdoor patio is open during nice weather. Crème de la Crème

is a pleasantly surprising family-owned bakery in an area full of chain restaurants and big-box stores.

Dan the Baker
1028 Ridge St., Grandview
(614) 928-9035
www.dan-the-baker.com
Tucked on a side street just off Dublin Road is a small but mighty bread shop, where Dan "the Baker" Riesenberger sells high-quality loaves and pastries until they run out. The menu changes weekly, but there are a few staples that remain the same, such as the olive polenta bread, baguettes, and various croissants. The shop is open from Thurs through Sun from 8 a.m. to 2 p.m., so get there early to score your favorites. Dan has recently added a few bread-baking classes to the menu.

Der Dutchman
445 Jefferson Ave., Plain City
(614) 873-3414
www.dhgroup.com/restaurants
If you want a stellar pie or homey Amish sweets, head west to the suburb of Plain City where Der Dutchman restaurant has a wholesale bakery that carries incredible (and huge) whole fruit and cream pies, muffins, donuts, and seasonal specials. The bakery is open from 7 a.m. until 7 p.m., closed on Sun.

Fox in the Snow
1031 N. Fourth St., Italian Village
(614) 826-0007
www.foxinthesnow.com
Fox in the Snow Cafe is a bakery and coffee shop serving up rustic-style baked goods and hand-poured drinks. It is beloved among locals and has been featured in national media outlets as one of the best breakfasts in Columbus. Other locations can be found in German Village, Historic Dublin, and New Albany.

Graeter's Ice Cream
Several locations
www.graters.com/columbus
Black Raspberry Chocolate Chip is Graeters all-time best-selling flavor, which has several locations

throughout the Columbus area. The Bethel Road store offers free tours of the ice-cream-making process and has a giant indoor playground for the kiddos; call (614) 442-7622 to schedule a tour.

Jeni's Ice Cream
Several locations
www.jenisicecreams.com

The ice creams and sorbets served up at these Columbus locations are handmade with unusual, sometimes savory ingredients; signature flavors include Salty Caramel, Brown Butter Almond Brittle, Gooey Butter Cake, and Milkiest Chocolate.

Just Pies
736 Northfield Rd., Westerville
(614) 818-9300
www.just-pies.com

This specialized bakery carries over 25 varieties of award-winning pies and has received national attention from Oprah and the Food Network, but what makes them so good? The fruit pies are stuffed with strawberries from California and raspberries from Oregon. Meringue and whipped cream are made daily from scratch. The secret? It's all in the crust. You'll never eat another pie once you have one of these. You can order three different-size pies, and seasonal pies show up through the year. Just Pies are carried at local markets like Weiland's and the Hills Market. Gluten-free pies are not available.

Krema Nut Company
1000 Goodale Blvd., Grandview
(614) 299-1636
www.krema.com

While shopping, try not to miss some of the local businesses that have become Columbus institutions. The city is home to the nation's oldest commercial peanut butter manufacturer, the Krema Nut Company, where you can take a tour and see how peanut butter is made. The company has been working with nuts since 1898 and specialize in the production of gourmet nuts, trail mix, hand-dipped chocolates, and all-natural peanut butter. Throughout most of the year, gourmet PB&J sandwiches are served in the store, where

---

TOP 10 ICE CREAM SHOPS

Whit's, Rita's, Shake Shack, and DQ make a strong showing in Columbus, but there are great family-owned ice-cream shops and fun milkshake bars to facilitate a brain freeze.

Coppa Gelato, Westerville
CRMD Ice Cream Shop, Short North
Diamonds Ice Cream, Sawmill Rd.
Graeters, many locations
Handel's Homemade Ice Cream, Hilliard and Powell
Jeni's, many locations
Johnson's Real Ice Cream, Bexley
Little Ladies Soft Serve, Westerville
Toft's Grand Scoop, Grandview
The Yard Milkshake Bar, Short North

---

you can shop for all sorts of nuts, nut butters, and other nutty gifts.

Pattycake Bakery
3870 N. High St., Clintonville
(614) 784-2253
www.pattycakebakery.com

The vegan, organic baked goods that come from Pattycake are "conscientious sweets handmade with love." As a "worker-owned cooperative," the team of bakers contribute different items, with some "house favorites" regularly on the menu. All the ingredients are 100 percent natural. It is carry-out only, with a small amount of outdoor seating.

Pistacia Vera
541 S. Third St., German Village
(614) 220-9070
www.pistaciavera.com

Pistacia Vera is the total dessert experience. Pastry chef Spencer Budros was a 2020 James Beard semifinalist in the Outstanding Baker category, which explains why this sweet kitchen turns out some of the city's most beautiful and artisanal desserts, especially the macarons. The menu includes an ever-changing selection of eclairs, tarts, pastries, and dessert breads. It also serves a short list of classic croques, quiches, and salads for brunch and lunch. The shop is open seven days a week from 7 a.m. until 3 p.m.

Resch's Bakery
4061 E. Livingston Ave., Whitehall
(614) 237-7421
www.reschbakery.com

As one of the longest-operating bakeries in Columbus, the Resch family has been serving cakes, pies, breads, donuts, and other desserts since 1912. The bakery has been in its current quaint storefront since the 1960s. The donuts are among the most popular items on the menu, so be sure to get there early if you want the favorite cinnamon or bow tie donuts. You can't go wrong with any of the old-school European-style Danishes, turnovers, cream horns, eclairs, or coffee cakes. Resch's also makes wedding cakes and other special-occasion cakes as well as seasonal desserts. The bakery is open unusually long hours, Mon through Sat 8 a.m. until 6 p.m., closed on Sun.

Schneider's Bakery
6 S. State St., Westerville
(614) 882-6611
www.schneiders-bakery.com

Schneider's Bakery has been a local favorite in Uptown Westerville since 1957. Donuts, pastries, pies, and tarts are among the freshly baked goods made on-site. It's the sort of place generations have been taking their kids to with memories of hauling away big boxes of donuts. It's that kind of place.

The Original Goodie Shop
2116 Tremont Center, Upper Arlington
(614) 488-8777
www.theoriginalgoodieshop.net

Though some people come here for fresh quiche and chicken potpie, dessert is always the main course. Glass cases are lined with colorful frosted cookies, cupcakes, and fruit squares. Kids love the frosted, flavored bubble gum, and everyone loves the buckeyes. The non-yeast, salt-rising breads are

a must, but the most popular temptation is the cinnamon sticks. Made with butter, cinnamon, and butterscotch, they double as breakfast or dessert.

Tous les Jours
2852 Olentangy River Rd., University District
(614) 372-5158
www.tljus.com

Tous les jours means "every day" in French, but the French-Asian bakery (albeit franchised) turns out anything but your run-of-the-mill desserts. The bread is baked every day and the dessert cases hold an impressive number of daily-made artisan pastries, cakes, and other sweet and savory items, also baked in-store. It also serves very nice coffees, espressos, and smoothies.

Woodhouse Bakery and Coffee Shop
19 W. Russell St., Short North
(614) 972-6069
www.woodhousevegan.com

The intimate fast-casual bakery and cafe located off a side street in the Short North serves up vegan specialties. You can get your hands on great scones, coffee cakes, and crumbles among the daily bakes and oat milk lattes and other dairy-free drinks for dine-in or carryout. Woodhouse never uses animals, eggs, or animal milk.

COFFEE AND TEA SHOPS

Caffeine junkies can get their fix quite effortlessly in Columbus. With no fewer than 40 Starbucks and about a dozen Dunkins, it is easy to do the drive-through in a pinch, but there are so many wonderful local coffeehouses where you can have a local caffeinated experience. Coffee aficionados may want to try out some of the independently owned spots around town that roast their own beans and serve delicious house-made pastries and sandwiches.

Columbus has many casual coffee shops perfect for intimate conversations on overstuffed sofas or cozy patios. There are plenty of spots in which to study or work the day away, knowing your next jolt of caffeine is just a few steps away. Whether you want tea or coffee, you can have a perfect pour in any sort of environment you prefer. Most listed here carry some sort of food or snacks and usually have Wi-Fi.

Brioso Coffee Bar
53 N. High St., downtown
(614) 228-8366
www.cafebrioso.com
Second location at 329 E. Long St., downtown

Coffee Connections
4004 Main St., Hilliard
(614) 664-3993
https://connections.coffee/

Crimson Cup Coffee and Tea
2468 Northwest Blvd., Upper Arlington
(614) 641-7020
www.crimsoncup.com
Second location at 4541 N. High St.,
    Clintonville

Fox in the Snow
1031 N. Fourth St., Italian Village
www.foxinthesnow.com
Other locations in German Village, Historic
    Dublin, and New Albany

German Village Coffee Shop
193 Thurman Ave., German Village
(614) 443-8900
www.gvcoffeeshop.com

Java Central Café and Roaster
20 State St., Westerville
(614) 839-0698
https://javacentral.coffee/

Kafe Kerouac Coffee House and Bar
2250 N. High St., OSU Campus
(614) 299-2672
www.kafekerouac.com

Little Moon Café and Tea
2899 N. High St., Clintonville
(614) 956-6468
www.littlemooncolumbus.com

Mission Coffee Co.
2060 S. High St.
(614) 300-0648
www.missioncoffeeco.com

Parable Cafe
149 S. High St., downtown
(614) 972-6001
https://parable.coffee

Qamaria Yemeni Coffee Co.
3221 Hilliard Rome Rd., Hilliard
(614) 742-7110
www.qamariacoffee.com

Roaming Goat Coffee
849 N. High St., Short North
(614) 294-2489
www.roaminggoatcoffee.com

Roosevelt Coffeehouse
300 E. Long St., downtown
(614) 670-5228
www.roaseveltcoffee.org
Other locations in Franklinton and Lewis
    Center

Stauf's Coffee Roasters
1277 Grandview Ave., Grandview
(614) 486-4861
www.staufs.com
Other location in German Village and
    Victorian Village

ZenCha Tea Salon
982 N. High St., Short North
(614) 421-2140
www.zen-cha.com

WINE, BARS, AND BREWERIES

Columbus, like any other big city, has the whole gamut of drinking possibilities. Pick your poison and pick your people. It's likely you'll find something that tickles your fancy. There are noisy pubs for the rowdy, and sophisticated wine bars for the restrained. There are sports bars and pick-up bars. There are places you can hunker down all night and areas you can bar-hop until your coach turns into a pumpkin. All you need to know is what you enjoy.

For the restless soul who likes a change of scenery throughout the course of the evening, there are a few areas with a concentrated number of bars and pubs within a few blocks' radius. Grandview and the Short North are good neighborhoods to park and walk to multiple locations. Grandview is quainter (and a little more residential) than the trendy Short North, but both have equally established watering holes that cater to a wide range of thirsts and budgets.

The Arena District is known for its lively bars hosting a younger crowd who want to drink and carouse. German Village and the Brewery District are home to several longtime established taverns. Fabulous rooftop bars have come into being as new hotels have been built taller than ever.

This chapter does not list every watering hole in town, but instead pinpoints the drinking establishments unique to Columbus and popular within different age groups. For consistency, the bars are listed in their respective neighborhoods, while The Ohio State University chapter has its own section dedicated to the pub crawl.

You may notice the drinking chapter is not as long as the dining chapter. That blurry fusion of restaurant and bar makes it tough to determine where to list some places. Many of the restaurants in the previous chapter have full-service bars that are frequented more for their drinks than their food. Likewise, many of the bars in this chapter can satisfy your hunger well into the night. Many of the entries here are bars with great food.

Basically, if the word *pub* or *tavern* is in the name, it's in this chapter. If the bar is well-known for tailgating or game-day specials, it's in this chapter. More and more places in Columbus have outdoor patios with happy hour deals, music, and activities during the summer months. They too are included here.

Hopefully, this cross section of drinking establishments will illustrate the abundance of carousing that is to be had in our city. Normally, you can carouse till midnight or 1 a.m., but check the websites to be sure.

Whatever your capacity to imbibe, do so with responsibility. As anywhere, drinking while driving is prohibited and strictly enforced. Please see the Area Overview chapter for alcohol-related statistics and laws. If you happen to overindulge, remember that Columbus rideshares exist for a reason. Just let the hosts or bartenders know, and they will help you find a ride home.

DOWNTOWN/FRANKLINTON

Places in downtown Columbus tend to close down in the 10 o'clock hour, but the breweries and some bars do stay open later. The bars listed here are long-established watering holes along with some newer hot spots. Of course, all the major hotels have their own bars, but only those with rooftop bars or interesting spaces are included here.

Rehab Tavern
456 W. Town St., Franklinton
(614) 220-5665
www.rehabtavern.com

They tried to make me go to rehab; I said, "Let's do it!" The hole-in-the-wall neighborhood dive bar has all the grit and character of one that has been here for 50 years, but the interior is clean and updated while preserving the earlier bar features. Rehab serves craft cocktails, domestic and hand-crafted beers, and mason jar cocktails. The small menu has some of the usual pub grub appetizers and a list of paninis. The vibe is a combination of local yocal and a little hipster. The old-school bar has a juke box, trivia games, and an outdoor patio.

The Ringside Café
19 N. Pearl St.
(614) 228-7464
www.ringsidecolumbus.com

This 125-year-old tavern, once a speakeasy during Prohibition, is arguably Columbus's oldest sports bar. The dark bar, full of antiques and weary business folk, is tucked in a little alley between all the big buildings. It has decent happy hour prices, and the menu consists of sandwiches and burgers named for famous boxers. The Ringside is more of a lunch and happy hour spot and closes around 8 p.m. It is not open on Sun.

Slammers Bar
202 E. Long St.
(614) 221-8880
www.slammersbar.com

Every night is ladies night at Slammers. The casual LGBTQ+-centric bar has been around for 30 years, making it one of Columbus's oldest lesbian bars, yet welcomes everyone. Slammers can become quite busy, and the patio can be packed in the summer months. The kitchen turns out pizzas, subs, and a selection of typical bar bites as appetizers. Street parking is available, but pay attention to the paid parking zones.

Stories on High
404 N. High St.
(614) 4845285
www.storiesonhigh.com

Zip up to the 28th floor of the Hilton downtown for stellar 360-degree views over Columbus from the city's highest rooftop bar. The decidedly Asian-inspired menu has tapas-style shareables with a heavy nod toward Japanese items like sushi, yakitori, and wagyu dishes. The bar has a well-rounded selection of handcrafted cocktails, wine, interesting beers, ciders, and sakes by the glass. The views are unrivaled. Guests must be 21 or older to enter.

BREWERIES

Columbus has a number of breweries that have been around for a while, with Columbus Brewing Company (CBC) being the granddaddy of them all. Others made a name for themselves more recently or have moved into the Columbus market from other Ohio locations. Most places listed here either serve food, allow patrons to bring in food, or arrange for food trucks to be nearby.

BrewDog, Franklinton, Short North, Canal Winchester
Columbus Brewing Company, West Side and Historic Trolley District
Combustion Brewery and Taproom, Clintonville
Derive Brewing Company, Clintonville
Endeavor Brewing and Spirits, Grandview
Hoof Hearted Brewery, Italian Village
Jackie O's, Downtown
L. Hoster Brewing Company, Whitehall
Land Grant Brewing Company, Franklinton
Ohio Brewing Company, Italian Village
Seventh Son Brewing Co., Italian Village
Wolf's Ridge Brewing, Downtown
Yellow Springs Brewery Taproom, Clintonville

Tip Top Kitchen and Cocktails
73 E. Gay St.
(614) 221-8300
www.tiptopcolumbus.com

Tip Top has been a downtown neighborhood bar for the past 15 years. Its quirky name came from local TV celebrity Flippo the Clown's old show called *Tip Top Bandwagon*. Historic photos, paintings, pottery, and randomly donated paraphernalia deck the walls of the extremely casual bar. It serves great whiskey concoctions and other fine libations, including PBR always for $2. The menu consists of "Ohio Comfort Food," including a pot roast sandwich that sits comfortably in the belly. Check out brunch on Saturday and Sunday.

The Walrus Kitchen and Public House
142 E. Main St.
(614) 817-1710
www.thewalruscolumbus.com

The downtown pub offers more than 30 beers on draft, a full wine and bar list, and a menu full of nicely done comfort food. You can get your karaoke and trivia on throughout the week and catch some live music on the weekends. The lively bar has a huge number of big-screen TVs, so it's a great place to watch a game with friends or play a round of pool or Ping Pong.

Wolf's Ridge Brewing
214 N. Fourth St.
(614) 429-3936
www.wolfsridgebrewing.com

The popular downtown brewery boasts an extensive beer selection and is also a beloved restaurant for its better-than-average brewpub menu. Brunch and dinner are served in the dining room with menus focused on seasonal flavors using Ohio ingredients. Each month the dining room features a fun thematic prix fixe menu like New Orleans or Asian street food. The more casual taproom serves up small plates, flights of beer, ciders, cocktails, and beer and wine by the glass, which are discounted during weekday happy hours. Check out Wolf Ridge's sister bar, Understory at the Open Air School, 2571 Neil Ave.

GERMAN VILLAGE/BREWERY DISTRICT

The brick streets and cozy brownstones are a reminder that this historic district is home to some of the oldest taverns in Columbus. Parking can be a challenge, but you are never far from a popular watering hole. Merion Village is just south of German Village.

Antiques on High
714 S. High St.
(614) 725-2070
www.antiquesonhigh.com

The sister brewery to Seventh Son Brewing focuses on producing tart and wild beers, hazy IPAs, and pale ales. Wine lovers will find a nicely curated selection of California and Italian wines, and the craft cocktails here are dynamite! The food menu consists of tapas-style small plates and snacky charcuterie offerings.

Classic Victory's Sports Bar
547 S. High St.
(614) 225-1577

German Village's divey sports bar is a village fixture. Victory's is nothing fancy, but it's an easy, casual place to catch a game on one of the many bar TVs, play some pool, and share standard bar food, like pizzas and wings, on the covered patio. It can get pretty hectic during Crew matches and Buckeye games.

DISTILLERIES

Columbus boasts several micro-distilleries, craft spirit distilleries, and a meadery.

451 Spirits, Clintonville
Brother's Drake Meadery, Old North
Echo Spirits, Grandview
Highbank Distillery Co., Grandview
Middle West Spirits, Old North
Watershed Distillery, Old North

Club 185
185 E. Livingston Ave.
(614) 228-3904
www.club185.com

This friendly neighborhood bar was established in 1954 and attracts a wide demographic of clientele, from young professional 20-somethings to fun-loving retirees, politicians, hipsters, and everyone in between. In typical German Village style, the interior bricks are exposed, the bar is dark, and the ceiling is tin. Folksy art and window nook seating provide a certain amount of coziness. The atmosphere is convivial, but there's no escaping the noisiness of the place. When it comes to food, it's known for its tasty scratch-made family recipes that your arteries may rebel against. You can get food until midnight.

Ferdinand Lounge
491 S. Fourth St.
(614) 928-3898
www.bistrolino614/ferdinand

The eclectic lounge is adjacent to Bistrolino Old World Kitchen and named for the owner's favorite bar in Beirut. This cozy venue is an easy place to grab a handcrafted cocktail and hang out on one of the jewel-toned sofas or highback chairs. The drink menu excels with whiskey and scotch, while many local spirits are used in the creative drinks. It's a nice spot to end your evening after a lovely dinner in the German Village.

Hey Hey Bar and Grill
361 E. Whittier St.
(614) 445-9512
www.heyheybaroh.com

This is about as friendly-neighborhood-dive-bar as it gets. The mantra is "a bar so nice, they named it twice!" The service is great, and the drinks are strong. It's the kind of place you can do shots, play darts or pool, catch some live music, or enjoy a Saturday night heap of wings or a Sunday hangover burger. The outdoor space behind the brick building is quite large, with a fire pit and casual patio seating. Hey Hey is open into the wee hours of the morning.

ROOFTOP PATIOS

The past few years have seen a burst of rooftop restaurants and bars offering panoramic views around the city, Stories on High being most elevated on the 28th floor of the downtown Hilton.

Brass Eye, Junto Hotel, Franklinton
Budd Dairy Hall, Italian Village
Goodale Station, Hilton Canopy, Arena District
Lincoln Social Rooftop, Short North
Little Rock Bar, Italian Village
Lumin Sky Bar and Kitchen, AC Hotel, Downtown
Mandrake Rooftop, Short North
RH Rooftop Restaurant, Easton
Stories on High, Hilton, Downtown
VASO, AC Hotel, Dublin

High Beck Corner Tavern
564 S. High St.
(614) 224-0886

This lively (and dark) dive bar is one of the oldest watering holes in town. The clientele is unpretentious. A small patio out front overlooks High Street, allowing you to watch all the comings and goings. It's an easy place to grab a beer, pizza, and play a round of pool or Ping Pong. Food is available for lunch, and dinner is served almost until closing seven days a week. It is open from 11 a.m. to 2 a.m.

The Laundry/Hausfrauhaven
769 S. Third St.
(614) 443-3680
www.hausfrauhaven.com

The popular neighborhood wine bar draws a broad demographic of people ranging from their 20s into their 80s. As the name suggests, the last coin-operated laundromat in the area was converted into a sleek new bar serving wine by the glass or bottle, a few beers on draft, and limited munchies. Pick up a bottle from the wine shop, and for a small corking fee you can enjoy the vino at a table or the wine-tasting counter.

Law Bird
740 S. High St.
(614) 636-1053
www.lawbird.com
The cocktail and wine bar menu here is playful to say the least. The "weird, but good" cocktails are named things like Chaos Theory, Return of the Mack, and Thugz Passion—and the flavor combinations are no less quirky, but unexpectedly fun and tasty! The Stirred and Sophisticated cocktails incorporate tahini or cinnamon toast crunch into the cocktail bases, while Slam and Shake drinks are refreshing familiar flavors. Then there are the Weird and Wonderful drinks, where you have to just trust the cocktailian masters at work. As the sign in the bar reads, "not governed by reason." The bar menu has enough options to take the edge off your hunger and keep you thirsty!

The Old Mohawk
819 Mohawk St.
(614) 444-7204
www.theoldmohawk.com
The casual and friendly Old Mohawk is known for its horseshoe-shaped bar and Tiffany lamps with dancing turtles. Great service complements the hearty, rib-sticking food. As one of the village's oldest pubs, this neighborhood hangout has been acquiring all sorts of savory regulars since it opened in 1933. The menu has your usual collection of bar fare and entrees. Among the more popular items are the Mother Mohawk sandwich (a grilled roast beef and Swiss on rye) and the legendary turtle soup.

Plank's Biergarten
888 S. High St.
(614) 443-4570
This old-fashioned beer garden opened in 1960 and is known as much for its pizza as its large selection of beers and microbrews. Most of Columbus is familiar with the Plank family's name, but this sports bar is not to be confused with Plank's Cafe (same family). The atmosphere is casual, and the exposed brick walls and wooden floors are typical of German Village. One can veg out in front of the big-screen TV with "The Works," a pizza loaded with every available topping, then wash it down with one of the 10 beers on tap, or choose from the 40 bottles. During the summer months, move your party outside to the patio, where there are picnic tables and several TVs. Plank's Biergarten has live music on selected nights, and it delivers year-round.

Thurman Café
183 Thurman Ave.
(614) 443-1570
www.thethurmancafe.com
Thurman's began as a pub in 1937, so it has had almost 90 years to gather the eclectic memorabilia that covers the walls. It has garnered national attention for its Thurmanator, an insanely huge double-stacked burger. Most will agree that Thurman's makes not only the best burger in town but also one of the biggest (if you consider 28 ounces big). Vegetarians will, no doubt, take pleasure in the great steak fries. The worst thing about Thurman's is the wait for a table. The fun and casual atmosphere attracts people from all around Columbus. Food is served until 1· a.m., making it a great stop for a late-night snack and drinks.

Tremont Lounge
708 S. High St.
(614) 444-2042
www.facebook.com/TremontColumbus
Since 1987, this gay-owned LGBTQ+-friendly bar has been a cornerstone gay bar in Columbus. It serves what might be the cheapest drinks in town in a recently renovated but casual environment where you can also play pool.

ARENA DISTRICT

The Arena District is 1 block west of the Greater Columbus Convention Center and centered around Nationwide Arena and Huntington Park. Chain restaurants and bars have come and gone, but a few independently owned operations can be found. Parking options include surface lots, garages, and street meters.

Betty's Bar
435 W. Nationwide Blvd.
(614) 225-9195

Betty's Bar has been serving drinks and cheering on Columbus sports teams for more than six decades. The tiny house-like bar is tucked around the corner from the heart of the Arena District, so you could walk right by it. It's a friendly neighborhood bar that can get pretty rowdy during games.

Brother's Bar & Grill
477 N. Park St.
(614) 221-0673, (614) 232-9020
www.brothersbar.com

During the week, Brother's draws more of an after-work crowd with its TVs, pool tables, and happy hour specials, but come the weekend, think spring break. It seems everyone in Columbus who has recently turned 21 winds up here. Aside from the attractive 20-something crowd, the pool table and fire pits are the other big draws. With the summertime comes an outdoor patio for dining and drinking under the stars. The adjacent Gaswërks draws a slightly older crowd but is under the same ownership.

Gaswërks
487 Park St.
(614) 228-1988
www.gaswerksbar.com

The easy, casual bar is a good place to grab a drink and food before a concert, baseball, or hockey game or just belly up to the very big bar to catch a game on TV. Gaswërks has a youthful vibe and an arcade area. It also has an outdoor patio with seating and corn hole.

Parlay Sporting Club and Kitchen
570 N. High St.
(614) 812-0200
www.parlaycolumbus.com

The modern sports bar is not your average divey pub. It's a bright, modern space with 100 TVs, buckets of beer, and a full restaurant menu that serves slightly higher-end bar food. Parlay has private rooms where you can gather, or head into the man cave or sky lodge seating to watch any number of sports being broadcast, including hockey, soccer, golf, and motorsports. The menu offers an interesting mix of items, such as Bang Bang Shrimp and curry mussels, along with

LGBTQ+ Bars
Axis Nightclub, Short North
Boscoe's, Merion Village
Cavan Irish Pub, Merion Village
Club Diversity, Brewery District
District West, Downtown
O'Connor's Club 20, Old North
Slammers, Downtown
SouthBend Tavern, Merion Village
Tremont Lounge, German Village
Union Café, Short North

burgers, salads, handhelds, and pastas. Even the jello shots are house-made.

R-Bar
415 N. Front St.
(614) 221-4950
www.rbararena.com

The popular hockey-themed bar serves up typical pub fare in a bustling sports bar atmosphere. It shows all international and NHL games on more than 30 big screens, including on the outdoor patio. Daily drink specials and a full kitchen menu are available seven days a week.

i Pub crawlers never look out of place in Grandview, or in the Short North, during the monthly Gallery Hop or Grandview Hop. The Gallery Hop, which happens the first Sat of each month, is a fun way to check out local artisan craft stalls or visit retail shops and galleries that stay open later. The Grandview Hop is a summertime night market that takes place the last Sat of each month.

SHORT NORTH

The Short North Arts District is a fun place to people-watch and progressively eat and drink. Stroll 14 blocks to experience a melting pot of alternative and trendy, casual, and upscale watering holes. There are a few rooftop bars along High Street.

Barley's Brewing Company, Alehouse No. 1
467 N. High St.
(614) 228-2537
www.barleysbrewing.com

Columbus's oldest operating brewpub has been serving Barley's traditionally brewed ales, stouts, and seasonal beers since 1992. A rare, gas-fired brew kettle caramelizes the malt for their flagship ale, MacLenny's Scottish Ale, a must for beer lovers.

Barley's is situated across the street from the convention center, making it a convenient meeting point. The spacious oak bar and dining room have a lot of seating, TVs, and a few dartboards. The menu is varied and consists of reasonably priced American and British fare. Mildred's sauerkraut balls and the piled-high nachos top the list of popular appetizers. You can also take home a jug of your favorite Barley's brew in a growler, refillable as quickly as you can drink it.

Bodega
1044 N. High St.
(614) 299-9399
www.columbusbodega.com

Bodega, which means "corner store" in Spanish, is nothing of the sorts, but rather a small, Euro-style sandwich bar with more than 50 beers on tap—perhaps the most in Columbus—and a nice variety of wines. It has a laid-back vibe, and people more or less come here for the happy hour specials and beer varietals.

BrewDog
1175 N. High St.
(614) 908-3053
www.brewdog.com

Some of the best craft beer in Columbus is made by local beer crusaders BrewDog, whose huge main taphouse is outside the city in Canal Winchester. The Short North taproom carries two dozen beers on tap and offers weekday happy hours and wings, sandwiches, and appetizers by Ox-B's. What sets BrewDog apart is the Kennels Hotel attached to the taproom. In proper pub form you can enjoy some drinks and mosey up to your modern-industrial hotel room for a city stay. Of course, your furry friends are also welcome for a city stay, and dog beds can be provided.

Mac's Proper Pub
693 N. High St.
(614) 221-6227
www.macsproperpub.com

Mac's has the inviting nature and atmosphere of a true Scottish pub, not to mention a huge selection of imported and domestic beers that flow all day. The walls are decorated with paraphernalia from the British Isles and golf towels from various courses. Wooden floors and booths give the spacious place a pub-like warmth, while garage-door-style windows open the dining room to the sidewalk during warmer weather. Bring your best mate along for a Scotch egg or cottage pie, then shoot a game of pool in the back room. It's open seven days a week.

Press Grill
741 N. High St.
(614) 298-1014
www.pressgrill.net

This friendly neighborhood bar is the more-casual counterpart of the Rossi just up the street. The patrons range from groups and solo diners to businesspeople and late-nighters looking for a burger. The menu is full of simple but delicious comfort food at a decent price. The basic Press Burger with a fried egg is one of the most popular choices. You can even get Thanksgiving dinner every Thursday! The narrow bar is often crowded with drinkers till the wee hours, and lucky for them the kitchen is open till midnight.

Rossi Kitchen & Bar
895 N. High St.
(614) 525-0624
www.rossikitchenandbar.com

The Rossi is a longtime neighborhood bar with a bit of a supper club feel. The first thing that grabs your attention is the long, mahogany 1930s bar that looks straight out of Chicago—because it is! The clientele that packs into the Rossi is urban and professional, creating a cool vibe without being overly trendy. It's a comfortable place still buzzing with energy after all these years, the sort of place that entices you to belly up to the pretty bar and have a drink while waiting for your table.

Short North Tavern
674 N. High St.
(614) 221-2432
Some places never change. This Short North institution is the longest-standing neighborhood bar
in the Short North, so it is well lived in and loved.
It's been serving up soups, subs, chili, and pasta
for ages, and no doubt many a grandfather has
tied one on here. There are dartboards and the
space can get pretty noisy, which is a sign of a
good time being had by all. Food is available, but
be patient with the kitchen. The pizza is worth
the wait.

Union Café
630 N. High St.
(380) 239-2728
www.unioncafe.com
Dozens of TVs buzzing with music videos line
the walls of this longtime Short North gay bar.
Music videos, sitcoms, and OSU games are piped
in on a weekly basis, while karaoke takes over
Friday nights. This hot spot serves a full range of
home-cooked small plates, handhelds, burgers,
and entrees in a fun atmosphere. The drink menu
has an extensive selection of martinis, bombs, and
shots. Throughout the week expect happy hour
specials, drag shows, karaoke, trivia, and brunch.

ITALIAN VILLAGE

City Tavern
697 N. Fourth St.
(614) 826-2348
www.citytaverncolumbus.com
The spacious, laid-back pub serves craft beers and
burgers, sandwiches, and wraps in a somewhat
industrial-modern setting. The full bar has a wall
of whiskey and offers daily specials on old-school
beers like PBR and Miller High Life as well as daily
shots and a beer of the month. City Tavern hosts
trivia night and has several screens to watch the
games.

Little Rock Bar
944 N. Fourth St.
(614) 824-5602
www.littlerockbar.net

The hip little bar is a relaxed place to grab a craft
beer from a sizable beer list or a frozen cocktail.
Enjoy it along with some pubby shareables or a
pizza by the fire pit on the rooftop patio.

Seventh Son Brewing Co.
1101 N. Fourth St.
(614) 421-2337
www.seventhsonbrewing.com
One of the anchors of Italian Village, Seventh Son
has been serving up one of Columbus's most
popular local brews since 2013 from its rustic tasting room on Fourth. Seventh Son is known for its
bright IPAs and ales, including the popular easy-
drinking Nimbus. The taproom does not serve
food, but provides on its website a daily schedule
of food trucks that will be parked outside. Indoor
and patio seating is plentiful.

VICTORIAN VILLAGE

The Vic Village Tavern
251 W. Fifth Ave.
(614) 299-2295
www.thevvtavern.com
This neighborhood haunt stocks a lot of old-
school beers, like PBR, Blatz, and Miller High Life,
in a casual bar atmosphere. The exposed brick
walls lined with booths, mirrors, and beer signs
lend the space a pubby feel. Plenty of TVs around
the bar and dining area make this an easy spot to
catch a game.

Zeno's Victorian Village
384 W. Third Ave.
(614) 294-9158
www.zenoscolumbus.com
A little bit of trivia: This friendly neighborhood pub
in Harrison West lays claim to having the city's sec-
ond-longest bar. This is a fun, casual place, with a
dining room that serves chili, pizzas, salads, sandwiches, and the usual late-night nosh. The clientele is a mix of locals and students of all ages. The
lower level is home to Dick's Dive, a 1970s-inspired
bar with no windows, no frills, and groovy music.
The bar is open late from Thurs through Sun and
closes at midnight earlier in the week.

CLINTONVILLE/BEECHWOLD

Bob's Bar
4961 N. High St.
(614) 888-9073
www.facebook.com/Bobs-Bar.com

The local-yocal dive bar has dubbed itself the "Cultural Hub of the Midwest" for the lively patrons who have passed through its doors since opening in 1978. Blink and you might drive right by, but if you end up inside, you'll be faced with a wide variety of beers on tap, cocktails, and a full bar. The place is not fancy, and neither are the clientele, but expect the vibe to be cheerful and the demographics to be varied. Also appealing are the bar games and happy hour specials.

Yellow Springs Brewery Taproom
2855 Indianola Rd.
(614) 261-7128
www.yellowspringsbrewery.com

Another popular brewery from Athens, Ohio, has moved into the Columbus market. The casual tap-room has a beer menu with about a dozen offerings including ales, IPAs, and stouts. A handful of classic cocktails and a reasonably priced, but small snack and sandwich menu are also available. The seating indoors is plentiful, and picnic tables on the all-season patio are another option.

OHIO STATE AREA/OLD NORTH

Dick's Den
2417 N. High St.
(614) 268-9573

This cool neighborhood dive is a Columbus staple for jazz and live music among the over-30 set. The bar has been around since 1964, and the decor is a friendly reminder of this. Time-worn bar stools, picnic tables, and a jukebox that plays only vintage soul and jazz create a "Beat" atmosphere, which is only enhanced by jazz-backed poetry readings and annual tributes to Jack Kerouac. Cheap drinks, cheap covers, and loyal jazzheads add to the small bar's divey appeal. The musical smorgasboard at Dick's Den includes everything from jazz and blues to funk and folk, while local bands draw faithful followings. No worries about

the friendly fellas milling about the entrance. They are there to collect a nominal cover charge and card anyone who looks under 50!

Ledo's Tavern
2608 N. High St.
(614) 263-1009
www.ledostavern.com

This simple neighborhood bar on the corner of High and Duncan has been around forever and draws a young Clintonville and campus clientele. Ohio State students converge on the place later in the evenings, when each night brings different drink and food specials. You are also guaranteed plenty of drunken antics—sumo wrestling, anyone?—and sing-alongs. Ledo's has a small outdoor patio, and free pizza is provided during happy hour on Friday.

Rumba Café
2507 Summit St.
(614) 268-1841
www.columbusrumbacafe.com

It's all music, all the time. This relatively new live music venue sits on the cusp of Clintonville and Ohio State's campus, so the cheerful restaurant brings a good vibe to an area in need of development. Brightly colored walls, lizard motifs, and thatched umbrella tables set a jungle-like tone. The menu's bar food and pizzas are tinged with Caribbean flavors and generously portioned. The house band, Hoo Doo Soul Band, plays frequently, while other local bands make regular appearances during evening and happy hour time frames. Purchase tickets online, and if the music doesn't make you tap your toes, the happy hour specials will!

Understory
2571 Neil Ave.
(614) 972-6006
www.understorycbus.com

Three venues are housed within the historic Open Air School building overlooking the beautiful Olentangy Trail. The thoughtful renovation of the 1928 brick school building preserved much of its original character and made a lovely connection with the bike trail. The Lounge is an intimate ground-level craft cocktail bar serving reimagined classic cocktails, a small but focused local beer and wine list, and a menu with shareables, entrees, and weekly specials. The Common's restaurant serves a fast-casual menu alongside draft beer, wine, and cocktails. Its big glass windows open to the vibrant tree-lined Patio, which welcomes well-behaved dogs.

WORTHINGTON

Gallo's Tap Room
5019 Olentangy River Rd.
(614) 457-2394
www.gallostaproom.com
Located in Olentangy Plaza just off Highway 315, this upscale sports bar carries more than 65 beers and serves a variety of bar food and tasty homestyle entrees. Catch a game on more than 30 TVs; pool, shuffleboard, and darts will keep you busy in between games or for private events.

Worthington Tavern
671 High St., Old Worthington
(614) 396-6052
www.worthingtontavern.com
If you're in the mood for a pint and pizza or some good higher-end bar fare, head to the Worthington Tavern. The dining room can be accessed in the front of the building, while patio seating in the back can be accessed through a rear entrance. Shareables, sandwiches, and a mix of meat entrees and pasta offer a little something for everyone in a pubby bistro-like setting. The weekday happy hour include beer, wine, cocktails, oysters, and pizza.

WESTERVILLE

Jimmy V's Grill & Pub
1 State St.
(614) 865-9090
www.jimmyvswesterville.com
Jimmy V's has been around for a long time. The pub, located in the heart of Uptown Westerville, is casual and the menu is vast. It is a popular place to grab a beer and a burger, and the food leans heavily toward the flavors of Greece and the Mediterranean. The gyros, Greek salads and dips, along with paninis and calamari rank high with regulars. The restaurant has a ton of TVs, lots of beer options, and good happy hour specials. The outdoor patio is one of the prettiest in the neighborhood.

The Draft Room
570 Schrock Rd.
(614) 394-8788
www.draftroomcbus.com
Part bar, part bottle shop. The lively Draft Room packs in the beer lovers, who can choose from two dozen "taps of pure liquid bliss." The rotating options include Columbus-brewed beers and a curated selection of brews from around Ohio. Grab a pint for imbibing in the taproom, then take a six-pack home from the bottle shop.

Wendell's Pub
925 N. State St.
(614) 818-0400
www.wendells.net
Tucked in the back of a strip mall, this unpublicized pub can be a little evasive, but it's worth searching out when you are on this side of town. It serves up good fish-and-chips in a bistro-like atmosphere. The bar is large and offers a nice selection of draft beers and wines by the glass. You may eat in the bar area, the dining room, or on the outdoor patio, which is quite pleasant in the summertime, despite overlooking a parking lot.

NEW ALBANY/GAHANNA

Flanagan's Pub
3001 Reynoldsburg-New Albany Rd.
(614) 855-7472
www.flanaganspub57.com
At first glance, you may mistake this green, box-shaped building for a garage, but inside it's a friendly, casual bar that has been keeping men out of their wives' hair since 1957. Anything more than jeans and T-shirts seems overdressed, and anyone with a penchant for racing will take pleasure in the memorabilia covering the walls. The ambience is familiar and cozy. Many locals on this side of town swear by Flanagan's burgers.

Close-up

Feeling Fishy?

Ask anyone in the city where to get the best fish-and-chips, and most likely they'll say The Bag or The Bucket. The Old Bag of Nails Pubs are a charming group of English-style taverns that have become an institution throughout the Columbus community. The Rusty Bucket Corner Taverns are more of a hybrid pub-bistro and likewise command a faithful following. Die-hard aficionados and true veterans of English pubs might find both of these establishments contrived, but their fish-and-chips are generally a solid choice.

If you have ever ventured across the pond to London and wandered beyond Buckingham Palace, chances are you have encountered the Bag's namesake. Many Columbusites make the pilgrimage to the mothership, which is also where Paul McCartney met his first wife, Linda Eastman.

Of the half-dozen Bag of Nails locations, the flagship pub in Old Worthington is the closest to an authentic pub and is aptly named, as it was once part of the neighboring hardware store. Its dark, tight quarters are well lived in. Plan to wait a bit to be seated, especially on weekends. Never mind, though; the bar is more the focal point of this pub. The drink menu offers a long list of imported beers and has a nice selection of scotch. It's a good atmosphere in which to have a pint of Guinness, but not with a large group.

A few of the other locations are more accommodating to larger groups as they are more like pubby restaurants. If you prefer a more family-oriented atmosphere, the Bag of Nails in Upper Arlington, Hilliard, and Bexley offer a more spacious restaurant setting. Cozy booths and big tables give families the option of dining away from the bar.

The Rusty Bucket Corner Taverns can, quite literally, be found on the corners of several shopping plazas. They are by no means pubs in the purest sense of the word. They are spacious and airy, with a lot of light wood, and have plenty of big-screen TVs around the bar area. The fish-and-chips are one of the most popular menu items. Families are as much at home in these restaurants as single folk watching the game at the bar. Weekends can become crowded, but the regulars find it well worth the wait for a table.

One of Columbus's longtime chippy institutions is Marino's Seafood Fish and Chips in Grandview Heights. While it may seem like a glorified Long John Silver from the outside and the spartan interior is vintage, fish-and-chips reign supreme. You can't ask for better value and quality for under $10. They'll load you up on fried fish, chips, and hush puppies, but also offer healthier items such as poached, baked, or stuffed fish, chowders, and salads. Marino's has a handful of booths at which you can eat, but most people carry out. There is a reason its fish-and-chips are regularly voted best in Columbus, and that's because they are old-school good. Marino's Seafood is located at 1216 W. Fifth Ave., (614) 481-8428.

Other fish-and-chips that rank high among Columbus diners are from two other longtime establishments, the Red Door Tavern in Grandview (1736 W. Fifth Ave.) and Windward Passage in Upper Arlington (4739 Reed Rd.). Among the more modern restaurants where fried fish receives rave reviews are Kitchen Social (Polaris and Bridge Park), The Pearl in the Short North (641 N. High St.), and Kai's Crab Boil (839 Bethel Rd.).

Gatsby's
151 N. Hamilton Rd.
(614) 476-0088
www.gatsbys1977.com
Come to this friendly neighborhood bar only if you are in the mood to have a good time. The compact place is surprisingly equipped for game viewing and celebrating rowdy holiday like St. Patty's Day. There are pet-friendly outdoor patios and live music on many nights. It is also open for breakfast and lunch and is a popular stop for bikers.

Signatures Bar & Grille
94 Mill St.
(614) 532-0344
www.facebook.com/signatures tavern
This family-owned bar-restaurant fills up rather quickly on weekends, as many of the live bands draw a faithful crowd from all around town. The whole gang can be accommodated at wooden tables, and the food is above-average pub grub. The outdoor patio is one perk, and NTN trivia is the other.

Old Bag of Nails Pubs
www.oldbagofnails.com
663 High St., Old Worthington
(614) 436-5552

3240 Tremont Rd.
Kingsdale Center, Upper Arlington
(614) 486-6976

18 N. Nelson Rd., Bexley
(614) 252-4949

4065 Main St., Hilliard
(614) 777-0713

24 N. State St., Westerville
(614) 794-6900

4661 E. Broad St., Whitehall
(614) 655-2424

Rusty Bucket Corner Taverns
www.myrustybucket.com
180 Market St., New Albany
(614) 939-5300

1635 W. Lane Ave., Upper Arlington
(614) 485-2303

4109 N. High St., Clintonville
(614) 261-0385

73 N. Hamilton Rd., Gahanna
(614) 475-4435

6644 Perimeter Loop Rd., Dublin
(614) 889-2594

3901 Britton Pkwy., Hilliard
(614) 777-5968

7800 Olentangy River Rd., Worthington Hills
(614) 436-2626

2158 E. Main St., Bexley
(614) 236-2426

GRANDVIEW

Byrne's Pub
1248 W. Third Ave.
(614) 486-4722
www.byrnespub.com
Byrne's is an Irish pub in every aspect: a dark wooden bar, friendly bartenders serving up a bit o' blarney, and pints of frothy Guinness—the proper way. There is even Irish music on the jukebox. And Byrne's does not expect you to drink on an empty stomach. Fill up on free popcorn, or order pub favorites like bangers and mash, shepherd's pie, or sauerkraut balls from the pub menu. The outdoor patio is festive, and traditional Irish bands entertain on occasion.

Grandview Cafe
1445 W. Third Ave.
(614) 486-2233
www.grandviewcafe.com
The Grandview Cafe serves up comfort food, signature drinks, and a head-spinning list of whiskeys in a vibrant atmosphere. A large bar and booths fill the ground level, and it can become really busy during Buckeye games or other sporting events. Patrons can spill over onto an outdoor patio in the summer months.

Jimmy V's Grill & Pub
1788 W. Fifth Ave.
(614) 487-1717
www.jimmyvsgrandview.com
One side of this Grandview institution known as Jimmy V's is a traditional sports bar, complete with memorabilia, affordable booze, and flat-screen TVs. The other side is a dining area imbued with the smells of garlic, and more TVs. The service is attentive and the menu, which is heavy into burgers and pita sandwiches, has a Mediterranean flair. The kitchen is open until midnight. Jimmy V's other location is in Westerville at 1 S. State St.

Johnnie's Glenn Avenue Grill
1491 Genn Ave.
(614) 488-0151
https://johnnies-grill.edan.io
Not to be confused with Johnnie's Tavern across the river, Johnnie's Glenn Avenue is pretty much

a dive bar in a house on a quiet residential street. The bar is split into two rooms: one with the bar and a few tables and the other with a pool table. The floors are linoleum and the tables are Formica. The clientele come in all ages, especially since many of the older set have been imbibing here since their college days. Weekends can become really crowded, but it's the kind of place everyone is welcome to squeeze into. Outside food is permitted, as the only munchies on-site are bagged chips and Slim Jims.

Knotty Pine Brewing
1765 W. Third Ave.
(614) 817-1515
www.knottypinebrewing.net
Non-Grandview denizens might be surprised to learn that this space has been serving the neighborhood since 1935. The brewery serves its own beer along with fresh in-house-made pizzas, soups, and full entrees. The place attracts patrons from the surrounding area looking for a casual, friendly drinking environment. It is a nice blend of warm wood paneling and understated, modern decor. A big front patio is open seasonally, and the bar features flat-screen TVs.

Natalie's Grandview
945 King Ave.
(614) 297-8060
www.nataliesgrandview.com
Grandview's popular live music restaurant moved into this bigger space a few years back, so now it can bring more wonderful musicians to Columbus in a bigger space. The bar has an open, industrial-warehouse feel to it with a small stage for happy hour and solo musician performances. The larger space opens to a full, bi-level dining room and bar facing a large stage. The food is great! The menu's slightly upscale bar food is well priced, there are plenty of options for beer and wine drinkers, and cocktailians have a full bar to order from. Most of the shows are ticketed, but Natalie's also offers the occasional free happy hour show.

Red Door Tavern
1736 W. Fifth Ave.
(614) 488-5433
www.reddoortavern614.com

Some things never change. This old-school oasis among trendy Grandview eateries has remained unchanged since it opened in 1964. The Grandview landmark has a wood-paneled dining room, antiques, plenty of bar stools, and, of course, a red door. Those who wear jeans and drink domestic beer will feel right at home here. Be sure to look for the "jackelope" hanging on the wall.

UPPER ARLINGTON

Daily Growler
2112 Fishinger Rd.
(614) 656-2337
www.thedailygrowler.com
The craft beer taproom offers more than 40 beers on draft, as well as wine and spirits. Grab a growler to go and bring it back to try another beer. The Upper Arlington shop opens in the morning as an Upper Arlington institution with Colin's Coffee sharing space in the Daily Growler. So you can come for a bagel, then beer! Find other locations in German Village and Powell.

Gallo's Kitchen and Bar
2820 Nottingham Rd.
(614) 754-8176
www.galloskitchen.com
This casual neighborhood bar and restaurant is tucked on a side street just off Riverside Drive. Read more about Gallo's in the Restaurants chapter.

Wine Bistro
1750 Lane Ave.
(614) 485-1750
www.winebistrocolumbus.com
If you like to enjoy a good glass of wine, this great little bistro is the place to do it. With a carefully curated list of wines by the glass and hundreds of bottles in the shop, you'll find something you like among the well-organized walls of wine. The bistro serves up small plates of shareables, charcuterie, and flatbreads. It offers flights, hosts private events, and has very knowledgeable staff to help you select a fun case of wine. The flower-lined patio with umbrella tables is a nice place to enjoy a glass of wine on a sunny day.

HILLIARD

Johnnie's Tavern
3503 Trabue Rd.
(614) 488-0110

Somewhere between Hilliard and Upper Arlington, "Johnnie's on the Tracks" is quite literally next to a railroad crossing and is about as local-yokel as Columbus gets. This garage-sized bar has been slinging beer since 1948 and is an institution among those in the know. Don't expect the bar to have very high-end liquor or even white wine, but the prices are right, the drinks are stiff, and the crowd is friendly. The food menu is limited to a small selection of fried bar food, but the smashburgers are quite good, and some might say the best in town. The place is small and can get crowded around happy hour, but there are several booths and tables that are first come. Nothing fancy here at Johnnie's, just a classic dive with plenty of TVs to catch the game– and Jell-O shots.

DUBLIN

Coaches Bar & Grill
1480 Bethel Rd.
(614) 457-3353
www.coachesbarandgrill.com

This popular sports bar has a very homey feel to it and, despite its location in a big strip mall between Dublin and Worthington, has all the qualities of a local neighborhood bar, such as big-screen TVs, super-friendly service, and the occasional summertime cookout. The outdoor patio has three TVs and provides a quieter setting to catch that big game. Coaches sponsors softball teams and tends to draw the postgame crowd, drinking in victory or drowning their sorrows.

Dublin Village Tavern
27 S. High St., Old Dublin
(614) 766-6250
www.thedublinvillagetavern.com

The 125-year-old, ivy-covered building has served as a stagecoach stop, post office, and hardware store. It now serves the community in a different way, with tavern-style fare and daily drink specials. Regulars come for the burgers and congeniality.

George Killian Lett, the great-grandson of the founder of Killian's Brewery in Ireland, even made a personal visit shortly after it opened.

Flannagan's Dublin
6835 Caine Rd., at Sawmill Rd. and I-270
(614) 766-7788
www.flannagans.com

Who says you have to live in California to play beach volleyball? Irish-themed Flannagan's attracts a young, fun crowd with its sand volleyball courts, corn hole, live music, and, oh yeah, drinks. You'll find a large selection of bottled and draft beer at cheap prices. The massive outdoor patio has a full-service bar, TVs, and pool tables for those on the sidelines. A variety of live local and national bands pass through these doors. Flannagan's serves typical pub grub for dinner only.

NAPA Kitchen and Bar
7148 Muirfield Dr.
(614) 726-9799
www.napakitchenandbar.com

This Dublin favorite is both a bar and a restaurant serving upscale Mediterranean-inspired fare. The dining room is separated from the wine bistro by a double-sided fieldstone fireplace. It is a warm, inviting restaurant with a menu that pairs well with wines, such as build-your-own charcuterie boards, salads with optional proteins, and oven-fired flatbreads. The bottle room/lounge is full of overstuffed chairs and tables where you can uncork a bottle and enjoy conversation in the elegant space.

North High Brewing
56 N. High St., Old Dublin
(614) 756-0200
www.northhighbrewing.com

The brewpub is located in an 1890 home that is on the National Register of Historic Places in historic Dublin. It serves a large selection of its own beers and some wine in a cozy but modern space. The full-service menu features upscale bar munchies like beer cheese, wings, and pork rinds. Indoor and patio dining are available. Table reservations are strongly recommended.

NIGHTLIFE

When the sun goes down, do you go out? At the end of the day (and, hopefully, by the end of this chapter), the night owls of Columbus can find enough to keep them busy until the wee hours of the morning.

Those of you who have not yet retired your dancing shoes will be happy to know there are a handful of nightclubs to satisfy the "clubber," and many are in the downtown and Short North areas. Rather than create a separate listing singling them out, I have chosen to integrate them here and in the Wine, Bars, and Breweries chapter. Effort has been made to mention the alternative scene when appropriate.

As for live music, Columbus has plenty of venues, ranging from formal concert halls and amphitheaters to intimate bars and neighborhood taverns featuring national and local acts. Once again, the Brewery District, Arena District, and the Short North are the premier late-night entertainment districts where you can park and walk to some of the most popular live music venues in the city. The entries here will focus on those specific areas, while the clubs on campus are listed in The Ohio State University chapter.

If it's the theater arts you prefer, Columbus boasts five major downtown venues where the city's arts organizations perform year-round. The Ohio State University, Otterbein College, and Capital University each have their own campus theaters, while several communities and high schools put on annual productions. You can read more about Columbus's performing arts in the Cultural Columbus chapter, but they should not be overlooked as a fun night out on the town.

An alternative to a sophisticated evening out at the theater might be a raucous night of risqué *Saturday Night Live*–style skits and music at Shadowbox. Those looking for entertainment of an even more "adult" nature usually know where to find it, so I am only going to make the passing comment that strip clubs, gentlemen's clubs, after-hours clubs—what have you—do exist in Columbus, so just Google it; they are not listed here. Live music, comedy, and improv can be had almost any night of the week, but your best bet is to check out Columbus Underground of Experience Columbus, for the goings-on around the city.

Movie lovers have a variety of options, ranging from movies at mainstream multiscreen cineplexes, foreign and alternative flicks at the smaller independent Drexel Theatres, or avant-garde film festivals at the Wexner Center. Columbus can also brag a monstrous, state-of-the-art movie screen at the science center and an old-fashioned drive-in just south of the city.

And don't forget the bowling alleys, which are listed in the "Other Leisure Activities" section of the Parks and Recreation chapter. If, after reading through this introduction and the entries in this chapter, you can still find nothing to do after dark in Columbus, my final suggestion is to just go to bed.

CINEMAS

Several multiscreen Phoenix theater complexes, conveniently located around Columbus, offer the most recent releases of mainstream movies on regular and IMAX screens. There are 18 theaters at Dublin Village (Sawmill Road and I-270), about 30 at Easton Town Center, and 24 at Lennox Town Center (Kinnear Road). Movies-16 at 329 Stoneridge Ln. in Gahanna is another option for those on the East Side.

Drexel Theatre–Bexley
2254 E. Main St.
(614) 231-9512
www.drexel.net
If you prefer foreign-language films and artsy documentaries to Hollywood blockbusters, this is one of the only places to find them in Columbus (aside from OSU). The historic theater is atmospheric and old-fashioned, so the picture can be a little dim when compared to high-tech cinemas. Ginger Rogers even attended the opening of this theater. The attached cafe serves coffee, beer, wine, and snacks and has its own street-side entrance.

Gateway Film Center
1550 N. High St.
(614) 259-7182
www.gatewayfilmcenter.org
The newest Drexel is located on the upper level of the Gateway South Complex on Ohio State's campus. Seven screens run nonstop blockbusters as well as alternative flicks. It also has a cafe and lounge to grab a quick bite or drink during the show.

Grandview Theater and Drafthouse
1247 Grandview Ave.
(614) 670-4102
www.grandviewtheater.com
This Grandview landmark is one of Columbus's independently owned movie theaters. It shows alternative flicks as well as blockbusters on two screens. Like its sister Studio 35, it shows international flicks as well as blockbusters on two screens. The circa 1926 Drexel Theatres are a true celebration of film and have hosted regular cinematic events, like runs of screening conversation series, and movie marathons. It also shows superhero movies and first runs of Disney and Pixar films. The high-back chairs roll up to long tables for easy dining on pizza and subs while catching the flick. A great selection of beer and wine is also available.

John Glenn Theatre at the Center of Science and Industry (COSI)
333 W. Broad St.
(614) 221-2674
www.cosi.org
Educational and scientific movies are shown Wed through Sun on the seven-story extreme screen. These monstrous, head-spinning films about volcanoes, space, and world culture run about 40 minutes. General admission to COSI is not required, but discounts are given to science center ticket holders.

South Drive-In
3050 S. High St.
(614) 291-3297
www.drive-inmovies.com
The last traditional drive-in in Columbus is not going anywhere anytime soon because it's not in the most desirable part of town for developers. Tuning into the radio might be the better alternative to the old-fashioned speakers, as they don't work very well (we are probably just spoiled with high-tech theaters). It's open seasonally.

Studio 35 Cinema and Drafthouse
3055 Indianola Ave., Clintonville
(614) 262-7505
www.studio35.com
The longtime independently owned movie theater has two screens showing everything from first-run blockbusters and indie films to cult movies like *Rocky Horror* and movie marathons. The bar serves more than 40 draft beers and scratch-made pizza from its kitchen.

Wexner Center for the Arts
1871 N. High St., OSU Campus
(614) 292-3535
www.wexarts.org

As part of The Ohio State University, this is Columbus's foremost venue for contemporary and independent film and video. It sponsors several film series throughout the year that feature atmospheric international movies, classics, and documentaries on alternative and artsy topics. Visiting filmmakers will sometimes speak before the showing of their film. The theater is located in the film/video theater in the Wexner Center Building on OSU's campus.

CONCERT VENUES

Most of Columbus's major concert venues are located right in the heart of the city, so you'll never have to go far, but that's not to say you won't sit in traffic for a time. Some of these venues host sporting and other entertainment events aside from concerts.

Jerome Schottenstein Center
555 Arena Dr., just off Lane Ave., OSU Campus
(800) GO-BUCKS (462-8257)
www.schottensteincenter.com
Affectionately referred to as "The Schott," the Value City Arena is home not only to The Ohio State University's basketball and hockey teams but also to big-name concerts, Dancing with the Stars, and Cirque du Soleil. This facility can accommodate up to 21,000 people for concerts. Tickets can be purchased during normal weekday business hours at the Schottenstein Box Office in the southeast rotunda or online.

i If attending an event at the Schottenstein Center, pre-paid parking is available for most concerts and special events. For basketball games only, shuttles operate continuously from the northeast Buckeye parking lot beginning 90 minutes before tip-off until 1 hour after the game. General shuttle information is available at schottensteincenter.com.

KEMBA! Live
405 Neil Ave., Arena District
(614) 461-5483
www.kembalive.com

This indoor/outdoor facility, formerly Promo West, caters to concertgoers who prefer a smaller, more intimate venue accommodating anywhere from 500 to 3,000 people. General admission tickets to the indoor concerts translate to "standing room only," as most of the seating is reserved. There is no covered area outdoors, but there are a limited number of reserved seats down front. A majority of the outdoor seating is on the lawn. Kemba brings in newer, bigger names and emerging talent in comedy, rock, jazz, and country music.

Nationwide Arena
200 W. Nationwide Blvd., Arena District
(614) 246-2000
www.nationwidearena.com
When the Blue Jackets aren't playing on their home turf, the arena becomes a major concert venue for acts like U2, Elton John, and the Rolling Stones. You will also find a mixture of unusual events like rodeos, ice performances, and monster truck jams. Tickets may be purchased at Nationwide Arena's ticket office or through Ticketmaster.

Newport Music Hall
1722 N. High St., OSU Campus
(614) 294-1659
www.promowestlive.com
America's longest continually running rock club is located right in the heart of America's biggest university. Newport can hold up to 1,700 people, but most seats have good views of the stage, as it was once a theater. As old as it is, it shows no sign of slowing down and is still the venue where up-and-comers take the stage. The Grateful Dead, REO Speedwagon, Ramones, and even Jerry Lee Lewis played here back in the day. The Killers, Chris Isaak, and the Foo Fighters have also graced the stage. Though some college students might find the prices a bit steep, it is still one of the more affordable concert venues in the city.

GROUP ENTERTAINMENT

This section includes a variety of amusement places that can entertain couples and larger groups.

Axe Throwing

There are a few places in Columbus that your group can throw axes in a safe environment while enjoying drinks and food. Most have private lanes, leagues, and a variety of axe-throwing games.

Capital Axe Throwing
6124 Busch Blvd., Worthington
(614) 412-9167
www.capitalaxethrowing.com

Dueling Axes
309 S. Fourth St., downtown
(614) 221-1600
www.theduelingaxes.com

Throw Nation
6649 Dublin Center Dr., Dublin
(614) 389-0465
www.thrownation.com

Buckeye Raceway Indoor Karting
4050 W. Broad St., West Columbus
(614) 272-7888
www.buckeyeraceway.com
Feel the need for speed? Find it here by driving high-performance European electric karts around a challenging indoor course. The "clean green" karts can reach up to 45 mph on the different quarter-mile course formats. Individuals under 18 years old must have an adult guardian sign a release. Children 48 inches and 8 years old may drive the kids' karts, while those 56 inches and 12 years old may drive the adult karts. The fee includes helmets and headsocks. Racers receive live timing and standings after each race to see where you ranked. After the race, continue your fun with on-site axe-throwing, laser tag, or footbowling and a quick bite from the cafe overlooking the track.

Escape Room USA
459 N. High St., Short North
(614) 522-6692
www.escaperoomusa.com/oh/columbus
Challenge your group in an immersive game of discovering clues, solving puzzles, and accomplishing tasks to move through interactive rooms and ultimately escape within 60 minutes. The Escape Room is in a beautiful old building in the Short North and offers several unique adventures, including a *Titanic*, jail break, and night at the castle themes. This group experience is appropriate for most age levels and is great family fun.

The Funnybone Comedy Club and Cafe
145 Easton Town Center
(614) 471-5653
www.columbus.funnybone.com
National and local comedians perform live seven nights a week at this longtime Easton staple. Drew Carey, Jerry Seinfeld, Chris Rock, and Ellen Degeneres are among the biggest names to have played here since opening in 1987. Food and alcohol are served, and if you purchase the pre-show dinner package, you'll enjoy priority seating.

PBR Cowboy Bar + Smokehouse
3950 Gramercy St., Easton
(614) 487-3660
www.pbrcowboybar.com/Columbus
Hold on to your hats folks! PBR, named for the Professional Bull Riders spectator sport, is the city's first cowboy bar and the northernmost location of the Texas-based entertainment venue. Saddle up for a night out at PBR, where Buckle Bunnies serve cold beer and boozy milkshakes while local sports and, of course, bull riding play on the giant LED media wall and a dozen TVs throughout the cavernous space. PBR is home to the state's only league-endorsed mechanical bull, ensuring a buck load of fun. Country music lovers will appreciate the line dancing, DJ, and live music throughout the week. The smokehouse menu consists of traditional by-the-pound Texas barbecue, the usual Southern sides, burgers, salads, and shareables.

PINS Mechanical
141 N. Fourth St., downtown
(614) 464-2255
www.pinsbar.com
Duck pin bowling is fun! The space can become busy and crowded, but staff tend to cycle groups through the lanes efficiently. Just grab a drink and hang out in the throwback arcade where you can

play Donkey Kong and Galaga, to name a few. All the money spent on the arcade goes to the Ronald McDonald House. This location does not serve food, but food trucks are always outside. The second location is in Bridge Park, Dublin, and the third two-story PINS at Easton has a lot of lanes, bar games, a two-story slide, and loads of mostly free arcade games.

Shadowbox Live
503 S. Front St., Brewery District
(614) 416-7625
www.shadowboxlive.org

For 35 years, one of America's largest full-time resident ensemble theaters has been performing original comedy sketches, plays, theatrical shorts, musicals, and live rock music—upward of 400 shows per year. The venue, nestled in the Brewery District, offers a unique, sometimes hilarious and risqué alternative to traditional theater. Keep in mind some of the shows are not for the easily offended. Guests are seated cabaret table–style, and a full-service bar and menu are available just prior to the show. Shadowbox sponsors a summer bootcamp for high school–age performers.

Star Lanes
8655 Lyra Dr., Polaris
(614) 468-4830
www.starlanespolaris.com

The upscale bowling venue is a modern entertainment complex with billiards tables, 4D theater rides, Ping Pong, and a full arcade. Twenty state-of-the-art bowling lanes each have their own seating and dining area. There is both regular bowling and high-tech HyperBowling, which plays like a video game with different levels, targets, and an LED bumper system that is part of the game. The huge game room has more than 60 arcade and interactive games. The 4D theater allows you to compete against your friends in different action-packed movie adventures, fighting zombies, aliens, and other monsters. Gameplay doesn't get any more immersive than the 360-degree virtual reality videos. The food and full bar menu is available in the sit-down restaurant and can be ordered to the bowling lanes.

Topgolf Columbus
2000 Ikea Way, Polaris
(614) 317-1003
www.topgolf.com/us/columbus

Read more about Topgolf and other golf simulator locations in the "Driving Range" section of the Golf chapter.

ZipZone Outdoor Adventures
7925 N. High St., Worthington
(614) 847-9477
www.zipzonetours.com

The whole family will enjoy getting outdoors at ZipZone, just north of Worthington, off US 23. Here, you can soar through treetops on fully guided zip lines through 20 acres of forest. Some of the platforms offer views of Columbus and the Night Flight Tours allow you the experience of zipping through the forest at night. Challenge yourself on five different levels of adventure and rope course with more than 60 challenge elements in the Adventure Park, suitable for ages 7 and up. The ground-level Kid's Park, appropriate for children ages 4-7, is a scaled down version of the larger climbing and ropes course.

LIVE MUSIC AND DANCING
Downtown

The Bluestone
583 E. Broad St., downtown
(614) 884-4646
www.liveatthebluestone.com

A 19th-century former Baptist church is home to a live music venue featuring primarily country music and some blues, rock, and electronic music. Because it is a former church, the acoustics are great and it's an intimate space to see some big-name musicians.

Club Diversity
863 S. High St.
(614) 224-4050
www.clubdiversity.com

Everyone is welcome at Club Diversity, making this one of the more popular LGBTQ+ bars around. It is located in a building with a lot of old brewery charm and has a patio for outdoor imbibing. Club Diversity is known as a popular piano bar, and for its live music ranging from indie to classic jazz. Also of note are the great martinis! Throughout the week, you can get in on karaoke or movie nights in the summer.

The Forum
144 N. Wall St.
(614) 972-6004
www.forumcolumbus.com

This cavernous, industrial club is an event space that hosts all sorts of ticketed shows throughout the year, ranging from smaller traveling acts to karaoke kickbacks. You can add a VIP package onto the ticket for reserved table selection and a private server.

German Village/Brewery District

Boscoe's Bar
1224 S. High St.
(614) 826-3758
www.facebook.com/Boscoes.Bar

Bring some color into your nightlife at gay-friendly Boscoe's, which serves up tasty libations along with spectacular drag shows, male revues, karaoke nights, drink specials, and the occasional celebrity guests. And if that isn't enough to keep you entertained, it also has dartboards.

Cavan Irish Pub
1409 S. High St., Merion Village
(614) 725-5502
www.cavanirishpub.com

Here's a claim to fame: Ohio's only gay Irish bar is in Columbus. It is popular for its friendly bartenders and huuuuuuuge karaoke library. Don't expect to see men in kilts, but it's a possibility, as is drunken karaoke-ing and showtune videos. Cavan's has a big, breezy outdoor patio and is open daily until 2:30 a.m.

Southbend Tavern
126 E. Moler St., Marion Village
(614) 444-386

The "Best Little Show Bar" in Columbus is a LGBTQ+-friendly bar with something happening every night of the week, whether it is a drag show,

pool tournament, bingo, or karaoke. It's a bit of a divey bar with a fun vibe and reasonable prices. Indoor and outdoor seating is available.

Short North/Italian Village

Axis Nightclub
775 N. High St.
(614) 291-4008
www.axisonhigh.com

The multilevel gay-friendly dance club has been keeping Columbus dancing for more than 20 years as DJs spin dance tunes on the weekends. It hosts weekly drag shows, special holiday events, dance parties, cabarets, and even a Sunday Church. Axis is becoming a staple of Columbus nightlife for gay and straight, men and women alike. The weekend crowd is still predominantly sweaty, shirtless dancing men. This minimalist, industrial dance club has several bars and a cabaret-style lounge with tableside service. Check the website as many of the events are ticketed and times vary.

Duecento IV
200 E. Fourth St., Italian Village
(330) 209-3069
www.facebook.com/duecentoiv

You can dance if you want to. The neighborhood cocktail bar with a sizable patio serves up live music, darts, happy hour specials, and fun cocktails at reasonable prices. It is open late on weekends and closed on Mon and Tues.

Surrounding Neighborhoods

If you thirst for consistently good live music, you will find local, regional, and national acts performing at plenty of places in Columbus. Most serve alcohol and some form of food. Check websites for ticketing, seating reservations, and happy hour performances. If they don't have a kitchen, a food truck is usually close by.

Dick's Den
2417 N. High St., Old North
(614) 268-9573
www.facebook.com/Dicks-Den

Natalie's Grandview
945 King Ave., Grandview
(614) 297-8060
www.nataliesgrandview.com

Rumba Café
2507 Summit St., Old North
(614) 268-1841
www.columbusrumbacafe.com

Skully's Music Diner
1151 N. High St., Old North
(614) 291-8858
www.skullys.org

Summit Music Hall
2210 Summit St.
www.thesummitcolumbus.com

Woodlands Tavern
1200 W. Third Ave., Grandview
(614) 299-4987
www.woodlandstavern.com

SHOPPING

To say shopping in Columbus is plentiful and varied is an understatement, and it won't take long to realize that you do not have to hop a plane to Chicago to do some good shopping (though it sounds fun!).

In the past 10 years, Columbus has experienced a retail building boom at Easton, the creation of a fashion district, and fun locally owned boutiques in the Short North, German Village, Grandview, and the Shops at Lane Avenue. Cute storefronts in Worthington, Dublin, and Powell attract shoppers to the northern and western parts of Columbus. Polaris Fashion Place continues to engulf half of Westerville, but Easton maintains its position as Columbus's shopping mecca.

This chapter, like most others, focuses on the independently owned shops, but it begins with the major, general shopping areas, briefly pointing out the suburban malls. It then categorizes the different types of boutiques, markets, and discount shopping.

The section titled "Specialized Shops" organizes entries by category rather than neighborhood. They range from antiques shops and booksellers to wine and garden shops. Clothing shops have not been included because there are just too many, nor has every cool and trendy boutique been mentioned.

Columbus is home to one of the most successful retail chains and global retailer of women's clothing in the world: L Brands, started as The Limited by Leslie Wexner in 1963. Easton also boasts luxury boutiques like Tiffany, Louis Vuitton, and Kate Spade.

Major department stores have a presence in Columbus, but most of them are at Polaris or Easton, like Macy's, Von Maur, Nordstrom, and Saks Fifth Avenue. Big-box stores are all over the city, while Kroger, Giant Eagle, Trader Joe's, and Meijer's are the primary grocery stores.

Columbus might have sprawling suburban malls and shopping centers, but there is plenty of unique shopping to be found all over town. Like its restaurants, many of these independently owned boutiques are clustered in the old downtowns of a few neighborhoods. German Village, Grandview, and Worthington are all good places to have lunch and leisurely stroll from store to store. The old-fashioned shopping experience is not lost on the ultra-hip Short North. High Street is lined with stylish boutiques, unique retail, and artsy galleries, all very walkable to one another.

Our location in the heart of prime farmland means there are fine farmers' markets that set up shop each summer, while Worthington maintains a winter farmers' market in a quiet shopping mall. The "Markets and Specialty Food Shops" section includes full-service gourmet food markets and fresh-food markets; the historic North Market is highlighted in a Close-up in this chapter as well.

Stores in Columbus do not go out of business nearly as often as restaurants do, but to be on the safe side, I suggest calling to make sure they are still open—especially if you have to drive across town. Hours of operation have not been included since they vary, but generally, most of the bookstores are open until 9 p.m. throughout the week, and the malls typically close around 9 p.m. You will have no problem finding somewhere in Columbus to spend your hard-earned dollars.

SHOPPING CENTERS

Easton Town Center
160 Easton Town Center, Easton
(614) 416-7000
www.eastontowncenter.com

The shopping mecca of Columbus is located about 8 miles northeast of downtown, just a few minutes from the airport and New Albany. The Limited developed this outdoor, boutique-style complex as a response to consumers' seeming boredom with traditional indoor malls. Georgian architecture, pedestrian-friendly strolling, wining, dining, and storefront boutiques attract more than 30 million visitors per year, making Easton one of Ohio's most popular attractions.

Easton's retail and office space encompasses more than 2.9 million square feet, making it one of the nation's largest mixed-use complexes—and still being developed. Needless to say, Easton isn't your quick in-and-out. It's a bit of a shopping commitment, but at least it's easy to get to. An interchange off I-270 leads right to its front door, providing easy access from all parts of town.

Statistics maintain that half of central Ohio visits Easton at least once a week in a 90-day period. And what's all the hubbub about? Eating, drinking, living, working, and shopping! There is so much to do here. You can read about Easton's locally owned dining options in the Restaurants chapter and its hotels in the Accommodations chapter. This entry focuses on Easton as a retail adventure.

Several department stores are located in Easton, including Macy's and Nordstrom. Easton has also attracted many upscale boutiques like Vineyard Vines, lululemon, and Tory Burch. The young and hip frequent J. Crew, Banana Republic, and Hollister. Eclectic and luxury goods are sold at shops like Swarovski, Tumi, and Sur La Table. Of course, many of The Limited stores are represented here, alongside a variety of shoe stores, jewelry shops, and children's boutiques, including an American Girl store.

The independent shops located within Easton Town Center are few, but Homage is a popular vintage-style T-shirt store celebrating all sorts of iconic people and moments in pop culture. The Diamond Cellar is one of the nation's largest independent jewelry shops, specializing in fine jewelry and watches. Celebrate Local is an ode to all things Columbus and Ohio. The store is one-stop shopping for local beers, artisan foods, and one-of-a-kind gifts under one roof.

Developers tried to avoid parking spaces in front of the buildings, and on weekends you might think they forgot about it altogether, but parking does exist. Large garages and surface lots throughout Easton are free, but the 1-hour street-side meters are enforced. However, a portion of the coins (from parking tickets) goes to charity.

Across Stelzer Road is Easton Gateway, with a Whole Foods, more shopping, and more restaurants. The west side of the town center is Morse Crossing, home to big-box stores, fast food, and car dealerships.

Lennox Town Center
Olentangy River Road and Kinnear Road, Grandview

This somewhat older shopping mall is located just off Highway 315, slightly west of the OSU campus. It is a popular place with students, and the retail options are a reflection of this. You'll find Target, Staples, Old Navy, World Market, and Barnes & Noble Booksellers, as well as a Phoenix (formerly AMC) 24-screen movie theater. Parking is plentiful in the lots.

The Mall at Tuttle Crossing
I-270 and Tuttle Crossing Boulevard, Dublin
(614) 717-9604
www.shoptuttlecrossing.com

Tuttle opened in 1997, so it feels a bit ancient. You can see this sprawling complex from I-270, but a more discreet entrance runs from Hayden Run Road. The mall is very quiet these days but is still anchored by JCPenney and some incarnation of a Macy's. It features the more affordable specialty stores, such as Claire's, Forever 21, and H&M. The busiest place in the mall is the freestanding restaurant, BJ's Brewpub, which makes great deep-dish pizza.

Polaris Fashion Place and Mall
1500 Polaris Pkwy., Westerville
(614) 846-1500
www.polarisfashionplace.com

The sprawling indoor mall opened in 2001 on the north side of Columbus, just off I-71, and now spreads the length of Polaris Parkway. The area is collectively referred to as Polaris Fashion Place. The mall is anchored by several department stores, including Saks Fifth Avenue, Von Maur, Macy's, and JCPenney. The website lists 190 specialty stores, including Madewell, lululemon, and Vans, a day spa, three sit-down restaurants, and a food court. Mall amenities include a fun children's play area designed in conjunction with the Columbus Zoo. Parking in the outdoor lot is free.

The Shops at Worthington Place
150 W. Wilson Bridge Rd., Worthington
(614) 841-1110

This enclosed mall is located near I-270 and High Street (US 23). It services north Columbus, and its anchors are shops such as Orvis, Talbots, Ann Taylor, and Kroger. A handful of interesting locally owned shops live here. ModeAlise is a unique women's clothing boutique, and Pizazz Gift Shop is a co-op run by local artists in the Worthington Craft Guild. Fantastic toys and kids' stuff can be found at Learning Express, and the kiddos might also delight in one of Paulette's Princess Parties. Like many of the antiquated suburban malls, it's been getting a much-needed face-lift.

Shops on Lane Avenue
1585 W. Lane Ave., Upper Arlington
(614) 481-8341
www.theshopsonlaneavenue.com

The longstanding mall in Upper Arlington is a go-to for shopping, dining, and exercise! Besides Whole Foods, there are several upscale women's clothing boutiques like White House/Black Market and Athleta, but locally owned Fabtique is the place to shop for fun, eclectic pieces and accessories. Recharge your shopping batteries with lunch at the Rusty Bucket or Sōw Plated, then burn off

i Those looking for factory or outlet shopping need only drive north or south on I-71. Tanger Outlets are 15 minutes north of Polaris Parkway in Subury while the Destination Outlets in Jeffersonville are an easy 45-minute drive south on I-71.

the calories at the Row House or Cycle Bar. Free parking is available in lots in front of and behind the plaza.

The Shops in Old Worthington
7227 N. High St., Worthington
(614) 841-2545
www.experienceworthington.com

A wander along High Street in Old Worthington passes by nearly 20 independent storefronts, ranging from jewelry stores and women's clothing at Birch to artisan foods at Speckled Hen, candles, wine, and more. House Wine is a bottle shop where you can grab a glass of wine, cider, or beer and enjoy it in-house or pick up a few bottles for home. Candle Lab sells more than 100 fragrances of premade candles and offers regular candle dipping classes. Fritzy Jacobs is an eclectic little store that carries whimsical home goods, baby items, and accessories.

Union Station Place–The Cap
N. High St., Short North

The innovative, pioneering project that came to be known as "The Cap" is one of the Short North's crown jewels—literally. The Union Station Place is located atop the bridge that crosses over I-670, linking the Short North with downtown both visually and literally. The barren bridge was once an eyesore and presented a disheartening walk from the Arena District to the Short North.

Now 27,000 square feet of retail and restaurant space totally eliminates the view of the interstate from High Street and actually encourages foot traffic between downtown and the Short North. People don't even realize they are crossing over a highway. The concept of retail shops built along a bridge is modeled after pedestrianized bridges in 16th-century England and Italy. Its architecture echoes the former train station, which once stood nearby, arches and all. Similarly European are the covered colonnades under which sidewalk cafes and patios afford views into downtown. The restaurants reflect the hip, urbane nature of the Short North and the Arena District—as does the coming and going of various retail shops here.

SPECIALIZED SHOPS

Antiques

Columbus Architectural Salvage
1580 Clara St.
(614) 299-6627
www.columbusarchitecturalsalvage.com
Artifacts and antiques abound in a huge warehouse/store near the Ohio State Fairgrounds. Spend time here if you are looking for one-of-a-kind architectural elements for your home. All sorts of interesting and unusual bits and pieces from buildings, homes, and other sites have dodged the landfill and landed in a shop where creativity knows no bounds. Mantels, lighting devices, wrought iron, columns, and stone sculpture are among the architectural elements you can find, but antique television tables, boxes, and dozens of bathtubs, doorknobs, and furniture are also among the treasures.

Grandview Mercantile
1489 Grandview Ave., Grandview
(614) 431-7000
www.grandviewmercantile.com
If you don't have anything specific in mind or just enjoy browsing antiques, vintage furniture, and eclectic decorative arts, you'll appreciate this fine consignment shop's carefully selected items. The mercantile carries a little bit of everything.

Greater Columbus Antique Mall
1045 S. High St., Brewery District
(614) 443-7858
www.facebook.com/GreaterColumbus
 AntiquesMall
Columbus's first (and largest) antiques mall is in a period building in the historic Brewery District. Five floors of antiques fill this 11,000-square-foot building, so give yourself some time to work your way through room after room of glass, furniture, and collectibles.

Magpie Market
1125 Kenny Centre
(614) 929-5264
www.magpiemarketantiques.com
This space in Kenny Centre Mall is not exactly an antiques shop, but rather a collection of vendors selling mixed vintage and retro items, cottage-style art, and mid-century pieces. Perfect if you're into "junkin'" or are not looking for anything specific but want a unique treasure for your home.

Bookstores

Book Loft of German Village
631 S. Third St., German Village
(614) 464-1774
www.bookloft.com
As the website suggests, this 1863 historic building has 32 rooms chock-full of coffee-table books, cookbooks, general fiction, and hard-to-find titles, making this one of the largest independent bookstores in the country. As you mosey through the maze of rooms, it may feel like a used bookstore, but everything is new—even some of the most recent best sellers are heavily discounted. Looking for something specific? A map breaking out the building into wings may prove helpful, but those preferring to wander will find the rooms nicely labeled according to special interest, and you may just encounter the resident cat snoozing on a shelf. Claustrophobic people should probably not shop here.

Cover to Cover Children's Books
2116 Arlington Ave., Upper Arlington
(614) 263-1624
www.covertocoverchildrensbooks.com
The independent bookstore carries books for young readers, parents, and teachers. The shop carries a variety of children's and young adult books, as well as offers reading clubs and writing workshops. It often hosts author and illustrator readings and signings.

Gramercy Books
2424 E. Main St., Bexley
(614) 867-5515
www.gramercybooksbexley.com
This beautifully curated bookstore features a broad selection of popular book titles (both fiction and nonfiction), classics, poetry, and fun, whimsical children's books and toys. Gramercy has extensive author programming and other events, as well as an on-site cafe to enjoy perusing your purchase over a coffee.

Prologue Bookshop
841 N. High St., Short North
(614) 745-1395
www.prologuebookshop.com
The indie bookstore features the latest fiction and nonfiction, children's and young adult books, games, stationery, and literary gifts. It carries lots of local authors as well.

Serenity Book Shop
1806 W. Fifth Ave., Grandview
(614) 525-0506
www.serenitybookshop.com
Enjoy a quiet reading party of one (or a few) in the serene hybrid space that serves coffee and tea with a backdrop of calming music. Bring your own book or purchase one in the shop, along with other book-related gifts, coffee mugs, plants, teas, and crystals. Be sure to check the website for book stock.

Crafty Shops

Global Gallery
3535 N. High St., Clintonville
(614) 262-5535
www.globalgallerycolumbus.com
As part of the Fair Trade network, this boutique's goal is to help people in developing countries by paying the artisans living wages for the crafts they produce. These objects, which include jewelry, wood carvings, ceramics, and textiles, raise money for a good cause. The gallery has supported changing exhibitions of more than 1,500 local and global artists from more than 45 countries. The inventory is ever changing, and pop-ups are common.

Helen Winnemore's Contemporary Craft Gallery
150 E. Kossuth St., German Village
(614) 444-5850
www.helenwinnemores.com
This contemporary craft gallery has been a landmark in German Village since 1938. Rooms are loaded with a variety of handcrafted items, including functional and wearable art, jewelry, and sculpture. It is considered one of the oldest stores of its kind in the nation. And you thought this was just a house on the corner!

Learning Express
3140 Riverside Dr., Upper Arlington
(614) 485-0005
www.learningexpress.com
These fantastic stores carry toys with a focus on education and creativity. As an independent franchise, the shops have a friendly neighborhood vibe and finger on the pulse of what's hot in kid-land. Shop by age or interest for games, stuffies, science and arts projects, pretend play costumes, and sports and action challenges. It also carries lots of STEM toys. Two other locations are in The Shops at Worthington and on Market Street in New Albany.

Penn and Beech Candle Co.
1255 Grandview Ave., Grandview
(614) 488-2009
www.pennandbeech.com
Beautiful hand-poured soy candles come in more than 100 scents and in many different sizes. Stop in to the cute boutique for just one candle or a collection of your favorite seasonal smells. Organize a date night or group outing to pour your own candles with a custom one-of-a-kind fragrance that you create. Two other locations are at 737 N. High St. in the Short North and 646 High St. in Old Worthington.

Pizazz Gift Shop
132 Worthington Sq., Worthington
(614) 781-1040
www.pizazzgiftshop.com
Pizazz features one-of-a-kind artworks and crafts made by a cooperative of Worthington-based artisans. The shop has been in The Shops at Worthington Place since 2010 and is operated by the Worthington Craft Guild, which also donates some of the profits to local charitable causes. Handmade jewelry, wood art, photography, and handbags are among the offerings.

Tiki Botanicals
650 S. Third St., German Village
(614) 674-2443
www.tikibotanicals.com
If you and your house want to smell heavenly, head to Tiki Botanicals for luxury handcrafted candles and bath, hair, and body care products.

The soy wax candles are all poured on location and come in a variety of sizes and signature scents. If you bring back your candle jar (or any favorite candle holder), they will re-pour it at a discount. The skincare lines include fresh and fragrant lotions, body oils, scrubs, and soaps. The bath bombs and shower steamers are high quality and add a touch of lux to your bath-time routine. Find a second smaller location in the Lane Avenue Shops in Upper Arlington.

Unique Boutiques

There are numerous wonderful independently owned women's, men's and children's shops that carry clothing, accessories, shoes, and certain home goods. A select few have been included here to point you to a cross section of unique boutiques that are easy to get to from downtown.

Fabtique
1657 W. Lane Ave., Upper Arlington
(614) 754-8472
www.fabtique.clothing.com
If you are tired of the same old stuff, head to the Lane Avenue Shops and check out this small but mighty women's boutique full of carefully curated emerging and established designers. Clothing, jewelry, and accessories are ever changing with the seasons.

Homage
783 N. High St.
(614) 706-4254
www.homage.com
The popular vintage-style T-shirt store celebrates all sorts of iconic people, sports teams, and moments in pop culture. Find "where's the beef?" tees, college and professional sports gear, colorful stadium caps, and tanks, hoodies, sweatpants, and backpacks printed with images and quotes that turn back time. Find a second larger location at Easton Town Center and the Homage Bar in the Graduate Hotel in the Short North.

LEAL
2128 Arlington Ave., Upper Arlington
(614) 488-6400
www.lealboutique.com
For 30 years, Leal has been the go-to store for high-end designer apparel. The shop carries dozens and dozens of famous and emerging names in clothing, shoes, bags, and accessories. Prepare to drop some coin here, but you will leave with something special.

Rowe Boutique
688 N. High St., Short North
(614) 299-7693
www.roweboutique.com
Rowe has been dressing the ladies of Columbus in contemporary women's fashions since 2007. If you are a sophisticated urbanite or modern suburban woman, feel fortunate to have one of Ohio's top women's boutiques in the Short North to keep you on trend.

Sampson: A Men's Emporium
694 N. High St., Short North
(614) 504-8038
www.sampsonmensemporium.com
Men's fashion and lifestyle reign supreme at Sampson, where the well-groomed gent will feel right at home in the dark-wood-paneled boutique with brassy accents and trunks of accoutrements scattered about the shop. The boutique is known for impeccable service and its thoughtfully curated wardrobe pieces and accents. Being dubbed a "modern general store," the Emporium also carries grooming products, gentlemen's accessories, and barware.

THREAD
1110 Chambers Rd., Grandview
(614) 906-3407
www.shopthreadonline.com
THREAD is a fashion boutique focused on designers with a relaxed "Bohemian chic" vibe. Flowing dresses, patterned sweaters, ruffles, fur, fedoras, and bell bottoms—you can find it all here.

Vernacular
661 N. High St., Old Worthington
(614) 547-7777
www.shopvernacular.com
East Coast meets West Coast in this colorful, chill lifestyle boutique that carries women's clothing,

accessories, fragrances, fun stationery, and home goods. The prices are reasonable and the service friendly. It's a great spot for a relaxed outfit or cheerful scarf.

Eclectic Shops

Big Fun
672 N. High St., Short North
(614) 228-8697
www.bigfuncolumbus.com

Here's a kooky place and most definitely the "funnest" store in town! To say it specializes in eclectic collectibles is an understatement. Big Fun is packed to the ceiling with the most incredible selection of vintage toys from the 1960s to the present. Star Wars and superhero fans will revel in the miniature and full-size figurines, some still in boxes. It is impossible not to revert into a giddy kid seeing all the Transformers, My Little Pony, comic books, and famous figure bobbleheads. It's a great place to stop in for funny greeting cards, goofy gag gifts, and drawers and drawers of vintage candy.

Celebrate Local
3952 Townsfair Way, Easton
(614) 471-6446
www.celebratelocalohio.com

Celebrate Local is an ode to all things Columbus and Ohio. The store offers one-stop shopping for more than 6,000 items like local beers, artisan foods, handmade crafts, apparel, and one-of-a-kind gifts—all under one roof. A stop into the family-owned store helps support local artists and small business.

The Flag Lady's Flag Store
4567 N. High St., Clintonville
(614) 263-1776
www.flagladyusa.com

Don't step foot in here unless you're proud to be an American—or at least a Buckeye. You'll find every size and type of indoor/outdoor American, state, military, and historical flag. You want the Betsy Ross or Spirit of '76 flag? You got it! Flagpoles, seasonal banners, sports, and college pennants are also stocked. In the spirit of democracy,

The Flag Lady doesn't limit you to just OSU flags. Yes, you can get a Michigan flag if you must. In fact, dozens of university banners are available, as are holiday, religious, seasonal, and LGBTQ+ pride flags. Individuals and businesses can customize your own. The store is one of the largest flag retailers in the country.

Fortin Welding & Ironworks
944 W. Fifth Ave., Grandview
(614) 291-4342
www.fortinironworks.com

Known for its ornamental ironwork, this family-owned iron and metal manufacturer has been designing, making, and standing behind its wrought-iron products since 1946. Step into the impressive showroom to see the variety of driveway gates, fences, railings, and trellises available. There are also a few lines of indoor and outdoor furniture and sporting equipment, like soccer and lacrosse goals. Whether you want small decorative pieces or large fences, you're guaranteed quality craftsmanship.

Fritzy Jacobs
635 N. High St., Old Worthington
(614) 885-8283
www.fritzyjacobs.com

This incredibly bright and cheery store is packed with unique designs and quirky decor for the home. You'll find everything from pillows to stationery to things for the garden. It carries a whimsical line of Cath Kidson's aprons, oven mitts, and handbags and have a room brimming with ideas for the wee ones. This is the sort of place where girlfriends buy gifts for girlfriends.

Morgan House Gifts
5300 Glick Rd., Dublin
(614) 889-0037
www.morganhse.com

The Morgan House, built in the 1860s and set on 6 acres, is both a restaurant and a gift shop that carries reproduction furniture and home accessories. It also has a wonderful gourmet food shop and full-service lunchtime restaurant on-site. It is available to rent for private events.

The Red Stable Souvenirs and Gifts
223 E. Kossuth St., German Village
(614) 867-5300
www.theredstable.com

Shop for Ohio-made and German-themed gifts created by local artists and vendors in a historic building in the village. Find everything from unique handmade jewelry, fine art, and clothing to pet accessories and cuckoo clocks direct from the Black Forest.

Tigertree
3284 N. High St., Clintonville
(614) 299-2660
www.shoptigertree.com

This hip boutique carries an eclectic mix of cool stuff ranging from men's and women's clothing, accessories, and vintage jewelry to unique household items and stationery. It's the sort of shop you go in looking for one thing and leave with a bunch more. Tigertree is a great place to shop for gifts, as its ever-changing stock brings in funky kitchen towels and artsy coffee mugs, interesting games, toys, puzzles, and DIY kits. Shopping here supports a beloved local business and nice owners, who also own the Cub Shrub children's store that recently moved into the same space.

Wild Birds Unlimited
6654 Sawmill Rd., Dublin
(614) 766-2103
wbu.com

This unique wildlife store specializes in supplies for feeding birds. The certified bird feeding specialists can help you develop a plan to attract a variety of birds, assist with selecting feeders, proper bird food, birdbaths, and binoculars.

Nurseries and Garden Shops

Flowerama
1600 Morse Rd., Columbus
(614) 256-6646
www.floweramacolumbus.com

You'll find a most beautiful and colorful selection of fresh flowers, plants, and silk arrangements from this second-generation family-owned floral design center. It has a strong online presence, but you can pick up bouquets, balloons, and cards at the four brick-and-mortar stores located in Whitehall, Westerville, Reynoldsburg, and on Morse Road.

Groovy Plants Ranch
4140 Cty. Rd. 15, Marengo
(740) 675-2681
www.groovyplantsranch.com

Half an hour north of the city is a groovy place for gardeners to shop for all sorts of interesting and eclectic house plants, air plants, and succulents. Groovy Plant Ranch sells ferns, cacti, hanging baskets, wind chimes, gardening gear, and even cow soil manure in a bag. Flower-centric events, classes, and workshops are offered throughout the year for all ages, whether it's crafting a succulent terrarium with your bestie or building a fairy garden with the kiddos. For rock collectors, the Holler Earth Rock Shop carries polished gemstones, tumbled rocks, fossils, shark teeth, and other collectibles for gardening. Head out back to the gem mine, where the littles or adults enjoy "mining" for gems and fossils in the water troughs.

Oakland Nursery
1156 Oakland Park Ave.
(614) 268-3511
www.oaklandnursery.com

Green thumbs swear by this award-winning nursery. Central Ohio's premier landscaping center, founded in 1940, encompasses 17 acres of competitively priced gardening products. You'll find all of your gardening needs and then some, including mulch, trees, exotic plants, birdseed, and water-gardening accessories. Aside from having the largest plant selection in Ohio, Oakland Nursery has the largest selection of roses in the

i Columbus's two major locally owned garden centers are Oakland Nursery (www.oaklandnursery.com) and Strader's Garden Center (www.straders.net). Each has multiple locations around the city that carry all your gardening needs and landscaping services. Oakland opens several satellite Christmas tree lots during the holidays, selling a variety of live trees, pine wreaths, and swags.

Also worth noting are several neighborhood floral shops with storefronts that carry bouquets, balloons, and other gifts.

April's Flowers and Gifts
1195 W. Fifth Ave., Grandview
(614) 488-5949
www.aprilsflowersandgifts.com

Christine's Flower Shop
2733 E. Main St., Bexley
(614) 235-4510
www.cuflowers.com

De Santis Florist
4460 Kenny Rd., Upper Arlington
(614) 451-4414
www.desantisflor.com

Griffin's Floral Design
45 N. High St., New Albany
(614) 855-7311
www.griffinsfloraldesign.com

Market Blooms
59 Spruce St., North Market
(614) 228-7760
www.marketbloomscolumbus.com

Milano's UpTowne Florist
2145 W. Granville Rd., Linworth
(614) 889-1001
www.milanoflorist.com

Olde Towne Flowers and Gifts
45 Parsons Ave., Olde Towne East
(614) 817-1766
www.facebok.com/oldetowneflowers.com

University Flower Shop
254 W. Tenth Ave., OSU Campus
(614) 421-1600
www.cuflowers.com

Midwest. The nursery runs seasonal specials, such as an annual spring fling in March, and has other locations in Dublin and Delaware.

Strader's Garden Center
5350 Riverside Dr., Dublin
(614) 889-1314
www.straders.net
Columbus's other garden center has four locations in the city, but this one is the primary nursery. The greenhouse carries a wide variety of fresh plants, trees, and herbs, as well as a nice selection of gardening tools and fertilizer. Bigger outdoor equipment, like lawn mowers, snowblowers, and grills, is sold seasonally.

Sunny Meadows Flower Farm
3577 Watkins Rd.
(614) 570-6719s
www.sunnymeadowsflowerfarm.com
The urban flower farm, just 6 miles from downtown Columbus, grows exquisite flowers using sustainable, organic practices. The seasonal fresh-cut flower arrangements, holiday centerpieces, and gorgeous dried wreaths feature flowers naturally in bloom at the time, so each bouquet pays homage to the current season. Find incredible bouquets and small bundles at local florists,

farmers' markets, and flower departments in some grocery stores. The farm stand is open Thurs and Fri from 11 a.m. to 5 p.m. and Sat 9 a.m. to 1 p.m., during which time pre-orders can be picked up, though home delivery is also an option. Among the most popular garden plants are the dozens of different dahlia, mum, and geranium rooted cuttings, as well as a variety of unrooted willow cuttings. Sunny Meadows' beautiful blooms are worth seeking out for a special occasion or just to bring a happy pop of color to your table.

Wine and Cigars

Aardvark Wine and Beer
2355 W. Granville Rd., Linworth
(614) 467-9800
www.aardvarkwineandbeer.com
Your friendly neighborhood wine shop is a great place to get an education along with a bottle of wine. Donnie Austin, sommelier-owner of the bottle shop, is a longtime fixture in the Columbus world of wine. Let the knowledgeable staff guide you to global varieties of wine, port, and bubbles, as well as beers, ciders, and hard seltzers. Public tastings are held every weekend along with private events and paired dining experiences.

Barclay Tobacco & Cigar
2673 Federated Blvd., Dublin
(614) 764-0300
www.barclaypipetobaccoandcigar.com

Put this in your pipe and smoke it—1,500 square feet of retail space, a 300-square-foot enclosed humidor, and cigar storage lockers available for monthly rental. This store is the larger of two locations; the original Barclay Pipe and Tobacco can be found in the Shops at Lane Avenue in Arlington (614-486-4243). Both Barclays carry their popular estate pipes and a full line of smoking merchandise.

Coast Wine House
75 S. High St., Dublin
(614) 553-7227
www.coastwinehouse.com

The bottle shop's cool coastal decor will entice you in to shop for some wine and stay for a meal. The small shop features approachable wines primarily from America's West Coast, but you can also find a selection of small producers from around the globe. Join the wine club and enjoy a cocktail and snacks in the comfy setting of Old Dublin.

Gentile's Wine Sellers
1565 King Ave., Grandview
(614) 486-3406
www.gentiles.com

Since 1954, Gentile's has been providing Columbus with fermented favorites from around the world. This full-service wine shop carries global wines and premium beers. Order ahead to pick up a Mama Mimi's Take'n Bake Pizza from the store's pizza shop. Check Facebook @gentileswine or Instagram @gentilesthewine for tastings and special events.

grain + grape
2780 E. Main St., Bexley
(614) 239 1011
www.grain-grape.com

Bexley's friendly neighborhood wine shop has been a purveyor of wine and beer for 40 years. Stop in to pick up a case of wine or cold six-packs of craft beer and cider, or stick around for a happy hour drink in the taproom or on the patio.

NAPA Kitchen and Bar
7148 Muirfield Dr., Dublin
(614) 726-9799
www.napakitchenandbar.com

Eat, drink, and be merry seems to be the motto at this wine bistro, located in the middle of an upscale strip mall near Muirfield. One part of the store is devoted to retail and the other to consumption. You can peruse the great selection of international wines for a few bottles to take home or settle down at a table to do a little sampling. There is a chic wine bar and small dining area where you can order light fare and have wines properly paired with the food. It offers regular wine tastings and classes. Another location is in Westerville.

Tinder Box
5911 Karric Square Dr., Dublin
(614) 761-3120
www.tinderboxdublin.com

Get all of your cigar, pipe, and tobacco needs at the Tinder Box, which carries dozens of brands of cigars at many different taste and price points. Pipe smokers can find bulk and tin tobacco brands, artistic pipes, and other accessories, like humidors, cigar cutters, and travel kits. Tindor Box also has a pipe and appraisal services and an on-site smoking lounge. They do not carry cigarettes, rolling papers, or vapes.

The Twisted Vine Wine Shop
1816 W. Fifth Ave., Grandview
(614) 488-6113
www.thetwistedvine.net

The service at this shop is outstanding! The wine specialists are happy to point patrons to a perfect vintage or direct beer-drinkers to the back of the shop, where a small selection of domestic microbrews and imports are tucked in the coolers. The curated collection of wine is impressive and the staff extremely knowledgeable. It's a great place to grab a glass or a bottle and hang out at the wine bar or on the small patio. The Twisted Vine also carries luxury specialty items like Luxardo cherries, various bitters, and a nice selection of vermouths. Call ahead and let them surprise you with a case of hand-selected wines.

Wine Bistro

1750 Lane Ave., Upper Arlington
(614) 485-1750
www.winebistrocolumbus.com

If you like to enjoy a good glass of wine, this great little bistro is the place to do it. With a carefully curated list of wines by the glass and hundreds of bottles in the shop, you'll find something you like among the well-organized walls of wine. The bistro serves up small plates of shareables, charcuterie, and flatbreads. It serves flights, hosts private events, and has very knowledgeable staff to help put together a fun case of wine. The flower-lined patio with umbrella tables is a nice place to enjoy a glass of wine on a sunny day.

Markets and Specialty Food Shops

Black Radish Creamery

59 Spruce St., North Market
(614) 517-9520
www.blackradishcreamery.com

One of the best cheese selections in the city is curated by Black Radish Creamery, which imports familiar and unusual global cheese and also creates fine handcrafted cheese in its state-of-the-art facility outside Columbus. Cheesemongers extraordinaire are at the ready in this North Market shop where you can taste samples, get suggestions, and accent your cheese purchases with the stem-to-spoon handcrafted fruit preserves. It's a fun shop to explore cheese from around the world.

The Butcher and Grocer

1089 W. First Ave., Grandview
(614) 454-6328
www.thebutcherandgrocer.com

You get what you pay for at the Butcher and Grocer: high-quality, 100 percent pastured, hormone- and antibiotic-free Ohio beef, pork, lamb, chicken, and cheese. Tony Tanner's boutique meat shop only deals in whole animal butchery that is never frozen. All the sausages are made in-house, and the market carries Ohio-centric products like eggs, honey, and craft beer.

CAM International Market

3767 Park Mill Run Dr., Hilliard
(614) 442-1888
www.huaxin.us/english/Location-Col.html

The Asian supermarket is one-stop shopping for all your Asian and some Southeast Asian needs. This is the place to find unusual produce, chilis, vegetables, and other fresh foods used in Asian cooking. Japanese, Korean, and Thai ingredients can be found throughout the store. The dry grocery area carries the full complement of seasonings, rice, noodles, and broths, while the extensive freezer department has every type of dumpling and microwavable dinner you can think of. Asian desserts and sodas have their own dedicated sections.

Carfagna's Kitchen

1440 Gemini Place, Polaris
(614) 846-6340
www.carfagnas.com

This third-generation Italian market-meets-restaurant is located just off Polaris Parkway. Carfagna's has kept Columbus in Italian specialties since 1937. You'll find a great selection of gourmet imports, cheese, meats, and pastas, along with a good selection of olive oils and wine. The family-owned store has an attached sit-down ristorante and bar reminiscent of a Tuscan ritrovo. It also hosts excellent cooking classes a few times a week in a villa-inspired teaching kitchen.

Frank's Fish and Seafood Market

5251 Trabue Rd., Hilliard
(614) 878-3474
www.franksfishandseafoodmarket.com

Frank Gonzalez, a longtime purveyor of fresh seafood from the East and West Coasts, has been serving Columbus high-quality fish since 1990. His market has expanded a few times over the years but remains in a building that is easy to drive by. The market is set back off Trabue Road in a bit of an industrial setting, but inside you'll find some of the best seafood in town. The cases and coolers are full of fresh fish, shellfish, and a few prepared foods like bacon-wrapped scallops and crab cakes. Frozen fish, smoked fish, and other grocery items, such as cocktail sauce, dips, and rubs, and even a wine room make this one-stop shopping for your next seafood feast. Frank's seafood is of the highest quality, wild caught or sustainably farmed, and worth the trek from any part of town.

The Hills Market
7860 Olentangy River Rd., Worthington
(614) 846-3220
www.thehillsmarket.com

This upscale, full-service grocer carries a great selection of specialty foods, wines, and high-end staples. It's known for its meat department, but with daily fresh fish shipments, the seafood selection is equally good, particularly the organic salmon and live lobsters, which they'll steam if you're a bit squeamish about that. The deli features cheese from around the globe, many varieties of Mediterranean olives, and a constantly changing menu of prepared foods. The Hills often hosts wine tastings and seasonal lobster rolls, and has a Value Wall, which carries a nice selection of wines for under $15. At the end of the day, the staff takes a lot of pride in customer service, knowing who you are and remembering what you like.

The Hungarian Butcher
2177 W. Granville Rd., Linworth
(614) 600-2254
www.hungarianbutcher.com

Chef Dan Varga's small shop carries a case full of cured, smoked, and freshly butchered meats. Whether you want classic cuts or high-end artisanal meats, the Hungarian Butcher does it all: steaks, chops, sausages, wagyu, corned beef, smoked turkey, pâté, terrines, wursts, and bacon. It offers a rotating selection of meats, as well as local farm market products and some prepared foods, like cabbage rolls and taco kits.

La Plaza Tapatia
225 Georgesville Rd.
(614) 276-0333
www.laplazatapatia.com

The region's largest Latino supermarket is just west of Columbus near the casino. Not only is it a grocery store, but it also has a restaurant, full bar, bakery brimming with pan dolce, galletas, and churros, and a cafe that serves ice cream. Marvelous Mexican ingredients range from produce

and meat to dairy and cheese for the quesadillas connoisseur. Kids will enjoy watching them hand-make tortillas on-site and be tempted by the aisles of sweets and sodas. The restaurant serves burritos and bowls, molcajete, tacos, tamales, and a variety of tortas.

Littleton's Market
2140 Tremont Center, Upper Arlington
(614) 826-1432
www.littletonsmarket.com

This gourmet neighborhood market is a beautiful spot to enjoy the experience of shopping for food. The open and airy store is packed with luxury food items, fabulous produce, and a dessert case that smacks you in the face as soon as you walk in the door. Do you need duck fat, lobster oil, or fancy French cheese? This is your place. The folks who work the meat, seafood, and cheese counters are longtime veterans and super knowledgeable when it comes to cuts and cooking ingredients. Cases tease you with house-made pasta, ravioli, charcuterie cones, salads, and sides. The executive chef cranks out fantastic prepared foods to grab and go. Littleton's also features small, changing menus for the cafe and bar, where you can enjoy a coffee or cocktail throughout the day. The outdoor patio is open seasonally.

Patel Brothers Indian Grocer
6600 Saw Mill Rd.
(614) 792-8484
www.patelbros.com

Having the right spices and grains is vital for Indian cooking, and you will find everything you need right here, along with other odds and ends from India including Bollywood movies. The shop is tucked in a small strip mall off Kenny Road, but this is where most of my Indian friends suggest shopping for both the basics and more complex Southeast Asian recipes.

Penzeys Spices
4455 Kenny Rd., Upper Arlington
(614) 442-7779
www.penzeys.com

If you've ever driven across Kenny Road and wondered what that weird round building is across from Iacono's Pizzeria, well, it's a spice store. With just a handful of shops in the Midwest, Penzeys is a mom-and-pop-type business where you can mail-order unusual spices from a catalog, or if you are lucky enough to have a shop nearby, you can buy them in person. Penzeys carries all sorts of interesting herbs, spices, meat rubs, and unusual seasonings. It also carries great hot chocolate, all sorts of jarred dried chili peppers, and a variety of salts and peppercorns.

Saraga International Grocery
1265 Morse Rd.
(614) 447-8588
www.saragaindy.com

This store is amazing, but it is also a commitment. Saraga is a large international grocery store that carries global specialties ranging from halal meats to every sort of tamarind a pad thai fiend might need. The store is organized by country and then by types of food. You can find every color of rice, spices at very good prices, noodles in all shapes and sizes, and international cooking tools. The periphery of the store has meat counters, live fish tanks, and seafood that may or may not be familiar. The few food windows serving Mexican and other immigrant street food can be quite busy at lunch or on weekends. From Argentina to Zimbabwe, you will likely be able to get the hard-to-come-by ingredients you need here. A bit of advice: come armed with patience, as it is frequently crowded with long lines. The employees often do not speak English, so asking for help may be futile at times. Prepare to use Google or a translator app to help.

Tensuke Market
1167 Old Henderson Rd., Upper Arlington
(614) 451-6002
www.japanmarketplace.com

Columbus can boast Ohio's largest Japanese grocery store. Sushi lovers need look no further than Tensuke (pronounced "ten-soo-key") for the freshest of fish, all forms of seaweed nori, sushi rice, and other bells and whistles to make a great Japanese meal. The grocery has a nice produce department with some Japanese-specific items, the freezer section has cases of dumplings, and the variety of soy sauce, miso paste, and sake is enough to make your head spin. The store also carries Japanese candies, drinks, wine, and household items. Tensuke is a quick place to grab more than 60 varieties of top-notch, premade sushi, tempura, and bento to go. The rolls, nigiri, chirashi, and combination packs are made fresh throughout the day, since the store is usually quite busy and the prepared food has a fast turnover.

Toro Hispanic Meat Market
1405 E. Dublin Granville Rd.
(614) 813-3082
www.toromeatmarket.com

Find organically grown meats and chicken, sustainable seafood, and high-end Mexican chorizo. Have any cut of meat prepared at the counter or pick up pre-marinated or seasoned meats. The supermarket carries a great selection of fresh organic produce, including specialty Mexican and South American imports, as well as cheese and beer. Pick up freshly baked breads and sweets from the bakery. Toro has two other supermarkets: at 5476 Westerville Rd. and at 704 Parsons Ave., just east of German Village.

Vincenzo's
6393 Sawmill Rd., Dublin-Worthington Area
(614) 792-1010
www.govincenzos.com

The amazing smells that waft through this bustling market will send you into a food frenzy, even if you aren't hungry. Shelves and counters are lined with daily scratch-made pastas, antipasti, baked entrees, marinated and roasted veggies, and heaps of olives. While some people get their dinners to go, others linger to shop for bread, cheese, and spiced meats. Vincenzo's is not a deli, but it does make wonderful hot and cold subs, calzones, and strombolis to go for gourmet meal replacement.

Weiland's Gourmet Market
3600 Indianola Ave., Clintonville
(614) 267-9878
www.weilandsmarket.com

Some things never change. Weiland's is that place everyone loves because they know what they are walking into: a specialty food retailer; meat, seafood, and produce market; destination wine shop; caterer; and friendly neighborhood grocer. This

70-year-old market is in a nondescript strip mall between Worthington and the OSU campus, but people flock here from all corners of town. Oddly enough, as one of Columbus's premier markets, there is nothing fancy or pretentious about Weiland's. It just sells great food.

Carnivores drool over the cases of deli meats, tenderloins, chops, and sausages. Lost children can usually be found hovering near the lobster tank while Mom and Dad wander through rows of marinades, salad dressings, global foods, and prepared dishes. It's almost cruel having so many cheeses to choose from. Fresh produce, breads, and baked goods round out the meal. Wine lovers are always pleased they don't have to make another stop, as Weiland's stocks more than 1,200 labels and a state liquor store is attached via hallway. Let's not forget a fresh bouquet of flowers for the table. This is top-notch, one-stop shopping.

Thrifting in Columbus

Whether you refer to it as thrifting, junking, or bargain shopping, there are plenty of secondhand shops to find clothing, household items, toys, and one-of-a-kind treasures. This section does not include flea markets, consignment stores, or antiques shops, but some of these stores might also have vintage or retro gems.

American Cancer Society Discovery Shop,
　Kenny Center Mall
Family Thrift, Whitehall
Good Life Thrift Store. Hilliard
Goodwill, multiple locations
Ohio Thrift Store, nine locations
Out of the Closet, Italian Village
St. Vincent de Paul, Reynoldsburg
Tri-Village Trading Post, Marble Cliff
Volunteers of America, Northwest Shopping
　Center

Farmers' Markets

I have listed a few of the more popular markets to which farmers from all over Ohio bring their fruits, vegetables, plants, and baked goods throughout the summer. The days and times vary. Check out "Things to Do" on the Experience Columbus

website at www.experiencecolumbus.com for an up-to-date comprehensive list.

Besides those listed here, Bexley, Canal Winchester, Franklin Park, German Village, Grove City, Hilliard, New Albany, and Upper Arlington all have nice weekly markets.

Clintonville Farmer's Market
3535 N. High St., Clintonville
More than 50 Ohio farmers and vendors come together every Sat from Apr to Nov. It has easy access from the Olentangy bike trail and is walkable to Northmoor Park, so grab some goodies from the market and go have a picnic by the river.

Dublin Market at Bridge Park
Longshore St., Dublin
(614) 333-8245
www.thedublinmarket.com
An outdoor farmers' market takes place every Sat starting at 9 a.m. Local farmers sell homegrown fruits, vegetables, flowers, plants, and herbs. Among the 120 vendors you might find baked goods, handmade foods, sweets, artisans, and some local retailers. The market also has events and activities for children. It is open from early May through Sept. Parking is free in nearby garages.

Pearl Alley Farmer's Market
Pearl Alley and Gay Street, downtown
(614) 645-5001
www.marketsatpearl.org
This festive urban bazaar is open from 11 a.m. to 2 p.m. on Tues and Thurs, May through Oct. Along with fresh produce and baked goods, merchants sell a variety of products ranging from handmade crafts and clothing to books, handbags, and jewelry. Street musicians and restaurant patios give the corner a lively atmosphere. Watch for special Sunlight and Moonlight Markets that have extended and unusual hours.

Worthington Farmer's Market
High Street, Old Worthington
(614) 285-5341
www.worthingtonfarmersmarket.com
This is one of Columbus's longest-running and most popular farmers' market. Booths and stalls

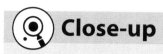 **Close-up**

The Historic North Market and Trolley District

The North Market (www.northmarket.com) is located at 59 Spruce St. in the Arena District, but this wasn't always the case. Local butchers, bakers, and farmers began selling their goods to the public in 1876 from a building nearby at 29 Spruce St., once the site of the city's public cemetery.

Though not in its original location, North Market is one of Columbus's two public markets to still be in operation. The original Central Market at Town and Fourth Streets was torn down a long time ago due to urban development. The West Market was converted into a Boys and Girls Club in 1926. The East End Market on Mount Vernon burned down in 1947, but has been resurrected as the East End Market in the Trolley District on Kelton Avenue.

After fire gutted the North Market in 1948, the city decided not to rebuild. Merchants pooled their money and purchased a temporary building to house the market, though the city maintained ownership of the property. Three decades later, after hitting rock-bottom and watching the old building fall apart at the seams, Nationwide Insurance sold the Advanced Thresher Farm warehouse to the North Market Development Authority. Columbus once again rediscovered its market roots and opened the doors of the current North Market in 1995.

On any given day, 30 regular merchants fill the indoor stalls, most of which serve finished foods. But you can find fresh seafood, cheese, and flowers, too. COLO Seafood Market and Oyster Bar carries fresh fish with daily deliveries from around the country and serves up a mean lobster roll. You'll find beautiful mixed bouquets at Market Blooms, a fabulous selection of wine and beer at Barrell and Bottle, and everyday essentials from the Mini-Super market. Black Radish's hundreds of imported and handcrafted cheese makes it one of Columbus's best sources, not to mention its interesting collections of fruit preserves, oils, and honey.

When it comes to prepared food, the North Market has many global offerings. Mediterranean, Indian, African, Vietnamese, and Thai food items are among the options. Many of the stalls not only serve premade meals but also sell basic ingredients for cooking at home. North Market Spices carries more than 400 handcrafted, high-quality spice blends, which solves your quest for the perfect rub. Some of the long-established and newer popular eateries in the market are Hoyo's Somali Kitchen (www.hoyoskitchen.com), COLO Market and Oyster Bar (www.coloseafood.com), Flavors of India (www.northmarket.org/merchant/flavors-of-india/), Nida's Sushi (www.nidassushinorthmarket.com), Momo Ghar (www.northmarket.org/merchant/momo-ghar/), Lan Viet (www.northmarket.org/merchant/lan-viet-market/) and Sarefino's (www.pastarianorthmarket.com).

A million people annually visit the North Market to eat, shop, or just people-watch. It is one of Columbus's most beloved landmarks but will be undergoing a major redevelopment over the next few years while a 32-story mixed-use tower is being incorporated to the current structure. The new Merchant Building marks the beginning of a new era for the North Market.

The Historic Trolley District on the near eastside of Columbus has recently been developed into a mixed-use complex that includes the East End Market. The once-abandoned site of the city's trolley car operation is still finding its footing, but nearly a dozen vendors have taken up residence in the cool brick building. Most of the vendors serve prepared foods, so do not come expecting a traditional market with produce and meat. You can, however, find fun plants from the Plant Gays or order nice Creole, Korean, Moroccan, or Middle Eastern food to enjoy inside the dining area up in the rafters or alfresco. Grab a drink from the Railhouse bar or the Switch speakeasy, or pop down to the Columbus Brewing Company beerhall with its large outdoor patio. The location at 212 Kelton Ave. is not on the site of the original East End Market but makes a valiant effort to maintain a tangible piece of Columbus's architectural history.

are set up along High Street in Old Worthington between 9 a.m. and noon every Sat throughout the summer. The season extends May through Oct, or later, depending on how the weather is. You'll find everything from herbs, honey, and fresh-cut flowers to vegetables, fruits, and quality artisan crafts and food products. No admission is charged, but parking can become competitive, as you have to park away from the town center and walk in. This is the largest year-round market; fall through spring, vendors move indoors a mile up High Street to The Shops at Worthington Place.

THE OHIO STATE UNIVERSITY

The Ohio State University (OSU) is among the biggest universities in the country. The fall 2023 enrollment stood at nearly 65,000, across all campuses. At last count, OSU has more than 39,000 full-time employees, property encompassing more than 17,000 acres, and an operating budget of nearly $10 billion—bigger than some small countries. The main campus alone has 53,000 students, making this one of the largest single campuses in the country, but don't let the size put you off.

According to *U.S. News and World Report*'s annual public university rankings, OSU is 1st in Ohio and 17th in the country. It is particularly noted for its industry-supported research and colleges of education, engineering, and business. In fact, 22 graduate and professional programs rank in the top 10, including Fisher College's MBA program. Ohio State has a huge study abroad program and produces top-ranked numbers of Fulbright Scholars and Peace Corps volunteers.

Despite fine academic reviews, the idea of being "just a Social Security number" at such a monstrous university scares more than a few students away. It's important, however, to recognize that one of the upshots to attending such a large public school is the amount of academic, athletic, and research resources available to students and faculty.

Upward of $2 billion in funding from external sponsors has helped The Ohio State University earn a reputation as one of America's preeminent research institutions. With over $130 million coming from the National Institutes of Health, it's no wonder the medical school rates in America's top 25 research schools and the College of Medicine and Public Health ranks 40th.

With extraordinary research expenditures, Ohio State is becoming one of the world's leading research universities, and it helps that its facilities and curriculum can support whatever it is that students need to do. For example, the OSU library system is ranked 5th strongest among public universities in the country by the Association of Research Libraries.

With more than 12,000 courses, Ohio State's academic offerings are as extensive as it gets, the athletic programs are world-class, and many of the facilities are brand-new and state-of-the-art, but the college experience isn't just about the academics. The university receives high scores with students for social and nightlife. No matter which way you slice it, OSU is a party school. All of its social offerings can be a distraction, of course, but it also offers a lot of variety to those students who can afford to eat out and the older crowd who can legally imbibe in alcohol.

The campus area has no shortage of ethnic eateries, 24-hour pizza joints, and cheap watering holes, some of which have been campus institutions as far back as the 1950s. Entries for pizza shops are listed here, while campus-area restaurants are covered in the Restaurants chapter. This chapter also includes a few of the drinking establishments that are identified with the Ohio State experience. You can't visit OSU without buying a pitcher of beer at the Out-R-Inn or basking in the shadow of the Horseshoe at the Varsity Club during a football game.

It doesn't take long to realize many of Ohio State's more popular traditions revolve around Buckeye sports, football in particular. Tailgating is a huge fact of campus life. Lane Avenue is blocked off while partyers spill onto the streets all around the stadium. Locals gladly partake of the pre- and postgame mayhem, which can leave quite an impression on out-of-towners—especially if you're from Michigan.

Anyone vaguely familiar with college sports understands the seriousness with which schools take their rivalries. Very few can match the animosity between The Ohio State University and the University of Michigan, which seems to grow even stronger once you graduate.

Stringent open-container laws are now enforced on football Saturdays. No more wandering across Lane Avenue with your open can of beer. No more verbally abusing Michigan fans slinking back to their cars for the drive north. While many of the responsible gamegoers are disappointed with these restrictions, it's all in an effort to curb offensive fan behavior.

For 150 years, OSU academics, traditions, and landmarks have become synonymous with Columbus. While not everyone is a Buckeye fan, it is impossible to separate the university from the city. Whether the Buckeyes win national titles or the media covers scandals that rip through various departments or OSU students find a cure for cancer, what goes on at The Ohio State University is a total reflection of our city and often defines Columbus in the eyes of the rest of the country.

The goal of this chapter is to provide general information and dispel some myths about America's largest university, offer pointers on how to get around and manage the campus sprawl, and make some sense of why so many locals are Buckeyes to the bone. We begin with a brief history of the university, but you can read more about William Neil, the man who donated the land, in the History chapter. The "Campus Today" section includes an overview of the student population, faculty, academics, and facilities. This is followed by a discussion about the Buckeyes and their traditions. The chapter ends with a listing of campus shops, pizza places, and the quintessential pub crawl.

HISTORY

President Abraham Lincoln's revolutionary Land Grant Act of 1862 laid the foundation for college education to be within reach of all high school graduates. Congress granted federally controlled

i The school is often referred to as Ohio State or OSU, but the proper name, when used as a noun, is The Ohio State University—as named in 1878.

lands to the states in order to establish institutions to teach the general population agriculture, mechanics, and military tactics. In 1870, the Ohio General Assembly established the earliest school that was to become what we now know as The Ohio State University.

The Ohio Agricultural and Mechanical College was first established on farmland bequeathed by Columbus businessman William Neil. As the name suggests, this college intended to matriculate students strictly in agricultural and mechanical disciplines. It opened its doors for classes in September 17, 1873, when 24 students met at the old Neil farm, 2 miles north of Columbus.

The college's curriculum was disputed among just about everyone. Some wanted to keep it devoted solely to agriculture, while others wanted to broaden the scope to include classical studies. In 1878, a vote was passed to include English and classical and foreign languages. It was at this time the college changed its name to The Ohio State University. Six of the men who began in the first class graduated this same year, while the first woman graduated from The Ohio State University in 1879.

CAMPUS TODAY
Faculty and Academics

The diverse range of studies envisioned by the first board of trustees at The Ohio State University continues to this day. Students have 200-plus undergraduate majors, 127 master's degrees, and 102 doctoral degrees to choose from with hundreds of specializations. Over 12,000 courses are offered in 200 fields of study. The original board would be proud.

Current president Walter "Ted" Carter Jr. and provost Karla Zadnik oversee the 14 different colleges and schools that make up The Ohio State University. The colleges range from architecture to engineering to veterinary sciences, and each has its own application and admission requirements.

Just have a look at the homepage of the department you are interested in, and you will find comprehensive faculty, admission, and departmental information.

Admission criteria vary for each school, but three primary factors are considered in the competitive review process: completion of a college preparatory curriculum in high school, grade point average, and SAT or ACT scores. The outlying regional campuses in Lima, Mansfield, Marion, Newark, and Wooster have their own standards of admission and deadlines. Links to each campus can be found on Ohio State's main website.

The student-to-faculty ratio is 18:1. Contrary to popular belief, only 5 percent of first-year classes have more than 100 students, while 89 percent have fewer than 50. The average class size is 25. The advanced undergraduate classes are even smaller, so that the ratio becomes even more manageable during junior and senior years. Yes, freshmen might have a few auditorium-size classes, but there are pointers on the website about how to make the most of this situation.

Many parents and students tend to forget about or overlook the esteemed faculty The Ohio State University employs. In classes with 100 or more, students may have trouble appreciating that these professors come from all parts of the world and from highly respected universities. They not only teach classes but conduct cutting-edge research, spearhead innovative discoveries, and create new art and technologies along with their students. Just read the laundry list of faculty members who have received the highest awards and honors within their fields.

One hundred twenty-six Ohio State faculty members have received the rank of fellow from the American Association for the Advancement of Science, 40 have received the prestigious Guggenheim Memorial Fellowship for humanists, and we can't forget to mention the 48 or so Fulbright scholars, making this one of the biggest producers of Fulbright scholars. Nearly three dozen faculty members are members of the prestigious American Academy of Arts.

Like all big public schools, the undergraduate program at OSU receives its share of negative publicity, but like anywhere, an education becomes what you make of it. It is the graduate schools, however, that have put The Ohio State University on the map. In 2003, Ohio State was ranked fifth in the nation for granting doctoral degrees. Nearly 3,000 graduate students taught 10,000 undergraduate students, making it a leader in graduate education experience.

For complete information, check out The Ohio State University website at www.osu.edu or call (614) 292-6466. For undergraduate application information, contact the admissions office at (614) 292-3980. For graduate information, contact the graduate admissions office at (614) 292-6031.

Students and Alumni

The current student population is made up mostly of Ohioans, with an almost even breakout of men and women. Admission to Ohio State is quite competitive with 72 percent of the entering freshmen in the fall of 2023 ranked in the top 10 percent of their graduating high school class, while 98 percent ranked in the top 25 percent. Thirty-nine percent were admitted into arts and sciences, while engineering and business came in a close second at 21 and 17 percent, respectively.

The annual tuition for a full-time undergraduate student in 2024 is around $12,900 for residents and $38,400 for nonresidents. The average room and board is about $14,000. This is not cheap for a public school education, but scholarships and federal and state financial aid are available.

Single full-time students entering college directly from high school are required to live on campus their first year, unless they are staying with parents and commuting. Living on campus certainly has its advantages both academically and socially. Ohio State's 42 resident halls are convenient to classes and within walking distance of athletic and art facilities, fraternity and sorority houses, and the restaurants, bars, and shops of High Street.

Some of the dormitories are new builds and offer a variety of room styles and living arrangements, including Live-Learning communities that cluster together students with similar academic and career goals. In addition to regular coed residential halls, the university has specialized living for students with similar heritage, same-sex residences, halls for upperclassmen only, and study-intensive environments for honors students.

Once you settle into your new home, getting around this sprawling campus can seem daunting, especially if you have to walk from class to class in a short period of time. The best suggestion to incoming students is to spread your classes out, allowing enough time to get from point A to point B. Also, keep a map of the campus buildings handy when scheduling, so you can see how realistic it is to make it to your next class on time. Many of the academic buildings are clustered around the Oval, so navigating this area generally isn't a problem.

The Campus Area Bus Service (CABS) is a free on-demand transit service with several routes that loop around campus and beyond. The Campus Connector and Campus Loop South each make stops throughout their respective sides of campus from 7 a.m. until midnight. The bus stops are well marked. The East Residential heads toward Indianola Avenue, east of High Street, while the Buckeye Express services the Buckeye Lot west of campus. Check out the website (www.ttm.ohio. edu) for detailed information about the routes.

Those who like to cycle will find plenty of bike racks outside most buildings. This is undeniably the best and quickest way to get around campus. It will also save you the hassle and expense of parking.

Driving and parking on campus can be tough at peak times. The general rule of thumb is the higher your student status, the better your parking options. There are surface lots, parking garages, and shuttles that go between central campus and west campus lots. Rates vary depending on where you want to park, but the closer you are to central campus, the more expensive it becomes.

The Ohio Union South and Tuttle Park Place parking garages charge a varying hourly rate for nonpermit holders. Students and visitors alike

i Ohio State's student identification card is called the BuckID. It functions as the official university photo ID, library card, meal plan card, campus and COTA bus pass, and, with appropriate funds, serves as a debit card accepted at many locations on and off campus.

should be warned: OSU takes parking seriously. In 2023 campus security wrote almost 80,000 citations and raked in almost $1 million in parking violations. Students cannot graduate or register for classes until their parking violations are paid or disputed and settled.

If students need a little extra academic support, contact Academic Services (614-292-5766), located at 1640 Neil Ave. in the Younkin Success Center. The "one-stop learning shop" provides students free tutoring, help with time or stress management, tips to improve study and test-taking skills, and instruction on how to take better notes. Free drop-in tutorial assistance is also available at the Mathematics and Statistics Learning Center, while appointments are required with tutors at the Writing Center, located at 4132 Smith Lab, to help students of all levels with their writing projects.

The Office of Student Affairs (614-292-8900) can provide information related to anything outside the classroom, from on- and off-campus housing, food service, and health issues to recreational activities. Its website (www.studentaffairs. osu.edu) has links to all the student organizations and services. The online student resource guide also discusses diversity initiatives, intramural groups, campus technology services, and the student code of conduct.

The Financial Aid Office (614-292-0300) assist in helping students manage their payment plans and eligible students to find jobs through the federal work-study program. There are plenty of non-university jobs to be had off-campus. Field-specific employment opportunities are sometimes posted in most of the academic buildings.

A variety of alumni services is available to those who survive their coursework, pay all their parking tickets, and go on to graduate: career services, networking, alumni clubs, and societies, to name a few. Rumor holds that somewhere in the world there is an Ohio State alumni meet-up taking place every 8 hours. It is fair to say you can go anywhere in the world and bump into one of OSU's 600,000 living alumni.

A quizzical eyebrow might be raised when you visit a remote island and encounter someone wearing a "Buckeye Dad" T-shirt or when you spot an "O" ballcap in a Tokyo train station, and it should never be surprising when you "O-H" at them and get an "I-O" in response. Take it from a former OSU student: No matter where you end up, once a Buckeye, always a Buckeye.

Diversity

The range of Ohio State's minority and international student body adds another dimension of diversity and culture to both the school and the city of Columbus. It also generates unique needs, so the university has focused on creating a campus environment that recognizes, respects, and appreciates cultural and religious differences. This is important since more than 6,000 international and 16,000 minority students are enrolled across all the campuses.

The Office of Diversity and Inclusion (614-292-0964) is a good place for minorities to find scholarship services, tutoring programs, and graduate or professional recruitment. The office is located at 154 W. Twelfth Ave. It also provides information about the extensive minority student organizations, such as the Indian Students Association, Asian American Association, and Turkish Student Association.

As part of the university's Diversity Action Plan, centers have been established to provide intellectual, cultural, and support programs for minority. students, women, faculty, and staff. Other inclusion offices focus on racial justice, advocacy, and community development for American Indian, Asian American, African American, Hispanic, gay, lesbian, bisexual, and transgender students. The office also houses the Rape Education and Prevention Program and Men's and Women's Student Services.

With nearly 2,200 staff and faculty members who are veterans, Ohio State is one of the few universities in the nation with a dedicated Veterans Affairs office to assist their employees. This office also serves as a focal point for veterans' advocacy, referrals, financial aid, and activities for students and staff alike.

Ohio State isn't just tooting its own horn. Outside sources are recognizing the university for its ongoing commitment to multiculturalism. The Ohio State University ranks highly as one of the

ⓘ The Ohio State University is among the top 5 higher education institutions for granting doctorate degrees to African Americans and in the top 20 for Hispanic students.

country's 50 best colleges for African Americans. The Frank W. Hale Jr. Black Cultural Center, located in the heart of campus at 154 W. 12th Ave., is open seven days a week. It hosts social, cultural, and educational programs focused on the African American culture and houses an impressive collection of artwork depicting the African American experience. The Black Studies Library can be found on the second floor of the main library.

A final testimony to OSU's diversity plan is the Kirwin Institute for the Study of Race and Ethnicity. This center brings together scholars from around the world to deliberate issues such as race, poverty, housing, and ethnic and religious conflicts. To learn more about diversity, affirmative action, and access for the disabled at The Ohio State University, read the diversity reports on the website.

Student Organizations and Activities

Being a student on campus or just being a resident of a large university town can be rewarding. Both students and the community reap the benefits of the endless number of campus programs available. The entire city can experience up-and-coming athletes, new artists, and fresh ideas turned out through various campus media. With 1,200 registered student organizations to choose from, you can find pretty much any activity you would want to be involved with.

OSU offers all the traditional college activities, like choral groups, musical ensembles, and a homecoming committee. Political types. may become active in one of the three student governments. There are almost 50 honor societies, as well as numerous local and national service and awareness organizations.

If you are looking for intramural sports or physical activity of some sort, there are hundreds of possibilities: ballroom dancing, ice hockey, bowling, and skiing, to begin with. There are too many to list here, but the Parks and Recreation chapter includes information and contact details of the more popular intramural and club sports offered at OSU. You can also check out the link to "Life on Campus" at www.undergrad.osu.edu.

From a social standpoint, one can understand the appeal of joining a fraternity and the sense of camaraderie it can create for a person who might otherwise feel lost at such a big school. Ten percent of the undergraduate population is part of Ohio State's Greek life. In order to receive a membership invitation to any one of the 29 fraternities and 17 sororities, students must maintain a GPA of 2.5 and have 12 credit hours under their belt.

While Greek life is most closely associated with partying and slacking, it also provides opportunity for community involvement and creates lifelong friendships. Statistics have shown that the overall GPA of OSU's Greek community (3.07) was higher than the overall university GPA (3.02). Who knew?

There are almost 50 faith-based organizations on campus. Many take advantage of the free meeting space in the Ohio Union, which also has a designated Interfaith Prayer and Reflection Room. The Campus Crusade for Christ (CRU) is the largest religious organization with more than 1,000 student members. Other spiritual groups focus on Catholic, Jewish, Coptic, Sikh, Pagan, Muslim and other global religions.

The *Ohio State Lantern* (614-292-5721; www.thelantern.com) is the university's official student newspaper. Established in 1881, the *Lantern* is one of Ohio's oldest newspapers and is editorially independent of the university. It is published daily when classes are in session and twice weekly during the summer quarter, covering all aspects of campus life and Buckeye sports. The *Lantern* also partially serves as a laboratory for journalism students and is consistently ranked among the best student newspapers in the country by the Society of Professional Journalists. The *Lantern* also supports Lantern TV studio productions.

Ohio State operates a public television station, WOSU channel 34. It has two public radio stations, 820 AM (NPR) and 89.7 FM, both with the call letters WOSU. AROUNSE OSU is the student-run online radio station.

This is just a sample of what the university has to offer. Check out the "Life on Campus" link

at www.undergrad.osu.edu for a complete listing and links to the different organizations.

Campus Buildings and Facilities

Many OSU students come from Smalltown, USA, and are sometimes overwhelmed with the sprawling campus—understandably so. Who wouldn't be intimidated by a campus with over 600 buildings, a city-size medical center, satellite communications center, supercomputer, polar research center, airport, wildlife preserve, and dairy farm? Situated on more than 1,700 acres, the school is as big as it sounds.

The Ohio State University is composed of the main campus in Columbus and four regional campuses. Collectively, Ohio State owns over 850 buildings, 42 of which are residence halls and 4 that are on the National Register of Historic Places. This doesn't include all the shops, services, and restaurants that line High Street, the school's always interesting "main drag."

If campus wasn't already big enough, don't worry, it's growing. Students who attended OSU a few years back won't recognize the "old" High Street thanks to all the development that is ongoing. The area along High Street between 8th and 11th Avenues is referred to as the Gateway, which serves as a transition from the Old North into the university area. This is where you will find the main university bookstore, rental housing, Gateway Film Center, and some retail and restaurant options.

No matter how much time you spend wandering the grounds and getting to know the campus, it never gets smaller, only more manageable. This section will provide a brief overview of only the primary facilities on the main campus. After a few visits and with a little familiarity, functioning in this 1,800-acre "city within the city" will become less intimidating. I promise.

Academic and Conference Buildings

Computing labs operate all over campus, but remote access is possible based on class and major. Printers have been centralized at a few locations for remote printing and is included in some courses.

The Faculty Club (614-292-2262; www.ohio-statefacultyclub.com) is a legendary private club for OSU faculty, staff, graduate students, and alumni. A one-time initiation fee is charged, and it is open to members for lunch and dinner. The Faculty Club also hosts special events like art exhibitions and receptions.

Fisher College of Business on Neil Avenue is more of a self-contained campus anchored by undergraduate and graduate program offices, a business research center, business library, and the 150-room Blackwell Inn and Conference Center.

Hayes Hall, named for President Rutherford B. Hayes, was built in 1893 and is one of the historic landmark buildings on campus. The iconic red brick building, situated on the Oval, has a special arch where whispers can be heard from one end to the other. The oldest building on campus is home to the history of art department, art studios, and the John C. and Susan L. Huntington Archive of Buddhist and Related Art.

Hopkins Hall on the north side of the Oval is home to the Department of Arts and many art studios. The galleries, featuring changing exhibitions of student artwork, is directed by the Urban Arts Space downtown.

Knowlton Hall houses the undergraduate and graduate programs for architecture, landscape architecture, and city regional planning. The award-winning modern building was dedicated in 2004 and houses the architecture library, exhibition space, fabrication labs, a cafe, and rooftop garden.

Mershon Auditorium (614-292-3535; www.wexarts.org), located at 15th and High Streets, is the campus's premier venue for dance, music, theater, and film. It has a capacity of about 2,500 people and plays host to national and international acts, as well as university performances.

The Ohio State University Wexner Medical Center (800-293-8000; www.wexnermedical.osu.edu) is a 900-bed hospital within a multidisciplinary academic medical and public health center. Located directly on campus are the full-service teaching hospital and the James Cancer Clinic, a leading cancer research institute, as well other medical research and teaching facilities.

The Ohio Union (www.ohiounion.osu.edu) is the primary gathering place for students, faculty, and staff. This building houses the Undergraduate Student Government, many student organizations, conference ballrooms, and Union Market. The building sits along High Street between 12th and 14th Avenues.

Orton Hall, home to the Department of Geological Sciences, is the second-oldest building on campus. Built in 1893, it's on the south side of the Oval and is supposedly haunted by its namesake, Edward Orton. This building's stone turret is one of the most recognizable landmarks on campus, and the bells chime every day, reminding you how late you are for class. Its geological museum is worth a look as it has a dinosaur and changing exhibitions.

Student Academic Services is the contemporary building that serves as the gateway to the heart of campus, literally and symbolically, as it houses the offices that help students navigate their university existence such as Financial Aid, Career Services, and the Registrar.

Thompson Library (614-292-6785; www.library.osu.edu) is the main library with 1.2 million volumes, a cafe, lots of different reading and study nooks, and a top floor with a beautiful view over campus. OSU's library system has nine libraries and nine specialized collections, which include architecture, fine arts, and science, and engineering libraries. The Moritz Law Library, business library, and medical libraries are among the graduate and professional libraries on campus.

The Veterinary Medical Center (614-292-3551; www.vet.osu.edu), located on the west side of campus, is both a research and teaching hospital. It also serves as a primary pet care facility for the campus and Columbus community. It offers walk-in emergency care from 8 a.m. until midnight.

The Wexner Center for the Arts (614-292-3535; www.wexarts.org) is a multidisciplinary contemporary arts center and museum. It features a broad range of art exhibitions, film· and video screenings, and music, dance, and theater performances in the Mershon Auditorium. Read more about the Wexner Center and its intriguing architecture in the Close-up in the Cultural Columbus chapter.

Athletic Facilities

OSU boasts one of the most comprehensive collegiate sports programs in the country. It offers 16 men's sports ranging from baseball, basketball, and football to fencing, golf, and hockey. OSU has 17 women's collegiate sports teams, including lacrosse, softball, and volleyball, and three coed teams. The athletic department operates on a budget in excess of $225 million and is spending another $100 million on upgrades to existing facilities and new builds.

The best source of information about Ohio State athletics is the athletics department homepage, www.ohiostatebuckeyes.com. Information has been included only for Ohio State's primary athletic buildings, but there are a dozen more not mentioned here.

Bill Davis Stadium is the home of OSU's men's baseball and women's softball teams, which play on Nick Swisher Field. It is located on the west side of campus near the Schottenstein Center just off Lane Avenue. Tickets to the games can be purchased online and at the gate an hour before the game.

The University's Golf Club (614-514-4653; www.ohiostategolfclub.com) is located 2 miles northwest of the campus at the intersection of Kenny and Tremont Roads. The Golf Club was established in 1938 and boasts two of the country's finest collegiate golf courses, the Scarlet and the Gray. National tournaments are held here, and anyone affiliated with the university can play either course. Its restaurant, overlooking the Scarlet golf course, is open to the public for lunch.

Jesse Owens Memorial Stadium is Ohio State's state-of-the-art athletic facility. It is one of the finest multisport facilities in the country. The stadium hosts track-and-field, lacrosse, and soccer events.

Jesse Owens Recreation Centers (614-292-7671) are located on the north and south sides of campus. They provide students with cardio equipment, free weights, and exercise machines. Outdoor basketball courts and table tennis are also available for pick-up games.

The Recreation and Physical Activity Center (RPAC) is the state-of-the-art multipurpose facility consisting of the main building with 25,000 square feet of fitness space, basketball and racquet courts, indoor tracks, and locker rooms. Additional amenities include athletic and personal trainers, massage therapy, babysitting, and a cafe. The McCorkle Aquatic Pavilion includes lap pools, leisure pools, a spa, and sauna. Students also have access to basketball courts, an indoor golf station and putting green, and a retail sports shop. Membership fees are built into students' costs. Faculty and staff can pay a quarterly membership fee to use the facilities and may add on their family. RPAC is located at 337 Annie and John Glenn Ave.

The OSU Ice Rink is located at 390 Woody Hayes Dr., right next to St. John's Arena. The facility is home to the ice hockey varsity and club teams and figure skating, and includes a warming room, locker rooms, training room, and pro shop.

The Schottenstein Center (614-688-3939; www.schottensteincenter.com) is home to the OSU men's and women's basketball and hockey teams. This distinct-looking arena is located off Lane Avenue, just west of campus. You can read more about "The Schott" as an entertainment venue in the Nightlife chapter.

Landmarks

The Lane Avenue Bridge is a state-of-the-art suspension bridge crossing the Olentangy River, making it easier to get from High Street to Highway 315 on the west side of campus. This cable-stayed bridge, opened in 2003, has six 12-foot-wide traffic lanes flanked by 12-foot-wide walking lanes. It is not only an iconic entrance to campus but also a necessary one.

Mirror Lake is Ohio State's oldest landmark, but underwent a modern renovation in recent years. The lake was originally fed by a natural spring, which figured prominently in the site being chosen for the university. Today it is a serene place to enjoy a stroll or sit on a bench along the banks. Several landmarks in their own right surround Mirror Lake Hollow: Browning Amphitheatre, Bucket and Dipper Rock, the Faculty Club, and Pomerene Hall.

The Oval is the heart of Ohio State's campus, but it's really more of a quadrangle. Buildings, pathways, and trees line this grassy hub of activity. Because of its centralized location, the Oval makes a great meeting point and is often the site of protests or rallies. In the summer months you'll see loads of college kids basking in the sun—with their books and iPads, of course.

The Ohio Stadium transcends athletic facilities. Its unique horseshoe configuration makes it one of the most recognizable stadiums in all of college athletics, hence its inclusion here under landmarks. With a capacity of almost 103,000 fans, Ohio Stadium is currently the third-largest in the Big Ten and fourth-largest college stadium in America. Even if you aren't a football fan, you can't overlook the nostalgia this building invokes.

Stadium plans were announced in 1919, and architect Howard Dwight Smith was hired. The animal husbandry department surrendered a pasture west of Neil Avenue in exchange for facilities west of the Olentangy River, which was later straightened and diked to prevent flooding. Ground was broken for Ohio Stadium on August 3, 1921, and the structure was completed in time for the 1922 football season. Its dedication game was held against Michigan on October 21, 1922, and the stadium was paid off a few months before the stock market crashed in 1929.

"The Shoe," the home of Ohio State football, retains its original U-shape and is on the National Register of Historic Places. It underwent $200 million worth of renovations in 2001 and hosted its largest crowd (110,045) on November 26, 2016, against the Michigan Wolverines. The notorious OSU–Michigan game continues to alternate every other year and takes place around Thanksgiving weekend.

BUCKEYE TRADITIONS

It all begins with Welcome Week, when incoming freshmen catch the Scarlet Fever. It doesn't take long to learn the fight songs and be sucked into the world of Brutus Buckeye, and the deep-rooted spirit doesn't stop at graduation. Even locals who attended other universities are often die-hard Buckeyes. Why? Because few schools can boast the successful sports history that the Ohio State Buckeyes can, and few have such deeply rooted traditions associated with it.

A century and a half of time-honored traditions is ingrained in the very fabric of our city. All true Buckeye fans will know who Woody Hayes,

Eddie George, and Brutus Buckeye are. They know where Block-O and the Buckeye Grove are located. They revel in the sound of the Victory bell. Buckeye fans defensively remind you that the school colors are scarlet and gray. Not red, burgundy, or silver—scarlet and gray. This section will clue you in to the most popular Ohio State traditions, so you don't make these kinds of mistakes.

"Across the Field"

Also known as "Fight the Team," this is the Buckeye fight song you hear played throughout the games by "The Best Damn Band in the Land."

The Best Damn Band in the Land (TBDBITL)

Founded in 1878, The Ohio State University Marching Band is a cornerstone of the university and has been dubbed by the fans as TBDBITL, or "The Best Damn Band in the Land."

Block O

This student cheering section has been around since 1938 and is OSU's largest and most recognizable student organization. Well known for their noisy antics during football games, they have had an increasing presence at the men's basketball games, and the women's basketball team also gets visits from the NutHouse. Block O has its own web page, www.blocko.org, which counts down the days, hours, minutes, and seconds until the next football season and cheers on all Ohio State athletes.

Brutus Buckeye

The school mascot is a nut! Brutus is one of the more visible and lovable symbols of Ohio State athletics. In 1965, an art student designed and introduced the first Brutus, while the name was chosen in a contest.

Buckeye Football

Where to begin? Baby Buckeyes are born every day. These fledgling Bucknuts quickly develop into full-grown football fanatics who will follow their team to the ends of the earth. Why? Because the Ohio State football team gives us something to cheer about.

OSU has one of the most storied football programs in the country. In the past 130 seasons, they have won over 900 games, including eight national championships: 1942, 1954, 1957, 1961, 1968, 1970, 2002, and 2014. To learn more than you've ever wanted to know about the team, you can go to the OSU website or visit the countless number of unofficial websites and social media dedicated to the Buckeye mania.

Buckeye Grove

Ohio State All-Americans are honored by having a buckeye tree planted in their name at the south side of the stadium.

Buckeye Leaves

In 1968, Woody Hayes started the tradition of placing buckeye leaves on the helmets of Ohio State players when they make a good play. When you see a sticker-covered helmet, you know you're seeing a good player.

"Carmen Ohio"

"Carmen Ohio" is the stirring alma mater of The Ohio State University. It is the oldest school song still in use. It was written by OSU freshman Fred Cornell in 1902, after a loss in Ann Arbor and can bring a tear to the eye of even the rowdiest of football fans.

Dotting the "i"

The grand finale of the band's famous "Script Ohio" is when a senior sousaphone player prances out of formation to "dot the i" in a most theatrical manner. The i dotter will kick, turn, and bow, causing the crowd to go completely giddy. A trumpet player first dotted the "Script Ohio" i on October 10, 1936. Decades later, this honor is familiar throughout the world but is typically relegated to band members. The few honorary nonband "i dotters" have included Bob Hope and Woody Hayes, and, on the 50th anniversary of "Script Ohio," members of the 1936 OSU Marching Band "dotted the i" en masse.

Gold Pants

A gold charm in the shape of football pants is given to players and coaches following wins over Michigan. The tradition began in 1934, when Coach Francis Schmidt was asked how OSU would deal with its archnemesis from Ann Arbor, and he replied that Michigan players "put their pants on one leg at a time just like everybody else." The Buckeyes then went on to shut out Michigan four consecutive times, prompting a group of businessmen to create the "Gold Pants Club," awarding these charms to all players who beat the Wolverines.

"Hang on Sloopy"

To an Ohio State fan, this song is much more than just a 1965 hit by the McCoys—it's synonymous with OSU football. "Sloopy" made its debut October 9, 1965, at the OSU–Illinois game and was a firmly rooted tradition by the end of that season. TBDBITL will break into riffs of "Sloopy" whenever something goes our way. It is also the official state "rock song." I wonder if Bruce Springsteen knew this when he played "Sloopy" at his last concert here and the crowd instinctively interjected the "O-H-I-O" chant.

OH-IO

What is the proper response to someone yelling "O-H" with their hands up over their heads like a ballerina? "I-O," of course. There is no limit as to where and when you can shout this chant during football season. You'll hear it echoed down the streets, between strangers at bars, and even via text.

The Ramp Entrance

One of the band's most famous traditions dates back to 1928. Band members and football fans let out a roar as the band parades down the ramp onto the field. The drum major struts triumphantly across the field and stops to execute the traditional back bend, touching his plume to the ground and sending the crowd into a frenzy. After a few rounds of "The Buckeye Battle Cry," a drum major baton performance, and a salute to the opposing school, the band performs the pregame show.

The Rivalry with the State Up North

Die-hard Buckeye fans can't even bring themselves to say the name "Michigan." They prefer to leave it at "the state up north." OSU and Michigan played their first game in 1897, and the annual Ohio State–Michigan football game was ranked No. 1 on a list of the "10 Greatest Rivalries in Sports" compiled by ESPN.com. The whole week before the Michigan game is devoted to mustering up school spirit. There simply is no greater rivalry in college athletics.

Scarlet and Gray

Scarlet and gray have been Ohio State's official school colors since 1878 and were chosen by three students because "it was a pleasing combination . . . and had not been adopted by any other college."

Script Ohio

The most famous tradition at The Ohio State University is the band's trademark "Script Ohio." After performing "Carmen Ohio" in a triple O formation, the band, led by the drum major, begins scrolling single file into a cursive spelling of the word *Ohio*. The "Script Ohio" formation was first performed during the 1936 season and takes three and a half minutes to complete.

Victory Bell

The Victory bell is located in the southeast tower of Ohio Stadium and is rung after every Ohio State victory. It was a gift of the classes of 1943, 1944, and 1945. On a calm day, it is said the bell can be heard 5 miles away.

Woody Hayes

I won't even try to sum up this iconic coach in one paragraph, other than to say he still embodies Ohio State football for many people today. His legendary temper ultimately cost him his job, but the football team enjoyed the best (and worst) of times while he was coach (1950–1978). He was

known for his love of competition and history and his hatred of Michigan and losing. Whether people liked or disliked him, his name is immortalized around campus.

SHOPPING

There are a number of retail stores, secondhand shops, tattoo parlors, and pharmacies located along High Street. Amazon has a pick-up center located on the corner of High Street and Lane Avenue.

Buckeye Corner
1315 W. Lane Ave.
(614) 416-2827
www.buckeyecorner.com
You'll be seeing red when you enter this mothership of all things Buckeye. You can find everything from Ohio State clothing to tailgating paraphernalia, including marching band CDs, jewelry, and flags. It is definitely a well-organized and highly stocked store, but it's a bit more expensive than its campus competition. There is another location in Easton.

College Traditions
286 W. Lane Ave.
(614) 291-4678
www.collegetraditions.com
This family-owned campus gift shop has a huge selection of Ohio State gifts and sportswear. You'll find limited-edition artwork, bobble heads, and national championship memorabilia. Even Fido will find something he likes. This is a great place for diehards to find yard decorations and bedroom ensembles.

The Ohio State University Bookstore
1598 N. High St.
(614) 607-6200
www.ohiostate.bncollege.com
The longtime family-owned bookstore is operated by Barnes & Noble College Bookstores. As one of the country's largest academic bookstores, students will find everything they need, from textbooks to computer supplies. It also carries a large selection of computer software, clothing, and dorm supplies.

University Flower Shop
254 W. 10th Ave.
(614) 421-1600
www.osuflowers.com

This florist is right in the heart of campus and will deliver to all student housing areas as well as the major hospitals. It carries fresh flowers, silk arrangements, balloons, and specialty baskets. This full-service FTD florist has another location in Bexley.

CAMPUS PIZZA PLACES

Just make your way along High Street or Lane Avenue and you'll eventually come across the standard pizza chains. Pizza Hut, Domino's, Donato's, and Papa John's are all represented somewhere in the vicinity of campus. So are plenty of good sub shops like Quiznos and Penn Station East Coast Subs. This section will suggest a handful of the more popular pizza places directly on campus. Most of them are open late and accept the BuckID.

Adriatico's New York Style Pizza
1618 Neil Ave.
(614) 421-2300
www.adriaticososu.com

This tiny pizza shop makes a big Sicilian pizza. The crust is thick, and the sauce is rich and garlicky. Though you can find cheaper pizza on campus, this is one of the favorites. The dine-in crowd is more the professor or graduate student types having pizza and beer. It also has a steady inflow of customers from residents of nearby Victorian Village. The tiny shop is located on the corner of Neil and 11th, across from the freshman dorms. Adriatico's delivers and accepts the BuckID.

Hound Dog's Three Degree Pizza
2657 N. High St.
(614) 261-4686
www.hounddogspizza.com

If the motto "Pizza for the People" isn't a dead giveaway that this campus institution dates back to the psychedelic 1960s, then the wall murals of a pooch smoking and drinking will. Despite ancient bathroom graffiti, the place is clean and

the ambience can be quite acceptable at three in the morning. Aside from several kinds of pizza, this sit-down restaurant serves edible pub grub, typical pizza shop fare, and beer. Expect to see a mix of young Abercrombie & Fitch–Urban Outfitters–Old Navy types hanging around the jukebox. Hound Dog is open 24 hours a day, every day, except major holidays, and accepts BuckID.

Tommy's Pizza
174 W. Lane Ave.
(614) 294-4669
www.tommyspizza.com

Tommy (well, at least an oil painting of him) greets everyone at the door. The full-service menu includes consistently good pizza that many say is the best in the entire world. The menu runs the gamut from subs to sandwiches to full Italian dinners. The place is decorated with Big Ten memorabilia on wallpaper covered with Ohio symbols, buckeyes, and footballs. Tommy's does not accept BuckID.

THE PUB CRAWL

The Library Bar
2169 N. High St.
(614) 299-3245
www.librarybar.com

This is an appropriate name for a campus bar located on the barhopping strip along High Street. The place has a lot of character, and two generations of Ohio State students claim fond memories of this bar. With a laid-back atmosphere and friendly staff, it gets very crowded, making it almost impossible to get a seat at the bar. But who goes to a campus bar to sit down? The upper level is lively with pool tables, foosball, and shuffle bowling. The lower level has darts and pinball, and the booths make this area a little quieter. It is well known that the Library has some of the best happy hour prices on campus. Live music and televised football games are the other draws.

> **i** OSU students can ride COTA buses for free anywhere in the city by showing their BuckID.

Out-R-Inn
20 E. Frambes Ave.
(614) 294-9183

This campus institution has been a gathering place since 1980 and continues to be for those who can't leave their college days behind. It's basically a two-floor house-turned-bar with two different outdoor spaces. Grab a table on the front porch or a picnic table out back, where there is a full-service bar and TVs on the fenced-in patio. There are pool tables and dartboards, and, after expanding to the adjacent building, pizza can be had, along with cheap pitchers of beer. Out-R-Inn is a campus mainstay and provides the absolute quintessential college-bar experience.

Skully's Music Diner
1151 N. High St.
(614) 291-8856
www.skullys.org

Situated in that transitional area between the Short North and Ohio State's campus is this eclectic dance-and-music venue that plays host to live alternative music on the weekend. It draws a diverse crowd, and the interior is funky, with a focus on leopard prints. Two bars, a dance floor, and a pool table will keep you entertained, but if you prefer to just hang out, there are sofas and tables inside and a small outdoor patio on High Street. Skully's has a full menu with daily specials and great happy hour prices, and serves food till midnight on weekends.

The Thirsty Scholar
2201 Neil Ave.
(614) 298-9805
www.facebook.com/The-Thirsty-Scholar

Studying makes you thirsty! The Thirsty Scholar has been around forever and is a campus institution located in a "Tudor-like" house at the edge of campus. It is your no-frills campus bar that serves cheap beer, strong cocktails, and hearty bar food. Happy hour specials run every day and are popular for group meet-ups—after studying, of course.

Varsity Club & Pizza
278 W. Lane Ave.
(380) 242-2056
www.varsityclubrestaurantcolumbusoh.com

You know you're in Buckeye territory the moment you walk through the VC's door, or perhaps even sooner. This scarlet-and-gray-painted building, which is pushing 50 years as a campus institution, sits in the shadow of the historic Ohio Stadium. One has to wonder how many times the jukebox here has cranked out "Hang on Sloopy" or people have shouted "O-H," "I-O" across the bar. Everything at the Varsity Club, from the menus to the decor, celebrates Ohio State sports—including the patrons. Don't even think about getting a seat here before or during a football game unless you come very early, and even then it will be a matter of luck. The usual pub nosh, along with pastas and subs, is on the menu. The food is quite affordable, as are the drinks.

Woody's Tavern
The Ohio Union
1739 N. High St.
(614) 292-9239

Located in the heart of campus, Woody's is a casual place in the Union to grab a sandwich and a drink (alcoholic or non), catch a game on the big-screen TV, or see a local band. It is usually closed during the summer quarter and accepts both BuckID and the university meal plan. Be sure to have a photo ID if ordering alcohol; everyone is carded.

GOLF

In general, Ohio does not have many upscale golf resorts, which is why the state's wealth of fabulous courses has often gone unrecognized. Columbus not only has a very rich golf history but also is somewhat a golf destination for travelers at certain times a year. There are more than 50 courses within a 15-mile radius of the city. Columbus is consistently home to two of the world's top 100 golf courses. According to the 2023 ratings by *Golf Digest*, which ranks America's top 100 courses, Muirfield Village Golf Club (Dublin) remains the highest at No. 17, The Golf Club (New Albany) sits at No. 44, and Scioto Country Club (Upper Arlington) landed at No. 68. Just outside the top 100 is the Double Eagle Club (Galena), which came in at No. 107. Each of these four courses is ranked among the best in Ohio.

Don't let these rankings scare you away. Columbus courses range from super exclusive country clubs with elite golf courses to relaxed semi-private clubs, but rest assured, you need not have membership anywhere to play golf on critically acclaimed, demanding, or picturesque courses. Columbus has one of the best samplings of "daily fee" golf courses in the country. The Irish-inspired Golf Club of Dublin, with its sod-lined bunkers and low stone walls, and the very popular New Albany Links courses are reminiscent of European-style golf courses. And you certainly shouldn't overlook the several inexpensive municipal courses where novices don't have to feel as if they are holding up the game while honing their skills. These are great places to learn the game without losing a load of balls in water and woods.

Columbus has long been a breeding ground for golfers. Just check out the roster. The Ohio State University golf team has nurtured the likes of Jack Nicklaus and Tom Weiskopf, both of whom were instrumental in bringing Ohio-born John Cook back to his old stomping grounds to attend OSU. No golf fan (especially not from Columbus) will forget local boy Ben Curtis bringing home the Claret Jug from across the pond after his low-key win at the 2003 British Open. Curtis is believed to be the first person since Francis Ouimet at the 1913 US Open to win a major championship in his first go. Interestingly, Curtis was so under the radar that many a Brit mistook his residence of Kent, Ohio, for Kent, England. And then there was Jack . . .

OHIO STATE PARK GOLF COURSES: A GOOD DEAL

Golf packages with optional lodging and meals are available through five of Ohio's state parks. They offer championship-quality, 18-hole public courses with golf cart rental and pro shops onsite. All five have been given three stars (very good) or four stars (outstanding) by *Golf Digest*. The state parks are an affordable place to get away for a day or a weekend or to hold a tournament. Season passes and gift certificates are also available. Contact individual parks for information, or view the website www.ohiodnr.gov.

Deer Creek State Park Lodge: (740) 869-3088, www.deercreekparklodge.com

Hueston Woods Resort and Lodge: (513) 523-8081, www.huestonwoodslodge.com

Maumee Bay State Park: (419) 836-1466, www.maumeebaylodge.com

Punderson Manor State Park Lodge: (440) 564-9144, www.pundersonmanor.com

Salt Fork State Park Lodge: (740) 432-7185, www.saltforkparklodge.com

DRIVING RANGES AND SIMULATORS

While many public golf courses like Champions, Wilson Road, and Raymond have their own practice areas, these facilities are dedicated driving ranges and entertainment simulators and might provide on-site instruction.

Caddy's Delight
1158 W. Third Ave., Grandview
(614) 725-4209
www.caddysdelight.com
Caddy's Delight offers all levels of golf instruction using golf simulators and offers a special opportunity to virtually "play" some of the world's greatest golf courses. Virtual tournaments and leagues are offered, and the facility is available for private parties and conferences.

The Fairway Golf Simulator and Lounge
1975 Henderson Rd., North Arlington
(614) 502-0729
www.thefairwaycolumbus.com
The family-owned, all-season indoor golf simulator venue allows you to play 9 or 18 holes on courses around the world without leaving the city. It's a great way to warm up your swing before going on a golf trip, or just "hit a bucket of balls" on a virtual driving range. The system keeps track of the score for you. The Fairway also hosts golf tournaments and leagues. Birdie's Grill in the on-site clubhouse serves American fare and handcrafted cocktails, among other drinks.

The Golf Center at SportsOhio
6100 Dublin Park Dr.
(614) 791-3002
www.thegolfcenteratsportsohio.com
Open seven days a week year-round, this facility has a 9-hole, par 3 Wee Links executive golf course. Perfect your swing on one of 100 natural grass tees and 36 covered, heated tees. Practice your short game in the chipping areas, sand traps, putting greens, and target greens. Buckets of balls range from $6 to $10. The facility also boasts a 9-hole foot golf course, miniature golf, pro shop, snack shop, and concession area. There is plenty else to do at SportsOhio, so read on

ℹ️ The Columbus Women's Golf Association offers women the opportunity to learn, play, and enjoy golf with other women through tournaments, outings, and leagues. Lady golfers can join the chapter via the website www.cwgaohio.org. Various municipal courses also have women's leagues open to the public.

about the batting cages, soccer, lacrosse, and extensive list of adult leagues, tournaments, and children's sports camps and clinics in the Family Fun chapter.

Golf Depot
789 Science Blvd., Gahanna
(614) 861-8200
www.thegolfdepotgahanna.com
The year-round practice facility is open until 8 p.m. seven days a week, offering 60 grass tee boxes and eight covered and heated bays. The huge putting and chipping greens allow you to work on your short game, or practice hitting from the rough and bunker areas. Several instructors are available through the on-site Hammond Golf Academy, which offers extensive individual and group lessons and golf academies. Buckets of balls cost between $8 and $20. Food and drinks are available through Barry's Grill and Pub, where you can enjoy post-practice beverages on the seasonal outdoor patio.

Topgolf Columbus
2000 Ikea Way, Polaris
(614) 317-1003
www.topgolf.com/us/columbus
Whether you take golf seriously or not, Topgolf is fun for couples, groups, or family outings. The three-story entertainment venue offers covered, heated bays for year-round fun. Each bay is rented in increments of hours and comes with HDTVs, sets of clubs, spacious sofas, and table service from a full food and bar menu. Choose from dozens of high-tech golf games that challenge your accuracy or distance as you hit micro-chipped balls into various-sized targets (or bunkers). The system keeps track of your score as you rotate through players. Virtual courses allow you to play

iconic golf courses from around the world as well. It's a fun way to hone your skills while having fun.

Westerville Golf Center
450 W. Schrock Rd., Westerville
(614) 882-9079
www.westervillegolf.com

The 120 lighted tees for nighttime practice, 80 grass tees, 40 covered heated tees, chipping greens, sand bunkers, and a putting green coupled with two 18-hole miniature golf courses (and eight batting cages) make this the largest driving range and family entertainment center in central Ohio. The facility is open year-round, golf clubs are available to rent, and there is no dress code. PGA-licensed instructors are also available by appointment. Be sure to pick up a frequent hitter card and earn savings on range balls.

X-Golf Columbus
1165 Yard St., Grandview Yard
(614) 549-7119
www.playxgolf.com

Whether you want to sharpen your golf skills or just relax with some friends, X-Golf provides year-round indoor golfing fun, food, and drinks. The sophisticated simulator tracks every statistic possible, from speed and impact to spin and impact. It keeps score and allows you to play scrambles, take mulligans, and choose from dozens of world-class golf courses.

GOLF COURSES

The following courses are located in Franklin, Delaware, and Licking Counties. The executive-length courses are marked with an (E) after the name. Assume the courses are 18 holes, par 72 unless otherwise noted.

Public Courses

Franklin County
Airport Golf Course (par 70)
900 N. Hamilton Rd.
(614) 645-3127
www.crpdgolf.com/golf-courses/
    airport-golf-course

Blacklick Woods Golf Course
7309 E. Livingston Ave., Reynoldsburg
(614) 861-3193
www.blacklickwoodsgc.com

Champions Golf Course (par 70)
3900 Westerville Rd., Westerville
(614) 645-7111
www.crpdgolf.com/golf-courses/
    champions-golf-course

Gahanna Municipal Golf Course (9 holes, par 35)
220 Olde Ridenour Rd., Gahanna
(614) 342-4270
www.gahanna.gov

Homestead Springs Golf Course
5888 London-Lancaster Rd., Groveport
(614) 836-5872
www.homesteadsprings.com

Mentel Memorial Golf Course
6005 Alkire Rd., Galloway
(614) 645-3050
www.crpdgolf.com/golf-courses/
    mentel-memorial

Raymond Memorial Golf Course
3860 Trabue Rd., Hilliard
(614) 645-3276
www.crpdgolf.com/golf-courses/
    raymond-memorial

Westchester Golf Course
6300 Bent Grass Blvd., Canal Winchester
(614) 834-4653
www.westchestergolfcourse.com

Wilson Road Golf Course (9 holes, par 30) (E)
1900 Wilson Rd., Hilliard
(614) 645-3221
www.crpdgolf.com/golf-courses/wilson-road

Delaware County
Arrowhead Lakes Golf Club (9 holes, par 36)
580 N. Walnut St., Galena
(740) 965-5422
www.arrowheadlakesgolf.com

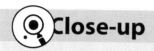

Jack Nicklaus: A Legend in His Spare Time

Few names are more synonymous with golf than Columbus-born and -bred Jack Nicklaus. When Tiger Woods was toddling around in diapers, our Golden Bear-turned-Buckeye was dominating the major championships like no one before. Born January 21, 1940, and raised in Upper Arlington, Jack's father took him to the golf course, where at age 10 he shot a 51 on his first nine holes and won the Scioto Club Juvenile Trophy. At 13, he broke 70. In 1959, at age 19, Nicklaus became the youngest player in 50 years to win the US Amateur. He won his second amateur two years later, and, after claiming he wouldn't turn professional, Jack left Ohio State in 1961. The Golden Bear became the Golden Boy!

Like his hero Bobby Jones, Nicklaus was a golf prodigy. Taking inspiration from Jones's 1926 US Open (or PGA) win at Scioto Country Club here in Columbus, Jack gave it his best to win the Grand Slam year after year. Nicklaus got a very special opportunity to take the four great tournaments in 1972, as they were being played at places he claimed were "good courses" for him. Good is an understatement when it came to his ability to play at Augusta, Pebble Beach, Oakland Hills, and Muirfield in Scotland. At these four courses some of the most famous shots of his career took place, putting Jack in the ranks alongside his hero.

Besides playing the game famously, the Nicklaus name is identified with all aspects of golf: course design, golf academies, real estate, clothing, golf equipment, and a museum. Not to mention the annual Jack Nicklaus Memorial Tournament, which draws the world's most famous golfers to Columbus for a week around Memorial Day.

Jack Nicklaus, the Memorial Tournament
Picture America

Winning the most major championships (18 PGA tours, 2 amateur events, and 8 Senior championships), 100 worldwide professional victories, an international conglomerate, and an annual tournament, Jack's renowned achievements go unparalleled. His status as a living legend was confirmed when named Individual Male Athlete of the Century by *Sports Illustrated* and one of the 10 Greatest Athletes of the Century by ESPN. Bobby Jones himself recognized Nicklaus's talents when referring to the 1965 Masters win: "Nicklaus played a game of which I am not familiar," but Juan "Chi Chi" Rodriguez summed it up brilliantly when he called Jack Nicklaus "a legend in his spare time."

The Jack Nicklaus Museum
2355 Olentangy River Rd.
(614) 247-5959
www.nicklausmuseum.org

Golf fans and museumgoers alike can immerse themselves in Jack Nicklaus's passion for the history and game of golf by visiting the museum, which is located between The Ohio State University campus and golf course. Exhibitions are dedicated to the legends of golf and the decades Jack Nicklaus transcended the game. There is a Memorial Tournament Gallery and Nicklaus Art and Design Galleries, as well as exhibitions about Ohio State's golf programs and the university's Turf Science and Management Program. Golf devotees are able to host a party or business event in this shrine.

The Jack Nicklaus Memorial Tournament
5760 Memorial Dr.
(614) 889-6700
www.thememorialtournament.com

It makes sense that Jack Nicklaus would conceive a golf tournament in the hometown where his legendary game has its roots. His desire to create an annual tournament that brings the world's best golfers together once a year was realized in May 1976. The tournament is played the weekend during or after Memorial Day at the Muirfield Village Golf Club in Dublin, a suburb of Columbus.

Nicklaus designed the Muirfield golf course, and it comes as no surprise that it is named for a most revered course on which he won his first of three British Opens in 1972 at Muirfield, Scotland. Jack's Muirfield was dedicated two years before the first Memorial Tournament on May 27, 1974, with an exhibition game between two former Buckeyes, Jack Nicklaus and Tom Weiskopf. The 220-acre course, which has been tweaked and its holes remade by the perfectionist, includes an 11-acre driving range, seven lakes, and streams winding through lush, manicured property (at least during tournament time) lined by homes that comprise one of Columbus's more affluent areas.

The general public can buy badges for the full week of events, which includes practice rounds for three days prior to the actual tournament. For those of you who may not be able to afford the full week, badges for just the practice rounds cost about $30. It's not nearly as crowded as during the tournament, so it lacks a bit of energy and excitement, but you can easily catch a glimpse of Ernie, Tiger, and Sergio doing what they do best. Weekend badges cost around $250. Keep in mind the golfers are not the only ones who make out financially during this tournament. Some of the money benefits charitable organizations in the central Ohio area. Since the tournament's inception, almost $6 million has been raised for Columbus Children's Hospital, the Memorial's primary beneficiary.

The Memorial Tournament, which remains one of the more popular stops on the PGA tour, is a reflection of Nicklaus's love and respect for the game, and it honors the memory of deceased and living golfers who distinguish themselves in the game. This is Jack Nicklaus's legacy to golf—and to Columbus.

There are only a few entry points to the Memorial Tournament. No outside food or beverages are allowed on the grounds. Souvenirs, food, and alcoholic and nonalcoholic beverages are available once on the grounds.

i The state of Ohio has the fifth-largest number of golf courses in the US. Three private clubs in the Columbus area are consistently ranked among America's top 100 courses by *Golf Digest*: Muirfield Village, Scioto Country Club, and The Golf Club at New Albany. For comprehensive information about golf in Ohio, course information, or golf instruction, check out www.ohiogolf.org or www.ohiogolfguide.com.

Bent Tree Golf Course
350 Bent Tree Rd., Sunbury
(740) 965-5140
www.benttreegc.com

Big Walnut Golf Club (9 holes, par 32) (E)
6683 Hwy. 61, Sunbury
(740) 524-8642
www.bigwalnutgolf.com

Golf Club of Dublin
5805 Eiterman Rd., Dublin
(614) 792-3825
www.golfclubofdublin.com

Hidden Valley Golf Course (9 holes, par 28) (E)
580 W. Williams St., Delaware
(740) 203-1470
www.delawareohio.net

Mill Creek Golf Club
7259 Penn Rd., Ostrander
(740) 666-7711
www.millcreekgolfclub.com

Oakhaven Golf Club
2871 US 23 N., Delaware
(740) 548-5636
www.oakhaven.com

Royal American Links
3300 Miller Paul Rd., Galena
(740) 965-1215
www.royalamericanlinks.com

Safari Golf Club
4853 Powell Rd., Powell
(614) 645-3444
www.safarigolf.com

Licking County
Clover Valley Golf Club
8644 Hwy. 37, Johnstown
(740) 966-5533
www.clovervalleygolfclub.com

Denison Golf Course (par 71)
555 Newark-Granville Rd., Granville
(740) 587-4653
www.denisongolfclub.com

Harbor Hills Country Club (9 holes, par 36)
225 Freeman Memorial Dr., Hebron
(740) 928-3596
www.harborhillscountryclub.com

Hillcrest Golf Course (9 holes, par 34) (E)
8866 Sportsman Club Rd., Johnstown
(740) 967-7921
www.hillcrest-course.edan.io

Kyber Run Golf Course
5261 Mink St., Johnstown
(740) 967-1404
www.kyberrungolf.com

St. Albans Golf Club (par 71)
3833 Northridge Rd., Alexandria
(740) 924-8885
www.stalbansgolfclub.com

Willow Run Golf Course (par 71)
Hwys. 310 and 161, Pataskala
(740) 927-1932
www.golfwillowrun.com

Other Nearby Counties
Darby Creek Golf Course
19300 Orchard Rd., Marysville
 (Union County)
(614) 349-7491
www.darbycreekgolf.com

Marysville Golf Club
13683 SR 38, Marysville
  (Union County)
(937) 642-1816
www.marysvillegolfclub.com

The Players Club at Foxfire
389 Canterbury Rd., Commercial Point
  (Pickaway County)
(614) 224-3694
www.theplayersclubatfoxfire.com

Private Courses

Franklin County
Brookside Golf and Country Club
2770 W. Dublin-Granville Rd., Worthington
(614) 889-2581
www.brooksidegcc.com

Columbus Country Club
4831 E. Broad St.
(614) 861-0800
www.columbuscc.com

Country Club at Muirfield Village
8715 Muirfield Dr., Dublin
(614) 764-1714
www.tccmv.com

Heritage Golf Club
3525 Heritage Club Dr., Hilliard
(614) 777-1690
www.heritagegc.com

Hickory Hills Golf Club (par 71)
3344 Georgesville-Wrightsville Rd., Grove City
(614) 878-0576
www.hickoryhills.com

Jefferson Golf and Country Club
7271 Jefferson Meadows Dr., Blacklick
(614) 759-7784
www.jeffersoncountryclub.com

Muirfield Village
www.mvgc.org

Muirfield Village Golf Club
5750 Memorial Dr., Dublin
(614) 889-6740

New Albany Country Club
5757 Johnstown Rd., New Albany
(614) 939-8520
www.nacc.com

Ohio State University Golf Club
3605 Tremont Rd., Upper Arlington
(614) 459-4653
www.ohiostatebuckeyes.com

Scioto Country Club (par 71)
2196 Riverside Dr., Upper Arlington
(614) 486-4341
www.sciotocc.com

Worthington Hills Country Club
920 Clubview Blvd., Worthington
(614) 885-9516
www.worthingtonhills.com

York Golf Club (par 71)
7459 N. High St., Worthington
(614) 885-5968
www.yorkgc.com

Delaware County
The Club at Tartan Fields
8070 Tartan Fields Dr., Dublin
(614) 792-0900
www.tartanfields.com

Delaware Golf Club (par 71)
3329 Columbus Pike, Delaware
(740) 362-2582
www.delawaregolfclub.com

Double Eagle Golf Club
6025 Cheshire Rd., Galena
(740) 548-5454
www.doubleeagleclub.org

Kinsale Golf and Fitness Club
3737 Village Club Dr., Powell
(740) 881-6500
www.golfkinsale.com

The Lakes Golf and Country Club
6740 Worthington Rd., Westerville
(614) 882-2582
www.lakesclub.com

The Medallion Club
5000 Club Dr., Westerville
(614) 794-6999
www.medallionclub.com

Rattlesnake Ridge Golf Club
1 Rattlesnake Dr., Sunbury
(740) 410-1313
www.rrgolfclub.com

Scioto Reserve Golf and Athletic Club
7383 Scioto Pkwy., Powell
(740) 881-9082
www.sciotoreserve.com

Wedgewood Golf and Country Club
9600 Wedgewood Blvd., Powell
(614) 793-9600
www.wedgewoodgolfcc.com

Licking County
Moundbuilders Country Club (par 71)
125 N. 33rd St., Newark
(740) 344-9431
www.moundbuilderscc.com

PARKS AND RECREATION

Parks and green spaces, along with an endless number of recreational and leisure activities, enhance the overall quality of life in Columbus. Several studies have concluded that natural settings reduce stress, stimulate good health, and elicit positive feelings, so it is safe to say you can find health and happiness somewhere in the 23,000 acres of parks in the Columbus area. Whether swimming, cycling, canoeing, or bird-watching, it can be done here. And much of it is free.

For those who like a good stroll in the park, Columbus has a variety of gardens, lake and riverside scenery, and an extensive city park system, as well as 15 Metro Parks, herb gardens, rock gardens, and the beautiful Park of Roses. Columbus also holds annual festivals dedicated to roses, violets, and tomatoes.

Active types who prefer cycling, roller blading, or running to a leisurely amble have plenty of opportunity to burn off energy in a number of places. One of this chapter's Close-ups features several multiuse biking and hiking trails throughout the city. A general listing of parks and community centers suggests where to swim or play tennis. Phone numbers and links to a variety of organized sports leagues, guided outdoor tours, and activities also are included here.

Getting outdoors makes you smarter, too. The Columbus Department of Recreation and Parks, the Department of Natural Resources, and the state parks offer educational classes that will get you back to nature. Go on a free guided canoe trip with an expert who interprets the local flora and fauna, or take a walk through one of the nearby nature preserves to find rare species of plants and animals. Several parks have nature and environmental study centers in which to watch for wildlife or experience hands-on learning.

If "dirt therapy" is your thing, there are a number of garden clubs and horticultural societies from which to learn the secrets to gardening in zone 5, or you can seek advice from the experts at OSU's Chadwick Arboretum. The Department of Natural Resources offers youth and adult educational gardening and nature programs, not to mention the numerous volunteer opportunities to help keep Columbus beautiful.

Despite seeming landlocked, Columbus has a lot of water in the tri-county area. Three of Ohio's 15 designated Scenic River systems are in the Columbus area. Twenty-two miles of the Olentangy River and 82 miles of Big Darby Creek, along with its tributary, Little Darby Creek, flow through the gently rolling Ohio River Valley.

Parts of the Olentangy River are flanked by dramatic shale banks, while the Darby Creek watershed is known for its abundance and diversity of aquatic and terrestrial plants and animals. The Darby is not only a State Scenic River but also a National Scenic River. To help keep the Darby ecosystem flourishing, a building moratorium and a push to block future building are under way.

This chapter is by no means exhaustive of all the activities that are available in Columbus, but read on to learn how much there is to do. It discusses the popular parks, expounds on many of the participant sports and leisure activities, and provides some practical information for boaters and bikers. No doubt there is something to tickle everyone's fancy in the following pages.

i The state of Ohio has wonderful natural resources. At least 20 of the 75 state parks and about a third of the 82 public nature reserves are within an hour's drive of the city. View maps and read more about the facilities, educational programs, and local wildlife at the Department of Natural Resources website: www.dnr.state.oh.us.

CITY PARKS AND URBAN GREEN SPACES

All parks listed here are free of charge and open from dawn until dusk, year-round, unless otherwise noted.

Battelle Riverfront Park

Battelle is located in downtown Columbus along Civic Center Drive. Several sculptures and memorials are incorporated into this urban park. It's a great starting point for a walking tour of Columbus's outdoor public art.

Bicentennial Park

Bicentennial Park was dedicated on Independence Day 1976 and, as part of the Scioto Mile, is conveniently located downtown along Civic Center Drive. Pools, a splashpad fountain, and benches offer a nice break from the office. This is also the place to be for downtown summer festivals or to just sit back and enjoy the views along the Scioto River from the restaurant Milestone 229.

Confluence Park

The park at the confluence of the Olentangy and Scioto Rivers offers commanding views of the city's skyline. It is a prime location from which to watch the Fourth of July fireworks. Popular with runners and cyclists, the trailhead for this portion of the Greenway Trail System is located at Spring Street and Highway 315, but parking is not readily available.

Frank Fetch Memorial Park

This 0.2-acre oasis in the middle of German Village is a tranquil little spot to take a stroll or walk your dog, as drinking fountains are available for your furry friends. It is lovingly maintained by village residents and was named for the "father of German Village," Frank Fetch, who helped make something pretty in the middle of an urban neighborhood.

Franklin Park

The largest of the city's parks is situated on 90-plus acres east of downtown on Broad Street. The sprawling grounds feature a duck pond, fishing pond, and Japanese garden, as well as basketball and tennis courts. It is adjacent to two smaller parks, Nelson and Wolfe, through which multi-purpose trails run. The Franklin Park Conservatory and David Youth Center also are located within the park.

Goodale Park

On the edge of Victorian Village, Goodale Park is Columbus's oldest park and one of the earliest urban public green spaces in the US. The 35 acres of land was granted to the Columbus community in 1850 by Dr. Lincoln Goodale and is now overseen by the Columbus Department of Recreation and Parks in conjunction with the Friends of Goodale Park. With majestic trees and lovely views of the skyline, Goodale Park is only a short walk from High Street, away from the hubbub of the Short North.

The park plays host to Columbus's Com-Fest and provides the backdrop for free concerts throughout the summer. Goodale is also a pet-friendly park, has an extensive playground area, tennis courts, a pond, and a gazebo, but parkgoers mostly come here to escape to peace and serenity in the middle of the city.

Livingston Park

Thanks to funding from various local organizations, recent beautification projects to Livingston Park earned the city top billing in the Keep America Beautiful program. Located on the near east side of Columbus, this 10-acre urban park is among Columbus's oldest. It is adjacent to Children's Hospital and features an adventure playground, interactive flower garden, and the standard athletic fields and picnic shelters.

Schiller Park

This 23-acre oasis in the middle of German Village has been a park since the early 1800s. After changing hands (and names) a few times, the villagers donated a statue of German poet-philosopher Friedrich Schiller in 1891, and the name stuck. The Huntington Garden Promenade was installed in 1993, and Schiller's quotes are etched into the granite as a tribute to the park's namesake. The perimeter of Schiller Park is lined with the Victorian homes that German Village is known for. It is a great place to take a walk and enjoy the architecture, do a garden tour, or let your children run loose in the playground. The Schiller Recreation Center offers arts and crafts classes, weight training, and other exercise and self-enrichment classes.

i In 1872 Canova's statue of the Greek goddess Hebe was installed in Schiller Park. It served a variety of functions, from drinking fountain to rain shield, until it mysteriously disappeared in the early 1950s. The sculpture *Umbrella Girl*, an updated replacement of the Hebe statue, was a labor of love by local artist Joan Wobst and was dedicated in 1996.

Scioto Mile

The ongoing riverfront development includes riverfront paths, fountains, a performance pavilion and a restaurant. It incorporates various urban parks that are linked via paths and bike trails.

METRO PARKS—OASIS IN THE SUBURBS

The Columbus and Franklin County Metropolitan Park District, known as the Metro Park system, was created in 1945. The district's commitment

Along the Scioto Mile
Amy Paulin

to conserving central Ohio's natural resources and providing the community with public parks and educational programs can be seen in the 20 beautiful and unique parks encompassing 29,000 acres in seven different counties. Each park has its own facilities, lodges, picnic areas, nature trails, activities, and rules.

The Metro Parks are all located within or very close to Columbus city limits. Most of them are situated off I-270 (the Outer Belt) and are well marked with brown attraction signs. They are not operated by the Columbus Department of Recreation and Parks, nor should they be confused with city parks. You can view a map and learn more about each individual Metro Park at www.metroparks.net.

Battelle–Darby Creek Metro Park, Galloway

The view across Big Darby Creek as it meanders through this park is beautiful. Both Big and Little Darby Creeks are home to several species of fish and freshwater mussels, some of which are listed as endangered or threatened. Battelle–Darby Park holds one of the largest areas of land in the surrounding watershed. The unique aspects of this park are its prairie habitats and wetland sites that have been replanted in recent years.

Activities include basketball, canoeing, cross-country skiing, sledding, and hiking. There are facilities for environmental studies and shelters with picnic and playground areas. Pets are welcome on the 1.6-mile trail but must be kept on a leash at all times.

Blacklick Woods Metro Park, Reynoldsburg

Blacklick Woods, the first Metro Park, was established in 1948 and has since grown to include 632 acres, including grassland, forest, and seasonal swamp pools. The 54-acre Walter A. Tucker Nature Preserve is a National Natural Landmark and has been designated an Ohio Watchable Wildlife site. City dwellers can view wildlife and nature without disturbing it by watching through a panoramic one-way window that opens to the forest and pond. If you must have a closer look, a 4-mile boardwalk and bike trail weaves through the woodlands.

i **A nature preserve is not the same as a state park, nor is it a recreational area. Some preserves are situated within parks (such as Blacklick Woods) but contain special wildlife, unusual plants, or unique geological formations that deserve an extra level of protection. More than 28,000 acres in Ohio are classified as protected nature preserve.**

Activities include basketball, cross-country skiing, sledding, and educational programs, as well as a lodge and picnic and playground areas. Golfers with an environmental conscience or environmentalists who like to golf will appreciate the course at Blacklick Woods. It won membership in Audubon's Cooperative Sanctuary Program for Golf Courses because of its environmental design.

Blendon Woods Metro Park, Columbus

Blendon Woods Metro Park opened in 1951 and contains another one of Ohio's 80 Watchable Wildlife sites. Bird-watchers have year-round access to two observation shelters overlooking the 11-acre Thoreau Lake, which sits within the 115-acre Walden Waterfowl Refuge. No fishing is permitted in this lake. The trails lead through the same maple and oak-hickory forests, open fields, and stream-cut ravines that once led the local Native Americans.

Activities include cross-country skiing, ice-skating, and educational programs. Facilities include shelters and picnic and playground areas, as well as a 3,500-foot disk golf course, youth group campsites, and a nature center. Goldenrod Trail is the 1.2-mile pooch path. Dogs must be leashed at all times.

Chestnut Ridge Metro Park, Carroll

Unfortunately, the native chestnut forest that was once here vanished due to a deadly fungus that was introduced years ago, but you can walk the Homestead Trail located high atop the ridge and see remains of Far View Farms, with its original fruit trees planted by the family.

Activities include cross-country skiing, fishing for those under age 15, and educational programs. Facilities include picnic and playground areas. The lake and neighboring wetlands can be appreciated from two docks where fishing events are held. An observation deck offers vistas across the trees into downtown Columbus. The foliage is quite a sight in the autumn.

Clear Creek Metro Park, Rockbridge

With nearly 5,000 acres, Clear Creek is the largest of the Metro Parks and was opened in 1996. Park naturalists teach cultural programs focused on the prehistoric, Native American, and European history and settlement of the area. Over 800 species of plants and 40 species of ferns, many of which are endangered, can be found while hiking the unimproved trails of this park's valleys, ridges, and sandstone cliffs.

Prairie Warbler Trail is appropriately named for the namesake critters that nest here. Clear Creek is stocked with trout, and the cold, tumbling water in certain spots makes great conditions for fly fishing. Fishing is permitted in Clear Creek, but bag limits allow 12-inch minimums and a maximum of two trout. Fishing rules are posted throughout the park.

Glacier Ridge Metro Park, Plain City

Glacier Ridge, once covered with farmland, is a constant work in progress and abounds with outdoor activities. Hiking, biking, and horseback riding trails wind throughout the 1,000-acre park just northwest of Dublin. The Honda Wetlands and prairie restoration is ongoing and attracts numerous birds, which are discussed in the Education Center. The unique features in the park are a boardwalk, ninja challenge courses, 25-foot viewing tower, and working windmill and solar panels that generate power for the park. Dogs are permitted on-leash on the trails, but can run free in the fenced 2½-acre dog park where there is a drinking fountain and bags to clean up after them.

Heritage Trail Metro Park, Hilliard

This 87-acre Metro Park is the trailhead for the 7-mile Rails Trail multiuse path that runs from Hilliard to Plain City. The walking/jogging/bike path in this park is paralleled for 4 miles by a horse

trail. More information about the Rails-to-Trails conservancy program is included in one of this chapter's Close-ups. Features include paved trails and a 4-acre off-leash dog park.

Highbanks Metro Park, Lewis Center

Highbanks Metro Park opened in 1973 and was designated a National Natural Landmark because of the beautiful 100-foot shale bluffs towering high over the banks of the Olentangy River. Two hundred six of the 1,200 acres of the park are also protected as the Edward F. Hutchins Nature Preserve. Take advantage of the observation deck to get a great view of the ravines and bluffs, or check out the Indian earthworks at three locations along the trail.

Activities include canoeing, fishing, cross-country skiing, sledding, and educational programs. Facilities include shelters and picnic and playground areas, an Environmental Study Center, a butterfly and hummingbird garden, and a nature center, at which you can see fossils from the park and learn about the Adena Indians who once inhabited the area. Two paved bike trails, Big Meadows Path and Oak Coves Path, are popular with bikers and runners. A primitive walking trail leads out to a large wetland area with a bird-viewing center. Dogs must be kept leashed while on the 3.5 miles of unimproved trail. Be advised that this trail is closed to hikers and pets when snow arrives in order to provide undisturbed ski tracks for cross-country skiers.

Inniswood Metro Gardens, Westerville

Active sports are not permitted at this park-within-a-park. Inniswood, one of the more manicured Metro Parks, is tucked inside a nature preserve, so hiking is the main activity that goes on here. Streams, woods, and wildflowers make up only part of this 123-acre park, which was opened in 1984. Inniswood's claims to fame are its collection of 2,000 species of plants and many themed gardens.

Among the feature gardens are a rose garden, a cutting garden, a white garden, and an herb garden with themed "rooms." There is also a 2.8-acre children's garden and a prairie garden

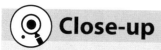

Close-up

Whetstone Park: Coming Up Roses

A sprawling 150-acre park is tucked conveniently off North High Street in Clintonville and runs along a very scenic part of the Olentangy River. The Olentangy was originally named Whetstone River by the early settlers because of the type of whetstones found in the area. The city bought this farmland in 1944 to turn it into what it is now: a free public park operated by Columbus Recreation and Parks. It includes the Whetstone Herb Garden and the Whetstone Park of Roses, one of the largest municipal rose gardens in the country.

Thirteen acres are dedicated to the cultivation of more than 11,000 rosebushes of more than 350 varieties. At the center of the garden is a beautiful fountain, but the focal point is really all around it. Roses in every color of the rainbow create a sensory overload from the moment you enter the park. The best time to visit is when they are in full bloom throughout June, but bloom time continues over several more months. Your senses can feast on fresh sights and smells through September.

The Park of Roses also contains a few specialized rose gardens, an arbetoreum, and an herb and perennial garden. Call (614) 645-3337 or visit www.parkofroses.org for information about private tours or to volunteer to help maintain the gardens.

The Whetstone facilities include a small yet photogenic wedding gazebo and shelter house that can be rented for events. Whetstone Park also contains athletic fields, ball diamonds, tennis courts, and a picnic area with a playground and shelter. Several paved bike trails pass through the park, and hiking paths meander along the banks of the river. Whetstone Park is the pride of Clintonville, and the Park of Roses shouldn't be missed.

highlighting species native to Ohio. The Memorial Garden caters to shade-loving plants, while the Woodland Rock Garden is a peaceful, natural area of waterfalls with woody and perennial species.

Three miles of paved trails run throughout the park, but leashed pets and bicycles are permitted only on Chipmunk Chatter Trail, which can be accessed at Sunbury Road. Several horticultural and natural history programs are available on-site. Inniswood Garden Society and volunteers do an outstanding job keeping up with the seasonal maintenance of the park so that everyone can enjoy beautiful grounds and natural areas year-round. Garden lovers shouldn't miss Inniswood. Visit www.inniswood.org for more details.

Pickerington Ponds Metro Park, Canal Winchester

Bird lovers, grab your binoculars and head over to Pickerington Ponds. This 1,600-acre Metro Park, which opened in 1989, protects a wetland and woodland area ideal for sighting some of the 260

bird species that have been spotted here. Call ahead for a daily recorded message of bird sightings, or go have a look for yourself. This Metro Park is a Watchable Wildlife site and has two observation decks offering views of Ellis Pond, from which you might spot songbirds, hawks, owls, and many other waterfowl. Hike along an uncovered boardwalk and trail to get a more personal wildlife viewing.

Prairie Oaks Metro Park, Hilliard

Some of Columbus's oldest nature can be found in this 500-acre Metro Park west of Hilliard proper. Prairie Oaks is a diverse natural area that falls within the highly protected Big Darby State and National Scenic River. The 30-acre Oak Savannah runs along the edge of the original forest, while nearly 500 acres of restored prairie and grasslands create a spectacular flower show in spring and summer. The meandering wetland restoration area allows for interesting species of sandpipers, plovers, waterfowl, and butterflies to be observed.

Seven trails of varying lengths snake through the varied landscapes, across the creek, and through woods and range in difficulty level. Wear appropriate shoes as the paths are mostly gravel, dirt, or grass.

Activities at Prairie Oaks are fishing, cross-country skiing, hiking along unimproved trails, fishing, and nonmotorized boating on Beaver and Darby Bend Lakes. Facilities include shelters and picnic and playground areas and a bridle trail for horses. Leashed pets are welcome on most trails, and your pooch can swim and dive at the dog beach on Darby Bend Lake.

Scioto Audubon Metro Park, downtown

The public park and nature preserve in downtown Columbus is part of the Scioto Mile network of parks and trails; just aim yourself toward the Metro Park water tower. The 119-acre park is set amid a once-industrial part of the Brewery District adjacent to the Grange Insurance Audubon Center (www.grange.audubon.org). Besides visiting the interpretive nature center and bird- and butterfly-watching, there is plenty to do in this urban preserve, ranging from boating and kayaking in the Scioto River to a challenging rock climbing wall and obstacle course. The dog park is fenced off for small and big dogs and has obstacle stations and jumping frames for your budding dog show winner.

Sharon Woods Metro Park, Westerville

Sharon Woods' 761 acres are enough to shelter you from the two major highways that pass nearby. Hike, bike, jog, or just wander the 3.8-mile multiuse trail winding through wetlands and woodlands. The park contains an observation deck overlooking an 80-acre field, and there are two sledding hills, one for children under age 10 and the other for teens and adults.

Activities include fishing on an 11-acre lake, in-line skating, sledding, and educational programs. The facilities include a lodge, shelters, picnic and playground areas, and four fishing docks for children under age 15.

Slate Run Metro Park and Historical Farm, Canal Winchester

The early settlers mistakenly named this park for the black sheets of rock found throughout the landscape, which they thought were slate. It should actually be called "Shale Run," but Slate Run it is. The park and living museum at Slate Run opened in 1981 and offer a glimpse into what family life was like on an 1880s farm. As the seasons change, so do the farm chores. Volunteers dressed up in period clothing manage the household, but visitors are more than welcome to participate in harvesting or canning produce when the season calls for it.

The park has a 2-mile hiking trail through woodlands and fields. The 2.5-mile horse trail has a parking lot with hitching posts and can accommodate horse trailers. The activities at Slate Run include in-line skating, educational programs, youth group camps, and fishing for children ages 15 and under at Buzzard's Roost Lake. The facilities include shelters, picnic and playground areas, and boardwalks with observation decks throughout the 156 acres of wetland. One of the unique features at Slate Run is Blackburn Bridge, a fully restored historic covered bridge.

Three Creeks Metro Park, Groveport

The Alum, Big Walnut, and Blacklick Creeks converge in this 1,300-acre park appropriately named Three Creeks. Once an illegal dumping ground, this Metro Park is now home to deer, mink, wood ducks, and other varieties of wildlife. Opened in 1999, the park provides a 9-mile, paved multi-use trail for those who want to run, bike, or in-line skate through grasslands and wetlands, past ponds and streams. With a name like Three Creeks, it isn't surprising the activities here include canoeing and fishing, as well as educational nature programs. Picnic facilities are available, and leashed pets are permitted on the trails. Just be sure to clean up after them!

Quarry Trails Metro Park, Marble Cliff

Columbus Metro Parks' newest, 182-acre park is located on the site of Marble Cliff Quarry, once the largest contiguous quarry in the country.

Situated between Grandview, Upper Arlington, and Hilliard, it is convenient to access from the highways and Riverside Drive, and includes trails, observation areas, a mountain bike trail, and a beautiful waterfall and lake. All the trails, ranging from 0.35 to 1-mile in length, are paved and the boardwalk is ADA accessible. General fishing is permitted in the quarry lakes, and Metro Parks does not require a fishing license, but does require catch-and-release, and no live bait may be used. Canoeing and paddle boating are permitted at Turtle Cove or on Swan Lake. The 0.75-mile mountain bike trail is rugged and only one lane, and in the winter, the park has one of the best sledding hills around. Your four-legged friends are permitted on the trails as long as they remain leashed and you clean up after them; a fenced-in dog park permits off-leash carousing for pups. One of the more unique features of this Metro Park is the 1,040-foot quarry face that can be climbed with a guide via online advance registration. The climb takes about 90 minutes and uses a suspension bridge and a series of rungs, ladders, and cables to ascend the wall.

GARDEN CLUBS AND SOCIETIES

Numerous garden clubs exist in the Columbus and central Ohio region; only a few are listed here to highlight a cross section of what is available. They range from Columbus chapters of national societies to specialized, local gardening clubs.

Botanical Society of America
(614) 899-9356
www.botany.org

Central Ohio Chrysanthemum Society
(614) 866-5010
www.mums.org

Central Ohio Herb Society
Inniswood Metro Gardens, Westerville
(614) 895-6216
www.centralohioherbsociety.org

Chadwick Arboretum & Learning Gardens
The Ohio State University
(614) 688-3479
https://chadwickarboretum.osu.edu

Greater Columbus Dahlia Society
(614) 891-5599
www.columbusdahlias.com

Herb Society of America
Central Ohio Unit
(440) 256-0514
www.herbsociety.org

Inniswood Garden Society
(614) 895-6216
www.inniswood.org

i Inniswood Metro Gardens etiquette: In-line skating and running are not allowed in the gardens, nor are food and beverages, but benches and tables are located at the entrance where refreshments can be enjoyed. Shirts and shoes must be worn on the grounds, and you must keep to the trails in the natural areas.

Worthington Hills Garden Club
(614) 885-9516
www.facebook.com/WorthingtonOhio
  GardenClub

COLUMBUS DEPARTMENT OF RECREATION AND PARKS

The folks at the Columbus Department of Recreation and Parks (614-645-3300; www.columbus recparks.com) seem to do it all! They keep us healthy and happy and playing outdoors through city parks, boat docks, golf courses, pickleball and tennis courts, and bike trails. They provide the community with athletic, artistic, and cultural classes, as well as facilitate gatherings of families and friends at picnic shelters, swimming pools, playgrounds, and softball diamonds.

Columbus has 30 neighborhood recreation centers, five athletic centers, and five public splashpads. Each facility offers a variety of services designed to meet the needs of children, adults, and families. These programs range from social programs, such as CRPD Therapeutic Recreation for the disabled community and the city's Free Summer Lunch Program, which provides meals for children, to leisure activities such as after-school projects and sports leagues. Some of these classes are free, while others are fee-based. There are also adult and senior athletic, exercise, and art programs.

There is no residency requirement to participate in programs offered by Columbus Recreation and Parks. However, the recreation departments of suburban neighborhoods may have different guidelines, such as resident and nonresident fees.

Check the Columbus Department of Recreation and Parks's website for a full list of centers and programs. The city also operates seven golf courses, which are listed in the Golf chapter. As you will see from the range of parks, recreational facilities, participant sports programs, and cultural activities, there is no age limit to enjoy a stroll in the park or to take a class for personal enrichment.

Community and Sports Centers

Many of the neighborhood community centers have adult leagues for a variety of sports. The Columbus Department of Recreation and Parks has adult leagues for football, basketball, softball, and volleyball. See its "Adult Sports" website for further schedules, fees, and online registration forms: www.crpdsports.org.

Berliner Park Sports Complex
1300 Deckenbach St.
(614) 645-3366
www.columbusrecparks.com
The 210-acre park is maintained by the Department of Recreation and Parks. Its indoor sports complex has basketball and volleyball courts, while the outdoor facility has 31 well-kept diamonds for softball and baseball, and areas for football, rugby, soccer, and walking. It claims to be the largest softball facility in the US and is located south of downtown Columbus off I-71 and Green-lawn Avenue. The Central Ohio Mountain Biking Organization maintains 4 miles of mountain bike trails to use at your own risk in non-muddy conditions, with the trailhead at Berliner.

Dublin Community Recreation Center
5600 Post Rd., Dublin
(614) 410-4550
www.dublinohiousa.gov
Dublin's recreation center is a central point for community gatherings. It has two swimming pools, a gymnasium, fitness area, jogging and walking track, extensive programming, such as aerobics classes, personal fitness, and swimming instruction, and an open gym, sports leagues, theater, and a community hall for meetings and classes. The fees are determined according to resident/nonresident status. On-site babysitting also is available.

Hilliard Recreation and Wellness Center
Scioto Darby and Alton Darby Creek Roads
(614) 876-5200
www.hilliardohio.gov
The new 105,000-square-foot Hilliard Recreation and Wellness Center, nicknamed "The Well," will open for business in 2025. It will include a gymnasium, indoor running track, fitness and weight room, aerobic dance and spin studios, classrooms, a 240-person community events room, commercial kitchen, child watch area, outdoor patio, and an aquatic facility that includes a lap pool, recreation activity pool, waterslide, and spa. Nearly 25,000 square feet of space within The Well will be dedicated to an integrated medical health and wellness center managed by The Ohio State University Wexner Medical Center. The center will offer rehabilitation and physical therapy.

Upper Arlington Community Center
3200 Tremont Rd.
https://communitycenter.upperarlingtonoh
.gov
The Bob Crane Community Center will open in spring 2025 in Kingsdale Center. The state-of-the-art space will offer an indoor pool, fitness and exercise spaces, three multipurpose gyms, a track, and e-sports room. Child care will be available, as well as an outdoor terrace, event and party space, and changing art gallery.

Westerville Community Center/Sports Complex
350 N. Cleveland Ave.
(614) 901-6500
www.westerville.org
This 96,000-square-foot facility has become the heart of Westerville's parks and recreation department. With a leisure pool and lap pools, tracks, fitness center, gymnasium, climbing wall, supervised room for children, lounge, and indoor playground, this facility caters to individuals and families alike. There are daily admission fees, or you can purchase individual and family PASSports. Keep in mind that nonresidents are charged a little more. Those who work full time in the Westerville area can take advantage of Westerville resident rates and attend no-sweat lunchtime exercise programs or squeeze in a quick workout before going home.

The Worthington Community Center
345 E. Wilson Bridge Rd., Worthington
(614) 436-2743
www.worthington.org/city/center.cfm
People who work full time or live in Worthington have access to this facility at a reduced rate. The center has two indoor swimming pools, a hot tub, fitness center, jogging/walking track, and art and childcare rooms. Individual and family passes are available, or purchase punch cards good for 10 or 20 individual visits.

OTHER LEISURE ACTIVITIES

Ballooning

For a bird's-eye view of Columbus and the surrounding area, call Columbus Aeronauts at (614) 699-1492 or view www.columbusaeronauts.com.

Boating

Boating, waterskiing, and tubing in Columbus can be a blast, but make sure your vessel is legal before having a boatload of fun. All watercraft, including kayaks, canoes, rowboats, and pedal boats, must be registered through Ohio's Bureau of Motor Vehicles; licenses are valid for three years. Fees range from $40 to $100 and help support Ohio's boating programs. Registration can

be renewed online at the Ohio Department of Natural Resources website at www.dnr.state.oh.us, or call (877) 4-BOATER (426-2837) with questions.

Once all the paperwork is in place, there are a handful of marinas at which you can dock your boat. The Columbus Department of Recreation and Parks operates Griggs Reservoir, O'Shaughnessy Reservoir, and Hoover Reservoir. Powerboats can take advantage of Griggs's and O'Shaughnessy's 40 mph open zones, while sailing and pontoon boats are more common on Hoover because of the 10 mph speed limit across the entire lake. Dock season runs from early May through late Oct, and a public lottery is held each spring for those wishing to dock at one of the marinas. Leaseholders are given first dibs to renew their space from year to year, but you can apply for dock space any time in the season.

A few private boat clubs operate around Columbus. Leatherlips Yacht Club (614-889-8997; www.leatherlips.com), Hoover Sailing Club (614-216-2679; www.hooversailingclub.com), and Scioto Boat Club (614-375-2628) are all membership-based private clubs. See the Sailing entry for more information, and don't forget the endless boating opportunities 2 hours north at Lake Erie.

Columbus Sail and Power Squadron
8492 Cotter St., Lewis Center
(614) 206-9651
www.columbussailandpower.org
The CSPS is the local unit of the world's largest nonprofit boating organization. With over 500 members in Columbus, it sponsors a wide range of boating activities, events, and educational and safe-boating classes and does free vessel safety checks. You must be at least 18 years of age to gain membership.

Bowling

There are quite a few bowling alleys around Columbus, but here is a short list for regular and duckpin bowling.

AMF Lanes
4825 Sawmill Rd., Dublin Area
(614) 889-0880
2434 Old Stringtown Rd., Grove City

(614) 875-4343
4071 E. Main St.
(614) 237-3723

Bowlero Columbus
4825 Sawmill Rd.
(614) 889-0880
www.bowlero.com

Columbus Square Bowling Palace
5707 Forest Hills Blvd.
(614) 895-1122
www.palacelanes.com

Holiday Lanes Bowling Center
www.holidaylanes.biz
4589 E. Broad St., Whitehall
(614) 861-1600
215 W. Johnstown Rd., Gahanna
(614) 471-1111

PINS Mechanical
www.pinsbar.com
141 N. Fourth St., downtown
(614) 464-2255
6558 Riverside Dr., Dublin Bridge Park
(614) 761-3933

Star Lanes
8655 Lyra Dr., Polaris
(614) 468-4830
www.starlanespolaris.com
Read more about the high-tech bowling and entertainment complex in the "Group Entertainment" section of the Nightlife chapter.

Ten Pin Alley
5499 Ten Pin Alley, Hilliard
(614) 876-2475
www.tenpinalley.com

Western Lanes
500 Georgesville Rd.
(614) 274-1169
www.western-lanes.com

Camping

The city of Columbus no longer operates public campgrounds, but the state runs campgrounds to accommodate all types of tents and trailers. At a minimum, state park campgrounds provide drinking water, restrooms or latrines, pads for parking a car or trailer, picnic tables, and fire rings. Campsites range from no-frills, walk-in tent sites to full-service sites for recreational vehicles with electrical and water hookups. Pets are allowed on designated grounds and must be kept on leashes at all times.

KOA has camping and glamping sites north in Sunbury and Mt. Gilead and east, conveniently located off I-70 near Buckeye Lake. The properties accommodate primitive tents or big rigs up to 85 feet. Some have on-site cabins, swimming pools, and showers. Cable, electricity, gas, and firewood are available for an extra charge. Call (740) 928-0706 or go to www.koakampgrounds.com to make your reservations.

Canoeing and Kayaking

Check out Paddle Ohio at www.ohio.org for extensive paddling opportunities throughout the state. Here in Columbus, the Department of Recreation and Parks offers group canoe trips, which can be found in its programming calendar, while Gahanna Parks and Recreation rents kayaks to explore Big Walnut Creek. Trapper John's Canoe Livery (www.trapperjohnscanoeing.com) makes a day out on Big Darby Creek easy for the whole family. If you don't have your own craft, rent one from the marinas at Alum Creek, Hoover Reservoir, Delaware State Park, or Buckeye Lake, which are all easy drives from Columbus.

Olentangy Paddle (www.olentangypaddle.com) is an outfitter that offers guided tours and kayak and paddleboard rentals to explore the downtown part of the Scioto River. Morgan's Ft. Ancient Canoe Livery will put you in a canoe for a trip through the breathtaking Ancient Valley River Gorge, an hour south of Columbus, or go and rent individual canoes, kayaks, and rafts. Check out the tours at www.morganscanoe.com or call (513) 932-7658. Also south of the city is Hocking Hills

Canoe Livery (740-385-0523; www.hockingriver.com), offering guided trips of different lengths for all skill levels. The Moonlight Canoe Ride on the Hocking River leaves at sunset and returns by the light of the moon to a toasty bonfire and marshmallows.

Climbing

Chamber Purely Boulders (1165 Chambers Rd.; 614-237-2377) gives climbers of all skill levels varied terrain on which to practice top-roped climbing and bouldering, and work on precision foot and hand work. It offers climbing classes for adults and youth, and group climbing parties. Day passes and multi-punch passes are available.

Another option is Columbus Outdoor Pursuits (614-442-7901; www.outdoor-pursuits.org), which has its own climbing facility as part of a rock-climbing program. Equipment is provided at no extra charge, but it is recommended you bring your own shoes. The Audubon Climbing Wall in the Scioto Audubon Metro Park downtown is a 35-foot structure not ideal for beginners, but the smaller boulder makes for a great starting point for young climbers to play around.

The newest Metro Park, Quarry Trails in Marble Cliff, has a vertical stone wall of more than 1,000 feet. It is a guided climb by advance reservations only. Read more about this experience in the "Metro Parks—Oasis in the Suburbs" section in this chapter.

Put your climbing skills to use in the great outdoors by heading to either Hocking State Forest or John Bryan State Forest. You are allowed, by permit, to rappel and rock climb in designated areas established within the parks.

Cricket

Several cricket clubs are active in the central Ohio region, and one of the oldest is the Columbus Cricket Club (www.columbuscricket.org). The Ohio State University has an intramural cricket club open to students, alumni, and staff. Contact Ohio State's Recreation and Physical Activity Center at (614) 292-7671 for further information.

i You can't live in Columbus and not know about Pelotonia, the annual cycling event that has raised nearly $300 million in the past 15 years for cancer research at the Ohio State Comprehensive Cancer Center–James Cancer Hospital. Each August thousands of cancer survivors, supporters, friends, and family donate money in support of riders pedaling various distances up to 101 miles. The ride weekend is an inspired three-day celebration of life and memory. People all along the route come out to cheer riders the whole way from Columbus to Kenyon College in Gambier, Ohio. Read more, donate, or register to ride at www.pelotonia.org.

Cycling/Mountain Biking

Under Ohio law, bicycles are defined as vehicles, and cyclists are obligated to adhere to the same rules as motorists. Bikers can be cited for speeding, drunk or reckless driving, and riding against traffic. The use of a horn, bell, or some sort of audible device is required, as is a light after dark. Some communities enforce their own rules, such as requiring helmets or limiting cyclists to dedicated bike paths. Just be conscientious of the rules if you plan to ride on a road shared with other vehicles.

The State of Ohio's website www.ohio.org/things-to-do/cycling-bike-paths is the best way to discover "Ohio's Bikeways" and download bike path maps, including those around Columbus. It also features dozens of statewide cycling tours, trails, and other resources. Adventure Cycling Association (800-755-2453; www.adventurecycling.org) organizes a laundry list of guided tours for cycling and mountain biking, including the Ohio to Erie Trail and the Underground Railroad Bicycle Route, which runs from Alabama to Canada, passing through Xenia, London, and Oberlin, Ohio.

Fishing

Locals fish everywhere, from the Olentangy and Scioto Rivers to the streams and ponds in some of the Metro Parks to the lakes and reservoirs surrounding Columbus. Large- and smallmouth bass, trout, and crappie are among some of the fish inhabiting central Ohio waters. The muskie, which is native to Ohio, is the largest of the Ohio game species. One of the best muskie resources is the Ohio Muskie Club at www.ohmci.org. The Ohio Department of Natural Resources (800-945-3543; www.ohiodnr.gov) is the most comprehensive place to read up on fishing resources and requirements.

Fishing licenses range from $14 to $25, and longtime residential licenses can be purchased for a few hundred dollars. Those over 65 can reap the benefits of being a senior and get a license for a mere $10. Fishing licenses are not required for those under age 16 or when fishing in private ponds and lakes.

Folf/Disk Golf

There are a handful of Frisbee golf courses in the area. The most popular city-operated disk golf course, located at 2933 Riverside Dr. on the east side of Griggs Reservoir in Upper Arlington, features an 18-hole course with large concrete pads and both open and wooded fairways. Blendon Metro Park is an 18-hole course perfect for beginners and charges a small fee per round to help maintain the course. Glacier Ridge Metro Park's 6-hole course is free, as are the two maintained by the city: the Hoover Reservoir Disc Golf Course on Central College Avenue in Westerville and Walnut Hill Disc Golf Course at 6001 E. Livingston Ave.

FootGolf at Sports Ohio in Dublin is a combination between soccer and golf and is played on a 9-hole, par 3 course and runs about $16 a round. Go to www.sportsohio.org for details.

Ice Hockey

Ice hockey has really taken off in Columbus. Men and women over the age of 18 can get involved in year-round adult recreational ice hockey leagues at one of the five Chiller facilities. They host special events, tournaments, playoffs, and championships, and the Columbus Blue Jackets Hockey School holds adult ice hockey and goalie camps at the Chiller rinks. People of any skill level can sign up as an individual or as a team. Contact the league at (614) 791-9999, or have a look at the Chiller website, www.thechiller.com, to register.

The Dispatch Ice Haus (614-246-3380), which is located inside the Nationwide Arena, is the practice rink for the Columbus Blue Jackets. Chiller Dublin (614-764-1000) has two NHL-size rinks and one of the largest learn-to-skate and junior ice hockey class programs in the country. Chiller Easton (614-475-7575) also is a dual-rink facility with one NHL regulation-size rink and the only Olympic-size rink of its kind in Ohio. Chiller North (740-549-0009), located in Lewis Center, has two NHL-size rinks and a pro shop. You might even be able to catch some curling going on here. These four facilities offer public skate sessions, skate rental, locker rooms, party and meeting rooms, and concessions. See the Family Fun chapter for information regarding youth ice hockey.

The Ohio State University has men's and women's club ice hockey teams, open only to OSU students, which play at the OSU Ice Rink. Learn more about the team and view their schedule at www.osuclubhockey.com or www.osuwomen-sclubhockey.org.

Ice Skating

Public skating sessions are held at the six Chiller ice facilities around the city. Information can be viewed online at www.thechiller.com. Chiller Dublin has two rinks and hosts many sessions per week. It has one of the largest learn-to-skate programs in the country. Chiller Easton also is a dual-rink facility, one of which is the only Olympic-size rink of its kind in Ohio. The OhioHealth Ice Haus (614-246-3380), which is located inside the Nationwide Arena, is the practice rink for the Columbus Blue Jackets and is sometimes open for public skating. All the above facilities offer skate rental, locker rooms, a party and meeting room, and concessions.

The Chiller Figure Skating Club, an organization helping skaters, coaches, and judges develop their skills, is a member of the US Figure Skating Association. Learn more about the instruction, clinics, exhibitions, and competitions at www.thechiller.com/figure-skating.

The Ice Rink at The Ohio State University also has open skating sessions a few times a week. Visit www.ohiostatebuckeyes.com for the schedule.

i The Adaptive Sports Connection in Powell offers people with physical or mental disabilities the opportunity to pursue outdoor activities, such as kayaking, cycling, and all sorts of other athletic adventures. Call (614) 389-3921 or view www.adaptivesportsconnection.org for program information, registration, or volunteer information.

Kickball

Seasonal kickball leagues are formed throughout Columbus during the summer months, and Columbus Recreation and Parks is a good place to start. One of the more popular spots to play is downtown at the Columbus Commons, where co-ed leagues play a few times a week. View www.columbuscommons.org to register.

Lacrosse

Lacrosse in Columbus is not quite a way of life as it is in, say, Baltimore or Long Island, but it is very popular here. If you are interested in playing in an adult lacrosse league, have a look at the Ohio Lacrosse Foundation's website: www.ohlax.com. This chapter of US Lacrosse provides links to regional club teams for adults, information regarding high school and college teams, and clinics and tournaments. The men's Columbus Club team is part of the Midwest Club Lacrosse Conference and has a winter indoor league. The Ohio State University has men's and women's varsity and club teams, as do several other universities in the area, such as Denison University, Ohio Dominican, Ohio University, Ohio Wesleyan University, and Wittenberg University.

Parachuting

For thrill seekers who want to try skydiving, the AerOhio Skydiving Center (800-726-3483; www.aerohio.com) is a good place to start. Weekday tandem jumping must be scheduled in advance, but walk-ins are welcome on the weekends. First-time jumpers have the options of accelerated freefall, tandem, or static line jumps, and for the experienced divers there are even more options.

Polo (Equine)

The US Polo Association has a chapter in Columbus that plays every Sunday afternoon (June–Sept) at the Bryn Du Polo Field in Granville. Pay a small fee to park and bring your own chairs, tent, food, and drinks, then help stomp the divots during breaks. View the Columbus Play Polo Club's website at www.playpoloclub.us, or call the club hotline at (614) 230-3342.

Pools

Swimming pools are located in the community centers listed in this chapter, some with indoor and outdoor pools, and throughout the surrounding neighborhood parks. The Columbus Department of Recreation and Parks operates eight pools and an indoor aquatic center offering swim classes for ages 6 months and up. Many neighborhoods, like Dublin, Grandview, New Albany, Worthington, and Upper Arlington also offer residential and nonresidential fee-based membership and daily entry passes. Check with each pool to make sure of the entry requirements as some, like Grandview pool, require pre-paid admission online and do not accept payment at the gate.

Racquetball and Handball

A good place to start is the Racquet Club of Columbus, which is located at 1100 Bethel Rd. The club has 4 Terstep panel racquetball courts, including two with glassed-in viewing, 10 Novacrylic tennis courts, and a fitness center. There are programs for men, women, and children. For membership rates or information on lessons and leagues, call (614) 457-5671 or view the website at www.racquetclub1.com.

Many private gyms and athletic facilities in Columbus have racquetball and handball courts, so contact the gym directly before joining. The Ohio State University has dozens of racquetball courts available to students and staff.

Rowing

If you want to learn the art of sculling, sweep rowing, or coxing, join the Greater Columbus Rowing Association (www.columbusrowing.org). No experience is required, as members are divided into categories of novice, intermediate, and advanced. Membership includes use of the boathouse, which is located on the Scioto River, and equipment. The association requires 5 hours of boathouse volunteer service, and members may get involved in competitive rowing and regattas.

The Ohio State University crew practices on the Olentangy River, as do many of the high school crew teams from Dublin, Upper Arlington, Wellington, or Westerville High Schools. Quite often you will see tournaments taking place along the riverfront and people cheering from the Fishinger Bridge.

For structured rowing exercise classes, head to Row House Fitness in the Lane Avenue Shops in Upper Arlington (614-321-2045; www.therowhouse.com). The fitness studio teaches different levels of rowing classes, some with built-in stretching and yoga components.

Rugby

Not only does Ohio breed amazing football players, but we churn out some good rugby players, too. More than 72 American and Canadian teams converge on Columbus every year for the Ohio Rugby Classic, which is held at Berliner Park. Men's and women's collegiate teams and high school teams compete in this round-robin tournament. The Ohio State University Rugby Football Club takes part in this tournament on top of its regular season schedule.

The Columbus Rugby Club is a Division III men's rugby team and its home field is in Obetz, Ohio. The CRC can be reached online at www.columbusrugby.org.

ⓘ Columbus Outdoor Pursuits (614-442-7901, www.outdoor-pursuits.org) is a nonprofit organization with outdoor programs for youths and adults. It offers basic and intermediate canoe and kayaking schools, low-budget boating trips, caving, rock climbing, hiking, backpacking, and bicycling programs, as well as winter activities like cross-country skiing.

Ladies, rugby isn't just for men! Information regarding the Columbus Women's Rugby Club can be viewed at www.cbuswomensrugby.com; no experience is required.

Running/Walking

The community and recreation centers listed in this chapter have paved or indoor tracks, but if you are interested in trekking through scenic areas rather than circling a track, read the "Happy Trails to You!" Close-up about various multiuse paths located throughout Columbus. The Central Ohio Greenways trail system (www.centralohio greenways.com) offers an extensive network of interlinked paths for walkers and runners.

Sailing

There are a handful of sailing options around Columbus. You can get details about the sailing at the Ohio Division of Watercraft by calling (614) 265-6480. Those of you who captain your own ships should have a look the Alum Creek Sailing Association (www.alumcreeksailing.com). It has a sailboats-only marina, a carry-on launch area for small beach craft, picnic areas, and shower facilities. The association sponsors races and offers both social and instructional programs. ACSA can be reached at (614) 467-9016.

The Hoover Sailing Club (614-898-9248; www.hooversailingclub.com), located at Hoover Reservoir, offers sailing instruction for adults and youth and plays host to weekly races and annual regattas. More links and general information can be found in the "Boating" entry.

Scuba Diving

Aquatic Adventures
3940 Lyman Dr., Hilliard
(614) 545-3483
www.aquaticadventuresohio.com
Aquatic Adventures is a full-service scuba center that which provides a wide range of aquatic training, from simple swimming lessons to PADI, SDI, and Master certifications. The retail shop sells swimming gear and scuba equipment and puts together dive trips.

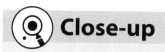

Close-up

Happy Trails to You!

Central Ohio affords cyclists and mountain bikers of all levels a pedal through some of Ohio's most beautiful scenery. The Central Ohio Greenways trail system consists of 150 miles of bike trails throughout the Columbus area, and more are being added regularly. Information about the individual multiuse trails and connectors can be viewed at www.metroparks.net. Eight different bike trails are linked to one another and into the major Ohio to Erie Trail. The Mid-Ohio Regional Planning Commission (MORPC) site's large, clickable map (www.morpc.org/central-ohio-greenways) shows existing and projected routes for the trails' continuous circulation around central Ohio.

East of the city is the 14-mile paved Thomas J. Evans Trail, which begins in Newark and winds along Raccoon Creek to Johnstown, Ohio. The 10-mile Panhandle Trail also leaves Newark but runs the opposite direction to the east. From this local trail you can connect to the scenic Blackhand Gorge Bikeway, which is part of the Rails-to-Trails conservancy program (www.railtrails.org, www.traillink.com). This nationwide network of bike trails is made from former rail lines, and many miles pass through Columbus.

Blackhand Gorge Bikeway, named for the outcroppings of bedrock called blackhand sandstone that occurs in this area, is located southeast of Columbus in Newark. It is a 4-mile asphalt path weaving through beautiful Ohio scenery, passing through thick woods, crossing streams, and running along the river. Keep your eyes open for cool rock formations.

The 12-mile Blacklick Trail follows Blacklick Creek while the Big Darby Trail runs for 3 miles along the State and National Scenic River. The Heritage Rail Trail is a 6.1-mile trail beginning in the historic district of Old Hilliard and ending west of Columbus near Plain City.

The I-670 Bikeway is a 3.5-mile asphalt pathway leading from the airport, through the city, and ending at Cleveland Avenue. It is recommended more as a commuter bikeway than a recreational path because it follows the highway, and riders must contend with curbs, bridges, and busy traffic conditions.

Olentangy-Scioto Bike Path was Ohio's first rail trail. Established in 1969, these two continuous paved trails run about 20 miles right through the heart of Columbus. The Olentangy-Scioto Trail mile marker 0 is located at Broad Street, and the miles are marked north and south of this point with either wooden posts set next to the trail or half-mile "ticks" on the pavement. Maps tend to divide this path into four sections: Upper and Lower Olentangy and Upper and Lower Scioto Trails.

Beginning at Frank Road, it passes through Berliner Park in German Village and heads north through downtown Columbus and the OSU campus. It passes through Clintonville and several parks before ending in Worthington Hills. This is one of the most popular multiuse trails in the city, used by bikers, joggers, walkers, and cross-country skiers (only in the winter, of course).

Outside downtown, Hilliard has about 35 miles of bike trails with a 6-mile stretch being part of the Heritage Rail Trail. Westerville has more than 50 miles of trails, with a few miles that is a rails-to-trails bikeway, part of the Ohio Erie Trail, which will run continuously from the Ohio River at Portsmouth in southern Ohio north to Lake Erie in Cleveland. Dublin's even more extensive recreational paths run 150 miles through parks and neighborhoods with a bike "pump track" in Emerald Fields Park.

Mountain bikers head north of Columbus to Alum Creek State Park for its 15 miles of wooded trails, perfect for beginning and intermediate riders. Berliner Park has a trailhead for 3 miles of trails appropriate for all skill sets. Several Columbus communities, including New Albany, Dublin, and Hilliard, maintain extensive bike paths throughout the neighborhoods.

For those who are not familiar with biking etiquette, a few pointers for trail usage could never hurt. Keep right, and pass on the left. More considerate cyclists have bells (or some sort of audible signal) to warn they are coming up from behind. The speed limit is 15 mph, and no motorized vehicles are permitted on any trails. Alcohol is strictly prohibited. Pets are permitted on the trails, but they must be leashed at all times. Happy trails to you!

Columbus Scuba
4680 Indianola Ave., Clintonville
(614) 353-7234
www.columbusscuba.com

Columbus Scuba offers both individual and small-group diving lessons in an indoor heated pool, professional and technical courses, and continuing education, but you must provide your own mask, fin, wetboots, and snorkel. It also sells diving equipment and organizes great dive trips.

Skateboarding

Skateboarders will be in concrete heaven at the city-run Dodge Skate Park at 667 Sullivant Ave. on the west side of Columbus. It has three in-ground bowls at 3, 4, and 6 feet deep, as well as a quarter pipe, bank ramp, and fun box. Purchase a required permit for use. The park is open from Apr to Nov. Skaters must wear helmets, and BMX bikes, boards, and roller blades are all welcome. The city also operates Tuttle Skate Park at 240 W. Oakland Ave. A few communities such as Upper Arlington, Dublin, Worthington, Gahanna, and Bexley have installed smaller concrete skate parks in the neighborhoods.

Skiing

Mad River Mountain
Bellefontaine
(970) 754-0005, (800) 231-SNOW
www.skimadriver.com

Mad River Mountain, Ohio's largest full-service ski and snowboard resort, is located at Ohio's highest point, an easy drive from Columbus on US 33. There are slopes for beginners and some new trails of varying difficulty for seasoned skiers.

i The Columbus Ski Club is an adult coed sporting league that reaches beyond the slopes. Really, it's all about the socializing! Check out www.columbusskiclub.org for local social excursions, national and international travel, adult leagues in a variety of sports, like volleyball, billiards, and tennis, and, of course, skiing. Call (614) 481-SNOW (7669) to find out more about the different activities.

Ski lessons and lift passes are among the services to check out online. A variety of food and drink is available at the base lodge, as well as a ski and snowboard rental shop, gift shop, game room, and children's zone on-site. No lodging is available at this facility.

Soccer

Adult men's and women's soccer programs are available at most of the recreation centers operated by the Columbus Department of Recreation and Parks. Call (614) 645-3300 to find out where the soccer leagues and organized practices meet and how to join. Youth soccer programs are listed in the Family Fun chapter.

Information regarding Columbus's Premier Soccer League can be found at www.columbus-premierleague.com. The Premier League, which is affiliated with the Southern Ohio Adult Soccer Association, the US Soccer Association, and the US Soccer Federation, has two divisions of men's teams.

Softball

Columbus is crazy for softball! It seems that every community, every business (big or small), and even the tiniest neighborhood bars all have softball teams. There are teams for slow-pitch, fast-pitch, beer drinkers, men, women, youth, gay, lesbian, the physically and mentally challenged— you name it, there is probably a league for it here. Just ask around to find out about teams in your community, or check with your place of employment. It won't take much legwork to find a team that's a perfect fit for you.

The Columbus Department of Recreation and Parks has both adult and youth softball leagues that play spring through fall. For information on city leagues, view the website at www.columbusrecparks.com for schedules and registration. Columbus Recreation and Parks also sponsors several tournaments throughout the year. The Columbus Lesbian and Gay Softball LGBTQIA+ open-division league is one of the largest gay softball organizations in the Midwest. They put together some fun organized tournaments and competitions that draw hundreds of people.

Tennis and Pickleball

Public tennis courts are common in Columbus, and pickleball courts are increasing in number. Most neighborhoods have courts within their parks or on school properties, some of which are lit in the evenings. Most of the parks and community centers listed in this chapter have tennis courts, so call the park to learn if there are any special rules or programs.

The Columbus Department of Recreation and Parks programs adult tennis leagues and lessons for those with varying skill levels, as well as pickleball instruction. Check out the department's website for information regarding the tennis program.

The premier tennis center is the Racquet Club of Columbus, located at 1100 Bethel Rd. The club has 10 Novacrylic tennis courts, 4 Terstep panel racquetball courts, including two with glassed-in viewing, and a fitness center. There are programs for men, women, and children. For membership rates or information on lessons and leagues, call (614) 457-5671 or view the website at www.racquetclub1.com.

For private or group tennis lessons, you may want to contact your local community center or high school to be put in touch with tennis instructors. A number of private clubs also have their own tennis courts, leagues, and lessons.

Pickleball has taken off in Columbus, with courts in neighborhood parks and a few indoor facilities opening in recent years. Pickle and Chill (205-354-6809; www.pickleandchill.com) at 880 W. Henderson Rd. in Upper Arlington has indoor and outdoor courts. The Jewish Community Center in Bexley and New Albany Tennis Center have indoor and outdoor courts as well, but you need to bring your own net.

Volleyball

The Ohio Valley Region of USA Volleyball (888-873-9478; www.ovr.org) is an amateur athletic sports association that gives players the chance to play in local, regional, and national competitions. The website has a comprehensive listing of programs, leagues, and tournaments, as well as general volleyball news and headlines. Another good place to inquire about adult leagues is the Columbus Department of Recreation and Parks. Call (614) 645-3300 to find out how to join. Volleyball enthusiasts can get on an email list at www.volleyball.org to receive email about local classes, clinics, tournaments, leagues, open games, and pick-up games and keep tabs on professional and collegiate volleyball events in the area.

If it's sand courts you're after, it is not unusual to see a rowdy, fun-loving crowd playing sand volleyball at a handful of bars around town, such as Gatsby's in Gahanna, Flannagan's in Dublin, and the several Goat locations in Gahanna, Dublin, and Hilliard.

PET-FRIENDLY COLUMBUS

We love our animals here in Columbus. Studies done by *Purina* magazine named Columbus among the Pet Healthiest Cities in the country, and we do what we can to keep it that way. Parkgoers shouldn't be surprised to find man's best friend running alongside his master on one of the trails or playing catch in many of the parks. But, given the large number of green spaces in Columbus, it is a bit surprising that there aren't more dedicated dog parks for our canines to frolic. While the Columbus City Council is addressing this issue, the section titled "Dog Parks" will point out a few places where owners tend to congregate, and some have designated times for dogs to run free.

Speaking of running free, the city of Columbus does not require leashes as long as the dog is under direct control of the owner (rottweilers being the exception), but leash laws do vary throughout other neighborhoods and in parks. Most of Columbus's city parks are, at minimum, dog friendly. Some of the city-operated parks expect you to have your dog under verbal control only, while others require they be kept on a leash of 6 feet or less. The rules are usually posted at park entrances.

Certain neighborhoods have mixed verbal and leash laws. Upper Arlington, Worthington, Bexley, Whitehall, Hilliard, New Albany, and Grove City are among the Columbus communities with some sort of animal control laws beyond the state code. The smartest thing to do is call ahead to confirm the rules at the park, or just take a leash along and check for signage.

This pet-friendly section will clue you in on where to go to adopt or track down your lost pet. One thing you may notice is that many of the rescue organizations work together in the best interest of all the homeless animals of Columbus, not just those in their own shelter. They pool their resources and facilities and cross-reference one another on their websites. If you can't find a pet that suits your household at one shelter, there is always the chance you are only a link away, so keep looking. Maybe pay a visit to one of the shelters; internet pictures don't always do justice!

Once you have that new family member, you will not be disappointed to learn that Columbus has the highest vet-to-pet ratio in the country due to the wonderful veterinary program and hospital at The Ohio State University. It's no wonder preventive health care is at the top of the awareness agenda.

With Fido or Fluffy home and healthy, it's time to spoil them rotten. Columbus has its fair share of animal mill chain stores, but there are plenty of locally owned boutiques where you can indulge your four-legged foodie's gourmet palate and haute couture style. One of the most fun places for Fido is the BrewDog Tap and DogHouse Hotel in Canal Winchester, with its pet-friendly guest room and restaurants and fenced-in dog park. Read more about it in the Restaurants chapter.

SHELTERS AND RESCUES

Columbus, like many other cities, has a severe overpopulation problem with cats and dogs. If you want to give a home to an animal, consider adopting from one of the many shelters to help reduce the euthanasia of thousands of cats and dogs every year. A good place to start is the Columbus Dog Connection (614-637-1342), which is a network of dog enthusiasts who alleviate some of the burden from shelters by providing foster homes for the animals until a permanent home can be found. The website www.columbusdogconnection.com has pictures of homeless dogs and cats, information about adoption, awareness events, and links to all the central Ohio rescues and shelters.

Another networking group to have a look at is Animal Outreach, based in Dublin. View its website at www.animal-outreach.org or call (614) 523-WAGG (9244) for links to shelters, veterinarians, and information about Animal Outreach's Spay Neuter Assistance Program, which helps subsidize the cost of a pet's spay or neuter surgery if you are unable to afford it.

Capital Area Humane Society
3015 Scioto-Darby Executive Court, Hilliard
(614) 777-7387
www.columbushumane.org

A state-of-the-art shelter with quality staff and volunteers makes this a safe haven for the many unwanted animals that come through its doors. Images of dogs, cats, rabbits, and pocket pets, such as hamsters and gerbils, can be found online. Keep in mind that not all are able to be photographed and displayed on the internet, so make a trip to the Humane Society to see if your pet is waiting.

Cat Welfare Association
741 Wetmore Rd., Clintonville
(614) 268-6096
www.catwelfareassoc.org

This shelter has been adopting stray, injured, or abused cats since 1945. All fund-raising money goes toward operating this no-kill shelter and helping maintain its feline residents. If you cannot take a healthy or special-needs kitty home, become a Guardian Angel by donating financial support to those cats that must remain on-site for health or behavioral problems. Adoption fees range from $25 to $40 and include vaccinations, microchipping, and various medical tests.

Citizens for Humane Action
3765 Corporate Dr., Westerville
(614) 891-5280
www.chaanimalshelter.org

The nonprofit shelter in northeast Ohio is funded solely through adoption fees and donations. It cares for mostly dogs and cats.

Cozy Cat Cottage
62 Village Pointe Dr., Powell
(614) 336-8510
www.cozycatcottage.com

The Cozy Cat Cottage is a nonprofit, no-kill cat adoption center, though there is one permanent shelter dog to make sure the felines are exposed to canines. The center relies on donations, adoption fees, fund-raisers, and boutique sales to help maintain this center for abandoned and abused cats. The adoption fees range from $80 to $90 and include medical testing, vaccinations, and spaying or neutering. Senior citizens can adopt a cat for free. Cozy Cat accepts monetary donations and has a wish list of supplies on its website for those who can donate goods. If you prefer to donate your time, any talent you have will be put to good use. Another special need is adopters who want to provide hospice care for terminally ill cats.

Franklin County Dog Shelter
4340 Tamarack Blvd.
(614) 525-4637
https://dogs.franklincountyohio.gov

Open seven days a week, this shelter lets you adopt a dog in less than an hour. The cash-only nonrefundable adoption fees range from $75 to $125, but this ensures your dog is spayed or neutered, microchipped, and has all its shots and license. Other services provided by the shelter are dog mixers, awareness programs, rabies clinics, and pet therapy. The shelter accepts donations in the form of money, dog food, carriers, blankets, and towels. If you are an animal lover but can't adopt, then sign up for some volunteer work.

Animal Control works in conjunction with Franklin County Dog Shelter, so check here or www.petfbi.com if your dog goes missing. Unfortunately, they are not able to accept cats at this shelter but are working with other shelters and

i Mingle with Our Mutts is a long-standing adoption event held at the Franklin County Animal Shelter the first and third Sun of each month from noon until 2 p.m. and at other locations. This event is coordinated in conjunction with the Columbus Dog Connection. Learn more by calling either facility or viewing the website at www.columbusdogconnection.com.

dog facilities toward becoming a no-kill facility. Definitely do not overlook the Franklin County Dog Shelter as a place to find your next pet.

Friends for Life Animal Haven
P.O. Box 7, Canal Winchester, OH 43110
(614) 837-6260
www.fflah.org
The Animal Haven is a no-kill animal rescue organization that takes in cats, dogs, kittens, and puppies. The rescues are placed in foster homes or live at the shelter in a homelike, open environment, as none of the animals are caged. The adoption fee, which includes a thorough examination, spay or neuter, worming, and up-to-date vaccinations, is $109 for dogs/puppies and $60 for cats/kittens. Sponsor a pet or volunteer your time. A special program at this shelter is the Forever Foster Program. You provide TLC and a foster home for a senior dog or cat to live out the rest of its life, and the Animal Haven will pick up the veterinary costs.

PetPromise
(614) 738-2149
www.petpromise.org
PetPromise is a nonprofit, no-kill animal rescue organization that focuses its adoption efforts on stray, abandoned, homeless, or abused cats and dogs. PetPromise functions solely on donations and the generosity of volunteers and foster

i All dogs three months of age and older must be registered annually by January 31 and immunized against rabies by a licensed veterinarian. The current year's license tag must be displayed on a dog's collar or harness at all times, even while the dog is on the premises of the owner.

parents. They do not yet have a shelter, though an effort to raise money for a no-kill sanctuary is ongoing. Until then, pets are placed in foster homes until permanently adopted.

Pets Without Parents Columbus
629 Oakland Park Ave.
(614) 267-PAWS (7297)
www.petswithoutparents.net
This nonprofit, appointment-only no-kill shelter accepts all breeds of dogs and cats. All pets are spayed/neutered and given their shots before going to their new home. Donations by way of money or supplies are always welcomed, and you can view a wish list at the website. Volunteering your time or any other talent is another wonderful way to contribute if you can't take a cat or dog home with you.

EMERGENCY AND VETERINARY SERVICES

The following lists just a select few of the many full-service animal hospitals around Columbus. Most of them have referral services, which can direct you to a specialist or a vet in your area.

Cats Only Vet Clinic
3416 Riverside Dr., Upper Arlington
(614) 459-4105
www.catsonlyvc.com

Easton Animal Hospital
2959 Stelzer Rd., Westerville
(614) 476-0000
www.eastonanimalhospital.com

Gahanna Animal Hospital
144 W. Johnstown Rd., Gahanna
(614) 471-2201
www.gahannaanimalhospital.com

MedVet Columbus
300 E. Wilson Bridge Rd., Worthington
(614) 846-5800
www.medvet.com

The Ohio State University Veterinary Hospital
601 Vernon Tharp St., OSU Campus

(614) 292-3551
www.vet.osu.edu

Upper Arlington Veterinary Hospital
1515 W. Lane Ave., Upper Arlington
(614) 481-8014
www.uavethospital.com

VCA Mill Run Animal Hospital
3660 Ridge Mill Dr., Hilliard
(614) 529-2222
www.vcahospitals.com

VCA Sawmill Animal Hospital
6868 Caine Rd.
(614) 766-2222
www.vcahospitals.com

Willow Wood Animal Hospital
5891 Zarley St., New Albany
(614) 855-3855
www.willowwoodah.com

KENNELS, BOARDING, AND DAY CARE

When it comes to boarding your four-legged friends, it seems there are nearly as many kennels as there are hotels in Columbus. This chapter provides just a handful of lodging options, but plenty more can be found in the Yellow Pages. If you feel better leaving your beloved family pet in familiar surroundings, you may want to start by checking with your veterinarian or contacting some of the animal hospitals listed, as many of them have on-site kenneling.

Canine Social Club
1103 Dublin Rd., Grandview
(614) 488-3647
www.caninesocialclub.org
The CSC comes highly recommended for the value and level of service provided to your pup. Day-care dogs are monitored by a dedicated staff in an open atmosphere at this indoor facility. There is no outside space due to city ordinances, but this doesn't detract from the fun to be had and the romping to be done. CSC offers kenneling and has a do-it-yourself dog bath on-site as well.

What sets this day care apart from others is that the staff works with Franklin County Dog Shelter to provide foster care for dogs until they are permanently adopted. Volunteers will also drop off and pick up Franklin County shelter dogs at the facility as a way to get them out of the shelter for a day and to allow interaction and playtime with day-care dogs.

Cheryl's Doggie Daycare
4712 Trabue Rd., Hilliard
(614) 527-1158
www.cherylsdoggiedaycare.net
If your dog suffers separation anxiety or you just want your dog in an environment where it can play and interact while you are at work, drop it off at Cheryl's Doggie Daycare. All dogs must be 12 weeks or older, spayed or neutered, on a flea control program, healthy and up to date on all shots, nonaggressive, and able to play well with other dogs and people. As a member of the North American Dog Daycare Association and Pet Sitters International, your dog will be well looked after by the professional staff certified in pet first aid. You can also contact Cheryl's for drop-in pet sitting in your home.

Homedog Resort
561 Short St.
(614) 525-0200
www.homedogresort.com
This dog resort is perfect for day care while you work or extended boarding while you play. The large facility provides plenty of space for dogs to roam in fenced areas divided by their size. Other services can be added on like training and grooming. It has easy drop-off and pick-up in the Brewery District.

i If you have a physical or cognitive disability, contact Canine Companions to get involved with a free program to be partnered with a highly trained dog to enhance your self-reliance. The North Central Regional Training Center of this national nonprofit organization can be contacted at (740) 548-4447 or www.canine.org/location/north-central.

Pet Palace
2800 Ole Country Ln., across from airport
(614) 471-6400
www.petpalaceresort.com
Conveniently located near the airport, dogs and cats are welcomed on a daily or long-term boarding basis at this pet hotel. Dogs are socialized in small playgroups within a controlled environment, while cats can bask in the sun of the Kitty Quarters. Rates vary depending on whether any additional services, such as grooming, extra playtime, or special treats, are added on.

The Pet Resort at Willow Wood
5891 Zarley St., New Albany
(614) 855-4800
www.petresortwillowwood.com
The Pet Resort at Willow Wood isn't cheap, but if your pampered pooch requires a vacation while you are on vacation, then look no further. The Pet Resort is the Ritz-Carlton of kennels. Besides an assortment of accommodations, other services such as grooming, "pet"icures, training, massages, and one-on-one cuddle time is available for a fee. For the dogs, there are runs of various sizes, deluxe suites, playtime, and doggie day care. Where else will your dog be walked several times a day, then bedded down to watch Animal Planet in the privacy of its own room? Cats, too, can have their own deluxe suites and climb the trees in the kitty playrooms. On top of all the good care they receive here, you can sleep soundly knowing Willow Wood Animal Hospital is in the adjacent building.

DOG PARKS

While stricter leash laws and a downtown dog park are being debated, dogs can live a pretty comfortable existence in Columbus. Dogs are required to be leashed and under control of the owner at all times when off property, but several neighborhood parks have specified times your pooch can run free.

One of the most well-attended dog parks is at Goodale Park in Victorian Village, where locals gather on a nightly basis for canine socializing.

i Waste bag dispensers are located in certain parks such as Whetstone, but be sure to take your own just in case. If you don't clean up after your pet in a public place, it could result in its impoundment. We can't have the hound in the pound!

Residents of German Village similarly converge on Schiller Park each evening. Jefferson Park in Bexley, however, is one of the few that do not permit pets at any time, but plenty of city parks nearby do, most of which are well marked with animal regulations.

One of the more popular spots for dogs is Antrim Park in Worthington, where man's best friend has been known to retrieve a stick or two from the lake. Despite the word on the street, all Worthington parks permit dogs off-leash at all times, as long as they are under verbal control of the owner. Control of one's dog is often a matter of opinion, but nonetheless remains at the owner's discretion.

Dogs are permitted off-leash before 8 a.m. and after 8 p.m. during daylight saving time at all parks in Upper Arlington, which includes Northam and Fancyburg Parks. During off-leash hours a pet owner must be able to demonstrate that the dog is under direct control.

Pets are permitted on the trails in most Metro Parks, but please see individual entries in the Parks and Recreation chapter for specifics. As long as dog owners are courteous to the non-dog people by cleaning up after Fido and keeping four-footed family members contained, good harmony can be maintained within the parks.

Alum Creek Dog Park
3992 Hollenback Rd., Lewis Center
www.alumcreekdogpark.com
Four acres along Alum Creek Reservoir accommodate small and large dogs in different fenced zones. The beachfront area gives your pooch water access directly from the beach. Other amenities include a dog wash station, drinking water for pets (and their people), waste disposal bags, and facilities for humans.

Big Walnut Dog Park
5000 E. Livingston Ave., East Columbus
www.columbus.gov/recreationandparks/
   parks/Big-Walnut-Park

Columbus's public off-leash park is situated on 3 fenced-in acres within Big Walnut Park. Dogs can take a dip in the pond, and it is lit to accommodate early morning and evening hours. The park is free of charge and open year-round from 7 a.m. until 11 p.m.

Brooksedge Bark Park
708 Park Meadow Rd., Westerville
(614) 901-6500
www.westerville.org

The city of Westerville's free off-leash dog park has a gated 1-acre park for larger dogs and a 0.25-acre gated area for smaller dogs. Both feature drinking fountains with water buckets, waste bags, and hydrants. The Westerville Convention and Visitors Bureau, along with Capital Area Humane Society, sponsors an annual event called the Dog Days of Summer, which includes adoption efforts and a Mutt March.

Mutt's Paradise AmuseMutt Park
1277 Hills-Miller Rd., Delaware
(614) 783-5638
www.muttsparadise.com

This private social club for dogs is located 18 miles north of Worthington off US 23. It is open almost year-round, 7 days a week, and provides 6 fenced-in acres where dogs can romp off-leash. Amenities include a swimming pond for the dogs and a picnic area for their people. Little dogs play in a protected, fenced-in area, and "play dates" cost $10 per hour per dog. An online scheduler allows you to secure a time frame, sign waivers, and submit proof of your dog's rabies and other vaccinations. This is a great way to socialize anxious dogs or give big dogs space to run.

Pizzurro Park Dog Playground
940 Pizzurro Park Rd., Gahanna
(614) 342-4250
www.gahanna.gov/facilities/facility/details/
   pizzurro-park-18

Pizzurro Park is a 4-acre fenced dog part where dogs are permitted to run off-leash in designated areas fenced off for different-size pets. The dog park also has an adjacent kids' playground where dogs must be on-leash. The dog park includes water fountains and water access to a creek. Access is free of charge from dawn till dusk.

SPECTATOR SPORTS

With no major-league football, baseball, or basketball teams, Columbus has forever been a college football town. There is no doubt Ohio State football is still the biggest draw, attracting crowds in excess of 100,000 to the games, but the city is now more than a one-sport town. If you want to watch professional teams play without having to leave Columbus, there are a few options.

The Columbus Blue Jackets play ice hockey teams from across the National Hockey League at the Nationwide Arena. And as hockey season winds down, the Columbus Destroyers arena football team takes over the space. The Columbus Crew hosts national and international soccer teams in their namesake stadium. The Columbus Clippers, the minor-league affiliate of the Washington Nationals, calls Huntington Park home. Scioto Downs features live harness racing, while Beulah Park, Ohio's first thoroughbred racetrack, is just a few minutes outside the city.

Columbus can also boast two relatively new sports arenas that double as entertainment venues: Nationwide Arena, home to the Columbus Blue Jackets, and the Schottenstein Value City Arena, where Buckeye basketball hosts a variety of national tournaments and concerts. The Ohio State University has a number of new and recently renovated athletic facilities for university sporting events. Tickets are typically available to the public; more information can be found in The Ohio State University chapter.

Ohio Stadium
OSU Dept. of Athletics

While the Buckeyes reign supreme, most other local universities have sports programs open for public attendance, some of which are quite good. The men's lacrosse team at Ohio Wesleyan University (740-368-3340) consistently ranks, if not wins, the North Coast Athletic Conference. The Ohio University football team made it the whole way to the 2006 GMAC Bowl, while Ohio State's golf team continually cranks out world-class players.

With all this talk of college sports, what do the locals do when they need an NFL, MLB, or NBA fix? They have to go to Cleveland or Cincinnati, but thankfully neither are very far, but just far enough to make a day of the event. Columbus natives seem to have split loyalties between Cleveland, home to the Browns, Indians, and Cavaliers, and the Cincinnati Bengals and Reds. Pittsburgh and Indianapolis is heavily represented in Columbus, and every so often you might even find a Seahawks fan in the mix.

Information about teams and athletic facilities in Cleveland and Cincinnati can be found in the Worth the Trip chapter, while the legendary Buckeyes are covered in both The Ohio State University and Parks and Recreation chapters. Columbus is big on participatory sports—golf, softball, and soccer—but read on for a listing of the spectator sports the city has to offer. For an up-to-date schedule of events, visit www.experiencecolumbus.com.

Columbus Blue Jackets
Nationwide Arena
200 W. Nationwide Blvd.
(614) 246-3350
www.nhl.com/bluejackets

The Columbus Blue Jackets National Hockey League team is based at Nationwide Arena. The Blue Jackets, in fact, are the only NHL team to play its games in the same facility in which they practice. The team's name was voted on by fans, and a cartoonlike bee is its logo and mascot. The Blue Jackets lost their first game against the Chicago' Blackhawks on October 7, 2000, and since then made the postseason playoffs six times. The team has yet to win a Stanley Cup, but at this point, Columbus hockey fans are just happy to have an NHL team.

The Blue Jackets play from Sept through Apr. Individual tickets can be purchased online or through the Blue Jackets' ticket office at (614) 246-3350. Individual ticket prices vary depending on where you want to sit in the 20,000-seat arena. Nationwide Arena is well designed; there isn't a bad seat in the house, even when stuck in peanut heaven.

Columbus Clippers
Huntington Stadium
330 Huntington Park, Arena District
(614) 462-5250
www.milb.com/columbus

Columbus has had a professional baseball team since the early 20th century, but the Jets pulled up stakes and moved away in 1971. After doing without baseball for six years, a push by Franklin County commissioner Harold Cooper brought about a new minor-league baseball team. The Clippers were the triple-A affiliate of the New York Yankees from 1979 until last year, when the team moved to the Washington Nationals. *Baseball America* magazine in its 20th-anniversary edition recognized the Clippers as the top minor-league franchise. The Clippers used to play on the west side at the old Cooper Stadium, but opened the 2009 season at their current home, Huntington Park.

Columbus Crew
Lower.com Field
96 Columbus Crew Way, Arena District
(614) 447-CREW (2739)
www.columbuscrew.com

We are the champions! After winning the MLS championship it is safe to say Crew tickets are going to be harder and more expensive to come by. The Lower.com stadium is a soccer-specific facility and home to the amazing Columbus Crew. Check out www.lowerfieldcbus.com for information about the venue. A little history of the Crew: The 1994 World Cup was held in the US, and Major League Soccer was born. The MLS is the fifth major professional sports league established in America, and Columbus's very own Black and Gold was one of the first 10 inaugural clubs.

Columbus Fury
Nationwide Arena
(614) 380-3879
www.provolleyball.com/teams/columbus-fury
Unleash the Fury! The women's professional volleyball team is Columbus's newest professional sports team. The Fury plays home matches at Nationwide Arena, and at $25 to $150 per ticket, this is about as affordable as professional sports gets in our town.

Eldorado Scioto Downs
6000 S. High St.
(614) 295-4700
www.caesars.com/scioto-downs
One of Ohio's five harness tracks is located 2 miles south of I-270 on US 23 (South High Street). Live harness racing is in season from May through Sept, but most patrons come for the state-of-the-art sports wagering. The grandstand has the best view of the homestretch during live races and can accommodate up to 3,500 fans, while the clubhouse is a full-service dining room and likewise provides good views of the track. A smaller cafe and brewpub also serve food, while the Veil Bar is the place to go for handcrafted cocktails and nice wines. When the weather cooperates, the outdoor patio puts you as close to the race as you can get. Simulcast of harness and thoroughbred racing is offered indoors where 1,800 slots and keno games keep the place lively.

Mid-Ohio Sports Car Course
7721 Steam Corners Rd., Lexington
(419) 884-4000
www.midohio.com

One of the nation's top road-racing tracks is located 60 miles north of Columbus. This 2.4-mile track hosts a variety of motor sports, such as motorcycle racing, CART, and Vintage Grand Prix, as well as the largest amateur car race in the world. General admission tickets for a three-day weekend give access to the entire area except the grandstand and paddocks. Prices range from $25 to $50. Individual day tickets run about $15 to $35. Children 12 and under are admitted free to the grounds and paddock areas, but tickets must be purchased for grandstand seating. Tent camping and motorhome camping passes are sold on a first-come, first-served basis, and cost varies depending on the event.

National Trail Raceway
2650 National Rd. SW, Hebron
(740) 928-5706
www.nationaltrailraceway.com
Every summer, you will inevitably notice an excessive number of vehicles towing hot rods and motorcycles along I-70. More than likely, they are heading to National Trail Raceway on US 40, just 20 miles east of Columbus. The National Hot Rod Association championship drag-racing track attracts hard-core drag racers to central Ohio for a variety of events, including super gas races and the popular Night of Thunder, an event full of jet cars and trucks with fire exhaust and fireworks. The facility accommodates crowds up to 40,000. General admission prices and gate times vary depending on the event.

CULTURAL COLUMBUS

In the past 25 years, Columbus has seen a proliferation of cultural organizations and an explosion of art galleries, theatrical troupes, and community-based cultural events. The city's steady growth and the influx of transplants have led to many positive outgrowths within the arts community: the diversification of audiences, new venues featuring all sorts of music, opportunities to hear authors discuss or read from their works, exhibitions by international artists, and world-class theater and dance.

The Columbus art scene is full of local talent and offers its residents access to emerging artists and famous traveling exhibitions. Performing arts take on a global and avant-garde perspective that one might not expect to find in the heartland of America. This is attributed partly to the young, growing, and highly mobile population of Columbus.

One of the drawbacks to this young, hip population is Columbus's arts seem to suffer a lack of regular subscribers and support on a younger community level. Columbus residents may not always be aware of the quality and variety of arts opportunities available to them. This chapter's goal is to show the depth and breadth of the city's rich art scene to both visitors and residents alike.

Art lovers will find valuable information at www.cbusarts.com. The CBUSArts site maintains a sophisticated and updated database of various performing and visual arts activities in the region. It provides contact details, hours, and links to the websites of literary, theater, dance, and visual arts organizations, as well as links to body art, sacred art, and graphic designers. A good source of event information is the Experience Columbus website, as mentioned throughout this guide.

Columbus supports a number of visual arts venues, including an eclectic concentration of galleries in the Short North. You can get a festive overview of these shops during the popular Gallery Hop, which takes place the first Sat of each month. Restaurants and shops stay open late, and many of the art galleries coordinate exhibitions and receptions around these weekends. It also is a great way to meet many of the artists whose work the galleries promote.

Art hounds looking to admire rather than purchase will find everything from sculpture and painting to photography and glass on display somewhere in the city. Dolls, railroad equipment, and early televisions are the focus of a few small, specialized museums. The Impressionist and German Expressionist collections at the Columbus Museum of Art are outstanding. The museum does not have very many Old Masters, but lovers of all things modern will appreciate the visual arts in Columbus.

When it comes to performing arts, Columbus is home to the Columbus Symphony Orchestra, BalletMet, Opera Columbus, ProMusica, Columbus Jazz Arts, and chamber music ensembles, along with professional and amateur theater groups. Many of them have formal seasons followed by a casual summer series. The more popular seasonal series have been included in this chapter.

A majority of performances are held at one of the three historic downtown venues: the Palace Theatre, the Ohio Theatre, and the Southern Theatre. The Davidson Theatre at the Riffe Center, the Columbus Performing Arts Center, McConnell Arts Center in Worthington, and the Jeanne B. McCoy Community Arts Center in New Albany offer intimate settings for smaller and local productions.

While traditional performing and visual arts are well represented, Columbus's contemporary art scene is thriving. The city's youthful demographics and reputable art schools provide both a breeding ground and a good audience for cutting-edge art forms.

The Ohio State University and the Columbus College of Art and Design are good places to watch for emerging artists in visual arts and fashion. They host student and faculty exhibitions throughout the year and keep the local art scene interesting. Capital and Franklin Universities also have their own art galleries. Likewise, one shouldn't overlook the colleges as a source of quality affordable theater. Otterbein College Theatre is quite reputable and offers subscriptions to a season of shows.

An increasing collaboration between the different art forms can be seen in the types of venues being developed. The Wexner Center, which is discussed in a Close-up in this chapter, offers an interdisciplinary approach to contemporary art. Rather than limiting itself to one specific art form, the center has exhibition galleries, performance spaces, and film theaters. The King Arts Complex is another example of a multidisciplinary venue with space for dance, visual arts, and educational programs.

Almost every major arts organization in the city has some sort of youth or adult art program. The Greater Columbus Arts Council website is the best place to search for community classes. A few adult programs have been mentioned here, but children's cultural activities are addressed in the Family Fun chapter.

Ultimately, the best approach to Columbus arts is to check out the suggested websites or weekly calendar of events on Columbus Underground (www.columbusunderground.com), 614NOW (www.614now.com), or Experience Columbus (www.experiencecolumbus.com).

ARTS ORGANIZATIONS

Columbus Association for the Performing Arts (CAPA)
39 E. State St.
(614) 469-1045
www.capa.com
Diverse musical programming makes CAPA one of the country's premier presenters of national and international artists. The various series cover a diverse mix of pop, folk, jazz, classical, and country entertainment. Comedy and theatrical performances are also given. Its crowning achievement in Columbus is saving the 1928 Ohio Theatre from the wrecking ball, but performances are held at all the major downtown venues and the Columbus Zoo Amphitheatre. CAPA's popular summer outdoor music series is held at the Columbus Commons, while its movie series of classics and family flicks is held at the Ohio Theatre.

The Columbus Foundation
1234 E. Broad St.
(614) 251-4000
www.columbusfoundation.org

As the country's top 10 largest community foundations, this unique organization provides financial support not only to the larger arts institutions but also to the small, grassroots arts groups, where funds might be limited. It offers grants to many of central Ohio's arts organizations, individual scholarships to artists and writers, and money for a huge scope of arts. The Community Arts Fund provides lesser grants to the small- and medium-size organizations that bring performance opportunities and arts education to the community. Some of these recipients are Glass Axis, Chamber Music Columbus, and The Actor's Summer Theatre Company.

Dublin Arts Council
7125 Riverside Dr., Dublin
(614) 889-7444
www.dublinarts.org
This local council offers high-caliber community classes in the performing, literary, and visual arts. Art shows, performances, and cultural events are held throughout Dublin, while changing art exhibitions take place in the Council Gallery. It is also responsible for funding public art sculptures

throughout the Dublin area. A variety of programming is available to adults, teens, and children.

Greater Columbus Arts Council (GCAC)
182 E. Long St.
(614) 224-2606
www.gcac.org
The Greater Columbus Arts Council can be thanked for its role in stabilizing and advocating the arts in Columbus beginning in the early 1970s. Originally responsible for managing only the Columbus Arts Festival and a calendar of events, the GCAC recognized the city's rich art scene and developed a long-range plan to promote Columbus through its cultural activity.

Realizing the economic impact the arts have on Columbus, the City Council developed a funding partnership with GCAC that currently distributes nearly $18 million annually between artists and organizations. This funding goes to support individual fellowships, grants, community arts education, business arts partnership programs, public art initiatives, and so much more.

Throughout its 50-year history, the GCAC has become one of the most highly regarded local arts councils in the country. Its website is a great place to look for information on grants, community arts education, and the Columbus Arts Festival.

Ohio Art League (OAL)
400 W. Rich St.
(614) 299-8225
www.oal.org
This nonprofit organization has been supporting and representing Ohio artists across all disciplines for nearly a century. The OAL introduced George Bellows and Roy Lichtenstein to the world. It promotes the arts through workshops, lectures, and publications. A prestigious biannual juried art exhibition, held at the Columbus Cultural Arts Center, attracts the best of local artists. Becoming a member of the OAL is a good way to stay abreast of the Ohio art scene.

Ohio Arts Council
30 E. Broad St.
(614) 466-2613
www.oac.ohio.gov
This state agency supports the arts throughout Ohio by providing financial assistance to artists and arts organizations. Funding comes from the Ohio General Assembly and the National Endowment for the Arts. Programming is focused on art access, innovation, and learning. The OAC's Riffe Gallery in downtown Columbus features changing exhibitions of Ohio artists and state museum collections.

PERFORMING ARTS

BalletMet
322 Mount Vernon Ave., downtown
(614) 229-4860
www.balletmet.org
The word *intelligent* is used to describe BalletMet's storytelling ability, and the desire to sit through intermission to discuss a brilliant performance is testimony to this. The company's dancers are known for their commitment to technique and

---

Makerspaces and Incubators

Columbus has several community spaces where developing artisans and creative types can find studio space, hone their craft through hands-on classes and lectures, hold exhibitions, and rent specialized equipment. Some require membership.

400 West Rich, Franklinton (www.400westrich.com)
Clay Café Pottery Studio, German Village (www.claycafecolumbus.com)
Columbus Cultural Arts Center, Downtown (www.culturalartscenter.org)
Columbus Idea Foundry, Franklinton (www.ideafoundry.com)
Franklin Art Glass, German Village (www.franklinartglass.com)
Glass Axis, South Columbus (www.glassaxis.org)
Makers Social, Franklinton (www.makerscolumbus.com)
Sew to Speak, Worthington (www.sewtospeakshoppe.com)
Terra Gallery, Dublin Bridge Park (www.terra-gallery.com)
Wild Goose Creative, Franklinton (www.wildgoosecreative.com)

The Columbus Symphony Orchestra
Tom Dubanawich courtesy CSO

the ability to handle the challenging and innovative choreography of artistic director Edwaard Liang. The troupe's repertoire includes classic, contemporary, and original choreography. The BalletMet season consists of half a dozen or so programs in addition to touring. The annual *Nutcracker* continues to kick off the holiday season.

In 1989 BalletMet made its international debut in Cairo, Egypt, and continues to entertain audiences beyond Columbus. BalletMet currently ranks among the top 20 largest ballet companies in the country, while its dance academy and outreach programs have an extended influence throughout the community. Performances take place at Ohio Theatre, Davidson Theatre, and the BalletMet's Performance Space.

Chamber Music Columbus
Southern Theatre
21 E. Main St., downtown
(614) 267-2267
www.chambermusiccolumbus.org
Nearing its 80th season, this organization remains one of Columbus's oldest and most inspired arts organizations. The CMC showcases national and international chamber music artists and ensembles. The season runs from Oct through May, and concerts are held at Southern Theatre and various other auditoriums. Many of the concerts are broadcast on WOSU-FM's station at a later date.

Columbus Gay Men's Chorus
Various venues
(614) 531-4272
www.cgmc.com
This choir includes mainly gay men, but it is open to all supportive individuals regardless of race, gender, religion, or age. Year-round concerts are held at various venues, such as local churches, the Columbus Performing Arts Center, and the Davidson Theatre in the Riffe Center. The three ensembles consist of the Full Choir, which accepts all musical skill sets; Illuminati, who perform sacred and spiritual songs; and Vox, which is the competitive singing group requiring audition. Tickets can be purchased online or directly from the chorus box office at the number above.

Columbus Jazz Arts Group
769 E. Long St.
(614) 294-5200
www.jazzartsgroup.org

This is the jazz lover's ticket to swing, jazz, and blues performed in a big-band setting. The CJO plays music of the legendary greats: Gershwin, Duke Ellington, Count Basie, and Ray Charles, among others. The orchestra has toured Europe and has featured world-class guest artists, such as Rosemary Clooney, Anita O'Day, Dionne Warwick, and Mel Torme, throughout the season. Performances take place primarily at the Southern Theatre and sometimes the Palace Theatre. Ticket packages vary in price and can be purchased online or at the theater box offices.

Columbus Symphony Orchestra
Ohio Theatre
55 E. State St.
(614) 469-0939
www.columbussymphony.com

Central Ohio's oldest, largest, and most visible arts organization calls the historic Ohio Theatre home. The symphony, under the guidance of its music director, Rossen Milanov, performs more than 100 concerts a year and reaches an audience of 250,000 with live performances, festivals, and programs and more than 2 million through broadcasts and online media.

The regular season includes classical music that can be subscribed to in a variety of packages.

Students with a valid ID can purchase discount memberships for Masterworks concerts. During the regular season, concerts are given in the evenings on Fri and Sat and matinees on Sun. The summertime series, which is slightly cheaper and more casual than the regular season, includes Picnic with the Pops and Popcorn Pops, a kid-oriented concert series.

Gallery Players
Jewish Community Center of Greater
  Columbus
1125 College Ave., Bexley
(614)231-2731
www.columbusjcc.org

For three-quarters of a century, the Gallery Players have been captivating Columbus audiences with community theater ranging from Pulitzer- and Tony Award–winning stories like the *Diary of Anne Frank* to swirling musicals such as *Joseph and the Amazing Technicolor Coat* and *The Carole King Musical*. Talent abounds in the diverse cast's high-level acting, singing, and dancing. At $25 per ticket, you will be hard-pressed to find a better theater experience at that price point.

Little Theatre Off Broadway
3981 Broadway, Grove City
(614) 875-3919
www.ltob.org

No need to venture all the way to New York for a Broadway show. Fine community theater is

Columbus Jazz Orchestra
Jazz Arts Group

offered year-round at the performing arts center in downtown Grove City. The Little Theatre Off Broadway features six audition-based shows per season—two dramas, two comedies, and two musicals—on the intimate stage where there are no bad seats in the house. The shows here are a little more off-beat, like *Little Shop of Horrors* and *Big Fish: A New Musical*. LTOB also hosts improv classes and private events. The theater does not sell alcohol like some larger venues. But you never know, the friendly resident ghost may even brush by you.

Opera Columbus
Ohio Theatre
55 E. State St.
(614) 469-0939
www.operacolumbus.org
Operas are performed in grand style at the historic Southern Theatre downtown. Opera Columbus maintains a traditional fall–winter season, with heavier performances like *Carmen* and *Don Giovanni*. Never fear, English subtitles are projected onto the screen above the stage. There is also no dress code for the opera, unless you feel like dressing up. We keep it casual in Columbus. Season subscriptions vary in price and can be purchased through the box office or online.

ProMusica Chamber Orchestra
Various locations
(614) 464-0066
www.promusicacolumbus.org
This professional chamber orchestra was founded in 1978 and has earned a reputation as one of the top chamber orchestras in the country. It plays Baroque masterpieces and global music, and works specifically composed for small orchestras. Collaborations with other arts organizations throughout the city, traveling to schools, and holding open rehearsals for seniors have helped broaden its audience. Various series and special events are offered throughout the season. Venues include the Southern Theatre, Franklin Park Conservatory, Alum Creek Amphitheatre, and various churches.

THEATER

The Actors' Theatre of Columbus
Schiller Park Stage
1069 Jaeger St., German Village
(614) 444-6888
www.theactorstheatre.org
With Shakespeare as its focus, this troupe brings outstanding public theater to central Ohio. The Actors' Theatre provides outdoor theater to the community on a "free-will donation" basis, which allows locals who may not have the means to go to a formal theater the opportunity to experience fine acting at a price they can afford—free. The season runs from May through Sept, and donations are accepted during intermission. There is no seating, so be sure to bring a blanket or chairs for theater alfresco at Schiller Park in German Village.

Broadway in Columbus
(614) 224-7654, (800) 294-1892
https://columbus.broadway.com
PNC Bank sponsors national touring Broadway productions in Columbus each year. Shows like *Moulin Rouge!, Phantom of the Opera*, and *The Lion King* are typically held at the Palace and Ohio Theatres. Prices vary. Tickets can be purchased online at Ticketmaster or the theatre box offices.

Capital University Theatre
2199 E. Main St., Bexley
(614) 236-6011
www.capital.edu
Capital University's theater department puts on four productions a year and works in conjunction with the Conservatory of Music to stage the occasional musical. Plays include classics, Shakespeare, and contemporary scripts. Parking is free at the university.

Contemporary American Theatre Company (CATCO)
77 S. High St.
(614) 469-0939
www.catco.org
A dynamic ensemble of players makes up Columbus's premier professional theater company. Scripts range from American classics like *Cat on a*

Hot Tin Roof to off-Broadway hits. Quirky, modern scripts by David Mamet and international plays are also part of the repertoire. This diverse theater company, which is becoming one of the nation's major regional theaters, can be seen in Studio One at the Riffe Center for the Arts. A variety of flex-ticket options and subscription packages vary in price for the seven-show season.

Curtain Players
5691 Harlem Rd., Galena
(614) 470-4809
www.curtainplayers.org
This award-winning not-for-profit theater group was established in 1943 and has been performing in a 78-seat church-turned-theater since 1981. It is the only community theater with a paid artistic director and boasts six high-quality productions per season. Shows have included *Cash on Delivery*, *Angel Street*, and *The Last Night of Ballyhoo*.

Lincoln Theatre
769 E. Long St., downtown
(614) 469-0939
www.capa.com
The unique, 582-seat Egyptian Revival–style theater anchors the King-Lincoln District and is equipped with a state-of-the-art sound and lighting projection system. For more than 40 years, the Lincoln Theatre provided stage and screen entertainment for Columbus's African American community, until the 1970s, when construction of a major highway displaced more than 10,000 residents and split the King-Lincoln District from downtown. It is now Columbus's jazzy urban performing arts and education center, which makes sense as Duke Ellington, Etta James, Miles Davis, and Columbus native Nancy Wilson once graced its stage. Today it hosts fantastic musicians and off-beat acts.

MadLab
227 N. Third St.
(614) 221-5418
www.madlab.net
The intimate theater has a resident troupe that performs several original plays per year, as well as shorts and improv. Local New Herring Productions

(www.newherring.org) performs plays that push boundaries and range in style and subject matter at MadLab.

Otterbein College Theatre
Campus Center Theatre
1 S. Grove St., Westerville
(614) 823-1109
www.otterbein.edu/theatre-performances
Otterbein's national reputation for truly outstanding students and faculty brings another level of theater to Columbus's art scene. The theater department's six annual productions range from Neil Simon plays to musicals like *Jesus Christ Superstar*. Individual tickets are reasonably priced in the $22 to $30 range and season subscriptions are available.

SEASONAL SERIES

CAPA Summer Movie Series
Ohio Theatre
55 E. State St.
(614) 469-0939
www.capa.com
During the summer, the historic Ohio Theatre reverts to its original function for CAPA's summer movie series. Classics like *The Godfather* and Hitchcock films, and family films like *Indiana Jones* are shown in the air-conditioned theater on the big screen. Tickets are $3 to $3.50 and can be purchased at the kiosk.

Picnic with the Pops
Columbus Commons, downtown
(614) 469-0939
www.picnicwiththepops.com
The Columbus Symphony Orchestra performs a variety of pop concerts under the stars on the lawn of the Columbus Commons throughout June and July. Highlights have included tunes from *Harry Potter*, jazz legends, Broadway under the Stars, and a special performance by the Ohio State Marching Band. The tickets are cheaper and the performances more casual than during the formal season. Table seating is also an option for bigger groups.

Shakespeare in the Park
Schiller Park, German Village
(614) 444-6888
www.theactorstheatre.org
Every summer since 1982, the Actors' Theatre of Columbus has taken the stage at Schiller Park Amphitheatre for the annual Shakespeare in the Park. Just bring a blanket and stretch out under the stars for a free dose of the bard's wit and wisdom. Schiller Park is located at 1069 Jaeger St.; plays begin around 8 p.m. Families are welcome, but it is suggested to keep the little ones under wraps and turn your cell phones off.

VENUES

Columbus Zoo Amphitheatre
9990 Riverside Dr., Powell
(614) 645-3400
www.columbuszoo.org
This intimate outdoor stage sits on the banks of the Scioto River and is a great place to catch a performance by the Columbus Children's Theatre or one of the CAPA-sponsored concert series. Parking is available on the zoo grounds for a fee, and it is suggested guests bring chairs or blankets for lawn seating. The Columbus Jazz Arts Group holds its annual Jazzoo series in July and Aug.

Davidson Theatre at the Vern Riffe Center
77 S. High St.
(614) 469-0939
www.capa.com
This intimate performance hall is located on the third floor of the Riffe building at the corner of High and State Streets. It is managed by CAPA, and smaller performances by BalletMet, local theater troupes, and touring productions like *Riverdance*, *Stomp*, and *Peter Pan* are held here. With seating for fewer than 1,000 people, there isn't a bad seat in the house.

King Arts Complex
835 Mount Vernon Ave., downtown
(614) 645-5464
www.kingartscomplex.com

This multifaceted facility is called the King Arts Complex for short. Built in 1925, it is on the National Register of Historic Places and is the only historic building in Columbus designed by an African American architect. Its cultural and artistic programs focus on the African American heritage and experience. Programming encompasses dance, music, and literary and visual arts. The Elijah Pierce Gallery showcases local and national artists, and there is ample free parking in the vicinity.

MadLab
227 N. Third St.
(614) 221-5418
www.madlab.net
This alternative venue welcomes all types of artistic disciplines. Hosting highly experimental art forms, like Japanese noise art and avant-garde dance, this innovative arts facility has the capacity to support multimedia theater, music, dance, visual arts, and any other "undefined" art form. Traditional theatergoers may find the productions a little weird, but the culturally advanced just might like the group's daring and progressive approach to the arts. This small, intimate theater suits local productions' budgets and need for flexibility.

The Ohio Theatre
55 E. State St., downtown
(614) 469-1045
www.capa.com
A "palace for the average man" was built in the Spanish Baroque style in 1928. It was originally designed as a Loews movie house and seats nearly 2,800 people. This beautiful building is located across from the state capitol and is on the National Register of Historic Places. The Ohio was saved from the wrecking ball in 1969 and was subsequently purchased and restored by CAPA. Today it is home to BalletMet, the Columbus Symphony Orchestra, and the Broadway Series and hosts over 100 classical, theatrical, and comedic acts per year.

i The world-renowned architect Thomas Lamb designed both the Palace and Ohio Theatres. The sweeping grand staircase of the Palace is proof of the inspiration drawn from the Palace of Versailles, near Paris.

The Palace Theatre
34 W. Broad St., downtown
(614) 469-9850
www.capa.com/venues/detail/palace-theatre

The sumptuous Palace Theatre first opened as a vaudeville house and cinema in 1926. Over the years, all the big names in entertainment have taken the stage, making the Palace the most active live-show theater in Columbus. Although this theater never faced the same potential fate as the Ohio and Southern, it was likewise purchased by CAPA in 1989, and is now home to Opera Columbus. The Palace hosts a year-round schedule of performances by all of Columbus's major performing arts organizations and CAPA-sponsored shows and concerts. Parking is available directly behind the Palace Theatre in the LeVeque Tower garage for $3.

The Southern Theatre
21 E. Main St.
(614) 340-1896
www.capa.com

The Southern Theatre opened in 1896 as part of the Great Southern Fireproof Hotel and Opera House. Its fireproof construction ensured structural longevity, but by 1979, the theater was in dire straits and closed. Like the Ohio Theatre, a public campaign saved the building, which was subsequently purchased and gifted to CAPA in 1986. A 14-month overhaul brought Columbus's only 19th-century theater back to life in a magnificent way. The intimate interior is striking, with its gold gilding, soft lighting, and electric blue curtain. The Southern is home to the Columbus Jazz Orchestra, ProMusica Chamber Orchestra, and Columbus Gay Men's Chorus and hosts several touring productions throughout the year. Its inclusion on the National Register now ensures the great Southern the legacy it was intended to have. Suggested parking is in the Commons garage across from the theater on Main Street.

VISUAL ARTS

Columbus Museum of Art
480 E. Broad St.
(614) 221-6801
www.columbusmuseum.org

The museum, established in 1878, is located 4 blocks east of downtown, and you'll know you've found it when you see the big bronze Henry Moore sculpture in front of the Broad Street entrance. With more than 10,000 works, the museum houses an outstanding collection of late 19th- and early 20th-century American and European modern art. Works by Degas, Monet, Matisse, Picasso, and Ernst make up an exceptional collection of modernism.

The two names one encounters repeatedly associated with the museum collections are Howald and the Siraks. The museum can thank Ferdinand Howald, an important collector of early 20th-century American and European art, for his contribution of 280 works in 1931. Sixty years after this gift, Howard and Babette Sirak gave their personal collection of 78 pieces of European Impressionism and Expressionism a new home at the CMA. More recently the museum was bequeathed a transformative gift of 27 contemporary artworks.

The Museum of Art is particularly well-known for its superb regional collections of Columbus's very own Elijah Pierce and George Bellows. The museum boasts the largest public collection of woodcarvings by folk artist Elijah Pierce, and also acts as repository for the world's biggest collection of paintings and lithographs by George Bellows, one of the finest American artists of his time. It also holds the world's largest collection of Aminah Robinson works.

Other highlights include pieces by Edward Hopper, Norman Rockwell, and Georgia O'Keeffe. Frederick Schumacher gifted his collection of 17th- and 18th-century works to the museum in 1957. The outdoor sculpture garden has a substantial collection of 20th-century pieces, while interactive and educational areas are open to children and families.

Visitors can dine at the Schokkp Café and browse the extensive Museum Gift Shop. Museum admission is $18 for adults and $9 for children, students and seniors. Sunday is free for everyone. CMA is closed Mon and stays open until 9 p.m. on Thurs. Parking is $7, but admission and parking are free for members.

Early Television Museum
5396 Franklin St., Hilliard
(614) 771-0510
www.earlytelevision.org
The free museum displays a fun collection of early television sets. Highlights include mechanical sets made between 1929 and 1932 and early color televisions from 1954. It is open only on weekends.

Ohio Craft Museum
1665 W. Fifth Ave., Grandview
(614) 486-4402
www.ohiocraft.org
This museum houses a permanent collection of contemporary crafts and hosts small changing exhibits and five major exhibitions per year. The Craft Research Library is on-site, and educational workshops are offered. The museum is closed on Sun, and admission and parking is free.

Ohio Railway Museum
990 Proprietors Rd., Worthington
(614) 885-7345
www.ohiorailwaymuseum.org
One of the oldest railway museums in the nation is here. This museum was founded in 1948 and houses a collection of 30 pieces of vintage railway equipment. Take a demonstration ride on one of the museum's streetcars or interurbans, and learn about the history of electric transportation. It is open Memorial Day through Labor Day, and a small admission is charged.

Old Rectory Doll Museum
50 W. New England Ave., Worthington
(614) 885-1247
https://worthingtonhistory.org/doll-museum
Whether you find them creepy or charming, nineteenth-century dolls and toys are on rotating display at this small specialized museum operated by the Worthington Historical Society. Highlights are American, French, German, and Parisian bisque fashion and milliners' dolls. Docent-guided tours may be arranged; otherwise, tours are self-guided. The museum is closed Sun and Mon but open year-round. A small admission is charged.

The Pizzuti Collection
632 Park St., Short North
(614) 221-6801
www.columbusmuseum.org
A ticket to the Columbus Museum of Art gives you entrance to the Pizzuti Collection in the Short North. The really cool three-story museum features contemporary art from Ron and Ann Pizzuti's collection and changing exhibitions. It is only open Fri through Sun and for special events, but is worth a look if you can catch opening hours. Separate admission tickets are also available online or at the door.

Riffe Gallery
Vern Riffe Center
77 S. High St., downtown
(614) 644-9624
www.oac.ohio.gov/riffe-gallery
This free gallery is sponsored by the Ohio Arts Council and features changing exhibitions by Ohio artists and collections from state museums. The exhibits are organized by guest curators through the Ohio Arts Council, which strives to present the breadth, depth, and vision of Ohio arts. Located in the same building as the Davidson Theatre, this open and airy gallery is a nice place to browse before a concert. It is open most weekdays noon to 5 p.m.; closed Sat through Mon.

GALLERIES

Several art and photography galleries are clustered in the Short North Arts District, but much of the gallery scene is spattered around the city. Check out www.shortnorth.org for a comprehensive list of galleries and artsy retail shops in the hip Short North. Franklinton also has an emerging arts district, with a few nonprofit galleries, a glass studio, and an arts center.

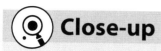 # Close-up

Wexner Center for the Arts

You're wandering along High Street and notice a huge skeletal, disjointed-looking building sprawling across the OSU campus. You stop and say, "What is this?"

Well, it's a lot of different things: a museum, a theater, a studio, and a library, but most importantly, it is a conversation piece. This experimental building is doing exactly what it was intended to do—make you think and talk.

The Wexner Center for the Arts is a multidisciplinary arts center conceived as a laboratory for contemporary visual and performing arts and film. The center opened in November 1989 after an unprecedented $225 million fund-raising campaign. Leslie H. Wexner, chairman and founder of The Limited, Inc. and one of America's top 50 art collectors, footed a large portion of the bill. His contribution earned him the naming rights, so the building is dedicated to his father, Harry L. Wexner.

The design of the building was selected through an international competition, after which architects Peter Eisenman of New York and Richard Trott of Columbus were chosen. Their goal was to create a revolutionary structure that forces people to look at the world in a different way. They were indeed successful. The building itself is an embodiment of what is inside. The architecture often generates the same (sometimes hot) debate as the art it houses. Both challenge us to look at new forms and consider what is art or, in this case, architecture.

The Wexner Center's location serves as an entry point to the university. It is situated where The Ohio State University intersects the community—both literally and philosophically. In some ways, it links Columbus to the rest of the world through its promotion of international art and ideas. The entry plaza lines up directly with the runway at the John Glenn International Airport, symbolizing artists coming from around the globe.

Architecturally, the building is full of symbolism. To put it simply, the slightly off-kilter nature of the building echoes the pattern of the campus's uneven street grid. Its scaffolding-like passageway represents the Wexner Center as an "unfinished" building, ready and willing to embrace new art. An effort to symbolically link the past with the future is seen in the castle-like towers on the south end of the facility. They are a visual reference to the turrets of the "Armory," a former campus building that once stood on the site of the Wexner Center.

Art Access Gallery
540 S. Drexel Ave., Bexley
(614) 338-8325
www.artaccessgallery.com
This fine-arts gallery, located in the heart of Bexley, was once a post office. It specializes in regional artists and carries an eclectic mix of oil and acrylic paintings, pastels, gouache, lithography, and sculpture. Exhibitions change each month.

Brandt-Roberts Galleries
642 N. High St., Short North
(614) 223-1655
www.brandtrobertsgalleries.com
This urbane, sophisticated art gallery deals in a variety of paintings focused on present-day social narratives and offers one of the area's largest selections of contemporary and post-war art. The gallery also provides art advising and framing services.

Contemporary Art Matters
243 N. Fifth St., Old North
(61) 313-4360
www.contemporaryartmatters.com
Working with emerging and mid-career artists, this gallery has been exhibiting contemporary painting, sculpture, and photography in Columbus since 1993. Exhibitions of contemporary art are presented in the Factory Gallery and Viewing Room spaces with public openings. Consulting and collection management services are also available for the novice and experienced collector.

The 12,000 square feet of gallery space has the capacity to handle all sorts of traditional and nontraditional media. The Wexner Center has featured everything from sculpture and photography to multimedia and video installations.

Music, dance, and theater offered by the Wexner Center are equally as wide ranging and innovative as the visual arts. Performances take place on a variety of stages around campus, but the Mershon Auditorium is the primary performing arts venue. Built in 1957, the Mershon was renovated into a world-class theater in 1996. Seating around 2,500, it features a generous stage with a 75-seat orchestra pit and, like many European opera houses, has a concert-quality pipe organ. Thrilling contemporary artists, classical musicians, pop stars, and even OSU graduates have graced the Mershon stage.

This strong and challenging facility requires strong artists and artwork able to hold its own. Since its inception, the Wexner Center has hosted a long list of emerging artists, contemporary masters, and cultural pioneers. The exhibition/show archive reads like a "Who's Who" list: Twyla Tharp, Merce Cunningham, Roy Lichtenstein, Julie Taymor, Andy Warhol, and on and on. Visiting filmmakers have also been known to introduce their own films prior to screening.

The Wexner Center offers year-round films and videos that you won't find anywhere else in the city. Everything from cinematic classics and rare documentaries to independent and international films has turned up on the movie schedule. Annual film festivals and themed series are also part of the programming. Screening takes place in the Wexner Center for the Arts' Film and Video Theatre.

The Wexner Center for the Arts has been a building shrouded in controversy since the beginning, from the selection of the controversial architect (chosen for that very reason) to the notoriety for its groundbreaking architecture that put The Ohio State University on the cultural map with cutting-edge art. Whether you love it or hate it, the Wexner Center is like any worthwhile piece of art—it gets a reaction.

The Wexner Center offers the community wonderful public programming and lectures. It encourages artistic experimentation through a variety of student residencies and fellowships. Everything you need to know about the Wexner Center is somewhere on the extensive but user-friendly website: www.wexarts.org. Contact the information desk at (614) 292-3535, or visit in person at 1871 N. High St. You can't miss it!

Franklinton Arts District
400 W. Rich St.
www.franklintonartsdistrict.com

A cluster of galleries, art incubators, and maker-spaces are located along West Rich, Walnut, and McDowell Streets. Longtime Wild Goose Creative is a neat arts incubator and creator's space offering exhibitions, lectures, and hands-on classes. Wild Goose is wildly popular! The Vanderelli Room features local and national artists, while ROY G BIV promotes emerging contemporary artists.

Glass Axis Studio & Gallery
2117 S. High St., south Columbus
(614) 291-4250
www.glassaxis.org

This nonprofit arts organization was established in 1987 as a place where students and members of the community can come together and exchange ideas about the medium of glass. This unique full-service gallery and studio has grown to include a cold shop, hot shop, and flame- and kiln-working facilities. Membership is offered to experienced students at discounted rates, allowing them use of the facilities, while members of the community can register for all levels of glassblowing classes. Demonstrations and fund-raising events are also held on-site.

Hawk Galleries
135 E. Main St., downtown
(614) 225-9595
www.hawkgalleries.com

This open and airy gallery features original blown-glass art and 3D art. It also carries contemporary ceramics, crystal, and metal sculpture. The gallery represents an impressive list of nearly 100 artists, including two of the world's foremost living glass artists: Dale Chihuly and Lino Tagliapietra.

Keny Galleries
300 E. Beck St., German Village
(614) 464-1228
www.kenygalleries.com

The brothers Keny have a treasure trove of American artworks packed into a quaint German Village town house. They deal in historic American paintings and 19th- and 20th-century folk art, but specialize in master watercolors by big names, like Winslow Homer and Alice Schille, as well as prominent Ohio artists like Edward Potthast and George Bellows. You'll also find works by contemporary folk artists and the great folk masters such as Elijah Pierce and William Hawkins. The prices are reasonable, considering the Kenys have been known to sell pieces to major museums, such as the National Gallery of Art.

Lindsay Gallery
986 N. High St., Short North
(614) 576-1973
www.lindsaygallery.com

This comfortable gallery is situated on the northernmost end of the Short North and features American folk and outsider art. Wondering what exactly outsider art is? Just pop in and ask Duff Lindsay. The owner is more than happy to oblige you with a definition by pointing out the pieces hanging on the wall. Given the vision and creativity, it's hard to believe most of the artists represented by this dealer are self-taught or have no formal training. There is a little bit of everything at this gallery; just take a peek in the back room!

i The legendary tradition of the Short North Gallery Hop is held the first Saturday night of each month. Restaurants, bars, shops, and galleries stay open late and host special exhibitions and entertainment.

ROY G BIV
435 W. Rich St., Franklinton
(614) 297-7694
www.roygbivgallery.com

This nonprofit public art gallery was started by a few Columbus College of Art and Design students and is considered one of the edgier galleries in town. It can afford to take more risks because Arts Council subsidization alleviates the need for pressure sales. ROY G BIV features many different types of media, including paintings, ceramics, mobiles, and sculptures, encompassing a variety of genres. Exhibitions change monthly.

Terra Gallery and Creative Studio
6631 Dale Dr., Dublin
(614) 726-9260
www.terra-gallery.com

Elevate your living space with one-of-a-kind custom artwork tailored to your home. Terra's team of artists collaborates with you to craft pieces that resonate with your style and preferences for your home, or help them design a mural, canvas art, or installation for a corporate space. Artists can also create custom house portraits. The gallery carries ready-made frames and does custom framing. Studio artists offer a range of art classes in landscape or oil painting, metal art classes, paper making, and even pet portraits.

ATTRACTIONS

If you are a tourist here to see the sights, you'll find Columbus an easy and unintimidating city to explore. We have plenty of world-class attractions, including the zoo, science center, and statehouse.

History buffs might be interested in Native Americans and check out one of the ancient Indian mounds located in and around Columbus. Contact the Ohio History Connection at (614) 297-2300 or www.ohiohistory.org for a full listing of mounds, earthworks, and Native American sites in Ohio. While not in Columbus, it is worth noting that an hour and a half south of the city is the sacred UNESCO World Heritage Site, the Serpent Mound. This ancient American Indian burial site is one of the world's largest geoglyphs (man-made design on the landscape) and is most clearly seen from an aerial view.

Some of Columbus's attractions are located downtown (or close by), while the rest are scattered about the city. This chapter's entries are divided into three categories reflecting this division: "Downtown," "Surrounding Neighborhoods," and "Farther Afield," meaning within an hour's drive.

Major public monuments are included here rather than the Cultural Columbus chapter because they have a broad appeal to a variety of people and are often located on public grounds. Amusements and attractions catering specifically to children have been listed in the Family Fun chapter, while places of interest over an hour away can be found in the Worth the Trip chapter.

Columbus has activities in all prices ranges. Admission to most of the attractions included here are under $20 per person. Rather than assign price codes, only the exceptions will be noted. Not much is free in Columbus, so if you live here or frequent the city, consider joining your favorite organization or taking out a membership that gives additional benefits and ongoing free entry.

As a final note, a few of the best sources of information on attractions in Columbus are Experience Columbus (www.experiencecolumbus.com), Columbus Underground (www.columbusunderground.com), and 614Now (www.614now.com). Experience Columbus has the most comprehensive list of sights and events, allowing you to sort by location and date.

DOWNTOWN

Center of Science and Industry (COSI)
  Columbus
333 W. Broad St., Franklinton
(614) 228-COSI (2674)
www.cosi.org

This hands-on science museum is currently celebrating its 60th anniversary and has shuffled more than 30 million visitors through its doors to discovery since opening in 1964. Aside from being one of the most popular attractions in Columbus, it is one of the more well-respected and largest science centers in the country. COSI is currently located in what was once the Central High School, but the grand classical architecture makes it look more like a majestic state building sitting along the banks of the Scioto River.

This living museum provides hands-on, discover-based exhibits, where kids of all ages (and parents) can explore how things work in the world around them. There are nine exhibition areas and more than 300 interactive experiences allowing visitors to conduct their own underwater experiments, explore space, or try their hand

COSI
Shawnie Kelley

at the country's only high-wire unicycle. The outdoor Big Science Park is a hands-on science laboratory for kids. COSI is also home to Ohio's largest planetarium and the John Glenn Extreme Screen Theatre showing mind-boggling scientific and *National Geographic* movies on a three-story screen. Admission for adults (13 and older) is $30, for children ages 2–12 is $25. Children under 2 are admitted free of charge. The annual membership levels vary in cost. The science center is generally closed Mon and Tues.

Greater Columbus Convention Center
400 N. High St., downtown
(614) 827-2500
www.columbusconventions.com
The Greater Columbus Convention Center is located in an area that was once Columbus's major railroad terminal. Architecturally, it strives to reflect this in the shape and pastel coloring of the rectangular buildings that, from the air, look like boxcars. This multipurpose facility straddles the Short North and downtown.

The center plays host to many of Columbus's biggest conferences, competitions, and expositions. It is conveniently located near the major entertainment districts and within walking distance of several reputable hotels and restaurants. It also has its own food court and shops.

Ohio Statehouse
Broad and High Streets
(614) 752-9777, (888) 644-6123
www.ohiostatehouse.org
The symbolic center of the city encompasses 10 acres called Capitol Square and is the country's eighth-oldest working capitol building. The statehouse, interchangeably referred to as the Capitol, has been used by legislators since 1857 and is recognized as a National Historic Landmark.

After the first statehouse on this site burned down, the current building was constructed of Columbus limestone in the Greek Revival style between 1838 and 1861. Prison labor from the penitentiary was used to construct the ground level of the building. An 1840s rumor held that all good stonemasons had to be very wary of the law. Otherwise, they would end up in jail for the silliest thing and forced to use their talent on the statehouse.

TOURS

Columbus Food Adventures
(614) 440-3177
www.columbusfoodadventures.com
One way to discover a city is through its food. Beginning in 2007, husband and wife owners Bethia Woolf and Andy Dehus have grown Columbus Food Adventures into one of Ohio's premier culinary tour companies. The tours showcase the city through a variety of walking or driving tours that are either centered in one neighborhood or have specific foodie themes, such as taco trucks, desserts, or immigrant food. The guided tours typically make about five or six stops, each involving nice portions of food and sometimes drinks, especially on the "Adult Beverage" tour. Bethia and Andy have spent years developing relationships with restaurateurs, so guests are greeted as friends. Beyond enjoying the food, you will learn a lot of about each culture, cuisine, and Columbus. The couple has spent the past 15 years chronicling the culinary changes in Columbus, so check out the Food Adventures blog and the original

Alt Eats blog at www.alteatscolumbus. com for an extensive listing of ethic and immigrant restaurants around the city. Also, follow them on Facebook for up-to-date discoveries and insights on openings and closings.

The Columbus Landmarks Foundation
57 Jefferson Ave., second floor
(614) 221-0227
www.columbuslandmarks.org
The Columbus Landmarks Foundation is a group committed to preserving the city's architectural heritage. The foundation offers various guided walking tours through many historic neighborhoods, such as Capitol Square, Old Beechwold, and the Brewery District. These tours run through the summer and cost about $12 per person. There are also biking tours, Halloween ghost walks and bus tours in October, and the annual candlelight tour, called the "Great Hallelujah Holiday Tour of Churches," in December. You can purchase tickets online or in person.

Nathan B. Kelly was the architect responsible for the design of the lavish center rotunda and cupola, along with other architectural improvements, such as installing a heating and ventilation system. Building resumed in the 20th century, with the judiciary annex finished in 1901; an atrium, built in 1993, connects the statehouse and Senate Building. Both buildings were restored to their original beauty in 1996.

Among the sights not to miss are the statehouse rotunda's lavish marble floor and stained-glass skylight; the reproductions of original desks, carpets, and chandeliers in the House of Representatives and Senate chambers; the marble map of Ohio in the Map Room; and the original mosaic tile floor of the Grand Staircase in the Senate Building.

The statehouse is open seven days a week between 8 a.m. and 5 p.m. Daily free 45-minute

guided tours provide an in-depth look at the history, architecture, and functions of the building. Information can be obtained in the rotunda, accessible from High Street, or the information desk at the Third Street entrance. Tours must be scheduled and are offered 10 a.m. to 3 p.m. weekdays and noon until 3 p.m. weekends. The visitor center, which includes a cafeteria and gift shop, is located on the ground floor of the building.

i Abraham Lincoln visited the statehouse three times. A plaque commemorates a speech he gave to Ohioans shortly after the Lincoln–Douglas debates in 1859. He addressed the legislature in 1861, and his final visit was on April 29, 1865. Lincoln lay in state for a day in the rotunda as his casket was transported to its final resting place in Illinois.

Thurber House
77 Jefferson Ave.
(614) 464-1032
www.thurberhouse.org

One of America's greatest humorists, James Thurber, and his family lived in this house during his college years at The Ohio State University (1913–1917). It has been lovingly restored as a literary center, museum, and bookstore and is on the National Register of Historic Places. Literary pilgrims can tour several rooms of early 20th-century period furnishings and may even bump into a few ghosts. Highlights include the typewriter Thurber used when working for the *New Yorker* magazine.

The gallery presents book-related exhibitions and year-round programs, which include writing classes for children, author readings, and Thurber celebrations. Thurber House programming goes beyond Columbus city limits by sponsoring the Thurber Prize for American Humor and an adult writer-in-residence. The bookstore carries all of

Thurber's books in print. The museum is open Tues, Thurs, Sat, and Sun from 1 to 4 p.m., and admission is $5. Guided tours are offered on Sun for an additional fee.

Topiary Garden
Old Deaf School Park
480 E. Town St.
(614) 645-6640
www.columbus.gov/recreationandparks/
** parks/topiary-garden-(deaf-school-park)**

This clever garden art is modeled after French artist Georges Seurat's late 19th-century painting titled *A Sunday Afternoon on the Isle de la Grande Jatte*. This Postimpressionist landscape painting is translated into a real landscape and is the only such re-creation in the world. The ensemble consists of 54 topiary people, 8 boats, 3 dogs, a cat, and a monkey, making it one of the nation's largest topiary gardens.

The garden is best viewed from the east, as the artist conceived the painting from a hill in the

Topiary Park
Amy Paulin

CSRAB

east overlooking the Seine River. This project was conceived by James Mason, an instructor at the Columbus Recreation and Parks Department's Cultural Arts Center. The topiary is maintained by the department, and the museum shop, which funds the garden, is located in the gatehouse and open Apr through Dec. Entrance to the garden is free.

SURROUNDING NEIGHBORHOODS

Chief Leatherlips Monument
Scioto Park
7377 Riverside Dr., Dublin
The Dublin Arts Council commissioned this 12-foot limestone sculpture in 1990 as the first in its Art in Public Places program. Each piece relates to Dublin history. This portrait memorializes Wyandot Native American Chief Leatherlips. Local history holds he was executed by fellow tribesmen near Scioto Park. Climb up into the open head and you'll get a great view of the river and amphitheater. Leatherlips was created by Boston artist Ralph Helmick and is located in Dublin's Scioto Park.

Field of Corn **Sculpture**
Dublin and Rings Road, Dublin
In celebration of Dublin's agricultural heritage, this display of public art was commissioned by the Dublin Arts Council in 1994. Columbus artist Malcolm Cochran cast 109 6-foot ears of white concrete corn that stand upright in rows at the intersection of two major roads. On closer look, the layout resembles the white grave markers in Arlington National Cemetery. Osage orange trees and office buildings serve as the backdrop,

but from certain angles this is quite a photo opportunity.

Franklin Park Conservatory and Botanical Gardens
1777 E. Broad St., Bexley
(614) 715-8000
www.fpconservatory.org
Three miles east of downtown is a classic turn-of-the-20th-century conservatory listed on the National Register of Historic Places. A plant house has been on this site since 1895. The conservatory biomes showcase more than 400 species of plants from a variety of climate zones. Highlights include large bonsai and orchid collections and the country's largest public display of poinsettias during the holidays.

The botanical gardens encompass 28 acres and include sculptures, fountains, a Japanese garden, and an outdoor amphitheater, which hosts summer concerts. Special events, such as an annual living butterfly display and changing art exhibitions, are held throughout the year. Admission is around $23.50 for adults and $16 for children. Students and seniors are given discounts with proper ID. It is open daily from 10 a.m. until 4 p.m., with special holiday hours.

Motorcycle Hall of Fame Museum
13515 Yarmouth Dr., Pickerington
(614) 856-1900
www.americanmotorcyclist.com
The headquarters of the American Motorcycle Association is located just 15 miles east of downtown Columbus and houses the two-story Motorcycle Hall of Fame Museum. On display are

Ohio Statehouse Monuments

There are several interesting monuments located on the grounds of the statehouse, making for a nice walking tour. The following is a quick explanation of the more interesting sculptures and their location.

Cannons: The four cannons, which consist of two Napoleon 6-pounders and two 12-pounders, were made of cast bronze at the Miles Greenwood foundry in Cincinnati, Ohio, in 1864.

McKinley Monument: On the west side of the statehouse is the 1906 monument to assassinated President William McKinley made by H. A. MacNeil, of New York.

Mount Vernon Sundial Replica: The Daughters of the American Revolution erected this sundial in 1932 on the north side of the statehouse.

Ohio Veterans' Plaza: This veterans' memorial was designed by Schooley Caldwell Associates in 1998 as a reminder that our government could not exist without the sacrifices of our veterans. It is dedicated to all Ohio men and women who have served in the armed forces since World War II. It also serves as the east entrance to the statehouse and features a drive-through, drop-off area.

Ohio World War Memorial: World War I American infantrymen are honored in this 1930 sculpture designed by Arthur Ivone. It is located on the west stairs of the statehouse.

Peace Statue: In 1923 the Women's Relief Corps of Ohio erected this statue by Bruce Wilder Saville on the north side of the statehouse in honor of Civil War soldiers.

These Are My Jewels Statue: The oldest monument on the statehouse grounds was designed by Levi Tucker Scofield of Cincinnati for the World's Columbian Exposition of 1893. Portrayed in the statues are Cabinet members Edwin M. Stanton, secretary of war, and Salmon P. Chase, secretary of the treasury; Presidents James A. Garfield, Rutherford B. Hayes, and Ulysses S. Grant; and Generals William Sherman and Phillip Sheridan. The female figure is Cornelia. It was moved to the capitol in 1894 and is now located at the northwest corner of the statehouse.

historical and classic through present-day bikes. There are also plaques with information about the inductees to the Hall of Fame. The museum is open regular business hours daily, and a small admission is charged. Seniors get a discount, and children 18 and under are free.

Ohio Expo Center
717 E. 17th Ave.
(614) 644-3247
www.ohioexpocenter.com
The 150-year-old Ohio Expo holds over 200 events year-round. This huge 360-acre facility is home to

half of the major events held in Columbus, with the Ohio State Fair and Quarter Horse Congress being the two largest. Other events range from horse, cattle, and dog shows to an antiques show and the annual crafts festival.

There are 20 buildings in the complex, with ties for 2,000 cattle and the capacity to seat up to 20,000 people. The center is located just off I-71, a few minutes from downtown and near the OSU campus. Parking rates vary per vehicle, depending on the event. Traffic becomes quite congested in this area before and after events.

Shrum Mound
Campbell Park
3141 McKinley Ave., Hilliard
www.ohiohistory.org

It is held that this ancient mound was built by the Adena Indians sometime between 800 BC and AD 100. Shrum is the last remaining conical burial mound in Columbus and is maintained by the Ohio Historical Society. Visitors are sometimes disappointed to see it is "just" a 20-by-100-foot mound of grass with stairs leading to the top, but it is the ancient and sacred nature of the site that makes it special. Entry is free.

Watch House Sculpture
Coffman Park
5600 Post Rd., Dublin

Symbolism abounds in this 1998 sculpture created by Columbus artist Todd Slaughter. A symbol of the connection between Dublin's past (the Native culture) and present (the contemporary culture) is seen in a copper house that sits atop an earthen Native American–inspired mound. Prairie grass and sunflowers refer to the garden crops of Ohio's first farmers. The windows cut out of the planetarium-like dome represent the expanding and changing nature of the landscape, people, and universe. Different aspects of the building reveal themselves as the viewer moves toward the artwork. Admission is free.

FARTHER AFIELD

Cuyahoga Valley National Park and Scenic Railroad
Rockside Station
7900 Old Rockside Rd., Independence
(330) 439-5708
www.cvsr.org

We are fortunate to have Cuyahoga Valley National Park less than 2 hours north of Columbus. It is a short distance to drive for outdoor beauty and adventure that feels a world away from the nearby major urban centers of Cleveland, Akron, and Columbus. The 33,000-acre park lies along the Cuyahoga River Valley through which the Ohio & Erie Canal once traveled, connecting Lake Erie with the Ohio River. By the mid-19th century, towns along the canal flourished because of the shipping industry, until the Civil War and railroads put the canal system out of business. A 4-mile section of the canal was made a National Historic Landmark in 1966, and Cuyahoga Valley was given national park status in 2000.

Explore the park on more than 125 miles of hiking trails that vary in difficulty and habitat. The Boston Mill Visitor Center is the place to borrow hiking poles, pick up trail maps, and learn where water and restrooms are located. The Brandywine Gorge Loop circles past a deep ravine with gorgeous views of Brandywine Falls. Cycling is permitted along the Towpath Trail—20 of its 101 miles are located within the park and shared with runners and other outdoor enthusiasts moving at different paces. Paddling in the Cuyahoga River is lovely, but at your own risk. Mountain bikers should hit the East Rim Trails for varied terrain requiring intermediate skills. Entry to the park is free.

Whether you are a train enthusiast or a family up for an adventure, hop aboard the Cuyahoga Valley Scenic Railroad, which makes stops at eight stations from Independence to Akron, Ohio. Tickets must be purchased in advance of boarding, but CVSR offers a variety of price levels ranging from plain old coach and first class to luxury seating in Premium Coach or the upper dome. The dome seating is on the upper level of the train and provides panoramic views through its big glass windows and domed roof. The cafe cart serves munchies and both alcoholic and non-alcoholic drinks, and bathrooms are found throughout the train. The ride is about 2 hours round-trip, but you can also ride your bike one way along the trail and hitch a ride back (for you and your bike) for a nominal one-way fee. Be sure to know the schedule. Parking at the train stations is free.

Hartman Rock Garden
1905 Russel Ave., Springfield
www.hartmanrocks.org

This quirky rock art garden was created by Ben Hartman between 1932 and 1944 using more than 250,000 rocks. The folk art garden was a product of his being laid off during the Great Depression and having a little time on his creative hands. The miniature larger-than-life backyard kingdom includes buildings, figurines, walls, bridges, and even a castle made from whatever he could get his hands on. Stone, metal, glass, and wood were turned into figments of his imagination taken from books, radio, and film. The garden was maintained by his wife for 50 years and is now in the care of Friends of Hartman Rock Garden, who offer 1-hour guided tours of the garden for a fee. Well-behaved children are permitted with adults. It is open from 8 a.m. to 8 p.m. daily, year-round. Donations are encouraged, but it is otherwise free. This is a nice stop to bundle with a trip to Young's Jersey Dairy Farm in nearby Yellow Springs.

Ohio Caverns
2210 E. SR 245, West Liberty
(937) 465-4017
www.ohiocaverns.com
The largest of Ohio's caverns is open regular business hours, year-round, and are located beneath the grounds of a 35-acre park with shelters and picnic areas. Visitors are guided through the colorful stalactite and stalagmite formations on a 50-minute, mile-long tour. The path is level and paved, but you should wear sturdy walking shoes. Regardless of the outdoor weather, the interior of the caverns remains a constant 54 degrees Fahrenheit, so bring a jacket. Admission is charged.

Olentangy Indian Caverns
1779 Home Rd., Delaware
(740) 548-7917
www.olentangyindiancaverns.com
Beautiful limestone passages were formed millions of years ago by underground rivers cutting their way through solid rock. They were used by local Native Americans and rediscovered in 1821 by J. M. Adams, a member of a westbound wagon train. Today, guided tours are offered through the winding maze of underground rooms, integrated with stories of ancient Indian lore. The tour features a "Council Rock" used by the Wyandottes for tribal ceremonies.

Artifacts and geological exhibits can be seen at the on-site museum, and goods can be purchased at the gift shop. Tours are offered Apr through Oct, and admission and activity fees range from $5 to $30. Those under 2 are free. An 18-hole miniature golf course, petting zoo, gem-mining, and picnic areas are also located on the grounds.

The Wilds
14000 International Rd., Cumberland
(740) 638-5030, (866) 444-WILDS
www.thewilds.org
Can't afford a safari? A day at The Wilds is nothing short of a trip to Africa! This 10,000-acre wildlife conservation park, tucked in the hills of Ohio, is the largest facility of its kind in North America. Year-round guided tours in open-air buses will allow you to see large groups of rhinos, giraffes, Asian wild horses, red wolves, mountain zebras, gazelles, and many other species. Bird lovers come to spot some of the 150 bird species documented here. In short, this place is amazing!

The safari-style tours allow for spectacular photography and wildlife sightings, while the observation decks along Lake Trail Mini-Park and the Outpost offer extended viewing areas. Dine in the Overlook Cafe or Terrace Grill and shop in the Gift Market, or better yet, stay the night in The Lodge at the Wilds or in a yurt on the property. A special Sunset Safari, which includes a twilight dinner and guided tour, is offered seasonally, as are winter tours, birding trips, and horseback safaris.

The Wilds is open daily, year-round. Admission ranges from $40 to $150 based on the length and type of safari. Annual memberships are available and discounts are given with Columbus Zoo memberships. The Wilds is located 20 miles southeast of Zanesville, about an hour east of Columbus.

Young's Jersey Dairy Farm
6880 Springfield Xenia Rd., Yellow Springs
(937) 325-0629
www.youngsdairy.com
This is a 150-year-old family-run dairy farm that does a huge ice-cream business—a destination dairy for dozens of flavors of farmstead cheese and house-churned ice cream, malts, and sundaes. The large restaurant also serves sandwiches and other hearty farmstead entrees. Just order at the counter and peruse the large gift shop until your number is called. There is plenty to do beyond the curds and cream. Take a lap through the barns to see (and smell) the cows and other farm animals. Kiddos will enjoy the playground, giant slide, miniature golf, and batting cages. Photo ops abound with tractors and hay bales to climb on. Young's hosts

year-round events beyond the usual fall festivals: Come for the popular wool gathering (you knitters can buy beautiful yarn!), spring Easter Egg Hunt, and summertime bike tour of the area. Young's is open daily until 8 or 9 p.m.

HISTORIC HOMES

History buffs will be excited to learn there are several preserved or restored 19th-century homes in and around the city, many of which are operated by local historical societies. Some of the homes included here are dedicated to interpreting 19th-century life in Ohio. Museum-style displays range from "old stuff" laid out on tables to period rooms with changing exhibits. Some provide costume-clad docents, and others have self-guided tours, but each gives you insight into a little piece of Columbus history.

Fletcher-Coffman Homestead
6659 Coffman Rd., Dublin
(614) 716-9149
www.visitdublinohio.com
This 1860s homestead, listed on the National Register of Historic Places, features guided tours through period rooms full of 19th-century furniture. The restored barn has a display of early Ohio farm machinery and barn furnishings. The Heritage Gardens have interesting heirloom and antique interpretive plantings, typifying American farm life in the mid-1800s.

i Columbus has 18 distinct historic districts with 82 buildings on the Columbus Register of Historic Properties and 176 properties on the National Historic Landmarks Registry. Some of the historic districts include the German, Italian, and Victorian Villages, the Brewery District, and East Town Street, Iuka Ravine, Hamilton Park, Old Oaks, and Bryden Road Historic Districts. Structures of architectural significance include the LeVeque Tower, Athletic Club of Columbus, Budd Dairy, Camp Chase, and Orton Memorial Laboratory at The Ohio State University.

Hanby House
160 W. Main St., Westerville
(614) 891-6289
www.ohiohistory.org/visit/browse
-historical-sites/hanby-house
The Benjamin Hanby House State Memorial is managed locally by the Westerville Historical Society. This former home of composer Benjamin Russell Hanby, known for his songs "Darling Nellie Gray" and "Up on the Housetop," was built in 1846. Furniture and personal items of the Hanby family, who occupied the home from 1853 to 1870, are on display. Highlights include a walnut desk made by Hanby, the original plates for the first edition of "Darling Nellie Gray," and a large collection of sheet music. The Hanby house was also a station along the Underground Railroad. It is only open by appointment, and a small admission fee is charged. Members of the Ohio Historical Society receive free admission.

Kelton House Museum and Garden
586 E. Town St., Olde Towne East
(614) 464-2022
www.keltonhouse.com
Lovers of all things Victorian should make it a point to stop in at this 1852 Greek Revival–style home located just east of downtown. Restored by the Junior League of Columbus, this was once the home of a prominent merchant family from 1852 to 1975. The museum conveys the story of 19th-century urban Columbus through period rooms and collections of lavish furnishings, decorative arts, and personal items from three generations of the Kelton family. Some of the highlights include a Duncan Phyfe lyre card table and a grandfather clock made circa 1790.

The Kelton family house was one of several Underground Railroad safe houses along East Town Street. Pearl Hartway, an escaped slave from Virginia, took refuge with the family for 10 years until she married Thomas Lawrence, a free black carpenter from Cadiz, Ohio. An Ohio Underground Railroad Association plaque on the museum grounds commemorates these events.

The Kelton House is open Thurs through Sun and for holiday and special events, including the occasional Afternoon Tea service. The entrance

Orange Johnson House, Worthington
Shawnie Kelley

fee is around $10, and a cute little museum shop is on-site.

Orange Johnson House
956 High St., Worthington
(614) 885-1247
www.worthingtonhistory.org
The oldest restored house in Franklin County began in 1811 as a pioneer cabin built by Aurora Buttles. Five years later, it was purchased by Orange Johnson, "the most prominent and prosperous businessman in Worthington." In 1819 a Federal-style wing was added, and the family resided here until 1863. The home is beautifully restored and features furniture of the Federal period, some connected to early Worthington families. The kitchen has a working fireplace, while many of the architectural features are original to the home. The O.J. House is open by advance reservation for guided tours. A $5 admission is charged.

HISTORIC TOWNS

Several restored villages and sites are within an easy drive of the city. Many provide costumed interpreters and craft demonstrations.

Clifton Mill
75 Water St., Clifton
(937) 767-5501
www.cliftonmill.com
At one time there were approximately 100,000 mills in this country, but now, fewer than 100 are still in original operating condition. Forty-five minutes southwest of Columbus is one of the largest water-powered gristmills still in existence, around which the village of Clifton grew. Clifton Mill was built in 1802 on the Little Miami River to take advantage of the concentrated water funneled through the gorge. A tour provides insight into one of America's earliest industries and explains the mill's involvement in the Civil War.

The Mill Restaurant offers beautiful views overlooking Clifton Gorge and serves home-cooked meals for breakfast and lunch. The pancake and corn bread mix is made on-site, and those who tour the mill receive a free sample bag. The Country Store carries jams, candles, dried floral arrangements, and Clifton Mills brand pancake mix, ground wheat, and cornmeal. The gallery displays a collection of 300 flour bags from different mills. The mill, gorge, and grounds are decorated with over 3.2 million lights each year to create a spectacular holiday illumination and waterfall of lights.

The Golden Lamb
27 Broadway St., Lebanon
(513) 932-5065
www.goldenlamb.com
Since 1803, the Golden Lamb has been feeding and bedding weary travelers, making this Ohio's longest continually operated inn and the state's oldest hotel.

Historic Lyme Village
5001 SR 4, Bellevue
(419) 483-4949
www.lymevillage.org
Historic Lyme Village was started by a group of individuals dedicated to "preserving yesterday for tomorrow." Many of the structures were moved to Lyme Village in the 1970s and 1980s. Pop into the visitor center for a map before touring the town's 16 19th-century buildings, which include log houses, barns, stores, and a one-room schoolhouse.

The Victorian Wright Mansion, built in 1882, houses the museum, and the 1836 Seymour House was the first building in the village. Events

i Escaping to the country was considered the highest form of sophistication among the 1940s New York smart set. Louis Bromfield's good friends Humphrey Bogart and Lauren Bacall were married at Malabar Farm on May 21, 1945. Exhibits related to their nuptials make this one of the most popular tourist attractions in northern Ohio.

such as Victorian Tea, Pioneer School, and Civil War reenactments are held throughout the year. Church services are held on Sunday at the New England–style Lyme Church. The Sunday school is the oldest continuous organization in Ohio.

Malabar Farm
3954 Bromfield Rd., Lucas
(419) 892-2784
www.malabarfarm.org
This 900-acre working farm is located in Malabar Farm State Park, about an hour north of Columbus. The 32-room Depression-era mansion was once the home of Pulitzer Prize–winning author and highly acclaimed agriculturalist Louis Bromfield. An extraordinary visitor center is a great place to start a tour as its interpretive exhibits tell the story of the life and legacy of Bromfield. Year-round guided tours of the "Big House" provide insight into Ohio's farming traditions, as well as Bromfield's glamourous Hollywood life and farming conservation philosophies. Tickets can be purchased online or at the gift shop. Seasonal wagon tours of the farm are offered for an additional fee.

Twelve miles of hiking, horse, and cross-country ski trails ensure there is plenty to do on the property, which is owned and operated by the state. Regular events include square dances, a maple syrup festival, Heritage Days, and wildlife weekends.

Roscoe Village
600 Whitewoman St., Coshocton
(740) 622-7644
www.roscoevillage.com
Roscoe Village, "America's Canal Town," was established in 1817 as Caldersburgh by James Caulder. It was renamed for abolitionist William Roscoe in 1830 and grew into the fourth-largest wheat port with the advent of the Ohio-Erie Canal. The prosperity of Roscoe declined with the demise of the canal industry in the early 20th century. Historic preservation began in the 1960s, and today Roscoe Village is a living museum—women with hoop skirts and all!

This charming restored 1830s canal town offers quaint shops filled with crafts, books, candles, and gourmet foods. Stroll the brick sidewalks, and explore pocket gardens and 19th-century buildings. The village's Johnson-Humrickhouse Museum has collections of American Indian artifacts and 18th- and 19th-century Asian, European, and American decorative arts. There is a small entrance fee for this surprisingly fine regional museum. Artisans such as blacksmiths, weavers, and broom makers offer live demonstrations in some of the workshops, while visitors can learn the art of candle dipping or tin punching for themselves. Independently owned shops line the charming brick streets. Add-on fees are charged for seasonal guided tours of the themed gardens and the 45-minute horse-drawn canal boat ride. "Living History" tickets can be purchased at the visitor center for individuals or family package deals.

Overnight guests can stay in the relaxed environs of the Apple Butter Bed and Breakfast via Airbnb. Dining options include the more upscale Huck's Tavern. Roscoe Village has a calendar full of events year-round, such as Apple Butter Stirrin', arts and crafts festivals, Civil War reenactments, and Christmas candle lightings.

Sauder Village
22611 Hwy. 2, Archbold
(419) 445-2231, (800) 590-9755
www.saudervillage.org
Forward-thinking Erie J. Sauder (1904–1997) turned his love of Ohio's history into a living museum. The dozens of buildings at Sauder Village are authentic 19th- and early 20th-century structures, disassembled and moved from their original locations around northwestern Ohio to create Ohio's largest living-history destination. The buildings, along with collections of agricultural equipment, textiles, and household furnishings, relate the story of how Ohio's earliest settlers transformed the Great Black Swamp into fertile farmland.

A costumed staff reenacts life in various historical settings and offers demonstrations such as spinning or old printing techniques and food preparation. Children will enjoy the hands-on activities at Little Pioneers Homestead. The village has a general store, quilt shop, herb shop, and gift center, as well as the family-friendly Barn Restaurant, bakery, cafe, and soda fountain on-site. The Barn offers a buffet and family-style meals, while the Doughbox Bakery sells pies Grandma would be proud of. There is both a campground and Sauder Heritage Inn at the village. Sauder Village is open seasonally, but the restaurant, inn, and bakery are open year-round.

Zoar Village
Zoar, 3 miles southeast of I-77
www.historiczoarvillage.com
Zoar Village was founded in 1817 by a group of peace-loving German separatists escaping religious persecution in their homeland. This self-sufficient community was one of the few experiments in communal living in the US that actually succeeded. With the passing of the Zoarite spiritual leader in the 1850s and the increasing influence from the outside world, the community voted to disband in 1898.

Today, you will find a mixture of privately owned homes and restored buildings operated by the Ohio History Connection. The gardens are beautifully maintained and serve as a focal point in the village. Architectural highlights include a cupola-topped assembly house, schoolhouse, town hall, meetinghouse, and The Number One House.

More information about visiting, adult art classes, antiques shows, and lecture series can be found on the website.

VINEYARDS

Ohio is one of America's top 10 wine producing states and turns out more than 500,000 gallons every year. The state has a rich winemaking history, which began in Cincinnati in the early 1800s. Three vineyards in the Columbus area have maintained that long tradition of growing flavorful grapes for quality wines. Check out www.ohiowines.org to explore Ohio's seven wine trails and to learn more about the vineyards and wine festivals. The website also has links to quick thematic guides and wine-soaked day trips.

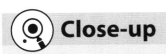

Close-up

A Little Monkey Business: The Columbus Zoo and Aquarium

A handful of animals were donated to the Columbus Zoological Park (now the Franklin Park Conservatory) in 1927, setting the direction for a fully planned zoo. Its current location swallows up nearly 600 acres of land and houses 800 species and 10,000 animals, making it one of the largest zoos in the country. Some 2 million visitors pass through the grounds of this world-class zoo, making it the eighth most visited zoo in the country.

Construction of buildings and the acquisition of animals occurred throughout the 1940s and 1950s. The 1970s brought about the implementation of an education department designed to promote awareness of human relationships to the natural world. But it was in the 1980s and 1990s that the Columbus Zoo came into its own. Director emeritus Jack Hanna built national recognition for the zoo through ongoing television appearances. Most people know him from *Late Night with David Letterman* and *Good Morning America*. Hanna, however, was not the zoo's first celebrity.

The year 1956 saw the birth of the world's first captive-born gorilla, Colo. She lived to be 60 years old, passing in 2017, but remains celebrated as the cornerstone of a groundbreaking gorilla breeding program. Colo foreshadowed the revolutionary facility the Columbus Zoo would become as a leading breeder of many endangered species. It is known worldwide for breeding lowland gorillas, cheetahs, polar bears, and 40 species of turtles. The zoo has reintroduced West Indian manatees, Mexican wolves, bald eagles, and Atlantic loggerhead and Pacific green sea turtles into the wild.

The zoo is broken up into various regions that simulate the natural environment of each animal's native continent. Educational signage is displayed throughout the exhibits. The 43-acre Heart of Africa Region is the zoo's largest. It features lions, bonobos, chimpanzees, ostriches, and leopards, to name a few. The North American Trek has been redeveloped in brilliant ways for visitors to see black bears, wolves, bison, bald eagles, and cougars. The Australia and Islands of Southeast Asia feature not only orangutans, kangaroos, and komodo dragons but also a boat ride through the islands.

Exhibition areas also are dedicated to specific species of animals. The Flamingo/Alligator Exhibit houses colorful birds native to the southeastern US and the Caribbean. The Humboldt Penguin exhibition provides underwater views of these birds that think they are living on the west coast of South America. The Discovery Reef is a 100,000-gallon aquarium designed to simulate a coral reef from a scuba diver's perspective. Colorful fish, stingrays, and sharks call this home.

When it comes to one-of-a-kind exhibits, the Columbus Zoo is one of only a few in the country that permanently houses koalas. It has the world's largest display of pachyderms and a collection of reptiles also among the largest of its kind. The Columbus Zoo is one of only three facilities outside Florida to exhibit the rare West Indian manatee.

The zoo is an incredibly interactive and hands-on place to take your family. Educational exhibits throughout focus on habitat preservation. The zoo has several exciting playgrounds for the kids, a petting zoo, the North American Train Ride, and pony and camel rides. The 1914 vintage carousel contains all 52 of its original horses. Year-round programs and special events are offered for adults and children. Several food courts and gift shops can be found throughout the grounds. The zoo also owns the Safari Golf Course. Read about the adjacent Zoombezi Bay Water Park in the Family Fun chapter.

The Columbus Zoo is located at 4850 W. Powell Rd. in Powell (614-645-3400 or 800-MON-KEYS/666-5397). It is open every day of the year. Admission is around $30 for adults and $25 for children. Children 2 and under are free. Various levels of membership include reciprocation to other zoos throughout the country. Parking is $10. For more information visit www.columbuszoo.org.

Buckeye Lake Winery
13750 Rosewood Dr., Thornville
(740) 246-5665
www.buckeyelakewinery.com
Buckeye Lake Winery is a restaurant that uses premium wines from Napa Valley vineyards and then blends and bottles about ten reds and whites on-site. You can enjoy a glass of pinot grigio, sauvignon blanc, or chardonnay or go with a red petite sirah or cabernet while enjoying a lakefront dinner or brunch. Wine with a view! Open Thurs through Sun.

Gervasi Vineyard Resort and Spa
1700 55th St. NE, Canton
(330) 497-1000
www.gervasivineyard.com
Read about the resort and spa located on a beautiful northeastern Ohio vineyard in the Worth the Trip chapter.

Slate Run Vineyard Winery
1900 Winchester-Southern Rd., Canal
  Winchester
(614) 834-5757
www.slaterunwine.com
Slate Run Vineyard is a small farm winery situated amid 4 acres of vineyards 19 miles from downtown Columbus. Wines are made from 60 varieties of grapes grown at Slate Run and fruits from other orchards. Highlights include fruit wines and German and Burgundy-style wines. There are also a cozy tasting room, gift shop, event house, informal tours, and picnicking.

Wyandotte Winery
4640 Wyandotte Dr.
(614) 476-3642
www.wyandottewinery.com
Gourmet fruit wines and award-winning table wines are made at the sister winery of William Graystone Winery in German Village. Along with grape wine, raspberry and cranberry wines are its specialty. Tours are given Tues through Sat. There is a tasting room and gift shop at this suburban winery, while pretty sister winery, Rockside Vineyards (www.rocksidewinery.com), is a short country drive just north of Lancaster.

TOURIST INFORMATION AND VISITOR BUREAUS

Figuring out what to do while you're in Columbus couldn't be easier. These visitor centers can be contacted for further tourist information about each neighborhood. I have included the city or chamber of commerce contact details when there is not a specific visitors bureau.

Bexley Area Chamber of Commerce
2242 E. Main St., Bexley
(614) 236-4500
www.bexleyareachamber.org

City of Grandview Heights
1016 Grandview Ave., Grandview
(614) 488-3159
www.grandviewheights.org

City of Hilliard
3800 Municipal Way, Hilliard
(614) 876-7361
www.hilliardohio.gov

City of Upper Arlington
3600 Tremont Center, Upper Arlington
(614) 584-5000
www.upperarlingtonoh.gov

Experience Worthington
777 High St., Worthington
(614) 841-2545
www.experienceworthington.com

Gahanna Convention and Visitors Bureau
116 Mill St., Gahanna
(866) 424-2662, (866) GAHANNA (424-2662)
www.visitgahanna.com

German Village Society
588 S. Third St.
(614) 221-8888
www.germanvillage.com

Italian Village Society
www.italianvillage.org

New Albany Area Chamber of Commerce
55 W. Main St., New Albany
(614) 855-4400
www.newalbanychamber.com

Short North Arts District
875 N. High St.
(614) 299-8050
www.shortnorth.org

i Discover Ohio by visiting www.ohio.
org for comprehensive visitor information, travel itineraries, things to do, and
events around the Buckeye State. Experience Columbus also provides an exhaustive
guide to events and attractions specifically in Columbus, which can be viewed at
www.experiencecolumbus.com, or call (614)
221-6623.

Visit Dublin
9 S. High St., Dublin
(614) 792-7666
www.visitdublinohio.com

Visit Grove City
3995 Broadway St.
(614) 539-8747
www.grovecityohio.gov

Visit Westerville
240 S. State St., Westerville
(614) 794-0401
www.visitwesterville.org

FAMILY FUN

Ask 10 different kids what they like to do in Columbus, and you'll get 10 different answers. The input from parents is as equally varied, but one thing can be agreed on: Columbus is a great place to raise a family. Many of Columbus's most popular family activities have already been listed in the Attractions chapter, but it is good to remember places like the zoo, the Center of Science and Industry (COSI), and the Columbus Conservatory, though catering to a broad audience, have extensive programming for kids. This chapter will present a variety of activities that target specific age groups, ranging from toddler to teen. A good place to start looking for children's activities is Experience Columbus (www.experiencecolumbus.com), which has a section about things to do with kids.

Events created specifically for children have also been included here, but many of the festivals listed in the Annual Events and Festivals chapter have specialized kids' booths and activities. Stalls at the Columbus Arts Festival allow children to create their own works of art, while the Dublin Irish Festival has a whole area for the wee folk. Some families enjoy special-interest events, like the annual train show, while others live for the Quarter Horse Congress. This is just a reminder not to overlook other chapters as a source for family fun.

This chapter focuses on amusement and seasonal activities, along with fun educational programs, popular athletic camps, and youth leagues. The city of Columbus places heavy emphasis on public green spaces, so there are plenty of options to get the family outdoors and active. The Parks and Recreation chapter includes information on bike trails, parks, and a range of sports the whole family can participate in.

You'll have no problem finding chain toy and clothing stores, such as Abercrombie Kids, Gap Kids, and Carters in most of the shopping centers, but there are several locally owned children's boutiques, bookstores, and toy stores that are noted in the Shopping chapter.

At the end of the day, it is just a matter of what you and your children like to do and how you define family fun. This chapter provides a kid's-eye view of the more popular activities, many of which come with recommendations from the younger crowd.

PARENT STUFF

A good place to find out what's going on in the Columbus area is *Columbus Monthly*'s go-to section for parents (www.columbusmonthly.com/columbus-parent). This monthly publication is full of informative articles targeting parents with toddlers through teens.

The Columbus Moms Network (www.columbusmomsnetwork.com) is a wonderful way to meet other moms while socializing with parents, kids, or the whole family. This organization holds play dates and Mom meet-ups, and provides information about community support

services, self-preservation and fitness, and even recipe round-ups. An updated calendar of kid- and family-friendly events can be found on the homepage.

Dads haven't been forgotten, either. Columbus Dads, part of the City Dad's Group (www.citydadsgroup.com), connects both online and real time at various locations around town, and like the Columbus Moms, it provides fathers with the opportunity to take an active role in their children's world with meet-ups, seminars, and group play dates. Connect with the Columbus chapter via Meetup, Facebook, and Instagram.

Educational activities abound at the local libraries. For example, Grandview Heights, Upper Arlington, and Westerville libraries have kids' educational programming, movies, and story times for toddlers. The Cover to Cover bookstore in Arlington and Gramercy Books in Bexley also host children's activities, readings, and book clubs. Impressively, the Book Loft in German Village has five rooms of children's books!

When it comes to children's haircuts, take them to a kids-only salon, where they'll experience the "funnest" haircuts in town. Cookie Cutter (www.cookiecutterscolumbus.com) is a favorite children's salon, with multiple locations. They've traded in barber chairs for planes, trains, and automobiles. Toddlers can sit in fun, animated seats while watching their favorite cartoon or film on TV. Polaroid pictures, along with a lock of hair, are included to commemorate kiddos' first haircut.

Cookie Cutter locations are in Hilliard (614-876-7700), Polaris Parkway (614-846-5610), New Albany (614-428-9999), Pickerington (614-522-0220), and Dublin (614-792-2899) and prefer advance appointments be made.

KID CULTURE

BalletMet
322 Mount Vernon Ave., downtown
(614) 229-4860
www.balletmet.org
Columbus's premier ballet company offers an extensive list of educational and academy classes. Children as young as 4 can enroll for beginner ballet, while a varied curriculum offers youth ages 6 and up everything from modern, jazz, and tap to Irish step, Pilates, and advanced movement. The YouthMet performs at special events, and the price of tuition ranges from $150 to $1,300.

Chamber Music Connection
700 High St., Worthington
(614) 323-1300
www.cmconnection.org
Young musicians flourish at the Chamber Music Connection. The CMC is a local organization providing all levels of chamber music education for students of all ages and abilities. The youth classes are small, and the programs are geared primarily for string, wind, and piano instrumentalists. The CMC sponsors several different ensembles for school-age students, various festivals, competitions, and scholarships. High-quality musical entertainment can also be hired through them.

Columbus Children's Choir
760 E. Broad St., downtown
(614) 220-5555
www.columbuschildrenschoir.org
Auditions are held annually for this independent, community-based children's choral program. Children in grades 3 through 12 are placed according to their grade and musical skill set in one of nine different ensembles. Enrollment lasts an entire season, and tuition costs between $450 and $775. They rehearse on a weekly basis throughout the school year, and members must re-audition each year. The Middle School Choral Fest is a full-day workshop open to choir members and non-member middle school singers each April, culminating in a few performances each semester.

Columbus Children's Theatre
512 N. Park St., Arena District
(614) 224-6672
www.columbuschildrenstheatre.org
Columbus Children's Theatre, founded in 1963, is the oldest and largest children's theater in central Ohio. The academy introduces kids ages 3 through 18 to all facets of the theater arts through creative drama classes, singing, dancing, and costume and prop design. The classes cost between $120 and $200. Aside from teaching young actors, CCT presents the community with fun live performances such as *Wicked*, *Willy Wonka*, and other plays and musicals geared toward family audiences.

Columbus Museum of Art
480 E. Broad St., downtown
(614) 221-6801
www.columbusmuseum.org
The Columbus Museum's kid-friendly programming is extensive. The kid-friendly Wonder Room

allows kids to interact, discover, and play with art in hands-on and creative ways. The Dreamy Room inspires imagination. Make sculptures, play in the treehouse, or build with Legos.

Channel their inner artist during Open Studio every Sat from 10:30 a.m. to 3:30 p.m. Each month highlights a different theme, such as landscapes or abstraction, through which kids are introduced to a variety of artistic styles and processes. Children ages 6 and older can explore the museum's collections and special exhibitions through self-guided activities. The museum is free for all on Sun.

Full- or half-day summer art workshops are also available for children in first through eighth grade, during which they learn about drawing, painting, sculpture, photography, and more.

Columbus Symphony Youth Orchestra
55 E. State St., downtown
(614) 469-0939
www.columbussymphony.com/education/
youth-orchestra.com
The symphony has been helping Columbus's youngest musicians find their inner maestro for 50 years now. Some 300 children grades 3 through 12 make up the five different youth orchestras. Junior Strings encourages the development of young string players in grades 3 through 7, while the Chamber Strings Orchestra is made up of talented players in grades 6 through 9. Both hold at least three concerts per season. The Cadet Orchestra is composed of students grades 7 through 10, who also perform three concerts per season.

One hundred young musicians in grades 9 through 12 form the primary Youth Orchestra, which has been nationally recognized and occasionally go on European tours. It is a big commitment to be involved in any of these orchestras, as members must take private lessons, participate in their school band, and attend weekly rehearsals. Tuition is around $500 per season.

Columbus Youth Jazz
769 E. Long St.
(614) 294-5200
www.jazzartsgroup.org/youthjazz
Get your young jazz cat into one of a few ensembles and labs. Middle and high school students in grades 7 through 12 can audition for the general CYJ orchestra, Big Band, Instrumental Lab, and Jazz Vocal Lab. Keep in mind this is a rigorous commitment, meeting weekly for 8 to 10 weeks at the Jazz Academy in the Lincoln Theatre, sometimes on Sundays. All this practice results in stellar instrumental and vocal performances by the jazz artists of the future.

Historical Dramas
Tecumseh!
Make learning history a little more fun by taking the family to the region's 90-minute outdoor historical *Tecumseh!* It is not recommended for children under the age of 5 or 6, as it depicts the epic struggles of Shawnee leader Tecumseh to defend his sacred homeland. The story is brought to life at Sugarloaf Mountain Amphitheatre in Chillicothe each summer, from June through Sept. Everything about *Tecumseh!* is top-notch: The script was written by Pulitzer Prize–nominated and Emmy-winning author Allan W. Eckert, the haunting music was recorded by the London Symphony Orchestra, and the story is narrated by Oscar-nominated Native American actor Graham Greene. It's no wonder this drama has received international acclaim during its 50-year run. Tickets range from $30 to $50 and can be purchased online at www.tecumsehdrama.com or by calling the box office at (866) 775-0700. Backstage tours and VIP packages are available, and the Gallery at Sugarloaf gift shop carries goods made by Native American and Indigenous artisans from around the country. The on-site restaurant is very casual, serving pizza, sandwiches, and pretzels. It is open each show night starting at 4 p.m.

Wexner Center for the Arts
The Ohio State University
(614) 688-3986
www.wexarts.org
Summer programming at the Wexner Center offers teens ages 13 to 18 the chance to explore their creativity through contemporary art forms, such as video, digital, sound, performance, and other alternative media. WexLabs for Teens are interactive studio workshops that integrate technology into art. Ohio Shorts encourages youth

under the age of 18 to submit original short videos for the annual competitions. YogArts is a series of yoga, art, and meditation workshops for families, while the film education programs introduce youth to filmmaking.

SPECIAL PROGRAMS

Kaleidoscope Youth Center
603 E. Town St.
(614) 294-5437
www.kycohio.org

KYC is a drop-in center for lesbian, gay, bisexual, transgender, or queer youth in the central Ohio area. This community center offers a supportive environment in which LGBTQ+ youths have a safe space to socialize, find community services, and foster a positive self-image that can be carried into schools and the world. There is also a library with internet access, discussion and support groups, and the occasional pizza party. The center is open to youth under the age of 24 and has links to mental and physical health and crisis resources.

Popcorn Pops
Columbus Commons, downtown
(614) 228-8600
www.picnicwiththepops.com

As part of the Columbus Symphony's Picnic with the Pops series, these special performances are intended for families with children ages 3 to 12 and are held on the lawn of the Columbus Commons. There are pre-concert activities and games. The shows have included music from *Harry Potter*, *The Wizard of Oz*, and Disney movies.

i Parents will be happy to learn that many of the Columbus area schools are connected with ROX (Ruling Our eXperiences). The free 20-week after-school program for girls in grades 5 through 12, run by licensed female professionals, helps girls learn to navigate academics, relationships, social media, body image, health, careers, and life in general. ROX empowers girls to rule their experiences. Non-school-related seminars for parents and parent-child workshops are offered throughout the year.

i The Columbus Youth Council is a group of high school juniors and seniors from across greater Columbus, who advise the mayor and city council on youth issues. The commission helps provide leadership in the development of priorities and a comprehensive agenda for the city's youth.

KID EVENTS

Gahanna Goblin Fest
Creekside Park, 123 Mill St., Gahanna
(614) 342-4250
www.gahanna.gov

All the little goblins come out one night around Halloween for a spooktacular family adventure. Gahanna Parks and Recreation puts on this free event for children of all ages, and while most kids come for the candy, some do come for the music and other activities.

Great Train Show
Ohio Expo Center
717 E. 17th Ave.
www.greattrainshow.com

Train enthusiasts can indulge their beloved hobby and escape the doldrums of winter during the Great Train Show, held in mid-Jan. The traveling two-day model train show draws exhibitors from around the country to show off operating model trains, provide workshops, and sell all the bells and whistles at hundreds of retail tables. Admission is $12 (cash only) at the door. Kids 11 and under are free.

Hayes Easter Egg Roll
Rutherford B. Hayes Presidential Center
Hayes and Buckland Avenues, Fremont
(419) 332-2081
www.rbhayes.org

Children between the ages of 3 and 10 are invited to participate in an old White House tradition started by President Hayes in 1878. There is no entry fee, but reserved ticketed entry is required. Each kid should bring three hard-boiled colored eggs for various races across the lawn. Prizes are awarded in different age groups, and an ℹ️ Easter egg hunts are held in various communities, like Grandview and Upper Arlington, as well as the Columbus Zoo (614-645-3550). Contact the Department of Recreation and Parks (614-645-3300) for dates and times for city egg hunts.

egg-decorating contest is also held. Children can visit with the Easter Bunny and receive passes to tour the Hayes Home and Museum.

Sun Watch Indian Village and Archaeological Park
2301 W. River Rd., Dayton
(937) 268-8199
www.boonshoft.org/sunwatch
This reconstructed 800-year-old village is a National Historic Landmark and gives visitors a one-of-a-kind glimpse into Ohio's ancient past. It hosts summer and winter solstice festivals and the Kids Dig Archaeological Festival. On Sat and Sun (Mar through Dec), families with children can explore Native American culture through themed demonstrations, activities, reconstructed buildings, and gardens.

Utica Ice Cream Festival
11324 Hwy. 13, Utica
(740) 892-4339, (800) 589-5000
www.velveticecream.com
Central Ohio has been celebrating America's favorite dessert for 30 years at the home of the Velvet Ice Cream Company, just east of Columbus. Operated on the site of an 1817 mill, this fourth-generation, family-run business has been cranking out the creamy confection since 1914. Ye Old Mill Ice Cream Festival, held in late May, kicks off with a parade and includes children's activities like balloon tosses, wheelbarrow races, sack races, a magic tent, and entertainment. Ice-cream-eating contests are sure to ruin appetites, as will the Root Beer Float Tent, but with such temptations like Olde Tyme vanilla, raspberry fudge cordial, and mint chocolate chip, how could you not let them indulge in dessert all day?

FREE FUN STUFF

Audubon Center, Downtown
Blendon Woods Metro Park Zip Line
Columbus Museum of Art Free Sundays
Glacier Ridge Metro Park Ninja Course and Zipline
Graeter's Lil' Pints Indoor Playground
Hayden Falls Park, Dublin
Homestead Park Train Station and Pond, Hilliard
Northam Park Playground Nature Hunt and Reading Garden
PBJ & Jazz for Kids, Topiary Garden/Lincoln Theatre
Planet Westerville Climbing Castle, Westerville
Scioto Grove Metro Park Playground
Scioto Mile Splashpad, Downtown
Summer Outdoor Movie Series, Columbus Commons, Bexley, Upper Arlington, Metro Parks
Village Green Park and Splashpad, Powell

KID PLAY

Amusement

Game Arena
1556 N. High St.
(614) 364-4747
www.game-arena.co
This high-tech gaming lounge offers dozens of PC setups and console stations, as well as the ultimate Red Bull Racing Experience. The individual and multiplayer game list is extensive, and retro games are also on the menu. The menu is better than average and has a cocktail list. Day passes and memberships are available.

Skate Zone 71
4900 Evanswood Dr.
I-71 and Morse Road
(614) 846-5626
www.unitedskates.com/skate-zone-71
Skate Zone features an old-school wooden rink for roller and in-line skating, as well as a designated skate area for beginners and toddlers. Note that you purchase tickets for blocks of time and must arrive for that specific session. Skates are available

to rent, while the Roller Cafe serves up typical rink snacks and drinks. The primary customers are kids ages 5 to 15, and though skating is the main attraction, toddlers will be able to participate with a skate mate to help balance. Older kids (and adults) can compete at laser tag in a black light arena or play popular video games at the arcade.

SportsOhio
6314 Cosgray Rd., Dublin
(614) 792-1630
www.sports-ohio.com
SportsOhio has several different facilities in one complex, including an award-winning miniature golf course, batting cages, and Can-AM Track Racers. Children under 58 inches tall can ride with Mom and Dad or go it alone in the Rookie Track Racers. The Midwest Gymnastics and Cheerleading facility, the Chiller Ice-Skating Rink, and Soccer First are also located within this sports campus. Each has its own schedule of summer camps, weekend clinics, and youth leagues.

ZipZone Outdoor Adventures
7925 N. High St., Worthington
(614) 847-9477
www.zipzonetours.com
Read about the zipline tours and kid's climbing course in the "Group Entertainment" section of the Nightlife chapter.

Zoombezi Bay Water Park
10101 Riverside Dr. (US 33), Powell
(614) 724-3489
www.zoombezibay.com
This combination amusement and water park once owned by Six Flags was purchased by the Columbus Zoo, and after extensive renovations opened in May 2008 with a fresh new jungle look and 15 new waterslides, a wave pool, fun rapids, and a lazy river. The park also features non-water entertainment, a kiddie pool, and other rides that appeal to the younger set. There is no shortage of dining options, and private cabanas are available for daily rental. Visit the website for information on entrance fees and annual passes. The Zoombezi season pass gains members entry into the zoo during the water park season.

Trampoline Parks and Ninja Courses

Columbus has a number of indoor trampoline parks, as well as different levels of obstacle and Ninja courses. Most of these facilities have a combination of activities like dodgeball, foam pits, race courses, and kids' areas. All are available to rent for parties. Pro tip: Fill out the liability waivers online before going to save time.

Big Air Trampoline Park
1400 Polaris Pkwy.
(614) 943-8703
www.bigairusa.com/columbus

Get Air Columbus
3708 Fishinger Blvd., Hilliard
(614) 355-9864
www.getairsports.com/columbus

Ninja Citi Adventure Park
2620 Sawmill Place
(614) 649-7700
www.ninjaciti.com

Urban Air
7679 Dublin Plain City Rd., Dublin
(380) 204-6390
www.urbanair.com/ohio-dublin

Summer Camps

If your children love the great outdoors, they may be interested in the programs offered at most of the Metro Parks. The budding naturalist (ages 3 to 5) and junior naturalist (ages 6 to 10) series allows children to explore fields, streams, forests, and ponds with Metro Park professionals. Blossoming green thumbs ages 11 to 17 can learn a thing or two about horticulture through the Junior Gardeners program at Inniswood Metro Gardens. The two-hour sessions highlight plant and animal life, their habitats, and, of course, gardening.

Metro Parks also offer year-round interactive classes that introduce preschoolers to nature through storytime and hands-on activities. Week-long summer camps at different parks are another option for children in preschool through ninth grade. Campers participate in age-appropriate activities, games, and crafts while learning about nature. Prices for the weekly camps range from $175 to $220, and children must bring a packed lunch. Find out more about the programs, campfires, and Friday night movies by calling (614) 891-0700 or looking online at www.metroparks.net.

The Columbus Department of Recreation and Parks offers a selection of summer camps for kids of all ages. Camp Buckeye is held at Tuttle Recreation Center just north of the OSU campus, where campers ages 6 to 12 join in a variety of sporting activities, such as tennis, softball, basketball, and hiking. The kids create works of art and finish each day off with a swim at the Tuttle pool.

Children ages 6 to 12 learn about Native American folklore and culture, study nature, do arts and crafts, and explore caves during 10 weekly summer camps held at Indian Village. Just look for the tepees on the west side of the Scioto River off Fishinger Road, and you've found the village. Parents will appreciate the high-energy recreation offered here. After a day full of fishing, canoeing, swimming, and boating, the kids will certainly come home tuckered out!

Indian Village also has a state-of-the-art multipurpose Indoor Recreation Center (614-645-5972), with a high ropes course, portable climbing wall, traverse wall, and fidget ladder. The facility, including tepees, is available for group outings, campouts, workshops, parties, and other educational programs.

Teens too old to attend Indian Village but not ready to give up their camping days can volunteer to be a counselor in training and share their knowledge with the younger kids. Application can be made through the Department of Recreation and Parks. Another option is the Teen Outdoor Adventure Camp. Each day begins in Franklin Park at the Indoor Adventure Center at 1747 E. Broad St., Bexley. Campers between the ages of 12 and 21 will be transported to various locations, such as Hocking Hills and Indian Village, for canoeing, orienteering, hiking, and rock climbing.

Youth of all ages will enjoy the Great Art Getaway. Children and teens can explore their creative side in a beautiful natural setting at Turnberry, near Pickerington. These weeklong sessions tap into the children's creativity and observation of nature through a series of art projects. Younger kids (ages 6 to 12) will learn how to make silkscreens, design T-shirts, fire ceramics, create sculpture, and put on theatrical productions. Teens will participate in additional activities, like macramé, mural painting, and beadwork. Also on the agenda are tours of the farm, a waterslide, and camping out. Parents have the option of transporting their children directly to the farm or dropping them off at several points around the city.

Each of the aforementioned camps costs around $230 to $275 per child per week, but there are many others to choose from. You can view the camp schedule and register online at www.columbusrecparks.com or by calling (614) 645-7000. Summer activities are also provided at many of the city's 55 neighborhood playgrounds, which are staffed with professional summer program leaders.

U-Pick Farms

As the seasons change, harvest activities start cropping up around Ohio—literally. Farms and orchards throw open their gates to visitors wanting to pick their own fresh fruits, vegetables, apples, and pumpkins. There is no shortage of traditional fall events like hayrides, bonfires, corn mazes, tractor rides, and apple cider donuts.

The Blueberry Patch, Mansfield (419-884-1797; www.theblueberrypatch.org)
Branstool Orchards, Utica (740-892-3989; www.branstoolorchards.com)
Cherryhawk Farm and Orchard (937-642-6442; www.cherryhawkfarm.com)
Circle "S" Farms, Grove City (614-878-7980; www.circlesfarm.com)
Doran's Farm Market, New Albany (614-855-3885; www.doransfarmmarket.com)
Hoffman's Farm Market, Galloway (614-867-7012, www.hoffmansfarmmarket.com)
Lynd Fruit Farm, Pataskala (740-927-1333; www.lyndfruitfarm.com)
Yutzy's Farm Market, Plain City, Ohio (614-873-3815)

Kid Science

Center of Science and Industry (COSI)
Columbus
333 W. Broad St., Franklinton
(614) 228-COSI (2674)
www.cosi.org

COSI offers a range of programming for children and their favorite adults. See the COSI entry in the Attractions chapter for more details.

4-H Club
2120 Fyffe Rd., OSU Campus
(614) 292-4444
www.ohio4h.org

This nonformal educational youth development program was started in 1902 in nearby Clark County as a way to teach school-age kids about agriculture and science through hands-on learning. 4-H now offers classes in more than 200 subjects that encourage youth to learn leadership, citizenship, and life skills.

Children ages 5 to 19 have the opportunity to experience organized activities, such as camping, workshops, and field trips, or get involved in specialized programs about flight, animal science, photography, and much more. Teens can develop their leadership and communication skills, travel abroad, or enter competitions at the Ohio State Fair. Project books have been developed for families so that parents can engage in activities with their kids.

The new Nationwide and Ohio Farm Bureau 4-H Center is located on the west campus of The Ohio State University, but there are branches in all 88 of Ohio's counties, as well as regional and OSU extension offices. 4-H membership is free, but you should check with each individual county about fees for certain classes or workbooks.

Franklin Park Conservatory
1777 E. Broad St.
(614) 645-3000, (800) 214-PARK (7275)
www.fpconservatory.org

Summer youth programs combine fun and education into half-day workshops. Children ages 4 to 14 will learn how to garden, investigate bugs, and try their hand at a variety of garden-inspired art forms, while Teen Corps gives high school–aged kids hands-on horticultural skills. Community Days, held the first Sunday of each month, are free to Franklin County residents. Read more about the Conservatory in the Attractions chapter.

The Ohio State University

The university's Department of Entomology offers tours of the conservatory and insectary. Budding entomologists can get a close look at over 130 species of insects, from tarantulas to hissing cockroaches to walking sticks. The conservatory features a tropical house, desert house, and over 1,200 other plant species. Tours must be scheduled a few weeks in advance, as this is an active research facility.

The Waterman Agricultural and Natural Resources Laboratory, on the corner of Lane Avenue and Kenny Road, offers guided tours of this working dairy farm. Kids can meet the 140-cow herd, tour the barns, and learn about various chores, such as milking cows and making cheese. Adults may be interested to learn about quality control, artificial insemination, and consumer issues. Your children just might leave knowing that chocolate milk does not come from brown cows! Call (614) 292-7234 to schedule a tour of the complex.

Orton Geological Museum
Orton Hall
125 South Oval Mall, OSU Campus
(614) 292-6896

Built in 1893, Orton Hall is one of the oldest buildings on Ohio State's campus and is home to the university's geology department. What many people don't know is that the first floor of this building also houses a small museum with one of the largest fossil collections in the Midwest. As you enter, the skeleton of a giant ice-age ground sloth greets you. This free museum displays prehistoric turtle shells, dinosaur eggs, and mastodon teeth. It also highlights Ohio's geologic history and exhibits one of 12 meteorites found in Ohio. OSU's first president, Edward Orton, donated the collection. Guided tours are available upon request.

KID SPORTS

If your children want to be involved in Little League baseball, softball, or football, you should check with city, school district, or community centers, as there are just too many to list here. The Columbus Department of Recreation and Parks offers a range of athletic summer camps at reasonable prices. For details about youth leagues and summer camps, call (614) 645-7000, or check out the activity guide at www.columbusrecparks.com. A wealth of organized summer camps and one-off clinics are offered in gymnastics, cheerleading, football, tennis, and track and field.

The co-ed Flag Football Camp held at Cleo Dumaree Athletic Complex on 276 S. Nelson Rd. in east Columbus gives boys and girls ages 7 to 14 the opportunity to learn the fundamentals of defensive and offensive football strategies while practicing all team positions.

Throughout the summer, kids can sign up for tennis instruction, drills, and games at Whetstone Tennis Courts in Clintonville. This tennis camp is appropriate for beginners and intermediate players. Novices are taught basic skills, while advanced players develop on-court strategies. Non-tennis activities, like wall climbing and picnic games, are offered during lunchtime.

The city has also developed therapeutic recreation camps that are modified to meet the needs of individuals with disabilities. Weekly sessions are held at Franklin Park Adventure Center at 1755 E. Broad St. in Bexley. The inclusive camps make every effort to accommodate a variety of special needs. Campers have the opportunity to take part in adaptive sports, fitness, arts and crafts, and photography and explore the great outdoors at various park systems. Some of the other fun events include picnics, parades, talent shows, and an overnight camp.

One of the advantages to having a champion major league soccer team in Columbus is access to great soccer camps and academies held throughout the summer and winter. National and international professionals teach the Crew Youth Soccer Camps during half-day to five-day clinics at historic Columbus Crew stadium. Campers of all skill sets are welcome to learn drills and develop ball skills. Check out www.thecrewyouth.com for information and pricing. Ohio Premier Youth Soccer Club (614-783-2237; opsoccer.com) offers kids 8 years old and above the opportunity to develop skills in a variety of age-appropriate academies.

Children ages 2 and up will receive top-notch soccer instruction at Soccer First, one of Ohio's finest indoor/outdoor soccer facilities, located at SportsOhio in Dublin. Ten outdoor fields, three professional-size indoor fields, training areas, and state-of-the-art equipment ensure a good starting point for new players and a premium environment for competitive players. Several group camps focus on the 2- to 10-year-old age group, while leagues and the academy cater to all age groups. Other leagues, instruction, and camps in lacrosse, flag football, and field hockey are offered at Soccer First. Get further information by calling (614) 793-0101 or going to the website: www.soccer-first.com.

Ice hockey has taken off in Columbus since the Blue Jackets came to town in 2000. The Youth Hockey Association is a great way for children and parents to learn the basics of skating, stick handling, and shooting. There are four Chiller Ice Rinks, where hockey leagues, camps, and clinics are offered throughout the year. One is located at the SportsOhio Complex in Dublin (614-764-1000), and the others are at Easton (614-475-7575), Lewis Center (740-549-0009), and the Ice Haus at Nationwide Arena (614-246-3380). You can view the website for youth programs in hockey and figure skating and the public ice-skating sessions at www.thechiller.com.

ANNUAL EVENTS AND FESTIVALS

Columbus loves festivals and celebrates everything from diversity to beer. According to a major National Endowment for the Arts survey, Ohio ranks second in the nation for attendance at festivals, and no doubt Columbus contributes a huge chunk to these numbers. Every weekend brings warm-weather celebrations or winter expos, for which venues, entry fees, and size vary dramatically. Certain events, such as the Pride Parade or the Asian Festival, draw a select crowd, while everyone in Columbus seems to turn up for Dublin's Irish Festival and Oktoberfest at the Ohio Fair Grounds. Thousands of people pass through the doors of the convention center and fairgrounds for huge annual events that have been going on, in some cases, for over a century.

Not every event is included in this chapter, but major marathons, ethnic festivals, and holiday celebrations are listed alphabetically in the calendar month they occur. Also included here are a few neighborhood arts festivals and street fairs that attract visitors from all over the state.

Smaller, more specialized events, such as music, home, and garden shows, can be tracked down at the convention center or expo websites. Various walks held by national charities are included on city calendars, as well as the specific charity website. One-time events and exhibitions are listed in *Columbus Underground* and *Downtown Columbus*, while seasonal series sponsored by Columbus's performing arts organizations are mentioned in the Cultural Columbus chapter.

Gallery Hop is a popular, ongoing monthly event held in the Short North the first Sat of each month. Art galleries stay open late and often feature new or special exhibitions. Restaurants and bars host live entertainment, and the area remains festive well into the night, particularly in the summer.

The city's website (www.columbus.gov) has a limited calendar of events, while Experience Columbus (www.experiencecolumbus.com) provides a comprehensive listing with short descriptions of upcoming events in and around the city. This chapter will point you in the right direction for planning your weekend or holiday itinerary in Columbus.

JANUARY

Columbus Golf and Travel Show
Ohio Expo Center
717 E. 17th Ave.
www.columbusgolfandtravelshow.com
Columbus is focused on its golf game, even in the dead of winter. Up to 50,000 people head to the convention center for one of the best golf expos in the Midwest. Check out hundreds of vendors, travel opportunities, PGA instruction, and golf-related exhibitions at this three-day exposition. Friendly competitions, putting greens, video games, and indoor driving ranges will get you itching for that next golf outing.

Great Train Show
Ohio Expo Center
717 E. 17th Ave.
(614) 644-3247
www.greattrainshow.com
America's largest national touring model train show rolls into Columbus for two days in mid-January. The show promotes the hobby of model railroading and features local and national sellers, hobby shops, train specialists, and

huge operating train displays. A highlight is the tiny "Magic Scale" trains that can fit in the palm of one's hand. Admission is $12 (cash only) at the door; children 11 and younger are free.

FEBRUARY

Arnold Sports Festival
Greater Columbus Convention Center
400 N. High St.
(614) 431-2600
www.arnoldsports.com
Columbus's Jim Lorimer and Arnold Schwarzenegger were the driving forces behind the world's largest fitness weekend formerly known as the Arnold Classic. What began as the Mr. World Contest in the 1970s has evolved into a world-class sporting event offering hundreds of thousands of dollars in prizes to competitive bodybuilders and martial artists.

Some 15,000 athletes and 150,000 spectators converge on Columbus in late February for 50 different sporting competitions, 14 of which are represented in the Olympics. Anchoring the weekend are the Arnold Classic and Ms. International bodybuilding competitions, but a short list of other events includes the Martial Arts Festival, the Cheerleading and Dance Team Championship, the Arnold Gymnastics Challenge, and the 5K Pump and Run. Boxing, archery, and fencing are also represented.

The Arnold Sports Festival is held at the Greater Columbus Convention Center, where the Arnold Fitness Expo features 650 booths of clothing, fitness equipment, nutritional information, and autographed merchandise. $35 gains you admission to anything in the hall, including certain preliminary rounds. Children under 14 are free. Tickets to the finals vary in price and can be purchased in advance through Ticketmaster or at the venue the day of the event.

MARCH

Columbus International Auto Show
Greater Columbus Convention Center
400 N. High St.
(614) 827-2500
www.columbusautoshow.com

Last year, nearly 500,000 visitors passed through the convention center's doors to see what's new in the automobile industry. Exhibitions include classic cars, luxury cars, and alternative-fuel vehicles. Major prizes are given away, and an activity center will keep the kids busy with a giant slide and moon bounce. The show lasts about 10 days, and the cost for admission ranges from $6 to $12.

Martin Luther King Jr. Day Events
King Arts Complex
867 Mount Vernon Ave.
(614) 645-5464
www.kingartscomplex.com
This annual birthday celebration is held at the King Arts Complex, Columbus's leading African American arts and cultural institution, located in the King-Lincoln neighborhood. The MLK Open House features a variety of performances, activities, speakers, and events commemorating the life of the late civil rights leader. A breakfast and a community march are held in his honor. Admission is free.

St. Patrick's Day Festivities
Downtown Columbus and Dublin
The Shamrock Club of Columbus (614-491-4449; www.theshamrockclubofcolumbus.com), a private social club founded in 1936, sponsors the city's annual St. Patrick's Day parade, beginning downtown on Broad Street and ending at the convention center. The suburb of Dublin fittingly goes all out for its patron saint. The Grand Leprechaun leads the parade from Metro Place to High Street in historic Dublin. Show up early for a St. Patty's Day breakfast and other pre-parade entertainment. Stick around afterward to hit Dublin's DORA (designated outdoor refreshment area) for a pub crawl along the Celtic Cocktail Trail, including Dublin Village Tavern with more than 40 types of Irish whiskey.

Other local bars that throw a good Irish bash are Byrne's Pub in Grandview, O'Reilly's Pub in Clintonville, and Cavan Irish Pub in Merion Village—the city's only gay Irish bar.

Capital City Half Marathon
Shawnie Kelley

APRIL

African American Heritage Festival
Ohio State University campus
(614) 688-8449
www.heritagefestival.osu.edu
The weeklong events, beginning in late Apr, include cultural dancers, storytelling, and dinners. Student organizations, BET (Black Entertainment Television), and nationally acclaimed speakers help celebrate African American history and culture with free events held across campus. A few of the formal dinners and parties charge for admission tickets.

Capital City Half Marathon
Downtown Columbus
www.capitalcityhalfmarathon.com
The Capital City Half Marathon is held in early Apr. The 13.1-mile run begins and ends at Lifestyle Communities Pavilion in the Arena District. Runners wind through scenic and historic areas of downtown Columbus, German Village, the Short North, and Victorian Village. A 2-mile lap through the OSU campus and around Ohio Stadium has been a welcome addition to the route.

MAY

Apron Gala at North Market
59 Spruce St., downtown
(614) 463-9664
www.northmarket.org
Each May, the North Market hosts a local food party that involves a multi-course meal, drinks, and entertainment. It's a ticketed event, so check online for various levels of admission. Dress is casual, but wear comfy dancing shoes and your most creative apron to possibly win a prize.

Asian Festival
Franklin Park
1777 E. Broad St.
www.asian-festival.org
About a dozen Asian American groups are represented at this two-day festival celebrating the rich heritage of various Asian and Southeast Asian cultures. More than 50,000 people attend this free festival that's been held around Memorial Day weekend for nearly 30 years. Enjoy traditional stage performances, authentic cuisine, and shopping in the Asian Market. Learn more about diverse cultures through hands-on activities, martial arts demonstrations, and educational cultural booths. There are plenty of activities to keep the kids entertained. Parking is free, with a shuttle provided between the park and various nearby parking lots.

Central Ohio Folk Festival
Highbanks Metro Park
www.columbusfolkmusicsociety.org
The Columbus Folk Music Society has been sponsoring some incarnation of this hootenanny for more than 25 years. While the two-day weekend lineup may include spotlight concerts, many go for the jam sessions and dozens of workshops. The whole family can get their fill of square dancing, banjo pickin', and bonfire singing, and maybe even catch the World's Worst Song Contest. Admission is free, but workshops range from $10 to $30.

Dandelion Festival
Breitenbach Wine Cellars
Old Route 39, between Dover and Sugarcreek
(330) 343-3603, (800) THE-WINE (843-9463)
www.breitenbachwine.com
The first weekend in May is the annual Dandelion Festival at Breitenbach Wine Cellars. It's everything dandelion, from cookbooks to wine to sangria. Those of you with the gift of culinary genius should try out your skills in the Great Dandelion Cook-off.

Herb Day
Gahanna Historical Society
101 S. High St., Gahanna
(614) 475-2509
www.ohioherbcenter.org

Celebrate spring in early May with an herb and crafts festival featuring fresh herbs, plants, and various demonstrations and lectures on herbal topics. Learn medicinal and culinary uses and get answers to gardening questions. You'll leave knowing why Gahanna was named the "Herb Capital of Ohio" in 1972. No admission fee is charged.

JUNE

Columbus Arts Festival
Downtown Columbus Riverfront
(614) 224-2606
www.gcac.org
This huge arts fair, which has been going on for almost 50 years, is organized by the Greater Columbus Arts Council and ushers in the summer for four days in early June. More than 250 artisans, craftspeople, and local restaurateurs sell their wares from booths along the Scioto River. Continuous art activities keep the children (and adults) busy, while nonstop entertainment on two stages keeps your toes tappin'. Admission is free, but expect to pay event parking prices.

Creekside Blues and Jazz Festival
Creekside Park, Gahanna
(614) 418-9114
www.creeksidebluesandjazz.com
This free three-day festival showcasing blues and jazz music is Gahanna's premier summer event. Aside from the music, you'll find arts and crafts, classic cars, children's activities, and the usual festival fare. Its location in Creekside Park allows for some interesting contests, including frog jumping and fishing contests and canoe races. It is held the third Sat in June.

Festival Latino
Downtown Columbus Riverfront
(614) 645-7995, (614) 645-3800
www.festivallatino.net
Spice up your weekend at Ohio's largest Hispanic/Latino event. International and regional artists perform on three different stages. Authentic cuisine, arts, crafts, and educational activities celebrate the diversity of Latin American cultures. Shop at the marketplace, learn the meringue, and help your children make copper bracelets.

i Stonewall Columbus (614-299-7764; www.stonewallcolumbus.org) is located at 1160 N. High St. and serves as a social and activity center for Columbus's gay community. It organizes a number of events in June, including the annual Pride Parade and Festival, rallies, concerts, and films.

Admission is free, and the festival is held all day Fri and Sat until 10 p.m.

German Village Haus und Garten Tour
588 S. Third St.
(614) 221-8888
www.germanvillage.com

Residents of German Village open their doors and gates for visitors to appreciate the design and restoration of a dozen homes and gardens. Admission is $15 in advance and $20 the day of the tour. Tickets can be purchased through the German Village Society.

Hilltop Bean Dinner Festival
Westgate Park, West Side
www.hilltopbusinessassociation.org

Civil War veterans had a tradition of reuniting over a bean social. A modern interpretation of the Bean Dinner was established in 1981 by the Hilltop Business Association on the west side of Columbus as a way to bring the neighborhood together. This daylong community event is held on the fourth Sat of June and includes music and, of course, beans!

Ohio Scottish Games
Cuyahoga County Fairgrounds
19201 E. Gagley Rd., Berea
www.ohioscottishgames.com

Kilt up and head to this traditional Scottish festival to see hammer throwing and Highland dancing at its best. Aside from professional and amateur athletic competitions, awards are given in various dance, harp, and fiddle categories. Explore your heritage at the genealogy tent, or find your family plaid on Tartan Days. And what's more Scottish than bagpipes and golf? These hallmarks of Scottish culture are celebrated with a golf outing and a tattoo performance. The festival is sponsored by the Scottish-American Cultural Society of Ohio.

Pride Parade and Festival
Goodale and Bicentennial Parks
(614) 299-7764
www.columbuspride.org

More than 700,000 participants attended the Midwest's second-largest gay pride march and festival in 2023. Stonewall Columbus, an organization that serves the central Ohio LGBTQ+ community, hosts a weeklong series of events in June that help raise awareness and celebrate gay pride. The massive festival begins with a rally for gay rights and ends in a Mardi Gras–style parade with a rainbow of floats and even more colorful people marching and dancing in the streets.

Worthington Arts Festival
Village Green, Old Worthington
(614) 885-8237
www.worthingtonartsfestival.com

This two-day juried arts-and-crafts show draws artists from all over the country. Works in a variety of media, ranging from clay and paint to metal and wood, are featured, along with jewelry and photography. The show is held Sat and Sun on the Village Green, and admission is free. Check the website for remote parking and shuttle options.

JULY

Comfest
Goodale Park, Victorian Village
www.comfest.com

Peace, diversity, and music prevail at one of the city's most popular festivals, and possibly the nation's largest non-corporate volunteer-driven urban music festival. This Community Festival (hence, Comfest) has been around for 50-plus years and is growing exponentially—and it's free! Local and national bands play on a variety of stages located throughout the park, while vendors of all things earthy, edible, and eccentric peddle their wares. Expect to find this festival's roots in civil rights, anti-war, and general social justice shining through.

Worthington Arts Festival
Experience Worthington

Doo Dah Parade
Goodale Park, Victorian Village
www.doodahparade.com

This zany Fourth of July tradition is a celebration of free speech, political satire, inspired (and sometimes stupid) lunacy, and opinionated people wanting to be heard. The only Independence Day parade in the city of Columbus is kicked off by a "less-than-grand" marshal organized by the DisOrganizers. Anyone with a daring, silly, funny, and/or good idea is welcome to participate free of charge. Actually, a bad idea might be even better for this parade full of bad taste, weird bicycles, clever political and religious commentary, and a world of impersonators.

Jazz and Rib Fest
Downtown Columbus Riverfront
(614) 221-1321, (800) 950-1321
www.hotribscooljazz.org

A fantastic free rib festival straddles both sides of the Scioto River for three days in the summer.

Nearly two dozen ribbers from around the country serve tons of mouthwatering ribs to the smooth beats of top local, national, and world jazz artists on multiple stages. Kids are kept busy in a wonderland of inflatable slides and bouncing buildings.

Red, White, and Boom
Downtown Columbus Riverfront
www.redwhiteandboom.org

Independence Day begins with entertainment, food, and a parade. It ends with the largest (and many say the best) synchronized music and fireworks display in the Midwest. The heart of the event is on the west side of the Scioto River near COSI, but the fireworks can be seen as far away as Ohio State's campus. There is no rain date and no charge for this event, but be prepared to wrangle with a hundred thousand people for parking spaces.

AUGUST

Dublin Irish Festival
Coffman Park
5200 Emerald Pkwy., Dublin
(614) 410-4545
www.dublinirishfestival.org
Dublin's festival is hailed as one of the largest and most popular Irish festivals in the country. More than 100,000 people turn up over the three-day celebration. Seven stages feature national and international Celtic bands. Cultural experiences include genealogy booths, dance instruction, and music workshops. Visitors can enjoy the art of storytelling or learn the traditions of an Irish wake in the Spoken Word Tent. Families can pay a visit to Brian Boru's Ireland in a re-created 10th-century village or partake of traditional arts and crafts in the Wee Folks area.

With over 90 stalls of unique imported goods, the expansive Marketplace is like an Irish arts festival unto itself. Vendors serve Irish beer along with authentic food from the British Isles. Traditional and pop Irish musicians play until midnight Fri and Sat. Sun is kicked off with three different masses: an Irish mass in Gaelic, a traditional mass, and an interdenominational service.

One need not be Irish to compete in the contests for reddest hair, greenest eyes, and most freckles. All entertainment and most activities are covered under a general admission ticket, which costs between $20 and $30 for adults.

SEPTEMBER

Columbus Italian Festival
St. John the Baptist Church
720 Hamlet St.
(614) 294-8259
www.columbusitalianfestival.com
Italian or not, you'll feel like part of the family at this festival that has been giving Columbus an annual carb boost for more than 40 years. There's no shortage of pizzas, home-style pastas, and Italian cookies. The whole family will enjoy the live entertainment and open-air market. Admission

Dublin Irish Festival
Shawnie Kelley

is $10 per person online or at the gate; children under 12 are free. Weekend passes are available.

Columbus Oktoberfest
Ohio Expo Center
717 E. 17th Ave.
www.columbusoktoberfest.com
Locals have been donning their lederhosen for nearly 60 years as German heritage and culture is celebrated for three days at the Ohio State Fairgrounds. Plenty of beer, brats, and bands abound till around midnight. Festival favorites include the stone hurl and Keg Toss and Press competitions, Kinderplatz for children, and the Beer and Wine

Garten for everyone else. Admission is free, but plentiful parking comes at a per-car charge.

Greek Festival
Greek Orthodox Cathedral
555 N. High St., Short North
(614) 224-9020
www.columbusgreekfestival.com
Labor Day weekend brings about a celebration of Greek heritage and the Orthodox Christian faith. Greek Festival dancers in full traditional costumes entertain guests as they indulge in handmade Greek food, pastries, and drinks provided by the church community. Highlights include a replica of

 **Close-up**

The Ohio State Fair: Americana-on-a-Stick

Almost half the state of Ohio is considered prime farmland, and one in seven people are employed in some aspect of agriculture. It's no wonder the state fair, which attracts over a million visitors, is among the largest in the country. For two weeks in August, a mix of special competitions, exhibitions, entertainment, rides, and thousands of animals showcase Ohio's agriculture and farming industry in an educational and fun way.

The fair began in 1850 and, despite its century of evolution, many of its early traditions have been preserved. The earliest fairs focused entirely on agriculture, but they quickly came to include food and entertainment. In 1896, Ohio's was the first fair in the country to be lit by electricity. The annual butter sculptures were first exhibited in 1903 and remain a popular attraction today. An All-Ohio Boys Band began performing in the 1920s, and its descendants, the All-Ohio Band and State Choir, are the fair's veteran performers as hundreds of high school instrumentalists and vocalists entertain fairgoers.

Not to miss is the time-honored "Butter Cow" sculpture, a tradition that began in 1903. Each year an artist creates a mystery butter sculpture that remains on display in a cooler exhibition case during the fair. More than 2,000 pounds of butter are sculpted into a variety of shapes that have included a giant Tonka truck, a bald eagle, an enormous ice-cream cone, and the Liberty Bell. You never know what the butter sculpture will be.

The schedule is packed with horse, dog, and livestock shows and cattle, pig, and poultry competitions. Big-name musicians take to the stages, kids take to the amusement rides, and local grillmasters take to the barbecue pits for a competition. Almost 200 vendors sell every type of fair fare imaginable, while three air-conditioned restaurants provide options other than deep-fried everything-on-a-stick. Hop on the Midway air gondola to sail above the fair from one end to the other and get a bird's-eye view of the action.

The Ohio State Fair is home to the largest Junior Fair in the nation, where thousands of youngsters exhibit everything from livestock to ponies. When the kids aren't competing and showing, there are magicians, a petting zoo, pig races, a farm animal delivery room, and a giant by-the-pound candy shop.

The fair is held for 15 days at the Ohio Expo Center, located at 717 E. 17th Ave. Check out the website at www.ohiostatefair.com for a full schedule of events. Adult admission is around $12, and seniors and children (ages 6 to 12) cost $10. Children under 6 are free; bigger families can save some money during Family Value Days. General parking is free.

Greek Festival
Chris Kanellopoulos

a traditional Greek village home, cooking demos, tours of the cathedral, and exhibitions of iconography and calligraphy. Admission is $5 for adults, $4 for seniors; children 12 and under are free.

The Little Brown Jug
Delaware County Fairgrounds
(740) 363-6262
www.littlebrownjug.com

The Little Brown Jug, held the third Thurs after Labor Day, is the Kentucky Derby of harness racing. The race, held during the Delaware County Fair, is part of the Triple Crown of the famed Grand Circuit. This pacing classic for three-year-olds is the most attended harness race in the country. The tailgating events have been called

i The state of Ohio is the country's leading producer of Swiss cheese, making about 138 million pounds annually. Sugarcreek is the center of Ohio's Swiss cheese industry, and Guggisberg is the home of the original Baby Swiss, earning the region the nickname "Little Switzerland."

"the biggest cocktail party in the state of Ohio," but you might want to save your sunhats and seersucker suits for the Kentucky Derby; people dress casually for this event. Jug tickets range from $60 to $375.

Ohio Renaissance Festival
2 miles off I-71 on OH 73
Waynesville
(513) 897-7000
www.renfestival.com

If you were born 500 years too late, fear not! For two months every autumn, you can be transported to 16th-century England, where you will rub elbows with royalty, banter with fools, and feast like nobility on turkey legs. This authentically re-created medieval village is a sprawling 30 acres of Renaissance cottages, craft shops, vendors, and stages.

Hundreds of costumed performers, storytellers, and musicians mill about the bustling lanes of the open-air marketplace and perform on 12 stages. Full-armored jousts, swordsmen, and an action-packed pirate show set the crowds cheering. People of all ages are entertained by games

The Ohio Renaissance Festival
Ohio Renaissance Festival, Inc.

of skill and human-powered rides. Try your hand at archery, or rescue the damsel in distress from the castle tower.

Every weekend has a different theme, such as the Highland Fling or Feast of Fools, so no matter how often you go, it's never the same. Tickets are $30, and children ages 5 to 12 cost $10. The festival runs from mid-Aug through the end of Oct.

Ohio Swiss Festival
Downtown Sugarcreek
(330) 852-4113
www.ohioswissfestival.com

More than 20,000 people attend this four-day festival at the end of Sept in Sugarcreek, Ohio's "Little Switzerland." There's plenty of cheese to go around, as well as polka bands, alpine horn players, and a yodeling contest. Other highlights include parades with cheese floats, a quilt auction, amusement rides, craft beer tents, and the crowning of Little Swiss Miss. The festival features two athletic events: the traditional Steinstossen, where men and women heave a heavy boulder as far as they can, and the Cheese Chase 5K. Admission is free.

Reynoldsburg Tomato Festival
Huber Park
1640 Davidson Dr., Reynoldsburg
(614) 322-6839
www.reytomatofest.com

Interested in tasting tomato fudge? Well, you can at this three-day festival celebrating the juicy fruit. Tomato exhibits, contests for the biggest tomato, a car show, a pickleball tournament, and the crowning of the Tomato Queen in the festival pageant are just a few of the highlights. Alcohol is sold in the Beer Garden, and nightly entertainment includes both local and national acts. Admission is free, and parking is free in nearby remote lots with shuttles running for those farther out.

Short North Tour of Homes
Short North and Victorian Village
(614) 228-2912
www.shortnorthcivic.org/home-tour

For 50 years, the tour has offered house gawkers an inside look at a dozen or so beautiful Victorian Village and Short North homes and gardens in various states of renovation. The event benefits the Short North Civic Association. Tickets cost $20.

Upper Arlington Labor Day Arts Festival
Northam Park
(614) 583-5310
www.upperarlingtonoh.gov

The Upper Arlington Labor Day Arts Festival features around 120 juried local, regional, and national artists in a variety of media. With activities and entertainment for the whole family, it is considered one of the best one-day arts festivals in the state. Admission is free.

West Jefferson Ox Roast
221 S. Center St., West Jefferson
(614) 879-8818
www.westjeffoxroast.org

Columbus's community of West Jefferson has been celebrating Labor Day since 1951 with a weekend full of fair games, rides, live entertainment—and 6,000 pounds of round roast! Sat and Sun are packed with parades, contests, dances, and concessions, but the real party begins Sun with the lighting of the Pit—a wood and charcoal fire is lit in a 140-foot-long, 4-foot-deep pit in the late afternoon. At 4 a.m. on Mon, the horn blows and the meat's on! The highly anticipated serving of the sandwiches begins late Mon morning as the festivities continue.

OCTOBER

All-American Quarter Horse Congress
Ohio Expo Center
717 E. 17th Ave.
www.oqha.com

With more than 26,000 horse show entries, the All-American Quarter Horse Congress is the world's largest single-breed horse show and the second-largest event held at the Ohio Expo. Over the course of three weeks, the congress attracts 650,000 people to the Columbus area, bringing more than $400 million to the local economy.

The daily schedule features horsemanship, roping, and racing events, as well as collegiate and 4-H/FFA horse judging contests. Other highlights include a Congress Queen contest, a youth tournament, and a horse bowl. Lectures and demonstrations provide educational information about the care and management of the American quarter horse. Commercial vendors sell western and English wear, towing vehicles and trailers, equine-related art, and jewelry.

The cost is $25 per vehicle for one-time admission and $75 for the entire show. No additional admission is charged on top of this fee. Additional charges apply for the Professional Bull Rider tour and the Freestyle Reining Performance.

Circleville Pumpkin Show
Downtown Circleville
(740) 474-7000
www.pumpkinshow.com

Ever seen a 2,300-pound pumpkin? If so, chances are you have attended "The Greatest Free Show on Earth," the Circleville Pumpkin Show. Every fall, over 400,000 people travel 45 minutes south of Columbus to the largest pumpkin festival in the country.

The show had humble beginnings in 1903, when the mayor of Circleville invited local farmers to exhibit their corn fodder and pumpkins in front of his office. A century later, the promotion of premium agricultural pursuits has been maintained. You'll see some of the biggest pumpkins on earth, not to mention indulge in edibles, such as (in the voice of Bubba Gump) pumpkin pie, pumpkin burgers, pumpkin bread, pumpkin ice cream, pumpkin waffles, pumpkin fudge, pumpkin pizza . . .

Pumpkin delicacies aside, the entire city center is blocked and converted into a mecca of arts, crafts, specialty stalls, and vendors selling the usual fair fare (corn dogs, fries, and funnel cakes). No alcoholic beverages are served on the streets.

Plenty of rides and games, parades, pie-eating contests, and musical concerts keep non-pumpkin connoisseurs occupied. You can even witness the crowning of Miss Pumpkin. Whatever level of pumpkin passion you may exude (or not), it is certainly worth a look at Ohio's oldest festival, which takes place the third Wed through Sat in Oct. Admission is free, but parking rates vary depending on proximity to the fair.

Columbus Marathon
Downtown Columbus and surrounding
 suburbs
www.columbusmarathon.com
More than 15,000 runners turn up for the flat, fast, and fun Columbus Marathon, which is consistently ranked as one of America's top 20 marathons by *Runner's World*. The Highlights' Kids Run, a half marathon, and the Jesse Owens 5K are also part of this nationally renowned event.

NOVEMBER

Scott Antique Markets
Ohio Expo Center
717 E. 17th Ave.
(740) 569-2800
www.scottantiquemarket.com
The Scott Antique Markets are the largest of their kind in the country and have become one of the Midwest's "favorite treasure hunts." The weekend show features 800 booths in two huge buildings. Admission is free, but parking at the Expo Center cost $5.

Wildlights at the Zoo
Columbus Zoo
4850 W. Powell Rd., Powell
(614) 645-3400
www.columbuszoo.com
Each November, the Columbus Zoo transforms itself into an illuminated wonderland and has been dubbed one of the top 10 holiday light shows in the country. A winter stroll through the zoo is enhanced with millions of sparkling lights, musical light shows, and live reindeer. Other

i One of America's largest outdoor holiday light shows is just under a 2-hour drive east of Columbus on WV 88 in Wheeling, West Virginia. Ogelbay Resort has been hosting this 6-mile drive through its spectacular "Festival of Lights" since 1985. The show remains fresh by adding a few new designs each year and special exhibits. Visit www.oglebay.com for details.

activities include ice skating on the frozen lake, magical train rides, and an appearance by Santa Claus.

Don't worry, the animals are not forgotten. Watch Santa Paws pay the animals a visit with specially wrapped treats in early December. Admission is regular zoo rates but free for zoo members. Wildlights is closed the evenings of Thanksgiving, Christmas Eve, and Christmas Day.

DECEMBER

Butch Bando's Fantasy of Lights
Alum Creek State Park
3311 S. Old State Rd., Delaware
www.butchbandosfantasyoflights.com
This drive-through light show runs seven days a week from mid-Nov until Jan 1. Depending on traffic, plan to spend 30 to 45 minutes enjoying the light show while tuned in to 88.3 FM to listen to the Fantasy of Lights radio station. Entry costs $20 per vehicle on weekdays and $30 on weekends. Tickets can be purchased online or at ticket booths near the entrance. Bathrooms are located at the end of the parking lot.

WORTH THE TRIP

If it's a change of scenery you're looking for, you'll be amazed at what you can experience within a few hours' drive of Columbus. Walk in the footsteps of an escaped slave along Ohio's Underground Railroad, or discover how the Amish maintain their simple way of life in this rapidly changing world. Ride the world's tallest roller coaster, or indulge in a five-star spa. No matter which direction you head, you are assured to find a good time outside Columbus that is worth the trip.

This chapter is focused on one-tank trips all within a few hours of Columbus. If you're not familiar with Ohio, you might be surprised at how varied the terrain and towns are, and how centralized the location is to other cities. You don't have to leave the state to find hills or valleys, lakes or beachfront, big cities or small villages. This chapter includes favorite perennial getaways, ranging from amusement and cultural attractions in nearby cities to a weekend on the Lake Erie Islands.

In 2 hours you can be at the Rock and Roll Hall of Fame or lying beachfront by Lake Erie. North on I-71 is the most direct route to Cleveland, but it isn't the most inspired landscape. You'll undoubtedly have a more scenic journey if you take the back roads through Ohio's heartland. Spend a day (or a weekend) in Holmes County, home to the world's largest Amish population; a visit here is like stepping back in time.

The drive south on I-71 is equally uninspiring, but once you hit south-central Ohio, everything changes. Lovely hills roll through state parks and continue to embrace Cincinnati, which is situated along the Ohio River. Here, you can take in one of the country's oldest zoos or catch a game at the Great American Ball Park.

If you fancy the great outdoors, check out the Parks and Recreation chapter for details about state parks and camping information. Historic towns such as Roscoe Village and Zoar are listed in the Attractions chapter, but this is not to say you shouldn't make a night of it. The same goes for Cleveland and Cincinnati. Both are only a short drive from Columbus and are equally good day trips or weekend getaways. Some of the cities included here have their own *Insiders' Guide*. So, if you are itching to explore beyond the surface, grab a guide, gas up, and get going!

DAY TRIPS

Ohio's Heartland: Amish Country

Amish County Tourism Bureau
6 W. Jackson St., Millersburg
www.visitamishcountry.com

One of the easiest and more unique day trips from Columbus is a visit to Ohio's heartland, also known as Amish Country. A leisurely drive through Holmes, Wayne, or Tuscarawas Counties will take you through numerous towns established in the 19th century by German and Swiss religious separatists such as the Amish and Mennonites. Known for their work ethic and peaceful existence, they shun most of the conveniences of the modern world. Horses and buggies carry them to church. Windmills power their homes. Crops are harvested the old-fashioned way—by hand. It doesn't take long to see how the world's largest Amish population (which equates to about 85,000) maintains their religious beliefs into the 21st century through their simple ways of life. Whether for a day or a weekend, it is worth the 80-mile journey back in time for a piece of cheese or a piece of tranquility. With names like Charm, ℹ️ Some fundamental observances when visiting Amish communities are to drive slowly and be cautious of the horses and buggies sharing the narrow roads. Respect the Amish religious beliefs when taking pictures, as for most of them it's against their faith to be photographed, and ask permission if you think they might be in your photo. Finally, some businesses are open on Sunday but may have limited hours. Be sure to check beforehand.

Berlin, Walnut Creek, and Sugarcreek, you'll not want to miss any of these delightful villages!

Attractions

Alpine Hills Museum and Information Center
16 W. Main St., Sugarcreek
(330) 852-4113
www.alpinehillssugarcreek.com
There is no missing this colorful museum in downtown Sugarcreek. Three floors of exhibits and audiovisual displays explain the Swiss and Amish heritage, cheese making, and farms of the area. A fun time to visit is during the Ohio Swiss Festival on the last weekend of Sept. The corner of Main and Broadway is home to the *Guinness Book of World Record's* world's largest cuckoo clock, which is more than 23 feet tall and 24 feet wide. The bird pops out and a couple polkas around the clock every half hour.

Behalt Amish and Mennonite Heritage Center
5798 County Rd. 77, Berlin
(330) 893-3192
www.behalt.com
Make this your first stop in Amish Country. The 265-foot cyclorama, one of only three in America, interprets the Amish-Mennonite history through a series of pictures. There is also a video presentation, pioneer barn, Conestoga wagon, and information center on-site.

Breitenbach Wine Cellars
5934 Old Rte. 39, between Dover
(330) 343-3603
www.breitenbachwine.com

As you enter the property to this award-winning winery, it seems you've turned the corner into a little Swiss village. The rolling hills of Breitenbach Valley provide lovely views if you choose to sip your wine on the patio, while an indoor tasting station allows you to sample before buying. Take in the beautiful views from the outdoor wine bar from May through Oct. Peruse the gift and cheese shop, grab a bottle of wine, and enjoy some grilled food in a tranquil setting.

Guggisberg Cheese Factory
5060 Hwy. 557, Millersburg
(330) 893-2500
www.babyswiss.com
If you thought Baby Swiss cheese came from Switzerland, think again. After years of experimentation, the original Baby Swiss was born here in Millersburg. Guggisberg is now one of the largest manufacturers of Swiss cheese in the country. The factory has over 40 varieties of cheese, as well as Swiss chocolates, beer steins, and cuckoo clocks. You can even watch the cheese being made during weekday business hours. It's closed Sun.

Schrock's Heritage Village
4363 SR 39, Berlin
(330) 893-3051
www.schrocksvillage.com
As one of Holmes County's top five attractions, there is something for everyone on this Amish homestead. You can take the kids on buggy rides, tour an Amish home, or pet the animals. The village has a variety of shopping including a craft mall, antiques center, leather shop, pet supplies, and a Christmas shoppe. Spend the night at the Schrock's Guest House and check out the Amish Country Theatre (www.amishcountrytheatre.com) after a meal at the Olde World Bistro.

Shopping

Shopping in Amish country is an attraction in its own right. If you are looking for one-of-a-kind gifts or handmade furniture to serve as family heirlooms, you will find an enormous variety of Amish (and "English") goods, as well as a large number of gift barns, craft malls, and furniture outlets that have several rooms and floors full of shopping. Apple Creek has Coblentz Furniture, Loudonville has Miller's Furniture, and Berlin has Sol's Palace, which carries a variety of handmade furniture and goods.

Bunker Hill Cheese
6005 County Rd. 77, Millersburg
(330) 893-2131
www.bunkerhillcheese.com
Eight decades later and still having local products delivered by horse and buggy, Bunker Hill and Heini's Cheese isn't just a cheese shop; it's a cheese chalet. You can sample 50 different types of cheese, test out Heini's famous yogurt cheese, or indulge in some hand-dipped ice cream. The shop sells lactose-free, specialty, and snack cheeses as well as meats and locally made pantry items. It's closed on Sun.

Carlisle Gifts
4962 Walnut St., Walnut Creek
(330) 893-2535
www.carlislegifts.com
Shoppers are greeted at the door of this Victorian home with fragrant aromas, while pleasant music entices them to explore the three floors of gifts, home furnishings, and the Thomas Kinkade showcase gallery.

Coblentz Chocolate Company
4917 Hwy. 515, Walnut Creek
(330) 338-9341
www.coblentzchocolates.com
Chocoholics, fudge fanatics, and caramel connoisseurs will be in heaven at this old-fashioned store that carries colorful candies, brittle, bark, and flavored popcorn. Wooden floors and candy jars invoke a nostalgic sensation, while the cases full of chocolate cause a mouthwatering response. Even those with sugar-restricted diets will find a variety of sugar-free candies at Coblentz.

Kauffman's Country Bakery
4357 Hwy. 62, Millersburg
(330) 893-2129
www.kauffmanscountrybakery.com
This is the place to come for your holiday stollen bread. As one of the largest bakeries in Amish

Country, the Kauffman brothers have been turning out over 20 varieties of breads, bagels, rolls, strudel, cookies, pastries, and pies daily from old-fashioned stone hearth ovens for two decades. They also carry a large selection of jams, jellies, and apple butter. Kauffman's is closed on Sun.

Lehman's Hardware and Appliances
One Lehman Circle, Kidron
(330) 857-5757, (800) 438-5346
www.lehmans.com
Move over, Walmart! This Amish "superstore" carries the world's largest selection of authentic historical products for those seeking a simpler life. Since 1955, Lehman's has been preserving the past for the future. People like the Amish, environmentalists, homesteaders, and anyone who seeks items to lead a more self-sufficient lifestyle shop here.

Lehman's carries everything from buckets to board games. If you need a lantern, fireplace, or wood-burning stove, you'll find it here. You will also find all your cooking essentials, from the butter churn to the dinner bell. Lehman's products uphold the store's slogan: "More than a store, it's a way of life." Lehman's has a second store in Millersburg, and both are closed on Sun.

Miller's Drygoods
4500 Hwy. 557, Charm
(330) 893-9899
www.millersdrygoods.com
Holmes County's first quilt shop has a large selection of handmade Amish quilts, rugs, pillows, and wall hangings. It carries over 8,000 bolts of fabric and has an outlet in the basement. Anyone interested in quilting or sewing should definitely have a look here.

'Tis the Season
4363 Hwy. 39, Millersburg
(330) 893-3604
www.tistheseasonchristmas.com
You can have Christmas any time of the year at Ohio's largest year-round Christmas store, located on Schrock's Amish Farm. You will find three floors of holiday collectibles and over 200 decorated trees. Ornament collectors spend hours searching through thousands of ornaments for that special

i Ohio leads the country in Swiss cheese production and ranks in the top five for overall cheese-making. With 13 Swiss cheese factories, Ohio produces 138 million pounds each year, almost a third of the nation's total output. Ohio's Amish Country was the birthplace of baby Swiss, developed by Alfred Guggisberg in 1950.

one. 'Tis the Season carries Lenox, Old World Christmas, Loony Tunes, and a huge selection of Christopher Radko ornaments.

Walnut Creek Cheese
2641 SR 39, Walnut Creek
(330) 893-3273
www.walnutcreekcheese.com
Get a serious taste of Holmes County. Walnut Creek Cheese carries the Amish area's largest selection of cheese, meats, and bulk foods. You'll find cookbooks, canned vegetables, and the exclusive Uncle Mike's smoked meats here. One might think this a popular place because they fulfill any cooking need, but I suspect it's the cafe's towering ice-cream cones.

World Crafts
13110 Emerson Rd., Kidron
(330) 857-0590
www.worldcraftskidron.com
This interesting shop is a demonstration of Mennonites practicing what they preach. The store was conceived as a way to aid people in need, so it carries fair trade merchandise such as jewelry, fabric, baskets, ceramics, toys, and wooden items by artisans from 35 developing countries, including Bangladesh, the West Bank, Kenya, Peru, Vietnam, and Haiti. It is managed and staffed entirely by volunteers, and the net profits are put back into projects that directly or indirectly help others in need.

Dining
There's nothing like a home-cooked meal in these parts, and trust me when I say there is no shortage of buffets or spacious, family-style restaurants. Most of the restaurants listed here have what is called the "Amish family-style" or "sampler" options on

their menus, meaning you can select two or three meats to accompany vegetables, real mashed potatoes, and an all-you-can-eat salad bar. With words like *alpine* and *chalet* in many of the restaurant names, you'll probably succumb to the wiener schnitzel, but don't plan on washing it down with a German beer. Most family-style restaurants are dry.

Another unique aspect to the dining experience is that many restaurants are part of a larger complex with gift shops, an inn, or a general store, or at least within easy walking distance of such. Entries have been included for several places that will afford you this "one-stop shopping": food, stores, and lodging, all on the same premises. Many restaurants in Amish country are closed on Sunday, so it is important to call ahead if you are visiting during the weekend.

Amish Door Restaurant and Village
1210 Winesburg Rd., US 62, Wilmot
(330) 359-5464
www.amishdoor.com
The village complex includes the family-style Amish Door Restaurant serving lunch and dinner, the Amish Door Marketplace, a coffee shop, and the 52 room Inn at Amish Door. You will find everything from wooden toys to bulk fabric in the Amish Village. It is possible to spend hours (or days) here if you like to eat, shop, and relax.

Der Dutchman Restaurant
4967 Walnut St., Walnut Creek
(330) 893-2981
www.dhgroup.com
If you don't mind sharing the place with buses full of tourists, you will not be disappointed. Despite the throngs of people, you will find consistently good food and service here. The dining room has a beautiful view of Genza Bottom Valley, and the restaurant is situated amid the shops on the main drag in Walnut Creek.

Dutch Valley Carlisle Inn, Restaurant & Shops
1357 Old Rte. 39, Sugarcreek
(330) 852-2586
www.dhgroup.com
This huge complex houses not only a family-style restaurant and bakery but also Dutch Valley

Furniture, Dutch Valley Gift Market with its three floors of home and garden accessories, and Dutch Creek Foods (www.dutchcreekfoods.com), which carries fresh meats, cheese, jams, and candies. Everything is closed on Sun.

Lodging

The Close-up in the Accommodations chapter highlights the inns of Amish Country. Keep in mind there are dozens of guesthouses in the tri-county area, so check out individual city websites to learn of other options.

Canton: Football Hall of Fame

Canton/Stark County Convention and
   Visitors Bureau
222 Market Ave. N., Canton
(330) 454-1439
www.visitcanton.com

As the birthplace of the National Football League and home to the Professional Football Hall of Fame, Canton holds a special place in the hearts of sports fans, but be assured the city is more than just a shrine to America's favorite pastime. Canton is the birth and burial place of 25th president William McKinley, and an imposing hometown memorial serves as a tribute. Canton can boast five arts organizations and three times as many golf courses in the area. "Sweeping changes" began here with the advent of the Hoover (electric vacuum) Company. If you appreciate sports, fine performing arts, or unique historical sites and museums, a visit to Canton is worth the 90-minute drive.

Attractions

Canton Classic Car Museum
123 Sixth St.
(330) 455-3603
www.cantonclassiccar.org

Housed in the 1915 showroom of a Ford-Lincoln dealership, this little museum has a lot of nostalgia. Among the 50 antique and classic cars, you'll find a 1901 Olds Surrey, a bulletproof gangster car, and Johnny Carson's 1981 DeLorean.

Cultural Center for the Arts
1001 Market Ave. N.
(330) 452-4096
www.culturalcenterforthe arts.com

This is one of the few centers in the country that house all the city's major art disciplines under one roof. The Canton Museum of Art (www.cantonart. org) has seen its share of high-profile exhibitions in its 90 years. The permanent collections focus on American watercolors and contemporary ceramics. The Canton Ballet (www.cantonballet.com) offers public performances several times a year, while the Canton Symphony Orchestra (www.cantonsymphony.org) holds around 50 concerts annually. Finally, the Canton Players Guild Theatre (www.playersguildtheatre.com) is one of the nation's oldest and largest community theaters.

First Ladies' National Historic Site, Library and
   Museum
205 Market Ave. S.
(330) 452-0876
www.firstladies.org

The center is housed in two historic buildings and serves as a tribute to the achievements and contributions of each first lady and other important American women. The City Bank Building houses the National First Ladies' Library Education and Research Center, with a replica of the first White House library. The Saxton House is the physical home of the library and has been restored to its original Victorian splendor. It is worth a look for the authentic period furniture and re-creation of President McKinley's study.

Gervasi Vineyard Resort and Spa
1700 55th St. NE, Canton
(330) 497-1000
www.gervasivineyard.com

You will forget you are in Ohio at Gervasi's Vineyard Resort and Spa. Just a short drive northeast lands you at a beautiful estate set with a rolling 55-acre vineyard that channels the Tuscan countryside. Gervasi's four-diamond luxury lodging makes a perfect escape for a romantic weekend or girlfriend getaway. The Casa, with its white stucco Italian-style entry, is an upscale boutique hotel with only 24 rooms. Each room has a patio with a view over the lake, king-size beds, and fireplaces. The four freestanding villas each have four suites, also with cozy fireplaces, covered patios, private living and dining areas, and heated floors—ideal for that winter weekend retreat. Breakast for two is bundled into the price.

Larger groups up to eight can experience a piece of history by staying in the restored original 1830 farmhouse. Four bedrooms, two bathrooms, modern rustic living and dining room spaces, and a full kitchen allow your family and friends to exist in a closed universe together for a few nights. It too offers views of the beautiful spring-fed lake.

After settling in, surrender to relaxation and tranquility at the Spa at Gervasi. The full-service spa indulges guests with a welcome wine and warm neck wrap to loosen you up. Then on to massages, skin and body treatments, facials, glam packages, or body wraps. A private suite is also available for couple's massages. After your treatment, chill out in the warm and cozy co-ed lounge overlooking the property.

Whether you prefer a casual lunch, romantic dinner, or a meal alfresco, there are four dining options to choose from. The Bistro is a rustic upscale Italian restaurant that serves antipasti salads, brick-fired pizzas, and other full entrees. A family-style brunch is served on Sundays. The more casual Crush House is a wine bar and eatery featuring appetizers, soups, salads, sandwiches, and pastas. The Still House doubles as a coffee bar and a cocktail bar, offering an extensive menu of brunchy items earlier and upscale bar food later in the day. The Piazza is the seasonal outdoor patio where guests can dine alfresco.

Gervasi's award-winning wines range from bold, dry reds to crisp whites and sweet dessert wines. The 30-plus varietals are grown on the estate and are well suited to the Ohio terrain and climate. Choose from Estate, Select, and Classic wines made on-site or from one of the several imported Italian private label wines made especially for Gervasi to round out the Tuscan-inspired experience.

Harry London Candies
5353 Lauby Rd.
(330) 494-0833
www.visitcanton.com
Canton has yet another Hall of Fame dedicated to another of America's favorite pastimes—chocolate. The Chocolate Hall of Fame is located at one of Ohio's largest chocolate factories. Take a tour to learn how these gourmet chocolates are made, then shop for a mouthwatering souvenir from the Midwest's largest chocolate store.

MAPS Air Museum
2260 International Pkwy.
(330) 896-6332
www.mapsairmuseum.org
The Military Aviation Preservation Society (MAPS), located on the west side of the Akron–Canton Airport, is dedicated to preserving historic aircraft. This hangar-turned-museum houses permanent collections of vintage war birds and civilian aircraft. Learn the history of aviation and its impact on society through the displays of fighter, bomber, and transport aircraft, or observe restoration in progress. Watch the historic birds in flight at the Aero Expo, which is held each June.

Pro Football Hall of Fame
2121 George Halas Dr. NW
(330) 456-8207
www.profootballhof.com
Did you know football was born on November 12, 1892? You can see its "birth certificate" in the form of the payment voucher to William "Pudge" Heffelfinger for $500 to play in a single game. Since then, football has become the most popular sport in the US, and this 83,000-square-foot shrine is dedicated to the great game and its great players. You can learn general football and team-by-team history here or watch National Football League footage in Cinemascope at GameDay Stadium, the state-of-the-art turntable theater.

The Hall of Fame is a complete chronicle of football and is ever changing with new exhibits and mementos, and don't forget the annual induction ceremony held every Aug. A weekend full of events, culminating in the Hall of Fame football game, is a good time to rub elbows with the full spectrum of NFL alumni. This world-class museum is open every day of the year except Christmas, and the gift shop is the only one in the country that carries merchandise from all 32 NFL teams.

Cincinnati: Sports, Arts, and OTR

Visit Cincy
525 Vine St.
Fifth Third Center, Fountain Square
(513) 621-2142
www.visitcincy.com
Cincinnati is only an hour south of Columbus, but it couldn't be more different. Nestled in a scenic bend of the Ohio River, the city's riverfront location held a pivotal role throughout history. From the inception of the city through its steamboat, pork-packing, and industrial heydays, the river brought prosperity to its residents. It also brought freedom to thousands of slaves who crossed over into the free states of the North.

The river is the natural boundary between Ohio and Kentucky, but Greater Cincinnati straddles the two states. The airport is on the south side of the river, so don't panic when you fly into Cincinnati and see a Welcome to Kentucky sign. As you cross into Ohio, you're greeted by the city's beautiful skyline and the neighborhoods seeping into the surrounding hills.

The downtown area has been undergoing a renaissance for several years, which means entertainment districts have been developed, the arts are flourishing, and riverfront stadiums are a big draw. The city has plenty of riverboat cruises, cultural events, and attractions to keep you busy for a day or a week.

This section focuses only on the Ohio side of the city, including Over the Rhine (OTR) neighborhood, a lively hub of dining and nightlife.

Attractions

Cincinnati boasts groundbreaking attractions and offers plenty of year-round family fun and sporting events. The Delta Queen Steam Boat Co., America's oldest continuously operated cruise line (www.deltaqueen.com), is based in New Orleans but makes regular stops in Cincinnati. You can learn more about the overnight packages on these paddle wheelers by viewing the website.

Cincinnati Art Museum
953 Eden Park Dr.
(513) 721-2787
www.cincinnatiartmuseum.org
The Cincinnati Art Museum opened in 1886 and is one of the country's oldest visual arts institutions. Collections span the globe and represent 6,000 years of world civilization. The museum has a display of Cincinnati's own Rookwood pottery, carved furniture, and paintings from the city's golden age (1830–1900). European artworks include old masters such as Titian, Rubens, and Gainsborough, as well as modern masters Picasso, Braque, and Chagall. The American galleries show works by Copley, Wyeth, Hopper, and Rothko. The museum is not downtown, but rather up a winding hill in Eden Park. General admission to the museum is free, but donations are encouraged. The CAM is closed Mon.

Cincinnati Museum Center
1301 Western Ave.
(513) 287-7000
www.cincymuseum.org
This is the first place hotel concierges suggest to visitors with families. The complex is located in the historic 1933 Union Terminal and houses six different museums. Detailed re-creations of Cincinnati's heritage tell the city's story at the Cincinnati History Museum. Kids can explore the world at CINergy Children's Museum. Step into the Ohio Valley's ice age in the Museum of Natural History and Science, or check out the free African American Museum of the Arts on the lower level. The facility also has an OMNIMAX theater and houses the Cincinnati Historical Society Library.

Cincinnati Zoo and Botanical Gardens
3400 Vine St.
(513) 281-4700
www.cincinnatizoo.org
The world-famous Cincinnati Zoo and Botanical Gardens is the No. 1 attraction in the city and consistently ranks among the top zoos in the country. It is internationally known for its successful protection and propagation of endangered animals such as rhinos and cheetahs. Opened in 1875, this is the nation's second-oldest zoo, and the 1905

i You can't leave the "Chili Capital of America" without trying Cincinnati's signature dish: spicy ground beef ladled over a plate of spaghetti. Order a "three-way" and you'll get mounds of shredded cheddar; throw in some onions, and it's a "four-way." Add beans, and it's a "five-way."

Elephant House is a national landmark. The zoo is open every day. Cash is not accepted for parking.

Harriet Beecher Stowe House
2950 Gilbert Ave.
(513) 751-0651
www.stowehousecincy.org

The author of *Uncle Tom's Cabin* lived in Cincinnati for 19 years, and her home-turned-museum displays family photos, journals, manuscripts, and artifacts from African American history.

Over-The-Rhine (OTR) Neighborhood
www.downtowncincinnati.com/districts/
  over-the-rhine

The preserved and restored 19th-century working-class German neighborhood is home to the bustling Findlay Market, Ohio's oldest market hall. The craft breweries, hip gastro pubs, and trendy bars and restaurants are easy to get to without a car via the Bell Connector Light Rail. The area is believed to have the largest collection of 19th-century brewery buildings in the country. OTR is bustling at all hours of the day, so enjoy a wander around the vibrant, eclectic neighborhood.

Paramount's King's Island and Boomerang Bay
6300 King's Island Dr., Mason
(513) 754-5700
www.visitkingsisland.com

King's Island is a huge amusement park an hour south of Columbus that is known for its many thrilling roller coasters including the classic "Beast" wooden coaster and the high-thrill Banshee, Diamond Back, and wild Invertigo, whose name says it all. The "littles" will enjoy the Peanuts-themed kiddo rides. The whole family can beat the heat at Soak City Water Park, with more than 30 water rides, including water funnels, lagoons, and a water fortress. The park is open daily spring through Labor Day and weekends only through Oct. If you plan to go more than once in a summer, consider getting season passes. Children under age 3 are free.

Taft Museum of Art
316 Pike St.
(513) 241-0343
www.taftmuseum.org

A small yet superb art museum is located in one of the finest examples of Federal architecture in the Palladian style. The 1820 Baum-Longworth-Taft house, a National Historic Landmark, contains 700 works of art encompassing European masters, exceptional Chinese ceramics, early American painting, and furniture. It's closed on Tues.

William Howard Taft National Historic Site
2038 Auburn Ave., Mt. Auburn
(513) 684-3262
www.nps.gov/wiho

The restored birthplace and childhood home of the 27th US president and 10th chief justice of the Supreme Court, William Howard Taft, commemorates his life and career in four period rooms and various exhibits. The Taft house is open seven days a week, and admission is free.

Performing Arts

Cincinnati is home to some of the oldest and most respected performing arts organizations in the country. The mid-February Fine Arts Sampler Weekend is a great way to get an overview of what the "Queen City" has to offer.

The Aronoff Center for the Arts (513-977-4150; www.cincinnatiarts.org) is located in the heart of downtown Cincinnati at 650 Walnut St. This state-of-the-art facility has three stunning performance spaces and features the Weston Art Gallery. It hosts Fifth Third Bank's Broadway in Cincinnati. View www.broadwayacrossamerica.com for more information about touring productions. The Cincinnati Ballet (513-621-5219; www.cincinnatiballet.com), one of the country's top 10 professional companies, performs a repertoire of classic, neoclassic, and contemporary dance at the Aronoff Center more than 30 times annually.

The Music Hall, built in 1878, is the grande dame of Cincinnati arts venues (513-744-3344; www.cincinnatiarts.org). This landmark building is well known for its colorful history, stunning architecture, and fine acoustics. Located at 1241 Elm St., the hall is the home of the country's second-oldest opera company and fifth-oldest orchestra. As one of the nation's leading opera companies, the Cincinnati Opera (513-241-2742; www.cincinnatiopera.org) puts on several productions each summer. The Cincinnati Symphony Orchestra (513-621-1919; www.cincinnatisymphony.org) performs under the direction of Cristian Macelaru, and the season runs from Sept to May.

Sports

If you don't know much about Cincinnati, you've still probably heard of the Bengals and the Reds, or at least know of Pete Rose. This section will focus on the two great American sports born right here in Ohio: football and baseball.

Cincinnati is home to the oldest franchise in professional baseball. The Cincinnati Reds' home, the Great American Ball Park (513-765-7000; www.cincinnatireds.com), pays tribute to the city's great riverboat history with a set of stacks that shoot off fireworks after home games. It also pays homage to the Reds' rich past with statues of famous players, famous-date banners, and the Reds' Hall of Fame and Museum. Fans are treated to interactive displays and exhibits offering a comprehensive look at baseball's development, beginning with the first professional team, the Cincinnati Red Stockings of 1869. Guests are welcome to keep foul balls. No alcohol is sold after the seventh inning.

The Cincinnati Bengals plays in its waterfront home, Paycor Stadium (513-621-8383; www.bengals.com). The stadium has 50-plus concession stands, the Bengals Museum, and a FieldTurf playing surface and is open at the end zones, providing views into the city and over the river. The plaza located on the southeast corner of the stadium hosts a three-hour pregame event with music, food, and drinks in the Jungle Zone.

Cincy Classics

Arnold's Bar & Grill
210 E. Eighth St.
(513) 421-6234
www.arnoldsbarandgrill.com
Cincinnati's oldest tavern, established in 1861, is located in a quirky old building and retains some of its 19th-century decor. The historic eatery has long been one of Cincinnati's finest saloons, and legend holds that, during Prohibition, the second-floor bathtub was used to make gin. The walls of this spirited place are covered with paraphernalia, while the menu features traditional Italian and American cuisine.

Montgomery Inn at the Boathouse
925 Riverside Dr.
(513) 721-7427
www.montgomeryinn.com
Montgomery Inn's famous ribs and sauce are a Cincinnati institution. There are several locations throughout the city, but the Boathouse sits just east of the city and provides beautiful views of the Ohio River and northern Kentucky.

Accommodations

Cincinnati is an easy day trip from Columbus, but if you decide to spend the night, you'll have no problem finding bed-and-breakfast inns, historic hotels, and an endless number of chain hotels. Downtown is home to the historic Hilton Netherland Plaza and the huge Millennium Hotel, while the area just north of the city is loaded with mid-priced hotels servicing King's Island. Listed here is one of the more reputable and interesting options downtown.

Cincinnatian Hotel
601 Vine St.
(513) 381-3000
www.hilton.com
This landmark four-diamond/four-star hotel, built in 1882, is the only small luxury hotel in the city. It has been rated by *Condé Nast Traveler* magazine as one of America's top 25 hotels. Guests are showered with royal treatment, so it's no wonder the likes of Ronald Reagan, Tom Cruise, and the Rolling Stones have stayed here. Armoires, spacious

(Q) Close-up

The Road to Freedom

More than 150 years ago, 100,000 enslaved African Americans sought freedom through the Underground Railroad. The symbolic name was given to the northbound route slaves followed to gain their freedom. A clandestine network of safe houses, operated by abolitionists, whites, free Blacks, and Native Americans, helped runaways make their way as far north as Canada. Whispers of the Underground Railroad became reality when escapees crossed the Ohio River from Kentucky, first stepping foot on free soil in southern Ohio.

With one of the most important Underground Railroad stations in nearby Ripley, Cincinnati is a befitting place for the National Underground Railroad Freedom Center. This cultural icon stands as the nation's celebration of freedom and is the largest museum dedicated to the Underground Railroad. It opened August 24, 2004 (the day the United Nations celebrates the international abolition of slavery), to rave reviews and quickly become a national treasure.

African American architect Walter Blackburn of Indianapolis designed the distinctive center. The three buildings symbolize the cornerstones of freedom: courage, cooperation, and perseverance. The curved architecture echoes the winding river and philosophically reflects the precarious, changing path to freedom. During construction, representatives from worldwide freedom organizations added containers of soil from their sites to symbolically represent the free soil the slaves struggled to reach. The center sits between the Great American Ball Park and Paycor Stadium, overlooking the Ohio River toward Kentucky. Visitors can stand on an open deck and imagine the perilous escape thousands of slaves made across the river.

Through interactive exhibits and basic storytelling, the museum uses the power of the past to convey a simple yet profound message promoting human rights and freedom for all. See and touch the walls of a slave jail dismantled and moved from Kentucky. This emotional centerpiece served as a pen for slaves prior to being taken south for human auction. Other artifacts of interest include a first edition of *Uncle Tom's Cabin* and male slave trousers made of "Negro cloth," a coarsely woven cotton cloth purchased in large quantities by plantation owners.

The Freedom Center also highlights Ohio's position and unique historical contribution to the Underground Railroad. It brings to life the struggles for freedom not only in our country but also around the world and throughout history, including the present day. "The Struggle Today" spotlights the legacy of the Underground Railroad and freedom movements in contemporary society. The Hall of Heroes honors many people, ranging from those who helped American slaves in the 1800s to those who are currently fighting Asian sex slavery. Appropriately enough, the Freedom Center host seminars on cultural diversity in schools and many other relevant topics.

This 19th-century freedom movement challenged the way Americans viewed slavery and human rights. You will not leave this place without examining your own attitudes about freedom in the past, present, and future. And like the Underground Railroad, the Freedom Center's effect is felt far beyond Cincinnati. For more information regarding hours and admission, view the website at www.freedomcenter.org or call (513) 333-7500 for information.

The National Underground Railroad Freedom Center
FeinknopF Photography

dressing rooms, sitting areas, and writing desks give the 147 guest rooms more of a residential feel. You do, however, pay for Cincinnati's foremost address.

Cleveland: Art, Football, and Rock 'n' Roll

Cleveland Visitor's Center
334 Euclid Ave.
(216) 875-6680
www.thisiscleveland.com

It's a nondescript, two-hour drive north to Cleveland, bearing in mind traffic on I-71 is often thick and congested, but once you get there, the journey is well worth it. Cleveland extends 100 miles along the southern shore of Lake Erie, making it the largest lakefront metro area in the country. Geographically speaking, Lake Erie is the country's largest freshwater resource and provides year-round entertainment for mariners and landlubbers alike. Marinas, yacht clubs, restaurants, and museums take advantage of the lakefront views.

A few things can easily be packed into a one-day trip, but it is always tempting to stay the weekend. More akin to Pittsburgh than Columbus, Cleveland has all the trappings that come with having once been a great manufacturing and steel city: a rich 200-year history, old money, interesting architecture, a thriving arts community, professional sports teams, and multicultural neighborhoods, many with their own distinct heritage and lots of good eating! Whether you come to shop at the West Side Market, take in a show at Severance Hall, or go to a Browns' game, there is plenty that will keep you returning to Cleveland.

Attractions

The *Lady Caroline* (216-696-888; www.ladycaroline .com) longship sails along the coast, offering panoramic views of the city during lunch, brunch, and sunset dinner cruises on Lake Erie.

African American Museum
1765 Crawford Rd.
(216) 721-6555
www.aamcle.org

America's first museum dedicated to the African American experience offers four core exhibits reflecting on Black life in Cleveland, scientists and inventors of African descent, and civil rights moments. It also offers a glimpse into the African American role in the US by exploring the past and present.

Cleveland Botanical Garden
11030 East Blvd.
(216) 721-1600
www.holdenfg.org

The 10 acres of landscaped gardens include an award-winning children's garden, Japanese garden, and a new, one-of-a-kind glass house featuring two of the world's most delicate ecosystems: the desert of Madagascar and the cloud forest of Costa Rica. Fifty species of butterflies, birds, and insects are also exhibited. The gardens are open daily.

Cleveland Metroparks Zoo and Rainforest
3900 Wildlife Way
(216) 661-6500
www.clemetzoo.com

This 168-acre zoo is home to 3,300 animals, of which 84 are endangered species. It also has the largest collection of primate species in North America. The zoo features Wolf Wilderness, Australian Adventure, and the 2-acre indoor Rainforest. It is also a botanical garden.

Cleveland Museum of Art
11150 East Blvd.
(216) 421-7340, (888) 262-0033
www.clevelandart.org

This highly acclaimed museum has more than 45,000 works of art spanning 6,000 years. The 70 galleries feature ancient Egyptian and Roman sculpture, Renaissance armor, and Impressionist paintings. Be sure to venture out the back door to see Rodin's most famous sculpture, *The Thinker*. The CMA's collections of pre-Columbian and Asian art are unrivaled. Admission is free; the museum is closed on Mon.

Cleveland Museum of Natural History
1 Wade Oval Dr.
(216) 231-4600
www.cmnh.org

Explore the earth and beyond at Ohio's largest natural history museum. Discover prehistoric Ohio through dinosaur exhibits, gawk at the impressive collection of rare diamonds in the Gallery of Gems and Jewels, and track planetary movements and lunar events at the new Shafran Planetarium. This outstanding museum is open daily. Admission is $7 for adults, $4 for children.

Great Lakes Science Center
601 Erieside Ave.
(216) 694-2000
www.glsc.org
Learn about the Great Lakes, science phenomena, the environment, and technology at one of America's largest science museums. The center covers some 250,000 square feet, housing hundreds of hands-on exhibits and an OMNIMAX theater. The waterfront building is located between the Rock and Roll Hall of Fame and the Cleveland Browns Stadium. The science center is open daily, and parking is available (for a fee) in the attached garage.

Historic Warehouse District
www.warehousedistrict.org
Downtown's oldest commercial center now features trendy restaurants, wine bars, and live music venues. Some of the city's hottest restaurants, jazz bars, and lounges are found in converted warehouses in this area just east of the Flats. It is also home to art galleries, boutiques, and funky coffee shops.

Peter B. Lewis Building
11119 Bellflower Rd.
(216) 368-2000
www.case.edu/weatherhead
Just look for the dramatic, cascading steel ribbons on the campus of Case Western Reserve University, and you've found the most advanced management school facility in the world. Public tours of this stunning Frank Gehry building are available by appointment.

Playhouse Square Center
1501 Euclid Ave.
(216) 771-4444
www.playhousesquare.com
Five beautifully restored theaters are at home in Playhouse Square Center, making this the nation's second-largest performing arts center. The Allen, State, Ohio, Palace, and Hanna host most of Cleveland's major performing arts organizations. Tickets for the Cleveland Opera, dance, and Broadway can be purchased directly through the Playhouse Square website or at the box office.

The Cleveland Playhouse, located at 8500 Euclid Ave. in University Circle, is recognized as America's longest-running regional theater. Go to www.clevelandplayhouse.com for tickets. The Cleveland Orchestra (216-231-7300; www.clevelandorchestra.com) performs at the architecturally stunning Severance Hall, also in University Circle.

Rock and Roll Hall of Fame
1100 Rock and Roll Blvd.
(216) 781-ROCK (7625)
www.rockhall.com
Cleveland has always been a major force in music history and is the site for the Rock and Roll Hall of Fame. I. M. Pei's spectacular building rises above Lake Erie and boldly expresses rock's raw power. Permanent collections of music artifacts and changing exhibitions tell the story of the musical forces that have shaped our lives. The hall hosts annual inductions, music festivals, and traveling exhibitions. It is open daily. Admission is $35 for adults and $25 for youth; kids under 6 are free.

University Circle
(216) 791-3900
www.universitycircle.org
The cultural center of Cleveland is located 4 miles east of downtown on the campus of Case Western Reserve University. University Circle is an attraction unto itself, having more cultural and performing arts institutions packed into 1 square mile than anywhere else in the country. Cleveland's major museums and several performance halls are located within walking distance of one another through a beautiful park setting.

Sports
Cleveland is home to several professional sports teams, but baseball is one of the city's oldest traditions, dating to 1869. The Cleveland Guardians (216-420-4487; www.mlb.com/guardians) play at downtown Progressive Field. This urban

ballpark was built as part of the Gateway Sports and Entertainment Complex, which also includes Rocket Mortgage FieldHouse, home of Cleveland's professional basketball team, the Cavaliers. You can purchase Cavs' tickets online at www.nba.com/cavaliers.

The Cleveland Browns (www.cleveland-browns.com) have a pretty confusing team history. To the heart-wrenching dismay of the fans, this football franchise was moved to Baltimore in 1996, but the city of Cleveland rallied to keep the name, colors, and history of the Browns in their city. The team has since returned to the shores of Lake Erie and plays at the Cleveland Browns Stadium.

The official tailgate party takes place before and after each game on the north side of the stadium, but the party continues throughout the game in the rabid, fan-filled "Dawg Pound." Be prepared for a lot of barking and drastic mood swings when things don't quite go fans' way. Bone-chilling wind blows off the lake, so dress very warm for games.

Cleveland Classics

Downtown Cleveland is full of stylish restaurants, bistros, and microbreweries, particularly in the historic Warehouse District and the Flats. Stuff yourself on cannoli and biscotti in Little Italy or kielbasa and pierogies in Slavic Village. Whatever you want is on the menu somewhere in Cleveland.

Great Lakes Brewing Company
2516 Market Ave., Ohio City
(216) 771-4404
www.greatlakesbrewing.com
The GLB Co., founded in 1988, was the first microbrewery in Ohio. The brewers craft their beer in an environmentally responsible manner, recycle through their Zero Waste Initiative, and purchase organic, locally grown ingredients to support local businesses. The menu is loaded with upscale American pub food, and if their lofty social practices aren't enough, pints of beer are reasonably priced during happy hour.

Johnny's Downtown
1406 W. Sixth St.
(216) 623-0055
www.johnnyscleveland.com
This contemporary and vibrant restaurant is a popular spot in the historic Warehouse District. Pasta lovers will be pleased with the variety of classic Italian entrees and unusual appetizers on the menu. The ambience is warm and trattoria-like.

Pickwick & Frolic Restaurant
2035 E. Fourth St.
(216) 241-7425
www.pickwickandfrolic.com
Flatbread pizzas and comfort food are served in a modern, pub-like restaurant that is part of a larger entertainment venue. For a British-themed meal, try the fish-and-chips or ham and cheddar ale soup, then slip down to Kevin's Martini Bar for more drinks. Dinner/theater packages are also available at Frolic Cabaret and Frolic Comedy Club.

Tommy's
1824 Coventry Rd., Cleveland Heights
(216) 321-7757
www.tommyscoventry.com
You'll find the biggest and best selections of healthy foods in the funky Coventry part of Cleveland Heights. Tommy's offers a great selection of vegetable and "meatless" pies. The changing menu always has something new and unusual to tempt your vegetarian taste buds. Regulars swear by the vegetarian French onion soup.

Trattoria Roman Garden
12207 Mayfield Rd., Little Italy
(216) 421-2700
www.trattoriaromangarden.com
Frank Sinatra tunes and red wine flow in the three dining rooms and outdoor patio of this Little Italy institution. It's not a fancy place, but folks line up at the door for the eggplant Parmigiano. Parking is a challenge in this area, but the food is worth the effort.

Accommodations

There are a variety of lodging options in downtown Cleveland, ranging from mid-priced hotels such as the Comfort Inn and Hampton Inn to the Embassy Suites for extended stays. The two hotels included here are Cleveland's most reputable, but they are also the most expensive.

Renaissance Cleveland Hotel
24 Public Square
(216) 696-5600
www.marriot.com

This magnificent 15-story hotel, built in 1918, is a designated Historic Hotel of America and is located right in the heart of the city. It has an indoor pool and is connected to Quicken Loans Arena and Progressive Field by indoor, climate-controlled walkways. The hotel's Sans Souci restaurant serves classic French and Mediterranean fare in a truly ritzy setting.

Ritz Carlton
1515 W. Third St.
(216) 623-1300
www.ritzcarlton.com

Cleveland's only four-star/four-diamond property features 208 luxurious guest rooms and suites with scenic views of downtown and Lake Erie. This first-rate hotel is adjacent to the Tower City shopping center and connects via an enclosed walkway to Quicken Loans Arena and Progressive Field. It is within walking distance of the Rock and Roll Hall of Fame and all lakefront attractions. The Century at the Ritz is the hotel's elegant restaurant and sushi bar, which is open to the public.

Dayton and Springfield Area

Dayton Convention and Visitors Bureau
1 Chamber Plaza
(937) 226-8211
www.daytoncvb.com

One of the easiest day trips from Columbus is the 45-minute pilgrimage west to Dayton, home of the Wright brothers and the "Birthplace of Aviation." The area's premier attractions are mostly flight-related, but history and art buffs may be pleasantly surprised at what else Dayton has to offer.

Antiques lovers may want to stop off along the way at the **Heart of Ohio Antiques Center** in Springfield (937-324-2188; www.heartofohioantiques.com). Some 650 dealers from over 20 states are represented at this huge mall conveniently located off I-70.

When you make your way to Dayton, you can get your fill of flight at a bunch of places. Start off at the historic **Wright Cycle Company** (937-225-7705), located at 22 S. Williams St. It is here that Orville and Wilbur Wright managed a bicycle and print shop. In addition to antique bicycles, visitors can view machinery and see where the first flight tests were held.

Next stop: Wright Patterson Air Force Base. The **National Museum of the U.S. Air Force** (937-255-3286; www.nationalmuseum.af.mil) houses hundreds of aircraft, ground vehicles, flight equipment, and missiles, making this the world's largest aviation museum. Also at WPAFB is the **National Aviation Hall of Fame** (937-256-0944; www.nationalaviation.org), where America's air and space pioneers are honored in exhibits spanning the dawn of flight through the current space age. The more popular highlights include early Wright brothers' models and the plane that dropped the atomic bomb on Nagasaki, Japan, in 1945.

It seems that the Wright brothers were interested in more than just flight. They were also among the founding patrons of the **Dayton Art Institute** (937-223-5277; www.daytonartinstitute.org). This surprising little gem of a museum houses an impressive collection of 12,000 works ranging from early American furniture to Italian baroque paintings to 1970s pop art.

An entirely different Wright made a mark on Springfield, as legendary architect Frank Lloyd Wright was commissioned to design the **Westcott House** on 85 S. Greenmount Ave. in downtown Springfield. The Prairie-style home was built in 1908 for Burton Westcott and was one of Wright's earliest Japanese-influenced designs. Well-organized guided tours are offered daily ($20) through the fully restored home and gardens.

Granville

Village of Granville
141 E. Broadway St.
(740) 587-0707
www.granville.oh.us

Located just 30 minutes east of the city, this charming village is practically a suburb of Columbus. Anyone who has visited the cute, little downtown of Granville will understand when I compare it to the town in *It's a Wonderful Life*. You almost expect to see Jimmy Stewart running madly through the streets. Granville is full of restored 19th-century homes, quaint boutiques, and little pubs. It is also home to picturesque Denison University.

New Englanders from Granville, Massachusetts, and Granby, Connecticut, settled Granville in 1805. The Granville Historical Society at 115 E. Broadway St. (740-587-3951; www.granvillehistory.org) is a good place to learn about local history. The Robbins Hunter Museum (740-587-0430; www.robbinshunter.org) is located at 221 E. Broadway in the historic 1842 Avery-Downer home. The museum features 11 furnished rooms with 18th- and 19th-century American, European, and Asian antiques, paintings, sculpture, carpets, and furniture.

The Granville Inn (740-587-3333; www.granvilleinn.com), at 314 E. Broadway, is an English Tudor country manor–style building built in 1924. The boutique hotel offers fine dining and accommodations in the form of 39 rooms, including four suites, all decorated with an elegant rustic lodge style. The Oak Room restaurant is truly romantic with floor-to-ceiling wood paneling, cozy alcoves, and a huge hearth. It is open for breakfast, lunch, and dinner, and guests can cozy up to the beautiful bar in The Tavern throughout the day. An outdoor patio is an ideal spot to enjoy a drink or meal with views across the lawn into historic Granville.

Across the street, visitors feel the history at Buxton Inn (313 E. Broadway St.; 740-587-0001; www.buxtoninn.com). This former stagecoach stop dates to 1812 and has a fascinating history—and possibly a few friendly ghosts. The inn recently reopened after a massive fire ripped through the building destroying a large part of it, including the kitchen. As of this publication, the Tavern is open for drinks and the hotel is open for business. The kitchen is slated to reopen later in 2024.

The inn's 25 unique guest rooms, with private baths, colonial-style decor, and some period antiques, are located in four restored homes, all connected to the inn by formal gardens and walkways. One interesting piece of trivia is that Presidents William Henry Harrison, Abraham Lincoln, and William McKinley all spent the night here—and all died in office. Coincidence? Most likely.

Hocking Hills

Hocking County Tourism Association
13178 Hwy. 664 S., Logan
(740) 385-2750
www.explorehockinghills.com

The region just southeast of Columbus, known as Hocking Hills, beckons hikers and outdoorsmen into the foothills of the Appalachian Mountains. Mother Nature provides attractions in the form of 300-million-year-old hills, valleys, ridges, and cliffs.

Some 9,000 picturesque acres encompassing nine state parks and four nature preserves offer year-round outdoor activities. Try something different, like scouting for bald eagles or canoeing in the moonlight. In just an hour's drive you'll find hiking, fishing, horseback riding, rappelling, birdwatching, and boating in some of Ohio's most remote areas.

Attractions

The Hocking Hills Regional Welcome Center is located on OH 664 and US 33 in Logan and can provide comprehensive information and detailed maps of the region.

Ash Cave is in the southernmost parts of the Hocking Hills and is the largest and most impressive cave in the state. At 700 feet wide, 100 feet deep, and 90 feet high, Ash Cave provided shelter to the earliest inhabitants and a resting place for weary travelers. Its cascading waterfall and Pulpit Rock offer great photo opportunities.

Cedar Falls is in a remote and austere part of Hocking Hills, 1 mile west of OH 664 on OH 374. Towering rock walls and grottoes surround this wild and lonely chasm. The falls, which plummet

50 feet into a pool below, is the greatest in terms of volume in the hills.

Conkle's Hollow is a rugged and rocky gorge, just off OH 374 on Big Pine Road. The 200-foot vertical cliffs surround the trail, which leads through a ravine overgrown with ferns, wildflowers, soaring hemlocks, and birch trees. Adventurous hikers can circle the gorge on the highest cliffs in the area by taking the Rim Trail. Stunning views are guaranteed, but caution is a must, as this trail can be dangerous in all seasons.

Old Man's Cave, located on OH 664, is the most visited area and the heart of Hocking Hills. This magnificent 0.5-mile gorge is divided into five sections: Upper Falls, Upper Gorge, Middle Falls, Lower Falls, and Lower Gorge. The Upper Gorge contains the Devil's Bathtub, a swirling natural pool that local legend contends reaches into the depths of Hades, where the devil resides. The 6-mile Grandma Gatewood Trail runs from Old Man's Cave to Cedar Falls to Ash Cave.

Rock House is the only true cave in the park. Nature has carved a 200-foot corridor into the sandstone, replete with Gothic arches and massive columns. Native Americans used recesses in the rear wall as baking ovens. It is located on OH 374 and Thompson Road, north of Conkle's Hollow.

Dining and Lodging

If you need a place to stay while exploring Hocking Hills, check out www.hockinghills.com, or contact Explore Hocking Hills (www.explorehockinghills.com) to find vacancies or which places permit pets. State parks also offer lodging, which you can read more about in the Parks and Recreation chapter. There are loads of different cabins and cottages to choose from. Listed here are just a few of the reputable rental groups. From time to time, a restaurant is attached to the lodging, but most are self-contained cabins with fully equipped kitchens.

Chalets at Old Man's Cave
18905 US 664 S., Logan
(740) 385-6517
www.chaletshh.com

More guests stay at these wonderful chalets, log homes, and A-frame cabins than anywhere else in the Hocking Hills region. All are spacious one-, two-, or three-bedrooms units and come fully furnished.

Four Seasons Cabins
14435 Nickel Plate Rd., Logan
(740) 385-1687
www.fourseasonscabinrental.com

This secluded house is located on 55 acres, where you can hike, mountain bike, fish, or use the paddleboat. You'll find an outdoor hot tub, deck, grill, and wood-burning stone fireplace.

Getaway Cabins
Various parts of Hocking Hills
(740) 385-3734
www.getaway-cabins.com

These private, secluded cabins are a perfect hideaway from reality and allow for uninterrupted romantic weekend getaways. Check out the website or call for special packages.

The Inn and Spa at Cedar Falls
21190 Hwy. 374, Logan
(740) 385-7489, (800) 65-FALLS (653-2557)
www.innatcedarfalls.com

Located less than 0.5 mile from its namesake, this 1840s cabin offers guests a chance to dine from a seasonal menu and stay in the romantic Cozy Cottages and other nearby vacation rentals. Many of the cabins are decorated with antiques or rustic modern furniture, and have a whirlpool and king-size bed. Some of the lodging options include various-sized cabins, cottages, yurts, and geodomes. After a day of hiking, indulge in a massage or other spa treatments at the Spa at Cedar Falls. The Kindred Spirits restaurant and Urban Grille offer high-quality food at affordable prices right at the inn.

i Early settlers mistook hemlocks for cedars, therefore, misnaming Cedar Falls. The cool, damp climate of this gorge favors hemlock growth, so it's no surprise Cedar Falls claims the largest tree in Ohio—a giant, 150-foot hemlock.

Lake Erie Islands and Sandusky

**Sandusky/Erie County Visitors and
Convention Bureau
712 North St., Sandusky
Intersection at OH 2
(419) 332-4470
www.sanduskycounty.org**

Many people think of Ohio as a landlocked Midwest state full of corn and cows. Not obvious are the plentiful beaches of northern Ohio and the Lake Erie Islands. Just one ride up Cedar Point's roller coasters and you'll have a different perspective—a bird's-eye view out over one of the nation's Great Lakes. While Cedar Point might be an easy day trip from Columbus, many opt to spend the night in Sandusky or plan a whole weekend around fun in the sun.

A 2-hour drive north of Columbus will not only get you to one of the most popular theme parks in the country but also land you at Headlands Beach State Park near Mentor. It features the largest (1-mile-long) natural beach in the state and borders two state nature reserves. A third preserve in Mentor, the Lagoon Nature Preserve and Marina, encompasses 450 acres and includes 1.5 miles of shoreline, with 3 miles of hiking and biking trails.

Traveling along the Erie coast, there are no fewer than a dozen lighthouses, some of which are only visible from shore or accessible by boat, but several are located on the mainland and open to the public. The museum at Old Fairport Harbor Main Lighthouse (circa 1871), just east of Cleveland, houses Great Lakes artifacts. Farther west of Cleveland is the newly renovated Cedar Point Lighthouse and the Great Lakes' oldest continuously operated Marblehead Lighthouse. Both are open for tours during the summer.

Visitors to northern Ohio can reach the Lake Erie Islands by ferry or plane, but if you're lucky enough to have your own boat, there are plenty of places from which to launch. Cars are permitted on all the islands, but you'll have the most freedom to explore if you rent a bicycle or golf cart. Rental facilities are located near all the ferry docks, and you can learn more about these services by contacting the ferry services included here.

**The Islands
(419) 625-2984
www.shoresandislands.com**

Ferries leaving Sandusky, Port Clinton, Marblehead, and Catawba go to most of the Lake Erie Islands, which are still quite unspoiled. It helps that the entire island is on the National Register of Historic Places: The downtown area is most active in the summer months and has shops, restaurants, and bars within a few steps of the waterfront. The north side is less commercial, with an abundance of wildlife, beaches, and clean, clear water. Contact (419) 746-2360 or www.kelleysisland.com for information on activities and cottage rentals.

Put-in-Bay on South Bass Island is a party place, but the festive atmosphere often overshadows its family-friendly side. Victorian-style housing, restaurants, boutiques, arcades, and a waterfront park give it a seaside resort atmosphere. The island is also home to two museums, a winery, and the towering, 352-foot Perry Monument, which can be ascended for panoramic views of Lake Erie. South Bass Island State Park offers waterfront camping and a lovely beach. Have a look at www.put-in-bay.com, or call (419) 285-2832 for more information on year-round activities, including ice fishing.

Middle Bass Island is covered with vineyards, old cottages, summer homes, and a campground. Most of the attractions are natural and include a rocky shoreline with expansive vistas and the Kuehnle Wildlife Area. The interior wetland's 20-acre pond is a favorite among bird-watchers and anglers.

Ferry Information

**Jet Express
3 Monroe St., Port Clinton
(800) 245-1538
www.jet-express.com**

Hydrojet catamarans whisk passengers to Put-in-Bay on South Bass Island. It also provides early-morning and late-night service. Children under 12 ride for free.

Kelley's Island Ferry Boat Lines

510 W. Main St., Marblehead
(419) 798-9763
www.kelleysislandferry.com
Boats depart every half hour, year-round, and run well into the evening. Automobile transportation is also available.

Miller Ferries

5174 E. Water St., Port Clinton
(419) 285-2421, (800) 500-2421
www.millerferry.com
Ferry service carries both cars and passengers every half hour to South and Middle Bass Island on a daily basis in the spring, summer, and fall.

Attractions

Cedar Point, Challenge Park, and Soak Park

1 Cedar Point Dr., Sandusky
(419) 627-2350
www.cedarpoint.com
The prestigious *Amusement Today* magazine voted this 364-acre family amusement park the "Best Park in the World" for many of the past 20 years. As home to the largest collection of roller coasters and rides, there is something here for everyone.

Cedar Point has 69 rides and 18 coasters, with 5 hypercoasters more than 200 feet tall. Coaster enthusiasts love the Magnum XL-200, Millennium Force, Valravn, Steel Vengeance, and Top Thrill 2. Thrill seekers also swear by Corkscrew. Parents can take it a little easier with the younger children on 7 rides at Camp Snoopy, while scaredy-cats can play it safe in the self-paddle swan boats. Families can beat the heat on the inner-tube slides and wave pool at Cedar Point Shores, while waterslide lovers can get their thrills on the Point Plummet, a near-vertical free-fall drop into a tunnel tube.

Various passes and season passes can be purchased online. Cedar Point offers a variety of lodging options within walking distance of the park. Some have their own private beaches. Guests staying at Cedar Point resorts receive discounted admission and early entry to the park. There is so much to do here that two days is not unreasonable, but be prepared to spend half the time waiting in line if you don't add on a fast lane pass.

i Kelley's Island is home to the world's largest prehistoric glacial grooves. Heavy glaciers carved out the soft island limestone, leaving a fossilized record of marine life from millions of years ago. Perimeter viewing of the grooves is possible.

Pittsburgh: Historic Hotels and Markets

William Penn Hotel (530 William Penn Place; 412-281-7100; www.omnihotels.com) has been the Grand Dame of Pittsburgh since it was built by Henry Clay Frick in 1919. The nearly 600-room hotel is on the National Register of Historic Places and is well priced for the sophisticated atmosphere and central downtown location. The beautiful lobby sparkles with giant chandeliers and is an elegant spot to enjoy a coffee or cocktail. Warm colors and cherrywood furniture decorate the various rooms and suites, many offering lovely city views. Time has sort of stood still for this hotel. A more nuanced bit of history is that the bubble machine was invented by a hotel engineer for Cecil B. DeMille's 1947 premier of *Unconquered,* filmed in Pittsburgh. Fittingly, the William Penn is where the phrase "Champagne Music" was coined to describe band leader Larewnce Welk's sparkly music, which was like sipping the bubbly! Cue the bubble machine, which went on to become a famous element of the *Lawrence Welk Show*. The hotel serves traditional afternoon tea in the Palm Court Mon through Sat.

When in Pittsburgh, try to make it over to the Strip District, a "strip" of land along the river that was and still is a thriving wholesale and market district. Find magnificent seafood, sushi, and fish sandwiches at Wholey's, the wholesale fish market. Pick up colorful olives, house-made pita, and a huge bag of pecorino cheese from Stamooli Brothers Co. and house-made pasta sauce and other Italian specialties from the Pennsylvania Macaroni Company. Parma Sausage is a fun meat market experience where shoppers take a number and wait in line to order cured meats from the incredibly friendly counter guys. The Enrico Biscotti Bakery and Café is legendary and has been featured in many media outlets over the decades. The neighborhood pièce de résistance might just be the beautiful Italian *meles* and *sfogliatelle* from Colangelo's Bakery & Café, located on a side street. The Strip District is worth the trek to the outskirts of downtown. It's walkable in nice weather, but you might want to drive or Lyft if you are closer to the heart of downtown or not into walking a mile or so. Once there, the Strip has lots to offer in terms of retail, international and whole sale food markets, greasy spoons (try DeLuca's or Pamela's), global cuisine, local coffee shops and bars, and several outlets where sports fans can stock up on Steelers gear.

Stonewall Resort, West Virginia

Beautiful mountain vistas surround this lakeside lodge that is adjacent to Stonewall Jackson State Park in West Virginia (940 Roanoke Dr., WV; 304-269-7400; www.stonewallresort.com). The resort is quite large as it hosts conferences, but it makes a nice family or couple's retreat. The rooms are modest but clean and well-appointed. The pool is the type that is both indoor and outdoor with the ability to swim between; there are indoor/outdoor hot tubs as well. The poolside loungers can get a little competitive when it's busy, but there is plenty of Adirondack and table seating all around the lakefront patio. The main restaurant offers both buffet and a la carte breakfasts and dinners. The golf club just up the mountain has another restaurant and bar with gorgeous bird's-eye views over the lake and valley. Take a wander over the bridge to hike along a few of the golf course fairways, tees, and greens. If you are up for a challenging round of state park golf, you'll find it here on an incredibly undulating course, narrow in many spots, with lots of bunkers and tees over water. Stonewall is a surprisingly nice resort in the Appalachian Mountains that feels a world away from Columbus.

Lewisburg, West Virginia

Lewisburg in West Virginia is a surprisingly neat little city, which a Vogue article declares as "the coolest small town in West Virginia." The General Lewis Inn and Restaurant (1236 E. Washington St.; 304-645-2600; www.generallewisinn.com) is an easy place to stay and enjoy the town. The inn's

24 unique rooms are furnished with antiques and have a ton of character—squeaky floors and all. A few of the rooms are a bit more modern after renovations. The restaurant is very good, from the food to the cocktails to the service. Top-notch experiences the whole way around. After having a drink on the wraparound porch or a stroll through the back gardens, wander into town for a look around the independently owned shops, Civil War cemetery, and Carnegie Music Hall.

Dinner at The French Goat (290 Lafayette St.; 304-647-1052; www.thefrenchgoat.com) is a nice walkable option. The farm-to-table menu offers several classic starters, entrees, and desserts. The dishes are nicely conceived as traditional dishes with modern touches and presentation. During the summer, the gazpacho soup is special, as is the French onion soup. The fancy riff on steak frites and duck cassoulet transports diners to the French countryside. Overall, you can sleep and dine very well in the mountains of West Virginia.

GRAND DAME RESORTS

Bedford Springs Resort, Bedford, Pennsylvania

Bedford Springs is situated in the beautiful Allegheny Mountains of central Pennsylvania, where hot springs have drawn visitors to the region for 200-plus years. You will be treated to beautiful sunsets, luxurious spa treatments, and the most epic golf course! This is the sort of place you can visit any season as there is plenty to do—especially if you are interested in the spa and lounging around in style. Plus, the property is magnificent year-round.

The Bedford's architecture is colonial, as there has been a resort/inn on this site since 1796. It is owned by the independent hotel brand Omni Hotels and is landmarked as a Historic Hotel of America and on the National Register of Historic Places. Collectively, they maintain wonderful custodianship of Bedford Springs. The 2020 renovations have brought thoughtful design into the carpets, lighting, and general patterns throughout the resort. The indoor pool was opened in 1905 as one of the first indoor pools in the country. In warmer weather, the outdoor pool is open, and there are a few trails around the property that lead through miles of mountain scenery. The recreation center has a laundry list of activities, like archery, axe-throwing, carriage rides, and other outdoor activities.

After a full day of activities, head to Spring Eternal Spa for a bath ritual tradition that's been embedded in Bedford Resort since 1895: Exfoliate in the hot/cold deluge shower, take an eucalyptus steam in the wet steam room, then alternate between the hot mineral bubble pool (hot tub) and cool mineral pool soaks. Continue at happy hour in the co-ed lounge with fruit, granola, and tea and beautiful views of the mountains. The spa service is top-notch.

Rooms, viewing the golf course or into the mountains, are spacious and comfortable. The Tavern serves casual pub food with a pretty view. The 1796 Room is decorated in an early American style that is warm and sophisticated with fantastic service. It has a steak house and serves a decadent signature steak and lobster tail. The breakfast buffet is solid, as the food turns over quickly and comes out fresh on a regular basis. You don't need a birthday to indulge in the famous 17-layer chocolate cake—chocolate devil's food cake with alternating caramel and hazelnut mousse, topped with gianduja mousse (chocolate hazelnut paste). That's 8½ layers of each! You might even lick the plate. Bedford is about a 5-hour drive and makes for a romantic getaway or luxurious long weekend.

Greenbrier Resort: America's Resort
White Sulphur Springs, West Virginia

People have been "taking the waters" (to fix what ails them) in the sulphur springs as far back as when the Native Americans were here. The Greenbrier was built in the 1880s, when train travel became popular, and became an infirmary during World War II when Eisenhower took a liking to the place. After World War II and years of disrepair, famous designer Dorothy Draper brought the hotel back to life with exuberant color, fabrics, and patterns, which remain its hallmark to this day. The Lobby Bar has the magnificent 600-pound chandelier that was on the set of Gone with the Wind in Ashley Wilke's home, Twelve Oaks, also the name of the on-site steak house.

You will definitely get your 10,000 steps in while exploring the enormous 700-room resort, which has an upscale retail row, cafes, ice cream, and a casino in the lower level. The property is full of paved paths that go to the golf and tennis clubs and past the original hot springs. Stop to play a round of croquet or reserve time to play a round of golf on the simulator at the golf club. The resort has an indoor pool, but the seasonal outdoor infinity pool overhangs the golf course and offers gorgeous views into the Allegheny Mountains. Check out the website for all the different dining options, spa treatments, and getaway packages. The breakfast buffet is quite good, with blintzes, house-made sausage, lox, and the Greenbrier's renowned peach sauce as the standouts. If you can visit during the holidays, the lights and dozens of decorated trees will knock your stockings off.

The Homestead: Taking the Waters
Hot Springs, Virginia

This hotel recently underwent serious historic restorations, which is a wonderful thing given its incredible history. The Homestead is dubbed "America's First Resort," since the earliest lodge was built on-site in 1766 around the hot springs (even pre-dating the nearby Greenbrier by 20 years). Guests have been "taking the waters" at the Homestead since 1832. The approach to the Homestead is extremely striking, winding along a narrow mountain road down into the valley, where the Grand Dame's great tower emerges from the surrounding hills. The 256-year-old historic hotel lays claim to the title of "Oldest Resort in America," but after its face-lift boasting updated guest rooms, refreshed public spaces, and Southern hospitality, it is looking quite spiffy.

The sprawling resort has 483 elegant guest rooms and suites along with casual and fine dining options and poolside food service. The Jefferson Pool is the covered natural warm springs pool a few miles away and offers an authentic hot springs experience. Summer is a great time to hit the golf courses, pools, and waterslides, or have the concierge register you for outdoor activities like horseback riding, fly fishing, or shooting. Float in the lazy river by day and soak in the hot tub by night. Even during the winter months, there is no shortage of experiences, such as skiing, tubing, ice skating, snowboarding, and snowmobiles. In fact, the Homestead's ski resort is the first in Virginia, founded in 1959.

Any time of year is a good one to pamper yourself in the adult-only spa and Serenity Garden, with an outdoor pool, a hot tub, and the geothermal Octagon Pool, which is heated year-round at a steady temperature of 96–98 degrees. This quiet oasis at the edge of the resort features renowned mineral pools that Thomas Jefferson frequented to treat his rheumatism. The original guest books show his longest stay was 22 days in 1818.

The spa menu is extensive, ranging from Swedish massages and body wraps to Japanese rituals and couple's massage. The Aqua Thermal Suite is an interesting take on European-style shower environments using hot and cold temperatures (think hot sauna then plunge pool); it includes The Chill cold cabin, experiential showers simulating various storm effects and a Finnish sauna.

Golfers can get out into nature on the Old Course, which started life in 1913. The serene course is surrounded with mature wooded grounds and beautifully manicured fairways leading to challenging greens. The Homestead is about a 5-hour drive from Columbus, and Lewisburg, West Virginia, is a nice layover point if you want to break up the trip.

RELOCATION

Most of the communities that make up Greater Columbus lie within and just outside the I-270 beltway. When deciding where to live in Columbus, take time to explore different parts of town. Like many big cities, Columbus is made up of a string of neighborhoods, each with its own distinct identity.

The north and south sides of Columbus are like night and day, while the east and west sides are equally unalike. New luxury apartments are going up in the Italian Village, while unique historic homes can be found in Victorian Village and Worthington. Suburban housing developments sprawl farther from downtown Columbus, and businesses such as Intel are drawing population into the suburbs. There is a great diversity in architectural styles and housing options all over Columbus.

In 2023, Columbus homes averaged $275,900, down from the previous year and still below the national median. A variety of housing options are available in Columbus, but without waterfront property or scenic landscape features in central Ohio, developers rely heavily on golf courses, manicured green spaces, and private amenities to add value and aesthetic appeal to residential property.

The downtown condo scene is blowing up, with park- and waterview properties selling for upward of $1 million, while modern industrial condos and smaller lofts are also being built with anticipation of a growing population.

Golf course communities are popular, and home buyers do expect to pay a premium for these homes, but because of a growing and more diverse market, golf club living has become much more affordable than it used to be. These homes cost anywhere from $300,000 to $2 million and come in various living arrangements, such as patio homes, condos, and family houses. People are also willing to pay for the extra amenities that come with a planned community, such as a clubhouse, swimming pools, and tennis courts.

If your preference is for older neighborhoods, downtown Columbus has several landmark districts with big, old Victorian and Italianate homes begging to be restored. Italian Village and Franklinton are works in progress, while German Village and Olde Towne East are much more established as a historic district but also more expensive. You can still find homes that have original interiors and have stayed true to the original architectural style.

Falling somewhere in between are Victorian Village and Grandview. Both are safe residential areas, with homes requiring updates rather than a total overhaul. Each of these urban neighborhoods has tight lots and often competitive street parking, but farther outside the metropolitan area you will find bigger lots and bigger homes.

The northern and western suburbs of Columbus have developed over the past 15 years. Worthington, Westerville, and Dublin are home to the quintessential suburban cul-de-sacs, highly rated school districts, and plenty of country clubs, parks, and libraries. What differentiate these three neighborhoods from other suburban sprawl are their restored old town centers with pubs, boutiques, and historic homes. While each city encompasses a huge area, their historic centers, particularly in Old Worthington, quite often define them.

Upper Arlington has a distinctly suburban feel to it, but it is adjacent to Ohio State University and is only 10 minutes from downtown. The styles of homes are diverse, but most were built in the early to mid-20th century. Arlington has one of the highest-rated public school districts, a great park system, and the residents have a deep sense of community; because of this, Arlington homes sell very quickly.

Looking for that one-of-a-kind, multimillion-dollar mansion? Then head east to the tree-lined streets of Bexley. Want a Georgian home of 5,000 square feet? New Albany is your place. It seems the farther east you go, the larger everything becomes, but rest assured, more moderate-scale living can be found in Gahanna and Westerville. Unfortunately, in between all these nice, livable neighborhoods are not-so-nice pockets of urban dwellings. Bexley, for example, is a distinguished "old money" community surrounded by some run-down parts of the city, which are very slowly being gentrified. Tear-downs and new builds are also a booming business.

While stereotypes are not always fair or accurate, there is no getting around the fact that certain generalizations are made about each neighborhood. This chapter attempts to be honest about the demographics and socioeconomic status without pigeonholing the residents into one category. It provides a short synopsis of each neighborhood while highlighting its interesting features.

There are plenty of real estate agencies to help with the search, and this chapter includes the contact details for several of the more reputable ones.

DOWNTOWN

www.downtowncolumbus.com

Downtown Columbus is undergoing a renaissance, and the city has made urban living a top priority. A surge in residential building of brownstones and high-rise and non-high-rise condo communities anticipates huge growth in the next 10 years. In fact, the Neighborhood Launch has even created its own 9-block community of brownstone condos with a variety of floor plans and green spaces.

With a daytime working population of nearly 90,000, studies have proven that downtown residential living is in demand. Developers have wasted no time converted commercial buildings into much-needed housing. Downtown Columbus is creating an infrastructure to accommodate more downtown living with grocery stores, dining, and parking. It is bringing about an influx of new restaurants, bars, and shops to stimulate redevelopment of the west and south sides of the city.

i The Wyandotte building at 21 W. Broad St. was built in 1898 and was Columbus's first steel-framed skyscraper. It was built by Chicago architect Daniel Burnham, who also built New York City's landmark Flatiron Building and Columbus's Union Station.

The newest addition to the downtown area is the Market Exchange District. This area, which runs east along Main Street from Grant Avenue to the I-70/I-71 split, was once the primary downtown neighborhood. The bustling 19th-century Central Market, for which the Market Exchange is named, was located where the Greyhound bus station now sits. It totals just a few blocks in length, but it is being transformed into an upscale urban locale. It is now home to galleries, offices, boutiques, and restaurants. Various types of housing options are also being developed along East Main Street.

The Market Exchange District is conveniently located near the Columbus College of Art and Design and Franklin University. The area attracts a student crowd and businesspeople during the day. The nightlife in this little pocket is somewhat minimal, but there are a handful of bars and restaurants that stay open late enough to provide downtowners something to do.

This district may seem a bit incomplete right now, but what was a decrepit part of the city a few years ago is becoming a trendy one. This is one place to keep an eye on if you are considering making the move downtown.

THE "ORIGINAL" SUBURBS

Some of Columbus's earliest neighborhoods radiate around the city center; a few are renovated historic districts, while others are, unfortunately, very run-down. Most of the neighborhoods, which are now considered downtown, were the earliest "suburbs" of Columbus. During the mid-1800s, wealthy industrialists and bankers ventured eastward along Broad and Main Streets to build new mansions away from the hubbub of the city.

You will notice as you drive east out of the city that for every beautiful, renovated building, there are three or four in need of repair. It takes a lot of vision to see beyond the crime and boarded-up structures, but there is hope that this corridor between downtown and Bexley will someday be whipped into shape. While many of these near east communities have seen better days, some semblance of their former grandeur can be found in the majestic old homes lining the streets.

Historic Olde Towne East was once one of Columbus's wealthiest neighborhoods. The boundaries of this eclectic area are generally defined as East Long Street on the north, I-71 and I-70 to the west and south, and an eastern border of Winner, Miller, and Wilson Avenues. The population is a mix of different races, professionals, artisans, tradespeople, singles, couples, and families.

The buildings of Olde Towne East are, like its residents, a mixed bag, having both residential and professional functions. Over 50 architectural styles are represented in more than a thousand homes. Some of Columbus's oldest inhabited houses are in this part of town. They range from restrained Italianate to over-the-top Victorian; a few even date to the 1830s.

Olde Towne East has experienced hard times, but many of its magnificent old homes are making a comeback. The Olde Towne East Neighborhood Association (www.oldetowneeast.org) plays a big role in restoring many of the grand old houses while preserving what currently exists. This neighborhood organization offers an annual tour of homes and sells a publication titled *Historic Homes of Olde Towne East,* which details the 50 most notable houses.

Another near east side community, the Jefferson Avenue Historic District, has several landmark buildings and was added to the National Register of Historic Places in 1982. This small area is bounded roughly by I-71, East Broad Street, 11th

i The art deco building that dominates the Columbus skyline is the LeVeque Tower. It was completed in 1927 and remained the tallest skyscraper in the city until 1973. The LeVeque was added to the National Register of Historic Places in 1975 and now houses modern apartments, the boutique Hotel LeVeque as part of the Marriott Autograph collection, and The Keep restaurant.

Avenue, and Long Street. The architecture is primarily Italianate, and many of the buildings date to 1875–1899 or 1900–1924. The most notable historic structure in the area is the James Thurber House, but this 55-acre district also encompasses the Franklin House, Columbus Museum of Art, and Columbus College of Art and Design.

Until you reach Bexley, the east side statistics show high crime rates and low incomes in this part of town. There are, however, bright spots in the community. The Franklin Park neighborhood, also on the near east side, encompasses Franklin Park, which is home to the city's beautiful conservatory.

The west side of downtown Columbus is a different story. Franklinton, on the near west side, is the oldest part of Columbus, but few remnants remain of the early settlement. This area was nicknamed "The Bottoms" because of its low ground level and continual subjection to flooding of the Scioto and Olentangy Rivers. A floodgate remedied that 200-year-old problem, and since 2014, Franklinton has been undergoing a massive transformation.

It is hard to tell where the city of Franklinton begins and ends. The Scioto River to the east and north, I-70 to the west, and Greenlawn Avenue to the south roughly define the area. West Broad Street, which is the main corridor, is a clutter of shopping centers, apartment buildings, fast-food joints, and auto dealerships. Just to the west of Franklinton is a small group of neighborhoods referred to as "The Hilltop." Though steeped in history, this area is also steeped in crime. The area around West Gate is a nice neighborhood where homes are starting to be scooped up at good prices. History buffs seek out the ghosts of

Columbus's past at West Gate Park, the site of a former Civil War prison camp cemetery.

The Franklinton Post Office, built in 1807, is located at 72 S. Gift St. This dilapidated, shored-up structure was placed on the National Register of Historic Places in 1973 and, though not much to look at, is considered the city's oldest standing building. Franklinton Cemetery was established in 1799 and is central Ohio's oldest burial ground, but most of the bodies have been removed to Greenlawn Cemetery, including Lucas Sullivant and many of Columbus's early families. Both cemeteries are on the west side, but, unfortunately, not much else remains of the original city.

There are fun reasons to venture to the west side of Columbus. The Center of Science and Industry (COSI), Land-Grant playground, and Veterans Memorial are situated across the bridge on the near west side of town. The area around 400 W. Rich St. has been an art incubator for many years now, while the Gravity Project and Franklinton Development Association is breathing new life into the neighborhood with living communities anchored by popular breweries and independent restaurants and the Junto Hotel.

THE BREWERY DISTRICT

The Brewery District is located on the south side of I-70 and is primarily centered along Front Street and east of High Street. This neighborhood is immediately south of downtown Columbus and was settled by German immigrants in the 1830s. It consisted of family homes, churches, and family-owned breweries that thrived until World War I, after which anti-German sentiment and Prohibition forced many of the Germans out of business—and out of town.

Many of the buildings lay abandoned until the end of the 20th century. New life was breathed into the derelict brick warehouses and breweries during the 1980s, and by 1992, this neighborhood was saved as the Brewery District Historical Preservation District. Thanks to the ongoing efforts of the Brewery District Commission, development and restoration are ongoing.

Nightclubs, restaurants, and bars make the Brewery District more of a nightlife spot than a residential area, but this is changing with new apartments and condos and a full-service grocery store.

The Brewery District supports professional offices, such as architects, attorneys, and accountants, but farther south along High Street are the many homes of German Village and the contiguous neighborhoods of Schumacher Place, Merion Village, and Hungarian Village, which are starting to be developed with retail and dining.

GERMAN VILLAGE

www.germanvillage.com

German Village is without a doubt one of the most popular downtown neighborhoods in which to live. For residents, much of German Village's appeal lies in its old-world atmosphere. Sturdy brick cottages and charming brownstones line the brick-paved streets. Window boxes spill over with flowers, and chimney pots add historical detail. Columbus doesn't get any more picturesque than German Village.

For visitors, the appeal lies in the variety of eateries, shops, and galleries. Locals will come from miles around to eat at the many fine restaurants, drink at the long-established watering holes, browse the bookshops, or see a show at Schiller Park. The Village is a completely self-contained community, with professional offices, dry cleaners, banks, and even a veterinary hospital.

German Village is situated 6 blocks south of downtown Columbus. It is bound by Pearl Alley on the west, East Livingston Avenue on the north, Jaeger and Bruck Streets to the east, and Thurman and Mithoff to the south. Prior to its settlement, sewers and tanneries made this property, just outside city limits, undesirable and cheap.

In the early 1800s, poor German immigrants settled *die alte sud ende* ("the old south end"), but they made the most of it. By 1865, schools, churches, and family-owned breweries were prospering. More than a third of Columbus's population was of German descent. Many of the wealthier residents moved east, and with all the anti-German sentiment during World War I, even more German Americans left the village (and Columbus). The neighborhood subsequently fell into disrepair.

In the 1960s the German Village Society was formed to rescue this once-thriving community. Members undertook a fund-raising campaign that resulted in the largest restoration project in the country. Thoughtful renovations led to the entire neighborhood—all 233 acres—being placed on the National Register of Historic Places; it remains the largest privately funded historic district on the register and in the country.

The heritage and culture of the German immigrants who fashioned this neighborhood have been preserved in a few restaurants and German music choirs and organizations that uphold traditions like Oktoberfest, but that's about it. Yes, the street names are good and guttural, but flip through the German Village directories and you won't come across many Deutsch names. As for cuisine, you'll probably find more pasta and burgers than you will brats and sauerkraut balls. I am respectful, but unapologetic, when I say German Village isn't authentically German.

The demographics are predictable for such a popular (trendy) area. A majority of German Village residents are white professionals between the ages of 25 and 65. Plus, most residents of German Village don't speak a lick of German. But who cares? It's a lovely part of town, where homes average around $550,000. It's a living museum and a tribute to our city's heritage. A visitor center is located at the German Village Meeting Haus at 588 S. Third St.

ARENA DISTRICT

www.arena-district.com

The Arena District creates the transition from downtown to the Short North and is bordered by North High Street to the east, Neil Avenue to the west, Spring Street to the south, and railroad tracks to the north. This lively part of town is a total boom-or-bust neighborhood, driven mostly by the throngs of hockey fans attending Columbus Crew, Clippers, or Blue Jackets games.

The Arena District is situated around Nationwide Arena and was planned from the very beginning, so who better than the master urban planner Daniel Burnham to provide the symbolic gateway to this district? Columbus's last remaining limestone arch from Burnham's 19th-century

Union Station now stands at the end of a landscaped park, McFerson Commons.

The Arena District is home to a few interesting restaurants and bars, several live music venues, and Huntington Park. While the Arena District has a distinct warehouse feel to it, brick alleys provide pedestrianized zones between the restaurants and pubs. This coziness is occasionally interrupted by views of the Columbus skyline—a friendly reminder you are still downtown.

Walking is the way to go if you are living or staying in this area. The Arena District is a 5-minute walk into downtown or the Short North, and an easy jaunt to Victorian Village and Goodale Park. North Bank Park along the Scioto River provides urbanites with 14 acres of green space and bike trails right at their back door.

Luxury apartments and high-rise condos are located in the Arena District. Burnham Square Condominiums and Parks Edge Condos overlook McFerson Commons, while the Arena Crossing apartments are literally a few steps away from Nationwide Arena and the North Market.

THE SHORT NORTH

www.shortnorth.org

The Short North begins just north of the Arena District and has pushed its boundaries to the edge of The Ohio State University. It runs along High Street from Goodale Avenue to the evolving "Old North" at Fifth Avenue. This artsy neighborhood is both trendy and vibrant.

After going through a complete overhaul in the 1980s, the Short North has become one of the most diverse, eclectic urban neighborhoods in Columbus. It's lined with trendy boutiques, art galleries, modern theatrical venues, and some of the best restaurants in town. Wander off onto the side streets, and you'll come upon brick town houses and clever little green spaces, called "pocket parks," tucked into unexpected places.

The community's socially conscious and creative side shows through in the variety of murals painted on buildings in the Short North. Graffiti is given a new twist at 641 N. High St. with a modern depiction of George Bellows's *Cliff Dwellers,* a social commentary on urban living. Fresh interpretations of *American Gothic* can be found at 714 N. High St., and the *Mona Lisa* watches over the neighborhood from Warren Street. *Mona Lisa* has become synonymous with the Short North and makes for a good photo op.

The Short North is known particularly for its culinary and artistic offerings and its residents for their alternative lifestyles. There is a large concentration of gay- and lesbian-owned businesses in this neighborhood. This part of town is a colorful, offbeat, entertaining arts district.

VICTORIAN VILLAGE

Victorian Village is another trendy historic district located between the OSU campus and the Arena District. Its primary road, Neil Avenue, runs all the way from the campus into downtown, making this a popular location for professors, students, and historic home lovers. Officially, the village lies to the north of Goodale Avenue, south of West Fifth Avenue, and in between North High Street and Neil Avenue.

Unlike the Short North, which is more of an arts and entertainment district, Victorian Village is truly residential. It's quite lovely to walk around, and locals can walk to several good restaurants and friendly neighborhood bars. Many of the homes are within easy walking distance of grocery stores, coffee shops, and bus stops. There's also Goodale Park, which is covered in the Parks and Recreation chapter.

Prior to 1870, this area was farmland owned by the Neil family, but as the university and city developed, Neil Avenue became one of the major thoroughfares into downtown Columbus. By 1879, Victorian Village was a thriving and growing community, but with the introduction of the automobile, residents began moving to suburbia. By 1920, the decline of this near north side community was under way. Fortunately, its architectural value was recognized, and Victorian Village was designated a historic district in 1973. Now, more than 80 percent of the neighborhood has been renovated.

Victorian Village's close proximity to the university keeps its social makeup economically, racially, and religiously diverse. The median household income is about $80,000, and more than 70 percent of residents have college degrees. In fact, 10 percent of Victorian Village residents have a graduate or doctoral degree, which makes sense since a large number of Ohio State faculty and staff live in this area.

Catering to the student population, many of the houses along Neil Avenue are split into rental units. The homes farther south of campus and off the side streets are private residences. Impressive examples of Italianate, Queen Anne, Tudor, Greek, and Gothic Revival can be found throughout the area, while the biggest and most prominent homes are situated around Goodale Park. Take some time in September to go on the Victorian Village Society's Annual Home and Garden Tour to see how beautifully these homes have been restored.

In 1851, Columbus's first physician, Dr. Lincoln Goodale, donated 40 acres to the city. Goodale Park, in Victorian Village, became the nation's first tract of land to be used as a public park.

ITALIAN VILLAGE

www.italianvillage.org

Tucked between highways, railroads, and two major thoroughfares is another historic district being developed in great ways. Italian Village is technically part of the Short North. It lies to the east of High Street and south of Fifth Avenue, picking up where OSU ends. Summit and Fourth Streets run right through the heart of Italian Village into downtown Columbus.

The housing options in Italian Village are truly "metro" in style: close together, minimal grass, and lots of pavement. They range from duplexes and row houses to town houses and new apartments. Forty percent of Italian Village homes were built in the 1950s and 1960s, and quite a few are pre-1939. After several historic homes were leveled, residents began working toward revitalization and preservation. A few parts of Italian Village are now on the National Register of Historic Places, and others are currently being considered.

The area is making slow progress, but new townhomes, lofts, and single-family units being built are drawing restaurants, bars, and retail to this side of the neighborhood.

NEIGHBORHOODS AND SUBURBS

The Ohio State University Campus

www.osu.edu

If you read only the introduction to The Ohio State University chapter, you'll realize it's a big school. The heart of campus is loosely defined as lying between Indianola Avenue to the east and Neil Avenue to the west, Lane Avenue to the north and Ninth Avenue to the south. These boundaries include the Oval with its peripheral buildings, the medical center, Ohio Stadium, and fraternity and sorority houses.

It also encompasses dormitories, off-campus housing, restaurants, bars, and shops. It's basically a concrete jungle. Like any university town, there are the nice parts and there are the not-so-nice parts, but the redevelopment of south campus has reclaimed several blocks of ramshackle buildings.

Students who attend OSU usually live in one of three places: on campus in the dorms, off campus within a few blocks of High Street, or in one of the nearby neighborhoods of Clintonville, Grandview, or the Short North. It's not difficult to envision the campus itself as a neighborhood, especially if you have tried parking on any of the side streets. The apartment buildings and rental properties situated east of High Street are exactly how one might picture student housing: porches crowded with ratty sofas, empty beer cans in the front yards, and a rowdy bunch of guys tossing a football around.

This isn't exactly a dangerous neighborhood, but it has its moments—quite often alcohol-related college stupidity. The university publishes an annual crime report so students and parents can be aware of what is happening on this diverse and energetic campus.

Clintonville

More hippie than hip, Clintonville is a laid-back residential neighborhood to which OSU professors and postgraduate students migrate. Bungalow-style houses with big porches and tree-lined streets give it a suburban feel, but Clintonville is only 4 miles north of downtown and convenient to Ohio State, the main bus lines, and two major highways.

i Locals are certain to differentiate between Clintonville and Old Beechwold proper. This wooded pocket of interesting early 20th-century homes was placed on the National Register of Historic Places in 1987.

Having been established in 1847, many of Clintonville's unusual street names are derived from the earliest settlers' names, such as Brevoort, Chase, Whetmore, and Webster. It is tucked between Arcadia Avenue and Cooke Road and is bounded on the east and west by I-71 and Highway 315. The main artery through Clintonville is High Street, and like many other parts of town, it is undergoing major redevelopment.

Clintonville is one of the first suburban neighborhoods in which you encounter true Columbus natives with families more than one generation deep. Bob Vila types will be in their glory, as more than half the homes in the community are pre-1940. There is no shortage of house projects here. Clintonville housing options are typically not for transients. Apartment complexes are few and far between, but they do exist.

While not a destination shopping or entertainment district, Clintonville has a decent number of eclectic boutiques, locally owned eateries, craft beer taprooms, and specialty stores. It does not offer the most upscale dining, but some of Columbus's more popular restaurants, like Northstar Café and Hot Chicken Takeover, are located here.

Worthington

www.experienceworthington.com

Driving directly up High Street (US 23) from downtown will put you right in the heart of one of Columbus's oldest suburbs. Worthington is located 8 miles north of the city between Highway 315 and I-71. A group of New Englanders from the Farmington River Valley in Connecticut settled the village of Worthington in 1803, the same year Ohio became a state.

The two names that are most frequently associated with Worthington are James Kilbourne, the man who purchased the property, and Thomas Worthington, the land agent who pointed him to this site and for whom the town is named. Interestingly enough, Worthington had little to do with the actual settlement of the village.

Under the leadership of Kilbourne, a New England–style village was developed around a central public square. Despite a losing bid to become the state capital, Worthington became well-known for its religious diversity, emphasis on education, and antislavery position.

Some 200 years later, the city covers more than 5 square miles and is home to 1,400 businesses, 21 different religious congregations, and a population of 14,500. Its schools are always at the top of the heap, and despite the low crime, great parks, and excellent location, most locals still seem to define Worthington by 6 square blocks known as Old Worthington, the original village.

Old Worthington lies within Morning, Evening, North, and South Streets and has all the trappings of a lovingly restored New England village: antiques shops, a village green, brick-paved walks, charming restaurants with street-side patios, and, of course, a pub or two. Many of Worthington's historic homes are in this area, and the website has a nice walking tour with points of interest.

Worthington homes average around $450,000, but various housing options exist. Ranch homes can be found in the Riverlea section of Worthington, while Cape Cod–style bungalows dot the neighborhood. Rush Creek Village, located just east of Morning Street, is a wooded pocket of ultramodern homes based on the architectural principles made famous by Frank Lloyd Wright. Worthington, though known for its colonial ambience, has a little bit of something for everyone.

Westerville

www.visitwesterville.com
Ten miles northeast of downtown Columbus is the vibrant middle-class suburb of Westerville. It is one of the few communities located outside the I-270 Outer Belt that has been included in this chapter. It is easily accessible from all parts of Columbus by I-270, I-71, and OH 3, also known as Cleveland Avenue and Westerville Road.

Westerville is an attractive place to live and work for several reasons. First and foremost, it is affordable. The city boasts one of the lowest income tax rates in the region, and the average home costs around $380,000. The area has its own electric and water division, which saves residents and businesses money. It is home to Otterbein College, Mount Carmel St. Ann's Hospital, and Polaris Fashion Place, one of Columbus's biggest malls.

Families appreciate the excellent emergency response and community and city services. There is a large police presence in the area, making this a safe, family-oriented community. Westerville is often voted the "Best Place to Raise a Family" in central Ohio by national magazines.

Despite having a population of 38,000, Westerville retains a small-town feel. This is due largely in part to the historic "uptown" built around Otterbein College. B&Bs, landmark homes, antiques shops, galleries, and storefront eateries lend Uptown Westerville (www.uptownwesterville inc.com) a certain charm. To experience this side of the city, just park your car and wander around Main Street and College Avenue.

While you're wandering, have a look at the Anti-Saloon League Museum at the Westerville Public Library. You'll quickly learn that this small suburb, established in 1809, was once an epicenter of the Prohibition movement. Even more surprising is that Uptown Westerville only lifted the booze ban in late 2004 when the Old Bag of Nails Pub was approved to sell liquor. Alcohol or not, Westerville offers visitors and residents a good selection of eating and drinking—and even better shopping.

New Albany

www.newalbanychamber.com
What comes to mind when you think of planned housing developments? Now, put that out of your head and think Georgian manors. Think country estates. Think horse farms. The community of New Albany is a series of exclusive neighborhoods, each with its own distinct qualities, but all inspired by the American colonial and English Georgian style.

New Albany was founded in 1837 and until recently was just a small farming community.

Development of this rural area began in the 1980s and is still going strong. In fact, with a current population of 11,000 and homes averaging $500,000, this suburb attracts well-educated, affluent residents with a median household income well over $206,000. Some of Columbus's best shopping and dining are just 10 minutes away at Easton Town Center, and its close proximity to the airport makes New Albany convenient for those who frequently travel.

Aside from location, there are many things that make this gentrified community so appealing, the obvious being the architectural cohesiveness among the homes, professional buildings, and schools. Every little detail has been planned, right down to the hand-molded bricks chosen for all the buildings.

Forty miles of white fencing and acres and acres of green spaces, meadows, and streams allow New Albany to retain an ambling countryside feeling while only 15 miles from downtown Columbus. Many miles of trails meander through the village and will eventually link all the neighborhoods and parks together. New Albany is home to the state-of-the-art Aquatic Center and a beautiful country club with a 27-hole championship golf course designed by Jack Nicklaus. Retail boutiques, professional offices, and a branch of the Columbus Metropolitan Library are clustered around Market Square, which looks like an old town square.

While many Columbus natives aspire to live in New Albany, corporate relocation brings a large number of executives in (and out) of this community. One of the biggest draws is the school system. The New Albany–Plain public school district might be one of the fastest growing in Ohio, but its outstanding programs and beautiful campus rival that of any fine private school.

Most of the homes are detached, but new condominiums, apartments, townhomes, and even retirement communities are being developed in the surrounding area. Several real estate agencies represent homes within a 5-mile radius of New Albany, but New Albany Realty has been the community's premier brokerage from the very beginning.

Gahanna

www.visitgahanna.com

Gahanna is located 8 miles northeast of downtown Columbus and only 5 minutes from John Glenn International Airport. It offers easy access to I-270, I-70, and I-670. The main thoroughfare through Gahanna is US 62, also known as Granville Street.

Gahanna was founded in 1849 along Big Walnut Creek, and its name is derived from an Indian word meaning "three creeks joining into one." You will find reference to this on the City of Gahanna's official seal, which reads "Three in One" and depicts the confluence of three creeks.

Olde Gahanna is currently the site of urban redevelopment that uses the natural waterway as a focal point for downtown activity and business. The polluted creek was cleaned up, and a waterfall and river boardwalk were added. The 5-acre park is now a great place for picnics and fishing, and hosts many festivals and annual events.

The restored old town features antiques and collectible shops, restaurants, and pubs. The businesses along Mill and Granville Streets were given a face-lift, while a few decks and patios helped pedestrianize the area. The Gahanna Historical Society offers a 1-mile walking tour of the town's 16 historic landmarks, which include a log house, two historic churches, and several historic homes.

Olde Gahanna is quaint, but it's just a small part of the overall city. Currently home to more than 35,000 people, Gahanna has a low crime rate and is one of the more diverse suburbs in central Ohio. Homes average around $360,000, making this an affordable and very family-oriented neighborhood.

With more than 750 acres of parkland, Gahanna has more park space per capita than anywhere else in central Ohio. Bikeways and nature

ℹ In 1972 Gahanna was named the "Herb Capital of America" and subsequently established the Ohio Herb Education Center, at which gardening classes and cooking and craft demonstrations are available. Visit www.ohioherbcenter.org for more information.

paths run throughout the community, and there are a number of excellent golf courses located in the vicinity.

Whitehall

www.whitehall-oh.us

Six miles east of downtown Columbus, tucked between Gahanna and Bexley, is the urban community of Whitehall. This small municipality was designated a village in 1947 and a city in 1950. It was named for a local landmark, the White Hall Tavern.

The heart of Whitehall is around East Broad Street and Hamilton Road, but, unfortunately, this section of town can be a little rough at times. Statistics have shown that its property and violent crime levels are higher than Ohio's average, but Whitehall seems to get a far worse rap than it deserves. The residents of this community take a lot of pride in their city and are doing what they can to make it a better place.

Whitehall homes average around $183,000, and while many of them were built in the 1950s, several housing options do exist. Just drive along East Broad Street and you'll find apartment complexes and town houses in between the shopping centers and strip malls; you'll also find a lot of low-income housing in this part of town.

Whitehall's median household income is around $57,000, and it has a population of 20,000 that is a diverse mix of white, African or African American, Hispanic, Asian, and other races. Because of this diverse population, Whitehall has some of the most authentic ethnic eateries in town. Wander over to these parts for some Vietnamese or Ethiopian cuisine—you won't be disappointed.

Bexley

www.bexley.org

Whether you drive east out of Columbus on Broad or Main Streets, you will eventually enter the "old money" city of Bexley, and quite frankly, all 2.5 square miles of it is beautiful. A small population of 20,000, outstanding schools, and excellent city services make this one of the most desirable (and expensive) parts of the city to live in.

This quiet, dignified community is bordered by Alum Creek on the west, Livingston Avenue on the south, Chelsea Avenue on the east, and Delmar Avenue on the north. It is situated 4 miles east of downtown, and trust me when I say you'll know when you've entered Bexley and you'll know when you've exited it.

Urbanization of this area began around 1876 when Capital University moved from Goodale Park to its current location on Main Street. In 1905, several prominent families made an exodus from Columbus and built magnificent mansions in this new suburb. Bexley became a village in 1908, but not without having to wrestle with Columbus for that status. Bexley formally became the City of Bexley in 1932.

The prices of homes vary dramatically, between $100,000 and upward of a million dollars, with the average being around $500,000. Starter homes are located on beautiful tree-lined streets south of East Main Street, some of which can be quite large but are dwarfed in comparison to many of the Bexley estates. Multimillion-dollar mansions are concentrated north of Broad Street. Even if you can't afford to buy one, take a drive through the area just to appreciate the neighborhood.

Families move here for the school system. Bexley's public schools are exceptional, and three of Columbus's best private schools are located here. The fact that 90 percent of Bexley high school graduates pursue some sort of higher education says a lot. The library, parks, and proximity to hospitals and major highways also add to Bexley's appeal.

While most of the city is residential, East Main Street (www.bexleymain.com) contains a small business district, with restaurants, professional services, a great bookstore, and loads of galleries and boutiques. It is within walking distance of most residents. Despite being surrounded by some of Columbus's most run-down streets, Bexley remains safe and relatively self-contained. It is truly a one-of-a-kind neighborhood.

RELOCATION

Hilliard

www.hilliardohio.gov

Geographically situated outside I-270, between Big Darby Creek and the Scioto River, is the suburb of Hilliard. Originally settled by John Reed Hilliard in the 1850s, Hilliard's Station grew around the rail station. Main Street remained the center of town until the 1960s, when rail service ceased and the completion of the Outer Belt shifted the city's focus to newer residential subdivisions and commercial development.

Hilliard covers 15 square miles and is home to approximately 40,000 very diverse people. The housing options vary dramatically, from small starter homes to elegant stone houses, costing anywhere from $100,000 to $1 million, the average being $380,000.

Depending on where one lives, you could be very close to the west side of Columbus or very close to Dublin; you could be near the railroad tracks or nestled along the banks of the Scioto River. If you don't like what you see, drive a few miles, and there will be a complete change of scenery, but no matter where you live in Hilliard, it is only 13 miles from downtown Columbus and 18 miles from the airport.

Aside from location, Hilliard can boast one of the healthiest tax bases in the city, as 40 percent of its tax revenue comes from businesses. This translates to an ever-developing city. It also means there are a lot of strip malls and shopping centers on this side of town.

In the past few years, Hilliard has become one of the fastest-growing suburbs, primarily due to its good public schools. Hilliard is the 10th-largest school district in the state and is reputable both academically and athletically. The city has dozens of churches and an abundance of social and civic organizations, 25 parks, and a state-of-the-art community and wellness center opening in 2025. The revitalization of Old Hilliard has helped the city retain a small-town feel amid the sprawl of suburban development.

Grandview Heights

www.grandviewheights.org

Locals tend to shorten this small suburb's name to Grandview. Its location just west of The Ohio State University and less than 3 miles from downtown Columbus makes it one of the more popular urban neighborhoods for young professionals and students.

Grandview Heights was once part of the neighboring Village of Marble Cliff but became its own separate entity in 1906. Annexations expanded the city to its present-day boundaries, which are defined by Cambridge Boulevard to the west and the Olentangy River to the east. The northern boundary is around King Avenue, while the southern edge runs along Goodale Boulevard.

The homes in this predominantly residential neighborhood average $525,000. Grandview's population of 8,200 is a healthy mix of singles and families, professionals and students, with a median age of 37. It is a safe community with good public schools, pretty churches, and a deep sense of community and history.

The most popular aspect of Grandview for nonresidents is its downtown commercial area. While not as artsy as the Short North, it offers a good amount of eating and drinking in a concentrated area. Several trendy restaurants, bars, and retail shops line Grandview Avenue, while others straggle out along First, Third, and Fifth Avenues. Grandview is also home to popular Grandview Theater and Draft House with a full bar and food menu. It's a great part of town to go on a date or people-watch from a sidewalk patio. Grandview Heights is a classic community that has, luckily, remained unspoiled for the past century.

Marble Cliff

www.marblecliff.org

Consisting of only 175 acres and fewer than 700 residents, this tiny village is one of three "bedroom communities" that make up the Tri-Village area. Marble Cliff is tucked between the other two, Grandview Heights and Upper Arlington.

It was settled in 1890 and incorporated as the Village of Marble Cliff in 1901 (then including Grandview Heights). It detached from Grandview in 1902 and has remained its own picturesque neighborhood ever since. With only a handful of tree-lined streets, Marble Cliff is lovely, wooded, and private. One would never suspect it is less than 3 miles from downtown Columbus.

Marble Cliff residents have access to the Grandview Heights swimming pool and are allowed to participate in Grandview recreation programs at residential rates. Dogs are not permitted in Marble Cliff parks, and it's a dry community. The website for Grandview Heights Marble Cliff Historical Society (www.ghmchs.org) provides an interesting virtual walking tour of sights that may or may not still exist in this area.

Upper Arlington

www.upperarlingtonoh.gov

This bedroom community is one of the oldest and most prestigious suburbs of Columbus. It was established in 1913 by Ben and King Thompson as an idealistic country club district and was incorporated in 1918. Neighboring Marble Cliff was, at the time, named Arlington, so the area north of Fifth Avenue became Upper Arlington.

The original 840-acre village was developed (south of Lane Avenue) using the distinctive Pitkin Plan, which is seen to this day in the wide, curving, tree-lined streets and balanced layout of municipal, educational, retail, and residential buildings. The plan was tweaked in the 1920s to include the Mallway business district, and, after substantial population growth, Upper Arlington became a city in 1941. In 1985, the Upper Arlington Historic District was placed on the National Register of Historic Places. Over the years, Upper Arlington grew to encompass almost 10 square miles. Its current boundaries stretch from Riverside Drive (US 33) in the west to Kenny Road in the east, Fifth Avenue in the south to Henderson Road in the north. It is convenient to most of the city's major highways and two hospitals, and is literally a stone's throw away from The Ohio State University.

You'll also find medium-size shopping centers, small plazas, exclusive boutiques, and fine restaurants throughout the predominantly residential neighborhood. Though adjacent to the university, traditional student housing is not common in Upper Arlington. A majority of the homes in this neighborhood are private residences, but condos and town houses are being built along Lane Avenue and Tremont as the city develops.

The cost of Arlington homes ranges from $200,000 to multimillion, but don't expect to find many at the lower end. The average home costs $550,000. It is also well-known that Arlington has one of the largest higher-priced markets with homes over $500,000.

South of Lane Avenue is where to find the most dramatic stone houses, many of which are landmark buildings and all of which are expensive. South of Lane is where most of the oldest homes are situated. As you venture north along Tremont, Redding, and Reed Roads, the homes will vary in style, from two-story colonials and Tudors to Cape Cods and ranch style. There is, however, so much more to Upper Arlington than beautifully maintained homes and well-tended lawns.

It is a family-oriented community with several public swimming pools, 180 acres of parks (dogs are allowed!), tennis and pickleball courts, and excellent city services. It is extremely safe and has one of the highest-performing school systems in Ohio. Upper Arlington puts a strong emphasis on developing an already highly esteemed school system, and the proof is in the pudding. Ninety-five percent of UA high school graduates pursue higher education.

UA, as it is referred to, has a population of around 36,000. The residents' deep sense of community is reflected in the strong civic association and numerous volunteer, cultural, and recreational organizations. The city puts on a very reputable Labor Day Arts Festival, but its biggest community celebration is the Fourth of July parade and fireworks. From the very beginning, Upper Arlington has been fortunate enough to have people who care tremendously about the community—and it shows.

Dublin

www.dublinohiousa.gov

With a population topping 49,000, Dublin remains one of Columbus's fastest-growing suburbs. An average household income close to $150,000 and homes ranging $250,000 to $1 million (averaging about $479,000) make it one of the more prestigious neighborhoods as well. It is located 20 minutes northwest of downtown and is easily accessible by US 33 and I-270.

What we currently refer to as Historic Dublin was originally platted as Sells Mills by John Sells in 1810 and renamed Dublin by an Irish surveyor in 1815. Dublin was incorporated in 1881. It remained a rural village with a population of only 681 until the completion of the I-270 Outer Belt, after which people flocked to this new suburb in droves. An influx of big businesses transformed farmland into a suburban commercial center.

The development of the prestigious Muirfield Golf Club and its surrounding subdivisions put Dublin on the map as one of the Midwest's premier golf and residential communities. Muirfield Village is quintessential suburbia: big homes on quiet cul-de-sacs, golf course views, excellent recreational facilities, and private lakes. The annual Memorial Tournament draws the biggest names in golf to Columbus once a year.

Tourism has become one of the major underpinnings of Dublin's local economy. Its significant Irish heritage and charming historic district attract a lot of attention. The annual Irish Festival and St. Patrick's Day Parade draw more than 100,000 people to Dublin, while Columbus's most popular attractions, the Columbus Zoo and Zoombezi Bay Water Park, are both just a few minutes' drive north.

Historic Old Dublin is situated around the intersection of Bridge Street (OH 161 West) and High Street (not US 23). As one of central Ohio's oldest communities, it has more than 30 landmark buildings, many of which house pubs, restaurants, shops, and galleries. This a perfect place to stroll the brick-paved streets and cross the pedestrian bridge to the newest Bridge Park development.

The city is well-known for its excellent park system with 1,100 acres of developed parkland, world-class golf courses, shopping malls, and ·

i Two famous Jacks call Dublin home: golf legend Jack Nicklaus and "Jungle Jack" Hanna, television personality and director emeritus of the Columbus Zoo.

i The main post office for the city of Columbus is located at 850 Twin Rivers Dr. and can be reached at (614) 469-4516. To find the post office closest to your community, look it up online at www.usps.com.

extensive community programming. The Dublin City school system has a reputation for superior academics. Its rapid growth necessitated the opening of a third high school, but size has not detracted from the quality of education, as more than 85 percent of Dublin graduates move on to a four-year institution.

Now covering more than 25 square miles around the Scioto River, Dublin is one of the best-known suburbs in Columbus and one of the most progressive communities in central Ohio.

THE OUTSKIRTS

To the east of Columbus, outside the I-270 beltway, are the cities of Reynoldsburg (www.visitreynoldsburg.com) and Pickerington (www.ci.pickerington.oh.us). Both were settled in the early 1800s and remained rural communities into the 20th century.

Naturally, Reynoldsburg was developed first because it is closer to the city. It has a decent number of shopping centers, strip malls, and several parks. Pickerington is a bit farther east and remains a distinctively rural community. Both areas have a variety of housing developments, affordable golf course communities, and large but decent school districts. In between the two is the small suburb of Blacklick, with several new developments and homes averaging $300,000.

Grove City (www.visitgrovecityoh.com) is located 6 miles southwest of Columbus's Outer Belt and is a quiet little suburb with a population of 41,000 and homes averaging $300,000. It is considered the Southern Gateway into Columbus and is typical small-town America, with affordable family homes, low taxes, and relatively low crime. Grove City has been around for over 150 years, and its town center has been redeveloped to include specialty shops, pubs, restaurants, and a great farmers' market.

To the north of Columbus, the sprawling Delaware County community of Powell is growing exponentially. Homes vary from $200,000 to well over $1 million. It is a bit of a trek out of the city, but there are several nice independently owned farm-to-table restaurants, boutiques, and bistros.

Libraries

Bexley Library
2411 E. Main St.
(614) 231-2793
www.bexlib.org

The Bexley Library has been at its current location since 1929 and has undergone several expansions and renovations. Anyone who resides, attends school, or is employed within Franklin County may obtain a library card. Cardholders have access to a collection of 300,000 items, including 65,000 audiovisual items. Workstations and walk-in internet service are available free of charge. A 24-hour drive-up repository is provided for convenient return of materials.

Grandview Heights Library
1685 W. First Ave.
(614) 486-2951
www.ghpl.org

If this small, friendly neighborhood library doesn't have what you are looking for, staffers can probably track it down through the Central Ohio Library Consortium. Between the seven libraries, five branches, and two bookmobiles, you'll have more than 450,000 titles and a million holdings to choose from. There is no limit to the number of items you can borrow from the library. Computers are available to surf the internet, and a quiet room is available for serious work. The Grandview Heights Library has been in this same building since 1923.

Upper Arlington Library
2800 Tremont Rd.
(614) 486-9621
www.ualibrary.org

Once again, Columbus libraries are doing great things. Hennen's American Public Library Ratings ranked the Upper Arlington Public Library among the nation's best public libraries serving a community of its size (25,000–49,999). The UAPL system includes the main library and two small branches at Lane Road and Miller Park.

There are lots of things that set this library apart from others. Aside from the primary collection of 450,000 items, the library houses special collections of works by local authors, the Older Adults Collection, the Ohio Reference Room, and an impressive media services department. The children's area is equipped with computers, plenty of tables, and a play space.

Patrons can use the library's PC and Mac computers free of charge. If one of the internet workstations is not available on the ground level, try going downstairs, where there are a few dozen. If you bring your own laptop, free plug-in data ports and wireless internet are also available in the reference department. Your library card gives remote access to online reference databases and homework tutors and the ability to reserve books via the website.

In keeping with the city's deep sense of community, the library's Outreach Service will deliver books to homebound residents, care centers, senior residences, and children's day-care centers. Adult and youth classes, author lectures, and book clubs are just a few of the library's year-round offerings.

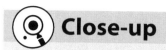

Columbus Metropolitan Library

The Columbus Metropolitan Library (CML) is often ranked first among the nation's public libraries serving a population of more than 875,000 and with nearly 1.5 million holdings. Among other things, this ranking is based on circulation and the number of volumes owned.

The CML system includes the downtown main library, 22 branches, and an Outreach Services Division, and jointly operates the Northwest Library with the Worthington Public Library. Holding a library card from any one of the libraries in the system allows you to borrow from any branch, return to and request items from any branch, and reserve books online.

The multistory main library houses a diverse collection of three million books, periodicals, maps, CDs, audio- and videotapes, and more. The variety of videos and DVDs available to borrow rivals Blockbusters. A coffee shop and gift shop are located on the ground level of the main library. Branches are located in just about every neighborhood, though the Bexley, Grandview, and Upper Arlington libraries are not part of the city system. They operate their own independent libraries, which are discussed at the end of the chapter.

Libraries are becoming much more than just a book-lending service. Having entered the information age, there is now a huge focus on electronic resources. On the most fundamental level, the library catalogs are now digitized and available online. No more manually searching through drawers of index cards! Self-check kiosks allow you to scan your card and check out the items you are borrowing.

Library users have access to other online services, including downloadable audio and e-books.

The depth and breadth of Columbus's library services are staggering and vary from branch to branch. Many of the libraries offer programs for toddlers, large-print books for seniors, and multilingual books and services for the growing non-English-speaking population. The main library and a few branches provide Homework Help programs for children in the Columbus school system. They also have outreach programs that will deliver books to nursing homes, hospitals, and private residences.

All these services mean growth, and all this growth means it takes a lot more money to run a library than it used to. The state of Ohio's funding is gradually shrinking. Thankfully, Columbus residents recognize the new role of the libraries and understand the need for these institutions in supplementing and supporting the community. This is why library levies do well at the polls with all age groups.

The Columbus Metropolitan Main Library (614-645-2275; www.columbuslibrary.org) is located downtown at 96 S. Grant Ave. The classic Vermont marble-and-granite building was constructed in 1904 through a gift from Andrew Carnegie, the father of public libraries.

Columbus Metropolitan Main Library
Rycus Associates

EDUCATION

Education was among the first institutions dealt with when Ohio became a state. Two hundred years later, many are left to wonder where it ranks next to new arenas, stadiums, highways, and shopping malls. It's no big secret that, not so long ago, Ohio was at the bottom of the barrel when it came to the quality of public school education.

Ohio public schools are funded largely by local property taxes, which in Columbus's case vary drastically across the city, as does the caliber of education students receive. Like any big city, some of the schools are very wealthy and capable of providing the best educations, while others leave a lot to be desired.

The city has tried shifting the demographics around by busing students to other schools, starting charter schools, and allocating tuition vouchers to low-income students so they can attend their school of choice, but change isn't happening on the scale that it needs to. Lobbyists and politicians have been working for years to bring about reform through budget and constitutional amendments, anticipating the day low-income, urban school districts gain equal footing with the wealthier suburban districts.

Ohio, in general, has shown steady improvement in many areas. Several urban, low-income school districts have moved out of academic emergency, sixth graders are reading better, and 89 percent of Ohio's schools earned overall grades of excellent, effective, or continuous improvement. But how does Columbus fare when compared with the rest of Ohio? In 2022, Ohio's state school system started using a star rating instead of a traditional A–F letter grade, with a maximum being five stars, to measure a school district in five categories: achievement, progress, gap closing, early literacy, and graduation. In recent years, the Columbus City School District has declined in enrollment, its graduation rate is 79.6 percent (lower than the state average of 87 percent), but previous chronic absenteeism is getting a little better. CCS received two stars overall for the year, but is focused on improving performance and addressing attendance and disparities.

The 2022–2023 report cards for Bexley, Dublin, Hilliard, New Albany, Olentangy, Upper Arlington, and Worthington public schools each scored between 4.5 and 5 stars across all standards.

PUBLIC SCHOOLS

The Columbus City School District contains 113 schools and around 46,000 students. South-Western City Schools is the second-largest public school district in Franklin Country, drawing on a large section of southwestern Columbus. Covering a sprawling geographic area, Olentangy, Dublin, and Hilliard school districts have multiple high schools and middle schools. Nearly every sport is represented in the high schools around Columbus, and there is an unending parade of athletes bringing home state championships on a regular basis. The following is a list of the public school districts around greater Columbus with their current 2023 report card rating by the State of Ohio's Department of Education.

Bexley City School District 5*
348 S. Cassingham Rd.
(614) 231-7611
www.bexleyschools.org

Columbus City Schools 2*
270 E. State St.
(614) 365-5000
www.ccsoh.us

Dublin City Schools 4.5*
7030 Coffman Rd.
(614) 764-5913
www.dublinschools.net

Gahanna-Jefferson Schools 4*
160 S. Hamilton Rd.
(614) 471-7065
www.gahannaschools.org

Grandview Heights City Schools 5*
1587 Third Ave.
(614) 481-3600
www.ghschools.org

Hilliard City School District 4.5*
5323 Cemetery Rd.
(614) 771-4273
www.hilliardschools.org

New Albany–Plain Local School District 5*
99 W. Main St.
(614) 855-2040
www.napls.us

Olentangy Local School District 5*
7840 Graphics Way, Lewis Center
(740) 657-4050
www.olentangy.k12.us

South-Western City Schools 3.5*
3805 Marlane Dr., Grove City
(614) 801-3000
www.swcsd.us

Upper Arlington City School District 5*
1950 Mallway N.
(614) 487-5000
www.uaschools.org

Westerville City School District 4*
936 Eastwind Dr., Westerville
(614) 797-5700
www.westerville.k12.oh.us

Worthington City Schools 4.5*
200 E. Wilson Bridge Rd.
(614) 883-3000
www.worthington.k12.oh.us

ALTERNATIVE PUBLIC EDUCATION

The Columbus Public Schools district has 21 alternative elementary schools, 4 alternative middle schools, 4 alternative high schools, and 2 kindergarten-through-eighth-grade schools. Alternative schools differ from traditional public schools in how the subjects are taught or in the focus of the instruction. Some schools engage students in their education by giving them higher levels of responsibility or by having students apply what they have learned in "real-world" settings.

The French immersion school Ecole Kenwood (614-365-5502) and the Columbus Spanish Immersion Academy (614-365-8129) are both tuition-free schools within the Columbus Public Schools district. Admission is by lottery. Children fortunate enough to be chosen won't just learn a foreign language, they will be taught in French or Spanish until the eighth grade, making them truly bilingual by the time they get into high school.

Also part of the Columbus Public School system are two Africentric Alternative Schools that provide an African-centered education using traditional and cultural guidelines, holistic perspectives, Kemetic principles, and historical knowledge as guiding tenets for teaching and learning. The elementary school (614-365-6517) with grades K–5 and the secondary school (614-365-8675) with grades 6–12 are both located at 300 E. Livingston Ave. The secondary school has an early college program that allows students to gain 45 to 90 hours of college credit. Admission to these schools is by lottery.

The Columbus Alternative High School at 2632 McGuffey Rd. (614-365-6006; www.cahs.info) was recognized as one of 200 outstanding high schools in the nation by the US Department of Education. It was also named an International Baccalaureate School, where students who fulfill program requirements can earn advanced credits for college.

Other school districts have their own alternative schools. Linworth Alternative Program

(614-883-3700) is an option for high school students in the Worthington City Schools but is not a separately chartered program, while Wickliffe Alternative (614-487-5150) is part of the Upper Arlington district.

PRIVATE SCHOOLS

Columbus has 30 private and non-Catholic parochial schools. Most of them charge some sort of tuition, have very small classes, and provide a broader and more balanced cultural and ethnic diversity than many of the public schools. There are 24 Catholic elementary schools and 5 high schools. To find out more information about Catholic education in Columbus, contact the diocese's Department of Education at (614) 221-5829. Following is a list of the direct contact numbers and websites for the private high schools only:

Catholic High Schools

Bishop Hartley
1285 Zettler Rd.
(614) 237-5421
www.bishop-hartley.org

Bishop Ready
707 Salisbury Rd.
(614) 276-5263
www.brhs.org

Bishop Watterson
99 E. Cooke Rd.
(614) 268-8671
www.bishopwatterson.com

St. Charles Preparatory School
2010 E. Broad St.
(614) 252-6714
www.stcharlesprep.org

St. Francis DeSales
4212 Karl Rd.
(614) 267-7808
www.sfdstallions.org

Other Private Schools

Columbus Academy
4300 Cherry Bottom Rd., Gahanna
(614) 475-2311
www.columbusacademy.org

Columbus School for Girls
56 S. Columbia, Bexley
(614) 252-0781
www.columbusschoolforgirls.org

Columbus Torah Academy
181 Noe Bixby Rd.
(614) 864-0299
www.torahacademy.org

Montessori schools
Various locations
www.montessori.org

Sunrise Academy
5657 Scioto Darby Rd., Hilliard
(614) 527-0465
www.sunriseacademy.net

Wellington School
3650 Reed Rd., Upper Arlington
(614) 457-7883
www.wellington.org

Worthington Christian Schools
6670 Worthington Galena Rd., Worthington
(614) 431-8210
www.worthingtonchristian.com

HIGHER EDUCATION

The Ohio State University isn't the only academic game in town. There are 16 universities in the Columbus metropolitan area, not to mention vocational and technical schools. The Ohio Department of Education can also help you find a postsecondary school suited to your needs.

Colleges and Universities

Capital University
1 College and Main, Bexley
(614) 236-6011, (866) 544-6175
www.capital.edu
Capital University was founded by the Lutheran Church in 1830 and is one of the largest Lutheran-affiliated universities in North America. This liberal arts school is known primarily for its conservatory of music, law school, and Center for Professional Development, which offers working professionals the opportunity to further their education. CU's 4,000 students can choose from 50 undergraduate majors and 8 graduate degrees in 6 schools of study. Students can get involved in a variety of campus organizations or become a Capital Crusader in 18 different athletic programs. A new Center for Lifelong Learning provides affordable undergraduate education to adult students in centers throughout Columbus.

Columbus College of Art and Design
107 N. Ninth St.
(614) 224-9101
www.ccad.edu
CCAD is one of the oldest and largest private art colleges in the US. It recently celebrated its 126th anniversary and is a recognized leader in visual arts education. More than 1,300 national and international students are enrolled in four-year programs of study resulting in a bachelor of fine arts degree in one of the seven majors. Students study everything from advertising and fashion design to traditional fine arts and industrial design. Students of photography, digital imaging, and film are also right at home at CCAD. Liberal arts courses are integrated into the curriculum to provide a well-rounded education. CCAD is a great place for the general public to attend special events and art exhibitions or to meet many up-and-coming artists.

Columbus State Community College
550 E. Spring St.
(614) 287-5333, (800) 621-6407
www.cscc.edu
Columbus State is the city's only community college, and the main campus is conveniently located downtown. Students can attend classes on a full- or part-time basis while working toward a career or technical degree in more than 40 fields. Many graduates receive an associate's degree in applied science or technical studies and go directly into the workforce. Others choose to transfer their credits to a four-year institution and continue on for a bachelor's degree. Community college is a great way to explore your options if you aren't sure what you want to study or to get the fundamental classes out of the way at a much cheaper rate than a four-year college. CSCC has about a dozen additional campuses, but those closest to Columbus are located in Dublin, Delaware, Gahanna, and Westerville.

Denison University
100 South Rd., Granville
(800) DENISON (336-4766)
www.denison.edu
This posh little school is situated on 1,200 rolling acres 20 minutes east of Columbus. Located in the charming village of Granville, it has close to 2,000 students. The Ohio Baptist Society founded Denison in 1831 as a theological institution for men only, but shortly after it became a private coeducational university and has since earned a reputation as one of the top 50 liberal arts colleges in the country. According to *U.S. News and World Report*'s annual rankings, Denison placed 50th among 217 schools.

Denison offers only undergraduate programs, and admission is extremely competitive. Its small student body, along with an 11:1 student-to-teacher ratio, allows for very personalized education. Students have more than 45 majors to choose from and a variety of clubs; Greek life, religious groups, student government, and multicultural events enhance campus life. Big Red athletics makes 11 varsity sports available to both men and women. Denison's excellent academic programs and New England–style campus don't come cheap.

Franklin University
201 S. Grant Ave.
(614) 797-4700, (877) 341-6300
www.franklin.edu

Franklin University originally focused on prelaw and law school but now offers 15 business-related undergraduate majors and 3 master's degree programs. Though 9,600 students are enrolled, the class size only averages about 18 students. Franklin is a good choice if you are a working professional wanting to continue school. It has concentrated on adult education by expanding night course offerings and giving "life experience" credit to mature students.

Franklin is conveniently located on 14 acres in the heart of downtown Columbus and has two additional suburban campuses in Dublin and Westerville. Franklin has one of the largest MBA programs in central Ohio, which can be completed at any of the three campuses or online via the Virtual Campus. Franklin University was one of the original 29 institutions selected by the US Army to deliver online education to eligible enlisted soldiers.

Muskingum College
163 Stormont St., New Concord
(740) 826-8211
www.muskingum.edu

Located an hour east of Columbus and founded in 1837 by a group of Scotch-Irish citizens in New Concord, Muskingum, meaning "a town by the river," retains its original affiliation with the Presbyterian Church. The college's 1,584 students can attain a bachelor's degree in more than 42 majors, while graduate students can earn a master's degree in education, teaching, or information strategy, systems, and technology. The school's low student-to-teacher ratio and solid curriculum, combined with a very low cost (as private colleges go), ensures Muskingum graduates an exceptional education at an exceptional value. Student life consists of more than 90 clubs and organizations, 6 sororities, 5 fraternities, and 17 men's and women's collegiate sports teams. The most famous Muskies include astronaut and former Ohio senator John Glenn, his wife Annie Castor Glenn, and the Columbus Zoo's beloved Jack Hanna.

Ohio Dominican University
1216 Sunbury Rd.
(800) 955-OHIO (6446)
www.ohiodominican.edu

Ohio Dominican University is a four-year, coeducational liberal arts college, founded in 1911 as an all-women's college. It became a university in 1968 and retains its Catholic and Dominican tradition. The university has approximately 3,000 students and is located in a residential suburb of Columbus. Ohio Dominican offers undergraduate degrees in 50 majors as well as 5 graduate degree programs. Students can participate in seven intercollegiate sports teams and a number of campus organizations, ministry, and outreach groups.

Ohio Wesleyan University
61 S. Sandusky St., Delaware
(740) 368-2000
www.owu.edu

Ohio Wesleyan was founded in 1842 by the Methodist Church to educate missionaries. It is now a private, coeducational liberal arts college associated with the Methodist Church only on paper. Its high selectivity and rigorous curriculum rank it among the best liberal arts colleges in the nation. OWU is nationally known for its blend of scholarship, teaching, and service. Graduates are no longer serving abroad as missionaries, but the university has been recognized for its extraordinary number of alumni who have served in the Peace Corps and are active in volunteer work within their communities.

The campus is located 20 minutes north of Columbus in Delaware, and the facilities range from 19th-century landmark buildings to state-of-the-art science centers and labs. Around 1,800 students are enrolled, half of whom come from Ohio. The school has more than 85 student organizations and 19 fraternities and sororities, and the Battling Bishops compete in a whole gamut of intercollegiate sports. The women's and men's soccer teams are the most recent teams to earn national titles.

Otterbein College
One Otterbein College, Westerville
(614) 890-3000
www.otterbein.edu

Founded in 1847, Otterbein was the first educational institution founded by the Church of the United Brethren in Christ, which later joined with the Methodist Church to form the United Methodist denomination. It was the first college to admit women without restrictions on what they could study, the first to include women on its faculty, and one of the first colleges to admit students of color.

This liberal arts school has about 3,100 students, and its program balances a classical liberal arts education with practical training, so it's no wonder *U.S. News and World Report*'s 2008 Guide to America's Best Colleges ranks Otterbein ninth among the Midwest's comprehensive colleges. It offers 49 undergraduate majors and can boast a 12:1 student-to-faculty ratio, but it is particularly strong in the performing arts. Students can choose from 12 fraternities and sororities, a number of service clubs, and Cardinal athletics. Those looking for a small-town college but wanting access to a big city will appreciate this school's location 20 minutes north of downtown Columbus.

The Pontifical College Josephinum
7625 N. High St., Worthington
(614) 885-5585
www.pcj.edu

The Pontifical College Josephinum is an international seminary that prepares Roman Catholic priests and missionaries. It is subject directly to the Holy See and is the only pontifical seminary outside Italy. The church requires a minimum of four years of theological study to enter the priesthood. Josephinum students can choose from two tracts: the College of Liberal Arts and the School of Theology. A master's of divinity is the highest degree offered.

Wittenberg University
200 W. Ward St., Springfield
(937) 327-6231, (800) 677-7558
www.wittenberg.edu

Wittenberg is located on a rolling 100-acre campus just 45 minutes west of Columbus in Springfield, Ohio. This nationally recognized college is affiliated with the Evangelical Lutheran Church. It was established in 1845 to train Lutheran ministers, and by the turn of the 20th century arts and sciences were integrated into the curriculum. Thanks to a sizable gift from Andrew Carnegie, Wittenberg's first science hall was built in 1908.

Until recently, the school's traditional strengths have been in the liberal arts, but the sciences, management, and education are becoming more popular majors for students. WU has also developed strong interdisciplinary programs in East Asian studies and Russian area studies. With more than 50 majors, including 8 preprofessional programs, Wittenberg students are exceptionally well prepared for postgraduate education, and it shows. About 70 percent eventually pursue graduate studies.

Campus life thrives, with more than 125 student organizations, 15 fraternities and sororities, and 22 varsity teams. Thirty-six percent of the student body partakes of varsity sports, making athletics the most popular campus activity.

VOCATIONAL SCHOOL

Aveda Institute
889 Bethel Rd.
(614) 291-2421
www.avedacolumbus.com

This popular beauty school offers two programs in beauty and personal care. The 42-week cosmetology program goes well beyond the study of hair and makeup. Classes in anatomy and physiology, aromatology, and skin care are also part of the curriculum. The esthiology program, which lasts 25 weeks, teaches skin and body care and makeup training, with an emphasis on pure flower and plant essences in treatments.

HEALTH AND WELLNESS

If you're going to get sick, Columbus is a good place to do it. The greater Columbus region supports 16 hospitals with a total of more than 6,000 beds. Many of the city's hospitals are well-known regionally and nationally for offering the highest-quality care and specialty services. The past few decades has seen the merger of several hospitals into bigger health-care alliances. OhioHealth (www.ohiohealth.com) is the organization with which Grant Medical Center in downtown Columbus, Riverside Methodist Hospital in northwestern Columbus, the Dublin Methodist Hospital, and both locations of Doctors Hospital are affiliated. The network includes 10 other regional hospitals, as well as many outpatient and urgent care centers and the McConnell Heart Health Center.

Columbus's other major hospital consolidation is the Mount Carmel Health System, which has three locations throughout the metropolitan area, including St. Ann's Hospital in nearby Westerville. It too has a network of outpatient surgery centers and family practices.

Columbus Children's Hospital is the second-largest pediatric health-care institution in the country. The R. David Thomas Asthma Clinical Research Center at Children's Hospital is one of only five such research centers in the country.

The Ohio State University Wexner Medical Center is gargantuan. It contains the university's College of Medicine, College of Public Health, five hospitals, two research institutes, and a network of more than 30 community-based specialty and primary care facilities. Ohio State's three-part mission of patient care, teaching, and research makes it the only academic medical center in the area. To obtain a physician referral from The OSU Care Connection, call (614) 292-4700.

If you're looking for a pediatric or family doctor, check out the Children's Hospital website, which allows you to search for doctors by a variety of criteria.

This chapter offers a brief overview of the city's major hospitals and also provides information on some of the more interesting alternative health-care options available in Columbus, along with a few ideas for rejuvenating your mind and body.

HOSPITALS

Doctors Hospital
5100 W. Broad St.
(614) 544-1000
www.ohiohealth.com/facilities/doctors

Grant Medical Center
111 S. Grant St.
(614) 566-9000
www.ohiohealth.com/facilities/grant

James Cancer Hospital
300 W. 10th Ave.
(614) 293-5066, (800) 293-5066

The James Cancer Hospital and Solove
     Research Institute
460 W. 10th Ave., Ohio State campus
800-293-5066
www.osu.edu

Mount Carmel Health System
www.mountcarmelhealth.com

Mount Carmel Hospital, East
6001 E. Broad St., Whitehall
(614) 234-6000

Mount Carmel Hospital, West
793 W. State St.
(614) 234-5000

Mount Carmel St. Ann's
500 W. Cleveland Ave., Westerville
(614) 898-4000

Nationwide Children's Hospital
515 E. Main St.
(614) 722-2000
www.columbuschildrens.com

New Albany Surgical Hospital (NASH)
7333 Smith's Mill Rd., New Albany
(614) 775-6600
www.mountcarmelhealth.com/na

The Ohio State University Wexner Medical
   Center
410 W. 10th St.
(614) 293-5123, (800) 293-5123
www.medicalcenter.osu.edu

Ohio State's Harding Hospital
1670 Upham Dr., Ohio State campus
(614) 293-9600

Richard M. Ross Heart Hospital
452 W. 10th Ave.
(614) 293-5123

Riverside Methodist Hospital
3535 Olentangy River Rd., Upper Arlington
(614) 566-5000, (800) 837-7555
www.ohiohealth.com/facilities/riverside

The University Hospital East–OSU East
181 Taylor St., East Side
(614) 257-3000

ALTERNATIVE HEALTH CARE AND BODYWORKS CENTERS

Alternative health-care practitioners treat the body and mind on a very integrated level. This section provides information about wellness centers and therapies that offer a more holistic approach to medicine.

A good source of information is *The Wellpoint* (www.thewellpoint.com), a free quarterly publication distributed at various health stores, healing centers, and libraries in the Columbus area. It is a centralized hub for news, articles, and advertisements related to holistic and alternative medicine in central Ohio. The Holistic Health Network (www.holisticnetwork.org) maintains a national, up-to-date listing of practitioners of alternative therapies.

Alternative Health Retreat
10225 Sawmill Pkwy., Powell
(614) 792-9295
www.alternativehealthretreat.com
Whole body therapies leading to a more balanced life and gut are offered at this holistic health center. Services range from colon hydrotherapy, cryotherapy, and IV therapy to infrared sauna, kinesiotaping, and NormaTec compression, as well as a variety of massages and cupping.

American Institute of Alternative Medicine
6685 Doubletree Ave., Worthington
(614) 825-6278
www.aiam.edu
Functioning as both a training center and clinic, the AIAM began as a massage school but has grown to teach acupuncture and *tui na*, a form of Oriental massage using soft-tissue manipulation techniques and acupressure points. The student clinic provides discounted massages, while professional massage and acupuncture are also available.

Being in Movement
3003 Silver Dr., Clintonville
(614) 263-1111, (614) 262-3355
www.being-in-movement.com
One can develop better breathing, body alignment, muscle tone, and flow of energy through the shape and quality of one's movements. This center offers a variety of body and movement awareness training, including the nonviolent martial art of aikido and three movement disciplines. Classes are available for adults and children

Clintonville Therapeutic Massage
3620 N. High St., Clintonville
(614) 558-8383
www.clintonvilletherapeutic.com
Clintonville Therapeutic Massage treats both your mind and body through traditional and cranial osteopathy, medical acupuncture, therapeutic medical massage, Reiki, and movement therapy using the Feldenkrais Method. These practitioners take a more multidimensional/multipractitioner approach to healing.

Healing Environments with Feng Shui
1373 E. Main St., Columbus
(614) 258-3299
www.healing-environments.com
One can derive healing environments by using the feng shui practices of balance and harmony. Reputable local feng shui master Sylvia Watson can provide consultations for your home, office, and gardens. She teaches workshops at various learning centers and presents at expos and conferences.

Inner Connections Holistic Center
1196 Neil Ave., near OSU
(614) 299-7638
www.innerconnect.biz
Inner Connections provides both familiar alternative bodywork, such as sports, pregnancy, and infant massage, and lesser-known forms of massage, like craniosacral therapy and polarity therapy, which integrate acupressure, reflexology, and meditation into massage sessions.

Wellness Works
4488 Mobile Dr.
(614) 329-0165
www.healthchanges.com
This holistic health and education center provides homeopathic and naturopathic health care. Among the massage offerings are therapeutic massage, Thai massage, and Reiki. Other therapeutic offerings include reflexology, hypnotherapy, and craniosacral therapy. Couples massage, yoga, and health-related classes are on the calendar.

COLUMBUS THE BEAUTIFUL
Salons and Day Spas

Charles Penzone
1356 Cherry Way Dr., Gahanna
(614) 418-5350
www.charlespenzone.com

Kenneth's Hair Salons and Day Spas
3134 Kingsdale Center, Upper Arlington
(614) 538-5800
www.kenneths.com
There are nine Kenneth's locations, including salons in Hilliard, New Albany, Westerville, and Dublin.

Open Sky Day Spa
1124 Goodale Blvd., Grandview
(614) 486-4520
www.openskydayspa.com

Panacea Luxury Spa
2130 Quarry Trails Dr., Upper Arlington
(614) 324-7777
www.panacealuxuryspa.com

W Nail Bar
160 W. Main St., New Albany
(614) 858-3223
www.thewnailbar.com
There are eight locally owned shops around Columbus, including in German Village, Powell, Bridge Park, and the Short North, and three salons in the Dublin, Easton, and Polaris DSW shoe stores.

Woodhouse Spa
19 N. High St., Dublin
(614) 790-8822
www.woodhousespas.com

MEDIA

Columbus Business First
300 Marconi Blvd.
(614) 461-4040
www.bizjournals.com
The primary source of economic development news and networking events in Columbus and around central Ohio.

Columbus CEO
62 E. Broad St., downtown
(614) 540-8900
www.columbusceo.com
This free monthly business magazine features articles on the business climate of central Ohio, including analysis of various sectors, management advice, and job listings. Libraries maintain current and back issues.

Columbus Dispatch
(614) 461-5000
www.dispatch.com
This is the city's only daily newspaper, which barely has a printed format, but you can sign up for various combinations of digital and/or printed subscriptions.

Columbus Monthly
62 E. Broad St., downtown
(614) 888-4567
www.columbusmonthly.com
Columbus Monthly has been the city's premier monthly magazine for nearly 50 years. It features restaurant reviews, business profiles, and articles on a variety of subjects, including political and civic issues. It continues to provide an alternative voice to the daily newspaper and is known for its well-written and heavily researched service pieces, like the "Best of . . ." series and school ratings. Individual issues can be purchased at most local news and magazine sellers or subscribed to at home. Libraries also maintain back issues.

BLOGS AND SOCIAL MEDIA SITES
614 Columbus
614 Eats
614Now
Alexis Nikole @blackforeger
Breakfast With Nick
Columbus Business News
Columbus Food Adventures
Columbus Navigator
Columbus on the Cheap
Columbus Underground
That Sandwich Dude
Yelp Columbus

LOCAL TELEVISION

Channel 4—WCMH
3165 Olentangy River Rd.
(614) 263-4444
www.nbc4i.com
The local NBC affiliate

Channel 6—WSYX
1261 Dublin Rd.
(614) 481-6666
www.wsyx6.com
The local ABC affiliate

Channel 10—WBNS
770 Twin Rivers Dr.
(614) 460-3700
www.wbns10tv.com
10TV is Columbus's CBS affiliate.

Channel 28—WTTE
1261 Dublin Rd.
(614) 481-6666
www.wtte28.com
WTTE is owned by the same folks who own the ABC affiliate.

Channel 34—WOSU TV
2400 Olentangy River Rd.
(614) 292-9678
www.wosu.org
The Ohio State University television station with educational and arts programming.

RADIO

89.7 FM—WOSU
www.wosu.org
The Ohio State University local NPR station

90.5 FM—WCBE
www.wcbe.org
WCBE is central Ohio's NPR station and provides a broad mix of local news coverage and cultural and world music programming. It is an eclectic station where you will find shows like *Fresh Air, All Things Considered,* and *BBC World Services.*

94.7 FM—WSNY
www.wsny.com
Sunny FM plays your standard elevator music. Beginning late November it plays holiday music 24/7 through Christmas Day.

97.1 FM—WBNS
www.97thefan.com
Sports radio

97.9 FM—WNCI
www.wnci.com
Top 40 pop music

99.7 FM—WRKZ
www.theblitz.com
"The Blitz" plays heavy rock and metal.

107.5 FM—WCKX
www.power1075.com
Current R&B and hip-hop

107.9 FM—WODB
www.b1079.com
Adult contemporary

WORSHIP

Regardless of one's religion, Columbus has a place for everyone. Naturally, as the city becomes more of a melting pot, a larger number of religiously affiliated groups are represented. It would be impractical to list the thousands of churches, temples, synagogues, and mosques in central Ohio, so this chapter just presents an overview of the religious scene in Columbus.

THE CATHOLIC COMMUNITY

A good place to begin a synopsis is with Columbus's Catholic population, which is around 300,000, making it the largest religious group in the city. The Diocese of Columbus (www.colsdioc.org) was established in 1868. Sylvester Rosecrans, the first bishop of Columbus, created many institutions within the new diocese, including parishes, schools, and its first newspaper, *The Catholic Columbian*.

During this time, he oversaw the construction of Columbus's first Catholic church, St. Joseph's Cathedral, on East Broad Street. It was consecrated October 20, 1878, and Bishop Rosecrans died a day later. The diocese now has 156 active priests and 108 parishes.

Education is discussed in a separate chapter, but this seems a logical place to mention that Columbus has 39 Catholic elementary schools and 11 high schools. To find out more about Catholic schools, contact the Department of Education's Catholic Conference of Ohio at (614) 224-7147.

Several institutions of higher education are directly affiliated with the church, the best known being the Pontifical College Josephinum in Worthington (www.pcj.edu), which trains Roman Catholic priests. This beautiful monastery is often home to art shows and classical music concerts, which give the public opportunities to visit the campus and chapels.

Capital University was founded as a Lutheran seminary in Canton and moved to Columbus in 1832. In 1959 the Evangelical Lutheran Theological Seminary and Capital University were separated. Capital is now one of the largest Lutheran-affiliated colleges in the nation, while Trinity Seminary continues to train church leaders. Unlike the Josephinum, Trinity admits women to the seminary.

Women also have a part in Columbus's monastic community. When the Diocese of Columbus was formed in 1868, the Dominican Sisters of St. Mary's of the Springs were given property in northwestern Columbus from which they continue to preach, teach, and reside. The Ohio Dominican University, a four-year liberal arts and coeducational college, was established by the Dominican community on property adjacent to the motherhouse.

THE NON-CATHOLIC CHRISTIAN COMMUNITY

While Catholicism claims the most members in Columbus, the evangelical Christian churches pack the most people in under one roof. Charismatics and Pentecostals might appreciate the old-fashioned preaching style at various Vineyard Churches (www.vineyardcolumbus.org) in Westerville, Sawmill, and Grandview. This church is known for its orthodox ministry and extensive musical worship.

Coming in a very distant second place to the Catholics, Methodists are the next largest religious group in Columbus, with a substantial number of United Methodist churches, as well as Free Methodist, Korean Methodist, and African Methodist Episcopal.

There are about 250 Baptist churches in the Columbus area to choose from, as well as 75 Lutheran and dozens of Presbyterian and

Episcopalian churches. Bible churches, Assemblies of God, Mennonite, Jehovah's Witness, and Eastern Orthodox churches, though not plentiful, also have a presence in Columbus.

The temples of the Church of Jesus Christ of Latter-day Saints are separate and distinct from their Mormon meetinghouses. There are thousands of Latter-day Saint churches and meetinghouses in the world but relatively few temples, and Columbus is fortunate enough to have one. Hilliard is home to the Columbus Ohio Temple (614-351-5001; www.churchofjesuschrist.org), which includes 18 stakes and more than 57,000 members.

Quakers have a number of options in central Ohio. Meetings are held every Sunday at 1954 Indianola Ave. (614-291-2331; www.northcolumbusfriends.com), just north of the OSU campus.

Columbus has several churches that not only accept but also advocate and openly support their LGBTQ+ members. The most comprehensive resource to find gay-friendly churches is Stonewall Columbus (614-299-7764; www.stonewallcolumbus.org). A list of churches that welcome gay Christians can also be found at www.gaychurch.org.

An increasing need for tolerance and compassion in our society is leading to the formation of several interfaith organizations. Students can get involved with spiritual organizations at their campus. The Office of Student Life (u.osu.edu/interfaith) supports the University Interfaith Association. Representatives of two dozen different faiths and churches come together to collaborate on the spiritual needs and issues of the student population.

The Spirituality Network (614-228-8867; www.spiritualitynetwork.org), located at 444 E. Broad St., maintains a referral list of spiritual guidance counselors within numerous Christian denominations. Some are ordained ministers, some are affiliated with specific religious orders, and others are laypeople. The network sponsors classes and retreats on spiritual transformation. This is the sort of place you can explore the "Sacred Feminine."

Many of the ecumenical and interfaith groups put their beliefs into social action. Habitat for Humanity is one of them. This nonprofit Christian housing ministry brings together volunteers of all faiths to help eradicate substandard housing in poverty-stricken and low-income areas. Volunteers help build affordable homes. To get involved with Habitat for Humanity, call (614) 422-4828, or check out the website, www.habitatmidohio.org.

THE JEWISH COMMUNITY

Columbus has a Jewish population of 25,000, and their heritage runs deep, particularly in Bexley. Founded 155 years ago, Temple Israel in Bexley was the first Jewish organization to be established in Columbus. There are now three synagogues in the city. Beth Tikvah is on the northwest side of Columbus, and Temple Beth Shalom is in New Albany.

The Columbus Jewish Historical Society is dedicated to documenting the history of the Jewish communities of Columbus and central Ohio. Aside from archiving the collections of local Jewish families, it maintains a library of oral histories, Jewish history books, and genealogies. You can contact the society at (614) 238-6977, or check out the website, www.columbusjewishhistory.org.

The Jewish Community Center of Columbus (614-231-2731; www.columbusjcc.org) is located at 1125 College Ave. and hosts a variety of recreational, cultural, theatrical, and educational activities, as well as fund-raising and outreach programs, that support the Jewish community.

If you are planning to relocate to Columbus and are looking to integrate into the Jewish community, a good source of information is the Columbus Jewish Federation, which has been around since 1926. Its extensive website (www.jewishcolumbus.org) offers a comprehensive listing of community and educational services, volunteer and advocacy opportunities, and synagogues throughout the city. It also provides links to national and international organizations.

OTHER RELIGIOUS COMMUNITIES

The Muslim community of Columbus is growing. The Islamic Center of Greater Columbus (614-253-3251; www.icohio.org) is a nonprofit organization that conducts religious, educational, cultural, and social activities in the best traditions of Islam. It also provides philanthropic and community services to those in need.

Buddhists will find about a half dozen meditational centers and groups that meet at various places around Columbus. The Shambhala

Meditation Center of Columbus can be reached at (312) 626-6799 or viewed online at www.columbus.shambhala.org. A statewide listing of Buddhist groups can be found at www.buddhanet.net.

Hindus from all over central Ohio worship at the Bharatiya Hindu Temple at 3671 Hyatts Rd. in Powell. It serves those who wish to live life in accordance with the Vedic dharma philosophies and traditions. For more information, call (740) 369-0717, or check out www.columbushindu-temple.org. There are a few more Hindu temples in nearby Dayton, Cincinnati, and Cleveland.

The International Society for Krishna Consciousness (ISKCON), better known as the Hare Krishna movement, was started in 1966. The Columbus Krishna House (614-421-1661; www.iskcon.org) was founded in 1969 as an all-female congregation. Men are welcome in the temple, which is located on the OSU campus.

Pagans and witches are right at home in Columbus, too. Pagan Nation (www.pagannation.com) is more of a social organization. The website has links to everything pagan, and it hosts the annual Real Witches Ball.

RELIGIOUS ARCHITECTURE

You don't have to go to church to agree that places of worship make for some of the most interesting architecture in any city. Columbus is no different. Included here are a few of the more outstanding and unique religious structures in the city. They have been singled out for a variety of reasons, including beautiful mosaics, a famous architect, and special gardens.

Annunciation Greek Orthodox Cathedral
555 N. High St.
(614) 224-9020
www.greekcathedral.com

Columbus's pièce de résistance as far as church architecture goes is the Annunciation Greek Orthodox Cathedral. This hulking building is situated in the Short North and belongs to the Greek Orthodox Metropolis of Pittsburgh. The current church was built in 1990 on the site of the original church, which was founded in 1922. You will never know from the austere exterior how lavish and impressive the interior is—unless you go in.

i ReStore is the Habitat for Humanity local retail center (614-737-8673) in Westerville and on Bethel Road. The center accepts donated goods and building materials, which are in turn sold to the public at deeply discounted prices. Drop off good-quality cabinets, doors, sinks, windows, and leftover remodeling supplies at 3140 Westerville Rd. in Westerville to help out the community.

Built in the traditional Byzantine style, its Greek cross floor plan dates back to the sixth century. The place is filled with symbolism, both within the architecture of the cathedral and its decoration. The floor symbolizes the earth, and the ceiling and chandelier represent the celestial universe with all its stars. Christian or not, you can't help but be moved by the powerful image of Christ looking down at you from the central dome.

The interior is covered with mosaics created by an Italian artisan from five million pieces of Venetian glass. If that isn't lavish enough, marble and 24-carat gold add to the glowing ambience. The choir screen is covered with icons, and the stained-glass windows depict scenes from the life of Christ and various saints. The church's website is beautifully done and provides an extensive explanation of the symbolism throughout the building. This is a must-see if you are staying in the downtown area. The church hosts the annual Labor Day Greek Festival and supports a variety of Greek cultural organizations and outreach ministries within the Columbus community.

Broad Street Presbyterian Church
760 E. Broad St., near East Side
(614) 221-6552
www.bspc.org

There are a number of interesting stone churches built along East Broad Street. The First Presbyterian Church is included here because it was designed by the famous architect Frank Packard in 1887 for the growing east side community. The church was completed in 1888, and like many of Packard's buildings it is a Victorian's interpretation of Gothic architecture.

In celebration of Columbus's diversity, Broad Street Presbyterian unconditionally welcomes anyone into its congregation and emphasizes social outreach. Practicing what it preaches, the church gifted 300 acres of Broad Acres land to Buckhorn Children's Center for at-risk children in 1989. Members also hand out food and provide day care for low-income families in the neighborhood and sponsor Habitat for Humanity projects.

First Unitarian Universalist Church of Columbus
93 W. Weisheimer Rd., Clintonville
(614) 267-4946
www.firstuucolumbus.org
The First Unitarian Universalist Church of Columbus ranks among the top 25 largest congregations of this more liberal religion. Combining reason in their approach to scripture and teaching freedom, tolerance, and unconditional love, Unitarian Universalist churches welcome all people regardless of race or sexual orientation. First Unitarian is located in the heart of Clintonville and has two lovely gardens on-site. The Memorial Garden is a tribute to life, while the walls containing the garden commemorate the church members who have died of HIV-related diseases. The Japanese Garden offers people a place to reflect and imagine.

Liberty Presbyterian Church
7080 Olentangy River Rd., Delaware
(740) 548-6075
www.libertybarnchurch.com
This laid-back Presbyterian church looks a lot older than it really is. A church was built on this site just after the War of 1812 as a tribute to the landowner's deceased sweetheart. In 1993 Amish barn-raising legend Josie Miller was hired to erect a duplicate of the original church, which is believed to be the largest bank barn in the country.

The church is constructed of hickory and hemlock. A 300-year-old oak (struck by lightning) was recycled into a beautiful pulpit. The sanctuary is decorated with Amish quilts and can accommodate 1,100. You'll find no pipe organ here, only string quartets playing Bach and a congregation clapping while they sing. The services are so informal that many members wear shorts to church. Come as you are!

You'll find the Liberty Barn situated at a very scenic corner of Olentangy River Road (Old Route 315) and Home Road, slightly north of Worthington. If the church is not open, it is still worth checking out the gardens and wandering through the old cemetery, where you'll find Lydia Sackett buried in the churchyard alongside her sweetheart, John Flanagan.

St. John's Episcopal Church
700 High St., Worthington
(614) 846-5180
www.stjohnsworthington.org
There's no mistaking the Connecticut roots of this church's founder. When you visit the first Episcopal church west of the Alleghenies, you'll swear you've made a wrong turn and ended up in New England. The current building was completed in 1831, but a church has been on this site since 1802.

James Kilbourne founded St. John's shortly after establishing Worthington. Its bell was rung for the first time on Christmas Eve in 1822. The exterior is made of handmade brick and the interior of hand-hewn wood, making St. John's well deserving of its inclusion on the National Register of Historic Places.

Worth noting is the labyrinth garden and cemetery located behind the church. The cemetery was once a community burying ground and includes five Revolutionary War veterans and seven veterans of the War of 1812.

St. Joseph's Cathedral
212 E. Broad St.
(614) 224-1295
www.saintjosephcathedral.org
This beautiful cathedral was started in 1866 and is built in the Gothic style. The glowing yellow stone of this bulky church helps it hold its own amid the skyscrapers surrounding it. The cathedral was consecrated in 1878 and was the first Catholic church built in Columbus. Its website has a nicely written history and listing of who's who on the stained-glass windows. There are three entrances from Broad Street and one from Fifth Avenue. The current seating capacity is around 700.

INDEX

INDEX

INDEX

ABOUT THE AUTHOR

Shawnie Kelley has lived in Columbus since 1997 and has called Upper Arlington home since 2002. She studied art history at Carnegie Mellon in Pittsburgh, The Ohio State University, and the University of Edinburgh, Scotland. Shawnie is the author of the first two editions of *Insiders' Guide to Columbus*, has written several books about Cape Cod, and has contributed food and travel-related articles to both national and international magazines. She owns Wanderlust Tours, a cultural and culinary travel company, and teaches cooking classes for The Mix at Columbus State. Some of her best times are just exploring the world, sniffing out regional food, writing about spas, historic hotels, and golf. Her favorite thing in the world is adventuring with her fun little family: Dan, Madalyn, and Gabe. She hopes the *Insiders' Guide* will expose Columbus as the international capital city it is becoming!